D1572838

THE FIRST
VICE
LORD

THE FIRST
VICE
LORD

Big Jim Colosimo and the Ladies of the Levee

ARTHUR J. BILEK

CUMBERLAND HOUSE
NASHVILLE, TENNESSEE

THE FIRST VICE LORD
PUBLISHED BY CUMBERLAND HOUSE PUBLISHING INC.
431 Harding Industrial Drive
Nashville, Tennessee 37211

Cover design: Gore Studio Inc., Nashville, Tennessee
Text design: John Mitchell

Library of Congress Cataloging-in-Publication Data
    Bilek, Arthur J., 1929–
        The first vice lord : big Jim Colosimo and the ladies of the Levee / Arthur J. Bilek.
            p. cm.
    Includes bibliographical references and index.
    ISBN-13: 978–1-58182–639–5 (hardcover : alk. paper)
    ISBN-10: 1–58182–639–7 (hardcover : alk. paper)
    1. Colosimo, Jim, d. 1920. 2. Criminals—Illinois—Chicago—Biography. 3. Gangsters—Illinois—Chicago—Biography. 4. Organized crime—Illinois—Chicago—History—20th century. 5. Prostitution—Illinois—Chicago—History. I. Title.
    HV6248.C577B55 2008
    364.1092—dc22
        [B]
                                                                        2008002673

Printed in the United States of America

1 2 3 4 5 6 7—14 13 12 11 10 09 08

CONTENTS

ACKNOWLEDGMENTS

This book could not have been written without the assistance of numerous family members, friends, associates, genealogists and researchers. I wish to give them all my sincere thanks and deep appreciation. Unfortunately, there are others whose names were accidentally lost or forgotten during the four-year development and writing of this book. My appreciation and thanks are also extended to them along with my apologies for the failure to list them here.

Very significant and valuable contributions to this book were made by:

My wife, Ellen Clark, whose unflagging kindness, patience, and support encouraged and enabled me to complete this work

My son Arthur John Bilek III, whose contributions, suggestions and repeated editing of the drafts moved the book to completion

My son Mark Bilek for his foresight, perseverance and assistance concerning my computer and software

My two daughters, Judy Zoromski and Mary Lu Bilek, for their unquestioning and loving support

Senior researcher and editorial associate Michael Schiltz for his genealogical and historical research

Newspaper research associate Jeff Thurston, who spent untold days and weeks in the newspaper-reference section of public libraries to provide the factual information for the story

Copy editor Bruce Clorfene

Map illustrator Lynda Wallis
Copy reviewers John Bilek, John Bender, Robert Lombardo, and
    Michael Schiltz
Image editor Dan Behnke
Italian editor Christina Colosimo
The Chicago Crime Commission
The Colosimo, Adamo, and Mascaro families
The Secret Six

In alphabetical order are many others who contributed greatly and assisted in a wide variety of ways: Ed Bauman, John Binder, Dr. Dominic Candeloro, Debbie Colosimo Hormel, Maria Statti Colosimo, Mariam Colosimo, Dr. James J. Conway, Genevieve Davis, J R Davis, Giuseppe De Bartolo, Michael Dooley, Mars Eghigian Jr., C. W. Bill Emblom, Thomas E. Gibbons, Lorenzo Gigliotti, William Helmer, Italian Cultural Center, Cheryl Kale, Nathan Kantrowitz, Rose Keefe, Jenny Khalaf, Richard Lindberg, Robert Lombardo, Matt Luzi, Elizabeth Mascaro, James McGuire, Ashley Meyer, Santino Pascuzzi, Dave Phillips, Mark Prow, Robert Reader, Paul Reda, Mimmo Rizutti, Tony Rose, Joe Walters, and Margaret Watkins. I owe each a considerable debt of gratitude and appreciation for the time and effort they expended and for their most gracious contributions to this book.

Special acknowledgment is made to Patricia Jacobs Stelzer who wrote "Prohibition and Organized Crime: A Case Study of the Life of John Torrio" in 1997 in partial fulfillment of the requirements for a master's degree at Wayne State University.

Special thanks to Chicago author Richard Lindberg for his longtime support and helpful suggestions as well as his line-by-line copy review of this mansuscript.

Queer things are said about Chicago,
I vow—I vow;
'Twas said she once was on the pork,
But now—but now;
They bring a charge
That's rather large,
And makes me cry: "Gee whiz,"
In point of fact
To be exact,
They say that Chicago is—
Wide open.
Wide open—wide open—
They say Chicago's wide open!
Each wild reforming son of a gun,
Says—places that we ought to shun,
And now, dear me, for every one—Wide open.[1]

— Paul James Duff,
Side Lights on Darkest Chicago

First in violence, deepest in dirt,
lawless, unlovely, ill-smelling,
irreverent, new
an overgrown gawk of a village,
the "tough" among cities,
a spectacle for the nation.[2]

— Lincoln Steffens,
"Chicago, Half Free and Fighting On"

INTRODUCTION

The life of a flawed Horatio Alger character is united with the most color-ful era in the history of Chicago to produce an adventure-filled tale replete with gaudy and garish characters. Chain-drive trucks slowly were supplant-ing the horse-drawn wagons rattling down the city's paving stone streets, and socialites earned their status by knowing gamblers and saloonkeepers by their first names. It was in this town that both "Big Jim" Colosimo and the famous red-light "Levee District" got their start, flourished and met their extraordinary ends.

The life of Colosimo and that of the Levee took place in a tightly confin-ing space known as the First Ward. This ward was the city's center for busi-ness, finance, and entertainment. It was also the center of drinking, gambling, and whoring.

Only thirteen years old, James Colosimo arrived from southern Italy hop-ing to plant his family's "flag" in Chicago. He found the Levee that boasted more than two hundred houses of ill-fame—from the grubbiest sheds to the gilded palace of sin—and hundreds of saloons, gambling houses, pawn shops, penny arcades, and hustle joints.

The Levee grew from a rag-tag collection of dirty, wooden shacks to stately two- and three-story stone buildings with every decorative fixture local and foreign artisans could produce. The reputation of the Levee reached his-toric proportions, and its fame spread throughout the United States and even across the Atlantic. This notoriety instigated its closing, bringing bands of reformers, crusaders, and investigators marching, singing and crashing through the gaudy streets.

Kingpin Big Jim Colosimo maneuvered through the maze of sin and politics, all the time rising in reputation and fortune. As his career was peaking,
true love claimed his heart. Beautiful and virtuous operatic soprano Dale Winter gave Big Jim the best reason to shed his role as vice lord to become a
celebrity restaurant and nightclub operator. He quickly made a series of moves
aimed at bringing him and his new bride happiness and respectability, but he
had let his guard down and his enemies took that opportunity to end his run.

The story is peppered with a motley collection of personalities, including
Aldermen Michael "Hinky Dink" Kenna and John J. "Bathhouse John"
Coughlin, evangelist "Gypsy" Smith, Rev. William Stead, Johnny Torrio, and
Mayors Carter Harrison Jr. and William "Big Bill" Thompson. In supporting
roles are hundreds of gamblers, bartenders, drunks, and several thousand
ladies of the evening, madams, cadets, panderers, and touts. Aiding and abet-
ting this cast of characters are crooked police captains, dishonest aldermen,
lazy political hacks, and disreputable boodlers and fixers.

All these people and their stories come together to form a boisterous
opera of the times—the tough, turbulent, noisy, wonderful years between the
1893 World's Columbian Exposition and the start of the bloody bootleg era of
the Twenties. The city was painfully and joyfully emerging as a metropolis and
leaving behind forever the days of Indians, fur traders, soldiers, and settlers.[*]

---

[*] AUTHOR'S NOTE: The vernacular of the times is used throughout this book. No intent exists to por-
tray any person or group in a dismissive or negative manner. Terminology some modern readers might
find offensive is used solely in an effort to be faithful to the nomenclature in general usage in Chicago
in the late-nineteenth and early twentieth centuries. Explanations and definitions of popular sayings,
words, phrases, and more from the era are provided in the Appendix.

THE FIRST
VICE
LORD

PROSTITUTION

A woman lurks in the dark and waits
To move on when a policeman heaves into view,
Smiling a broken smile from a face
Painted over haggard bones and desperate eyes,
All night she offers passersby what they will
Of her beauty wasted, body faded, claims gone,
And no takers.[3]

— Carl Sandburg,
Chicago Poems

A woman what hustles
Never keeps nothing'
For all her hustlin'
Somebody always gets
What she goes on the street for.
If it ain't a pimp
It's a bull what gets it.
I been hustlin' now
Till I ain't much good any more.
I got nothin' to show for it.
Some man got it all.
Every night's hustlin' I ever did.[4]

— Carl Sandburg,
Chicago Poems

Part One

CHICAGO— CITY OF OPPORTUNITY

Chapter One

ONE SPECTACULAR FUNERAL

Crooks and Dignitaries Carry the Casket

1920

Poor Jim—poor boy,
Affable and benign to all you always was
During your placid or cloudy days.
Now you are no more, my noble benefactor, my gentle friend.
My heart is broken by your horrible end.
In your own store an evil genius your precious life destroyed,
While real happiness you hardly enjoyed,
As if you was a toy.
Losing you, Jim, is a crushing blow to me—
Good as you was to me no one will ever be.
Poor Jim, poor boy.

— Raymond Regnella,
Bouncer at Colosimo's Café

The hearse carrying the flower-bedecked coffin wove slowly through the South Side streets that Big Jim Colosimo had known so well. The streets where he came of age. The streets where he ran dollar brothels. The streets where he cultivated political clout, became a vice lord, and ultimately, the king of Chicago's nightlife. The streets where he died.

There was a simple death notice in the newspaper:

Colosimo—James Colosimo, age 43 years, May 11, 1920, beloved husband of Dale Winter Colosimo, fond son of Luigi, and brother of Bettina,

Francesco, Anthony, and Maria. Funeral Saturday, May 15, at 9:30 a.m., from his late residence, 3156 Vernon av. Automobiles to Mount Carmel Cemetery.[1]

Colosimo's family met at the house on Vernon Avenue to plan what was to become the first of a series of showy mobster funerals in Chicago. They arranged a Catholic service in Santa Maria Incoronata Catholic Church at 218 Alexander Avenue and burial at Mount Carmel Cemetery, but Chicago's Catholic Archbishop George Mundelein gave a flat "no" to the plan. Archbishop Mundelein, who controlled all Catholic churches and cemeteries in Chicago and Cook County, decreed that any gangster viewed as a public sinner would be refused a Catholic burial. He issued an order forbidding Father Hoban, chancellor of the archdiocese, to permit the internment of Colosimo in a Catholic cemetery. The order noted that Colosimo had not abided by the dictates of the Catholic Church in his manner of living and had broken a sacred canon of the church by divorcing Victoria Moresco and marrying Dale Winter. The family hastily moved the service to the home and the burial site to Oak Woods Cemetery at 1035 E. Sixty-seventh Street with its 183 acres of winding roads and shady trees.

The newspapers made it a front-page epic with banner headlines and countless photographs. The expected mass of elected officials, appointed office holders, politicians, criminals, gangsters, mobsters, and hoodlums of all stripes guaranteed it would be a memorable event. It would be a long-remembered day when the close relationship between vice and city government was on display for all to see.

On the day of the funeral, every Italian living in the South Side would pay their respects to their murdered countryman. They would be joined by saloonkeepers, gamblers, madams, and pimps—all turning out one last time for the man they had known as the leader of their slice of society. All of the Levee residents and regulars—from lodging-house inhabitants to the marginally employed to drunks and bums—would be lining the streets to honor the memory of their friend, boss, and benefactor. The curiosity of the public would be drawn by the most important murder of the times, that of a man known from Hyde Park to Rogers Park. Big Jim's funeral would be the largest and gaudiest that Chicago had yet experienced.

The pallbearers were an amazing mix of all classes: Colosimo's lifetime friend and attorney Rocco De Stefano, state Representative John Griffin, First Ward saloonkeeper Patrick O'Malley, First Ward Democratic Club Secretary John Budinger, professional bondsman Ike Rodrick, Levee resort-keeper Mike Fritzell,[*] Alderman "Bathhouse John" Coughlin, and Colosimo's bookkeeper Frank Camilla.

The list of honorary pallbearers comprised a who's who of the era's famous, powerful, connected, and notorious:

Johnny Torrio, Colosimo's brothel and resort manager
Aldermen Michael "Hinky Dink" Kenna, Joseph Kostner, Dorsey
  Crowe, George Maypole, John Powers, Timothy Hogan, James
  Bowler, J. O. Kostner, and John Toman
Congressmen John W. Rainey and Thomas Gallagher
Judges John K. Prindiville, John R. Caverly, and Barnard P. Barasa
Assistant State's Attorney Dwight McKay
Former Assistant U.S. District Attorney Francis Borrelli
Democratic leader in the Thirty-fourth Ward Michael Rosenberg
South Park District Commissioner Louis J. Behan
First Ward precinct captain Edward Rexford
Political boss and former panderer Jakie Adler
First Ward politicians and dive keepers Andy Craig and Sol Van Praag

Two other politically connected honorary pallbearers were Anthony D'Andrea, Democratic committeeman of the Nineteenth Ward, and "Diamond Joe" Esposito, Republican committeeman of the Nineteenth Ward. Both of these powerful political bosses would meet bloody deaths in the violent years to come.[1]

The seemingly endless list of honorary pallbearers continued with Titta Ruffo, opera singer; Francesco Daddi and maestro Giacomo Spadoni of the Chicago Grand Opera Company; Mike Merlo, head of the Unione Siciliana; Mike Potson, manager of Colosimo's Café; Alfred Maggi, Big Jim's barber; Doctors Charles Volini, Anthony Ronga, F. C. Henmore, and A. M. DeVault; Norman Ballard, hotel owner at French Lick, Indiana; Edward Ballard, owner of Brown's gambling casino at French Lick; Ike Bloom, operator of the Levee's most infamous night spot Freiberg's Dance Hall; and George Silver, former resort-keeper and owner of the Friars Café.

One honorary pallbearer about whom much would be heard in the years ahead was state representative Michael Igoe, Democratic leader in the Illinois House of Representatives, South Park District commissioner and former assistant U.S. district attorney. He became the associate and lawyer for Al Capone's chief whoremaster Dennis Cooney. Later, he was the wheelhorse in the Nash-Cermak-Kelly political machine that sold out to the organized crime syndicate.[2] His last role was as a federal district judge appointed by President

---

* Resort is used here in the vernacular of the times to mean a brothel, gambling den, road house, or saloon.

Franklin D. Roosevelt. While sitting as a federal judge, Igoe was named in FBI wiretaps of the Chicago syndicate.

The pallbearer lists demonstrated the wide power and disparate relationships of Colosimo in his roles as vice lord, First Ward political leader, and restaurant owner. Some of his friends became well-known gangsters in the Prohibition era. Others were elected or appointed to high government offices. Some became wealthy and significant figures in the growth of the Chicago metropolis. A number died in bloody, unsolved murders. All owed something to a penniless immigrant youth from Colosimi, Italy.

In preparation for the funeral, the undertaker delivered the twenty-five-hundred-dollar casket to the darkened Colosimo home on Vernon Avenue on May 13, 1920. The heavy box was carried across the sidewalk, through the somber throng and up the steps to the front door. Widow Dale Winter, who had been resting inside, walked to the front door, but collapsed into a family member's arms when she saw the casket.

The next morning the door to the Colosimo home opened to the beginning of a virtually inexhaustible line of relatives, close friends, and business and political associates. Politicians from city hall and city, county, and state elected officials moved in and out throughout the day and evening. Detectives from the Twenty-second Street District Station guarded the doors and checked each package and floral piece as they arrived. Flower arrangements, wreaths garlanded with roses, and vases with cut flowers of every sort filled the house. In the living room the new widow was sitting in a soft chair. She wore a simple black dress covered by a black fur coat to ward off the spring chill that blew into the room with the crowd.

One of the bereaved, "Peg Leg Sam" Anderson, who had long lived in the Twenty-second Street area, hobbled to the casket. Many years earlier when he needed financial help, Big Jim had arranged for him to get into the pool-room business. He stopped in front of the body, and tears flowed from his one good eye, the other eye lost long ago in the Levee fight that furnished his nickname.

On the morning of the funeral, a large throng began to form along the sidewalk and across the street. Among the first to arrive were Aldermen Coughlin and Kenna, Big Jim's longtime personal friends and business associates. They soon were joined by delegations from the Union of Sicilian Sons,[3] Bellini Lodge No. 271 of the Knights of Pythias; the Trinacro de Union, and the First Ward Democratic Club. In the living room were Mike Fritzell; Ike Rodrick; Tom Chamales of the Green Mill Gardens; Sol Van Praag, who was long a power in First Ward politics; and three brothers of Victoria Moresco.[4] They were joined by Mont Tennes, operator of the Racing News service and head of all gambling in the downtown area.

Around the gilded casket were lighted candles and floral pieces of every size and description. A huge wreath from Dale held a photo of the pair in their happiest days, taken in front of the restaurant. One floral piece made from roses and sweetpeas depicted a giant clock with the hand stopped at 4:25, from the First Ward Democratic club. A full-sized floral harp came from the band at the café. A long blanket of roses from Tony D'Andrea and Mike Merlo lay across the casket. The largest display of flowers came from the Unione Siciliana.

After a male quartet sang several religious pieces, a brief service was held. Rev. Pasquale R. De Carlo of the Italian Presbyterian church, speaking with a thick Italian accent, gave a short reading from the scriptures and recited the Lord's Prayer. Coughlin knelt down and recited the Hail Mary prayer three times. The service was over. The shuffling of dozens of shoes began.

On a signal from the undertaker one of the bands in front of the house began to play Chopin's "Funeral March." Several men wearing badges carried floral pieces from the home and placed them in open-backed flower cars. Mourners from inside moved to the front porch and stood under the buntings of American and Italian flags. The men on the porch had never looked as sad and serious before in the presence of Big Jim. It was a dark day for all.

The heavy bronze casket was carried slowly from the home. Leading the procession was Coughlin, his face solemn and stricken. The pallbearers descended the steps slowly, followed by the widow in black with a long veil over her face and escorted by Rocco De Stefano and a brother-in-law. She walked as if she might faint at any moment. The family and close friends followed. All entered dark sedans that were parked in a long, silent line that wound into the next block. Slowly, the bands and the hearse and floral cars began to move. The mile-long motorcade followed, headed toward the Levee where most of Big Jim's life had taken place.

Watching intently and scribbling on their pads were reporters from all of the Chicago daily and weekly newspapers, the three national wire services, the *New York Times*, and other big-city newspapers with correspondents in Chicago. Their reports on Colosimo's funeral contained stories describing the bronze casket, the prominent persons in attendance, the two thousand mourners silently following the procession, the two brass bands, and the thousands of onlookers crowding the streets and roofs of buildings along the way from Colosimo's home into the Levee.[5]

The hearse led the way west on Thirty-first Street to Wabash Avenue and then turned north heading for the Levee. The cavalcade traveled slowly over streetcar tracks to the intersection of Twenty-second Street and Wabash Avenue. Almost ten thousand people lined the curbs and peered from tenement windows. As the hearse passed their vantage points, the male spectators took off their hats and caps and the women crossed themselves.

As the front of the procession reached the Levee, Coughlin and Kenna left their sedan and took their places on foot at the head of the one thousand members of the First Ward Democratic Club who were waiting on a side street to join the procession. Banners from the club and from Italian and Sicilian fraternal societies fluttered above the crowd in the spring breeze. The aldermen led the procession to Colosimo's Café at 2126 S. Wabash Avenue. The intersection of Twenty-second Street and Wabash Avenue was so jammed with mourners and spectators that neither streetcars nor automobiles could drive through. The honorary pallbearers formed a lane for the hearse, which stopped in front of Big Jim's restaurant. The two twenty-piece bands played "Nearer My God to Thee," and then the procession began the long drive to the cemetery.

More than two dozen newspaper photographers on top of buildings, in open windows, and on the roofs of cars and trucks took hundreds of pictures.

Twenty-four specially-rented cars had been parked on Wabash Avenue to carry mourners to the cemetery. They pulled from the curbs and joined the motorcade. The number of marchers swelled into the thousands as the Levee denizens fell in step with the slowly moving procession, following the cortege for a number of blocks. With the two bands providing solemn funeral music and sometimes playing pieces from Italian operas Colosimo loved so well, the cars moved south.

The procession ended at Oak Woods Cemetery at Sixty-seventh Street and Cottage Grove Avenue. Oak Woods was an old cemetery; the first burial was in 1865. There were 183 acres of winding roads and well-cared-for naturalistic grounds. In 1944 Big Jim would be joined by his last political partner, Chicago Mayor William Thompson, who was buried nearby.

The long funeral cortege rolled along the cemetery's tree-shaded roads. The cars parked, and the mourners slowly filed out. At the grave site, Rocco De Stefano, speaking in a halting voice, gave a lengthy and flattering eulogy. The service ended with the Apollo quartet reprising "Nearer My God to Thee." The widow needed help to return to her limousine, and the long, black car sped off to her empty house.

The day of the funeral the *Chicago Tribune* printed an editorial with the headline "The Vice King's Funeral":

> Following the body of "Big Jim" Colosimo to the grave today will move a cortege which should interrupt the complacent thought of Chicago. Three judges, eight aldermen, an assistant state's attorney, a congressman, a state representative and leading artists of the Chicago Opera company are listed as honorary pallbearers along with gamblers, ex-gamblers, dive keepers, and ex-dive keepers.

A cavalcade such as moved behind the funeral car of Caesar is to pay homage to the memory of a man who for more than a decade has been recognized as the overlord of Chicago's underworld. Such a tribute from men set up to make and enforce our laws, to a man who in much of his life was a law unto himself, is more than a tribute of friendship. It is a tribute to power, regardless of the source or justice of that power.

Jim Colosimo ruled in his world. Out of his rule came suddenly death to him. Raised to the throne of the half world, he was a maker and breaker of political aspirations. His methods were ruthless, considering the law only so far as to avoid its penalties. The penalty which came to him was not of the law but of the kingdom which he had built up. Yet it brings to his grave a concourse notable for its lights and shadows.

It is a strange commentary upon our system of law and justice. In how far can power be derived from the life of the underworld influence institutions of law and order? It is a question worthy of thoughtful consideration of those entrusted with the establishment of law and order, and of those dependent upon and responsible for such trust.[5]

After the funeral Bathhouse John Coughlin remarked, "There wasn't a piker's hair on Big Jim's head."[6]

Chapter Two

A BIRTH IN ITALY

Vincenzo Colosimo

1878–1891

An aggressive thug, Colosimo was to become Chicago's overlord of crime in a relatively short time. Today he is revered as the patron saint of the Capone syndicate.[1]

— Ovid Demaris, *Captive City*

The story to be told involves the First Ward—Chicago's hub of business, commerce, and frivolity; the Levee—the city's red-light district; and James Colosimo—the man who became the first vice lord.

The story begins in late nineteenth-century Calabria, a governmental region in southern Italy. This province sits between the Tyrrhenian Sea and the Ionian Sea near the toe of the so-called Italian boot. Very mountainous with thin lowland coastal strips along the seas, the region had several cities on the coasts and numerous small isolated inland villages connected by dirt roads that twisted up and down the mountainsides. Since the earliest of records the region was the most depressed economic area of Italy. The remoteness and seclusion of the towns promoted a strong sense of loyalty to family and place, but it also attracted bandits and brigands who lived in caves in the hills. These early gangsters specialized in robbery, extortion, and kidnapping for ransom.

In this mountainous area was a small town named Colosimi.[2] In the late 1800s there was one winding road leading into Colosimi. Inside the town were two smaller roads, one along the houses near the top of the hill and a second past the fronts of the houses near the bottom. Dirt paths connected the two roads. Almost three thousand persons lived in the homes of Colosimi. Many of the people from Colosimi bore the family name Colosimo. Names of other families were Maletta, Costanzo, Leo, Gigliotti, Mancuso, Perri, Talerico, Mirabelli, Rizzuto, Mascaro, Maraca, Burza, and Tucci.[3] They all were Catholics. They spoke Italian with a Calabrian dialect. Most had dark brown or black hair and brown eyes. Farming was the main industry. There were no school buildings; space for classes was rented in local homes. Students went to school Monday through Saturday. The church built in the sixteenth century was at the center of town.

Forests of pine had once covered the slopes of Calabria, but powerful feudal lords had cut the trees long before to sell for ship masts and construction in Rome. What remained were tiny farm plots that dotted the hillsides and valleys. Wheat farming and raising figs and olives were the principal economic activities. Some beans and potatoes were grown. Oxen and, later, mules were used to plow the fields. At sunrise the men would ride mules or lead oxen down the road to the small farms, work all day in the fields, and then at dusk lead their tired animals home.

When they were not having children, the housewives worked as weavers and seamstresses. The wives sewed all of the clothes for themselves and their families. They knitted socks and underwear. Some wove cloth for use in making clothes. Mothers and sisters used looms to make tablecloths, napkins, and sheets. There was bartering among families of food stuffs for services. The women and children cared for the chickens, goats, and pigs, the number of which depended on the means of the family. These small animals were raised at the side of or under the houses. Wealthier families had small wooden buildings attached to their homes for these animals. In tiny gardens the women raised kale, green beans, tomatoes, beets, and other vegetables. A few raised fruits such as apples, plums, and berries. The open fireplace in each home served as a stove for the daily meals and to boil the lye and animal fat or olive oil into the soap that the women used to wash clothes in the nearby river. The wives used wheat flower, rye, or corn to make the bread, which was baked every two weeks in one of the two town ovens. Families made bread on different days, and if one family ran out they borrowed from a neighbor.

Breakfast was a bowl of goat's milk with pieces of broken bread added. Other meals usually consisted of soup with potatoes, greens, beans, and other vegetables. Heat in the cold months came from the fireplace or heated coals placed in a copper bowl in the center of a wood brazier.

The children had little in the way of toys but made do by making certain of the house animals their personal pets. Some young boys raised birds as a hobby.[4]

The Colosimos were the dominant family in the town. In the 1800s the patriarch of the Colosimo clan was Antonio Colosimo, a wealthy landowner.

One of his sons, Luigi, married a woman named Santa, and they lived in the family home at 78 Fontana, today known as Vico Il Europa. The three-story house built of gray stone and concrete in 1750 by an earlier generation of the family was near the center of the village. The house still stands, remodeled and refurnished with money provided by Jim Colosimo during his lifetime. In 1871 the Luigis had a son called Antonio, named after his paternal grandfather. When Santa died, Luigi took a second wife named Giuseppina Mascaro. In 1876 Giuseppina gave Luigi a son, whom they named Francesco. Luigi was twenty-nine years old.

On February 16, 1878, Luigi presented a small male baby to the sindaco (mayor) of Colosimi. Luigi said that on the sixteenth of February his second wife Giuseppina Mascaro had given birth to a male son whom they were calling Vincenzo.[5] The baby's birth was recorded in the town's ledger, and the child was baptized Vincenzo in the town's church.

After Vincenzo, Giuseppina had two daughters: Maria born in 1880 and Elisabette, sometimes called Bettina, born in 1882. For a few years Vincenzo and his brothers and sisters attended school, but only Francesco and Elisabette learned to read and write.

When Giuseppina died, Luigi married a third time. His new wife was named Ursala. No children were produced during this marriage. After Ursala died, Luigi moved to Petilia Policastro, a small crossroads village twenty-five difficult miles east of Colosimi. Bettina moved with her father to Petilia Policastro, where she married an Italian. Her husband immigrated to the United States in 1898, and she joined him in Chicago in 1899. Later, Bettina's husband became involved in shady financial dealings that brought shame to the Colosimo name in America.

The economy worsened in southern Italy as the nineteenth century drew to a close. More and more of the men sailed to America in the hopes of making enough money to return home with a wallet filled with cash or to bring their family to the United States to live. Two factors brought many of these Italian immigrants to Chicago: its fame as a booming, growing frontier town and the building of a giant railroad network in America with Chicago as its hub. Luigi was faced with an economic dilemma. He was a widower with four children to raise. Luigi made a bold decision. He would send Vincenzo to America in the hope that he might become wealthy and support his father and the rest of the Colosimo family in Italy. Because Vincenzo was too young to travel alone, his half brother Antonio was to accompany him on the long and difficult trip.

Vincenzo was barely thirteen in 1891 when he and his twenty-one-year-old brother Antonio embarked on the arduous journey to the United States. At the time, people traveled between nearby towns on foot or by mule; a few rode in a small mule-drawn cart. Upon reaching Cosenza they took the steam railroad to Naples. They were limited in what they carried to a wooden trunk and hand baggage. Near the dock in Naples they purchased food for the voyage. There was no dining service for steerage passengers.

Antonio and Vincenzo boarded the steamship SS *Alsatia* in May 1891. Their ship sailed from Naples to Palermo and then Gibraltar. Leaving the Big Rock, the ship headed westward for 3,639 statute miles across the rough and turbulent Atlantic Ocean. Three long weeks after leaving Naples, and with many of the passengers suffering from a variety of illnesses, the SS *Alsatia* arrived in New York Harbor on June 3, 1891.[6] The pair disembarked in New York and set off by train for Chicago.

Antonio and Vincenzo Colosimo journeyed halfway across the continent to the burgeoning city on the southern edge of Lake Michigan. Luigi had likely made arrangements by letter with other recent immigrants from Colosimi so that Vincenzo could room in the new Italian neighborhood at the south edge of the downtown business district of Chicago. Antonio, who had dutifully brought Vincenzo across the ocean to Chicago on the directions of his father, had no interest in remaining in the United States. He returned to Colosimi, married a local girl, Jaquinto Parma, and remained there for the rest of his life.

Young Colosimo had landed in a world very different from the tiny town where he had spent the first thirteen years of his life. The new city had horse-drawn streetcars, steaming fire engines, peddler's wagons, and public and private carriages. The streets were made of paving blocks or cobblestone. State Street, the main thoroughfare, already was a bustling commercial success with large department stores on both sides. The crush of humanity and vehicles of all types and sizes that filled the downtown streets was barely kept under control by the Irish and German police officers in their tall, felt helmets. Chicago was bustling. The business and political communities were preparing busily for the great World's Fair that was coming in two years.

The young Vincenzo Colosimo moved into a crowded apartment and assimilated into his new land. He had nowhere to go but up. He changed his name to Jim Colosimo and began his way on a path that would turn him into Big Jim Colosimo, Chicago's first vice lord.

Chapter Three

EARLY VICE
IN CHICAGO

Fallen Women

1857–1892

And women tramp the streets so damp
Shorn of their modesty.
Their smile is hard, and their flesh wan,
And they cringe as they walk alone.
There's none of God in their sinful nob
As they hum a ribald song.
But these women tramp the streets so damp,
To the streets their kind belong.
There is much of woe, in their frozen hearts,
Where erst dwelt melody;
They've wedded shame, and lost their name,
For all eternity.
Always they tramp, the streets so damp,
Lost in iniquity.[1]

— Clem Yore, "The Women Who Walk"

Songs of the Underworld

At the turn of the century, Chicago had a growing population of well over 1.5 million. The police department of 2,430 patrol officers and 30 matrons had their hands full dealing with an increasing number of robberies, burglaries, batteries, and more than 100 homicides a year. The police had little time or resources to do much about the infant city's burgeoning prostitution industry. Streetwalkers strolled the wooden sidewalks along

Lake and Randolph streets in the business district, and shady ladies frequented the back rooms of stagecoach inns and rough-and-ready taverns along the riverbank. As the frontier town grew, the number of prostitutes grew. Low-down crib houses started popping up near the docks and warehouses along the main and south branches of the Chicago River.

In a few short years, as Chicago grew into a civilized city, the sordidness, visibility, and vulgarity of the prostitution trade became socially unacceptable. As early as the 1830s the city council passed ordinances prohibiting houses of ill fame and prostitution:

> Whoever keeps or maintains a house of ill-fame or place for the practice of prostitution or lewdness, or whoever patronizes the same, or lets any house, room or other premises for any such purpose, or shall keep a common, ill-governed and disorderly house to the encouragement of idleness, gaming, drinking, fornication or other misbehavior shall be fined not exceeding $200.
>
> All prostitutes, solicitors to prostitution, and all persons of evil fame or report, plying their vocation upon the streets, alleys or public houses in the city, are hereby declared to be common nuisances, and shall be fined not to exceed one hundred dollars for each offense.[2]

In spite of these ordinances, the city fathers chose to control rather than to eliminate prostitution. Based on the dubious but widely held belief that a little vice was good for trade, the business establishment struck a tacit agreement with local government to allow small pockets of vice to operate in areas adjacent to downtown. These areas became de facto segregated vice districts where brothels and prostitution were permitted to function without police interference. Although commercial sex was illegal by city and state law, these segregated vice districts were unofficially allowed to operate.[3] No one could have predicted it at the time, but these early districts were the seedbed that sprouted the notorious Levee that became the birthplace of the Chicago organized-crime syndicate.

One of the most important and destructive side effects of this segregated vice district policy was the virulent, corruptive influence on local government. The vice operations were so profitable that everyone tried to get a piece of the action. Corruption soon blanketed the police, the aldermen, the mayor, the vice-court judges, the city attorneys, the assistant state's attorneys, and the bail bond entrepreneurs.

These segregated vice districts attracted only the lowest class of economic activity. All types of shoddy businesses and illicit business practices soon emerged. Some of the worst brothels took to drugging affluent customers so that the prostitutes could steal their money, watches, and rings. There was no legal recourse for the unwitting victims whose wallets were lifted from the pile of clothes on a chair while their attentions were diverted. Confidence men and card sharks along the sidewalks and in the saloons had little or no interference from the police while taking special advantage of the unwary. The residents and visitors got drunk in the saloons and started fights that led to knifings and shootings.

Chicago's country-wide reputation as a wide-open town began in the 1850s. Travelers to the Windy City brought back stories of finding vice and crime in every imaginable form. Not only were there burglars and robbers, but there was a prosperous and booming trade in prostitution. During the Civil War, prostitutes invaded the city, lured by the free-wheeling, free-spending patrons enjoying Randolph Street's "Gambler's Row." As many as thirteen hundred women of easy virtue could be found in the saloons, dives, and bordellos and along the sidewalks in the Randolph Street strip of casinos and gambling houses.[4]

Throughout its early years Chicago had several areas where prostitutes plied their trade. One was in a unique spot on washed-up sand along the shore of Lake Michigan near the mouth of the Chicago River. Called the Sands, it was first noticed by the newspapers in the mid-1850s as the home of the city's lowest class of whores. There were a few crude, wooden shanties for whoring, gambling, and drinking. Drunks and bums lived in the area. At the urging of local do-gooders and wealthy business interests Mayor "Long John" Wentworth and a ragtag posse of police, firemen, and idlers tore apart and burned down the decrepit shacks of the Sands in 1857. The prostitutes moved to other areas.

Red-light houses could be found in the downtown business area along Lake and Randolph streets on the north and Adams and Wells streets on the south. Several brothels nestled among the saloons along State and Dearborn streets. After a few years, prostitution appeared at the southwest edge of downtown in an area called Little Cheyenne because of its wildness. There were vice areas on the Near West Side around Morgan and Lake streets and along the north edge of the Chicago River in the dark streets of the wharf district and along Dearborn Street.

Vice tended to locate where there was a ready supply of interested and moneyed men. The downtown business district provided a steady supply of Chicago businessmen and clerks for the brothels at its southern edge. In addition to the local traffic, every day the Dearborn Street railroad station provided hundreds of tradesmen, salesmen, and businessmen who hopped off their trains and walked through the vice area headed to nearby hotels.

The collection of brothels and women working in second- and third-floor flats at the south edge of downtown kept getting pushed further south by the ever-expanding economic engine that needed more space for banks, stores, and offices. Soon, these brothels were moved south to a vice district called Custom House Place, which was around Polk and Harrison streets and Clark and Dearborn streets. After a few years, the bustling red-light district around the Dearborn Street station made its final move and settled in for a very prosperous operation in the area bounded by Eighteenth Street on the north, Twenty-second Street on the south, Clark Street on the west and Wabash Avenue on the east.

Sometimes called the Twenty-second Street vice district, this sixteen-block area became commonly known as the Levee. The era of notoriety for the Levee lasted from the World's Columbian Exposition in 1893 to 1914. In 1911 and 1912, and finally in 1914, a series of dramatic shut-downs ordered by the mayor and the state's attorney turned off the red lights. The Levee's twenty-year run gave young Vincenzo Colosimo the perfect environment to become Big Jim.

Chapter Four

GROWING UP

An Immigrant Italian Boy Becomes
a Young Chicago Man

1892–1897

He was husky, handsome, cunning, literate, temperate and ambitious.[1]
— Jack Lait and Lee Mortimer, *Chicago Confidential*

The first step in becoming accepted in the big city for young Italian immigrant was taking an American name. Dropping Vincenzo, Colosimo began to use James or Jim. He also accepted the Americanization of his last name that in Italy was pronounced Co-LAHZ-i-mo but in Chicago became Col-o-SEE-mo.

Jim lived at 204 Polk Street, a few blocks south of the downtown business center, in a small colony of immigrant southern Italians.[2] Besides the oppressive poverty and intense overcrowding, this was one of the most openly and flagrantly vicious neighborhoods in Chicago. Social conditions could not have been worse. Tumbled-down sheds, dilapidated outhouses, uncollected garbage, and broken sewer pipes added to the squalor and stink. In the rear of many of the structures were foul-smelling stables for work horses with manure mounds in the unpaved alleys.[3] It was in this squalid neighborhood that Jim engaged in early forays into criminality such as pickpocketing and minor extortions from local merchants as one of a six-member band of *ruffianos*.[4]

In his first known legitimate job Colosimo joined the ranks of the illiterate, penniless Italian boys who rose at 2:30 a.m. to secure the first editions of the morning paper. Battling over street corners and hawking each edition as it was thrown off the newspaper trucks, he learned the language and the laws of the streets. He filled the time between editions by pitching pennies or shining the boots and shoes of the local business owners.[5] Colosimo also sold chewing gum and shoestrings on the street corners and ran errands for small-time gamblers and hoodlums from the seedy immigrant neighborhood. He briefly tried hard labor by digging ditches at the lowest of the trade wages. Colosimo's first full-time employment began when he started working as a water boy for a railroad section gang laying track.

At the age of fifteen Jim managed to obtain the position of gandy dancer—adjusting rails, smoothing ballast, and hammering spikes into ties on the railroad right-of-way. The gandy dancers were tough, iron-fisted men with great upper-body strength known for their profanity and drinking. Young Jim was known as the toughest, most fearless man in his work gang.[6] With his railroad pay, he sometimes went with other Italian men to the nearby saloons in the red-light district. Out on the town he was genial and happy-go-lucky, but when he became angered his temperament changed to unforgiving and murderous.

Jim had moved around the corner into the apartment of Emilio and Emmanuela De Stefano at 416 S. Clark Street. Emilio, a tall man of very honest character, was born in Laurenzana, Italy, in 1845. He ran a grocery and a private banking operation. Emmanuela had several children, including Rocco who was born in 1875. Jim spent almost ten years, off and on, living with the De Stefanos and forged a lifelong friendship with their young son Rocco. The young men choose different paths through life: Rocco entered the legal profession, and Jim turned to vice and the restaurant business with local political involvement along the way.

Jim learned many things from his foster parents. In their peaceful apartment he found a love for classical music and opera. Commercial integrity, a character trait in Jim nurtured by Emilio De Stefano, prevailed in Colosimo's business dealings throughout his life. There is no record that Jim ever cheated on a business obligation or failed to pay back a debt. He was known for always keeping his word to his friends and associates.[7]

The De Stefano family took their business reputation very seriously. When Emilio's father died in Italy he had owed money to several persons. Emilio took it upon himself to save sufficient funds to pay off these obligations. In 1889, Emilio returned to his hometown in Italy and, using his own savings, paid back the money his father had owed. In 1896, Emilio was operating a private bank at 416 S. Clark Street. Due to a financial panic, the bank had to close with twelve thousand dollars owing to depositors. Shortly afterward, Emilio died. Following their father's earlier example, Rocco and his two brothers, Louis and Edward, used their own savings to make good on those accounts.[8] Like his father, Rocco grew to be respected throughout the Chicago Italian community because of his good character and charitable activities.

On April 4, 1896, Jim completed the final papers for citizenship in the clerk's office of the Circuit Court of Cook County. He filed under a special provision that allowed minors to become citizens. Rocco witnessed the application and stated that Jim had behaved himself and was of good moral character. Circuit Court Judge Tuthill granted Colosimo citizenship on that same day. James Colosimo was officially an American citizen.

Jim saw many things on the streets and in the saloons of Chicago. Many colorful happenings took place in the red-light neighborhood near where he lived. Prostitutes solicited on the sidewalks and stood in the doorways. Sometimes the sordid business of prostitution had a lighter side. One day police raided several brothels and arrested a dozen scantily clad women. The officers grabbed the women as they exhibited themselves in the windows of the resorts. The captain decided that the best way to win convictions was to bring the women to court in their underwear. Municipal Court Judge Goggin, who heard the case, took an opposite view. He complained, "I don't believe that was good policy to take these women through the public streets. . . . The next time a thing like this is done ask the Civic Federation for paper sacks to cover the prisoners." Then the judge released the women while reprimanding the officers for the outrage of carting a lot of half-naked women through the city's crowded thoroughfares.[9]

In the 1890s Jim witnessed a Chicago that was extraordinary. Newspaperman George Ade said the city had nothing to learn from Port Said, Singapore, the lakefront at Buffalo, the seafront at Bombay, or the crib section of New Orleans, all of which had bad reputations for wild wickedness and lawlessness. In Chicago saloons were everywhere; most of them stayed open around the clock. The red-light districts adjacent to the respectable business section operated day and night.[10]

Jim heard on the street that State's Attorney Charles S. Deneen had said his job was as a prosecutor not a vice buster. Consequently, Jim observed that neither Deneen nor the police took action to clean up the widespread prostitution and gambling. Serving from 1896 to 1904, Deneen allowed vice to grow unhindered. Jim was learning about the prostitution business from a street-level perspective. For a brief period he became a small-time pimp and secured several girls to work for him, but after he had a brush with the police over his street ladies Jim decided to seek other employment.[11]

Chapter Five

WHITE WINGS

Colosimo Follows the Horses

1897–1901

More cunning than intelligent, something of a fist fighter, and above all peculiarly talented in the art of making friends, young Colosimo soon became immensely popular with his countrymen who represented a majority of the population.[1]

— Hal Andrews, *X Marks the Spot*

Chicago was a city of horses. Family-owned carriages, hackney coaches, and hansom cabs were pulled by horses. The single- and double-deck streetcars and five-cent jitney buses were pulled by horses. The drays, carts, and beer, ice, milk, and supply wagons that stocked businesses and markets were pulled by horses. The daily amount of manure deposited by these steeds was staggering in size and smell. In 1890, Health Commissioner Dr. Swayne Wickersham stated that there were one hundred thousand horses in the city and they deposited 750 tons of manure on the streets and alleys each day. As the city's population increased, the number of horses and the amount of horse manure deposited on the streets multiplied.

The high-toned ladies that shopped downtown did not relish the idea of stepping into that muck and mire. Lawyers and judges, accountants and stenographers, traders and buyers all suffered the same indignities when dodging the countless vehicles on the downtown streets. Newspapers editorialized, businessmen fumed, and powerful men's wives lobbied their husbands in their homes. Finally, on September 10, 1897, Mayor Carter Harrison Jr., responding to pressure brought by civic improvement clubs and society women with influential husbands, announced a new program to sweep clean the downtown streets and alleys. The mayor really meant to clean up the horse manure.

The press and the public nicknamed the street sweepers the white wings because the color of their coats, trousers, and round, flat-topped caps was white. The sweepers were equipped with a wide-mouthed shovel, a big push broom and circular wooden carts with very large steel-rimmed wheels. Because the program was initiated in the First Ward, the first sweepers were almost entirely recent Italian immigrants who lived in the ward. These immigrants obtained their jobs through the *padrones* who had influence with the precinct captains.

The local *padrone* obtained for young Jim Colosimo one of the positions as a street sweeper paying $1.50 a day. Each day, Jim pushed his two-wheeled cart behind the drays, carts, wagons, coaches, carriages, and streetcars proud of his title as a white wing.[2] Because of his strength and personality the other white wings looked up to him, and he soon organized his fellow Italian immigrants into a social and athletic club. On election days, the members voted for the candidates he selected.[3]

Jim's leadership role of the white wings and among the Italians in his neighborhood brought him to the attention of First Ward Alderman John Coughlin, nicknamed Bathhouse John, who appointed him to the political position of assistant precinct captain. Jim parlayed his new political clout into a promotion to foreman of street sweepers and a raise to two dollars a day. One of the many advantages of serving as an assistant precinct captain in the ward organization was virtual immunity to arrest.

Precinct captains and their assistants were the backbone of every political organization in the city. They personally registered each adult in their ward who could be relied on to vote for the party candidate. And on election day they turned out the vote for their candidates. In addition, they engaged in all types of voting frauds, from filling in blank ballots to arranging for beatings and kidnapping of members of the other party. They bribed the elections judges and clerks and physically discouraged opposition voters from participating in the election. Building on his new political role Jim was able to organize a large group of voters in the Italian settlement around Polk and Clark streets.[4]

Jim intuitively knew that local political power rested on the two Fs—friendship and favors. He was a friend to many people of all ranks; it came naturally to him. The Italian immigrants trusted him and in turn, through the power of Alderman Coughlin, he was able to provide his followers with city services and public jobs. He assisted them in obtaining admission to desired schools, passing license examinations, bailing relatives out of jail, and moving to the head of the line for admission to County Hospital and the Tuberculosis Sanitarium. Coming from an area in Italy where the feudal system held sway, it was natural for him to function within the feudal system that existed in the First Ward.

Jim used his connections to expand his income beyond his white-wing salary. In 1900, the U.S. Census shows James Colosimo's employment as "magician," which may have meant musician.[5] Jim Colosimo was the only Colosimi listed in the city of Chicago. However, the 1900 *Chicago City Directory* listed him as a saloon and restaurant owner. Many years later, social reformer Kate Adams, talking about Colosimo in his earlier years, said he ran a chop suey joint with prostitutes on the second floor. Maybe this was his first "restaurant."

In April 1901, Colosimo received another promotion in the street-cleaning operation to street and alley inspector. This was a plum job in political circles because inspectors usually did little or no work unless they were trying to shake down one of the local merchants. At that time Frank W. Solon, superintendent of street cleaning, was responsible for spearheading a clean-streets crusade. Colosimo, trusted precinct captain for Coughlin, was given the assignment by Superintendent Solon to clean up litter and trash in the downtown business district.

Colosimo working together with patrolman John Hogan began to look for violators of the clean streets and alleys ordinance. Together they wrote four citations for littering. Much to the distress of the four local businessmen caught by this diligent and hard-working team the offenders were actually arrested instead of being offered an opportunity to make an on-the-scene pay-off. Their cases were assigned to Justice Prindiville in Harrison Street Court. Those charged and their violations were:

> John Repakes—throwing garbage into the river.
> Tony Romagnono—sweeping rubbish into the street at 120 Clark
>   Street.
> John Lewis—sweeping papers into the street at Clark and Madison
>   Streets.
> S. W. Larson—sweeping rubbish into the gutter at 2 and 4 Clark
>   Street.

Judge Prindiville found all of the defendants guilty and fined them each five dollars. The irony of Big Jim Colosimo using his influence to clean up the streets of Chicago cannot be ignored.

On April 16, 1901, Jim was given a legal notice to be served on Andy
Craig at his saloon at 406 State Street. Craig was a longtime lieutenant of
Michael Kenna, nicknamed Hinky Dink, and a bail bondsman at the Harrison
Street police station. The notice required Craig to remove garbage from
behind his saloon. Colosimo, accompanied by Officer Hogan, inspected the
alley at the rear of Craig's very popular saloon and spotted a pile of garbage.
The pair went inside to notify the bartender that the mess had to be removed.
The bartender, a fiery Irishman by the name of Conroy, believed that the
political pull of Craig was stronger than that of this lowly street inspector. The
bartender unwisely placed his hands on Officer Hogan's chest, pushed him out
of the way and ran behind the bar. Hogan, thinking that Conroy was getting a
weapon, moved quickly and grabbed the bartender.

Even when Hogan told Conroy that he was under arrest, the bartender
resisted. He called to several bar patrons for assistance, and two inebriated
customers began to climb over the bar. Reaching for his revolver, Hogan
shouted, "If any of you come over that bar, you will be taking chances!"
They stopped. Jim got on the phone in the back of the saloon and called the
Harrison Street station for a patrol wagon. When it arrived, Hogan shoved
the bartender into the back of the police wagon. At the station, an unrepen-
tant Conroy was charged with disorderly conduct. That night Craig came to
the station and told Hogan, "You have been getting pretty gay, you had better look out."[6]

On the morning of April 27, 1901, Colosimo and Hogan testified before
Justice Martin in Harrison Street Court. Assistant City Attorney Terry R.
Gillan, apparently influenced by Craig, scuttled his own prosecution.
Through his questioning of Hogan, Gillian made it appear that Hogan had
been in the wrong. The defense presented no testimony at all, and Judge Mar-
tin discharged the case.

Colosimo promptly notified Superintendent Solon who became angered
at the attempt to obstruct the city's new clean streets program. He called in the
press. Solon told the reporters, "If the police we employ are not to be protected, and the man who has a little political influence can snap his fingers at
the law, we might as well stop work." Solon also fired off a letter to Chief City
Prosecutor Taylor:

> It was proved beyond reasonable doubt that Conroy was guilty of the dis-
> orderly charge preferred against him, and in the face of this evidence the
> justice, upon hearing the solicitation of Mr. Gillan, without hearing any
> evidence for the defense, discharged the defendant. If this department is
> to be so hampered is it absolutely useless for us to make any effort what-
> ever in having the violations of the street cleaning ordinance taken up.[7]

On April 23, 1901, the ordinance charge against Craig for littering came before a different judge, Justice Prindiville. Craig testified that the bricks and sand in the alley were not his and belonged to a nearby building under construction. Justice Prindiville ruled that it was a technical violation and fined Craig three dollars and costs. Justice was served, albeit poorly, but Colosimo would meet Craig again. During the early 1900s Craig operated a disreputable saloon in the Levee on Twenty-second Street.[8] When Colosimo was running the Levee Craig joined Big Jim's organization as a manager of vice resorts.

By 1902 Jim had expanded his business activities by opening a poolroom.[9]

Next, Jim turned his attention to a new source of income and power—the white wing social and athletic club. Working with Anthony D'Andrea in the Nineteenth Ward, "Dago Mike" Carrozzo, and Republican ward committeeman "Diamond Joe" Esposito, Jim transformed the social and athletic club into the first union of street sweepers in Chicago. The Chicago Laborers were the first step in Colosimo organizing or taking control of various laborers' unions composed of mainly Italian immigrants.[10] To run the union, Colosimo selected Carrozzo.[11]

Carrozzo, who came to Chicago from Montaguto, Italy, in 1906, was spotted early by Colosimo as Carrozzo shined shoes on street corners in the Levee. Colosimo liked the lad at once. He was impressed with his youthful enterprise and innate shrewdness and gave him a job as his messenger and errand boy. As Carrozzo grew up he became a tough street fighter, and Jim began to utilize him as a personal bodyguard. He taught Carrozzo how to win the friendship of the people in the Levee and how to do favors for them. Big Jim showed Carrozzo how to get the immigrants registered to vote and how to take those who were illiterate behind the curtain of the polling booth and to fill in their ballots for them. And finally, Colosimo instructed Carrozzo how to vote many times on election day for those who were too drunk, sick, or infirm to get to the polls.[12] Carrozzo, an apt student, went on to head twenty-five labor locals that made him a labor union czar and brought him untold dollars.[13]

In a second move into the trade-union field, Jim provided assistance to Joseph D'Andrea, brother of Anthony D'Andrea, to become business agent for the excavators' union. Because of his role in these two unions, Colosimo was able to expand his voting bloc beyond the Italian immigrants in the First Ward. Colosimo's power in the trade-union movement was described by labor-union author Robert Finch: "Al Capone gets too much credit [for his control over labor unions]. He simply added, by violent means, to a trade union empire that had been built from scratch in the Laborers by James 'Big Jim' Colosimo."[14]

The laborers' and excavators' unions remained firmly in the hands of the leaders of the Chicago organized-crime syndicate for the next seventy-five

years until the U.S. Justice Department decided to crack down on the LIUNA
(Laborers International Union of North America). The control of these
unions moved from Colosimo to Torrio to Capone to Frank Nitti to Frank
Rica to Tony Accardo to Momo Giancana to Joey Aiuppa, the legendary dons
of the Chicago Outfit.[15]

Jim's advancement in the First Ward Democratic Party and his employment and promotions in the white wings were due to the power of two men—
Coughlin and Kenna. They were the most colorful aldermen in the history of
Chicago. Rulers of the First Ward, their power to control the outcome of an
election was so great that for many years no mayor or backroom political boss
crossed them. The story of these men and how they gained control of the city
council is nearly unbelievable.

Chapter Six

TWO COLORFUL ALDERMEN

The Protectors of the Levee

1892–1904

Explaining why the two aldermen turned down bribe of $150,000 and other inducements offered by traction magnet Charles T. Yerkes for their votes for a fifty-year franchise of the city's traction system, the "Bath" said, "I was talkin' a while back with Senator Billy Mason and he told me, 'Keep clear of th' big stuff, John, it's dangerous. You and Mike stick to th' small stuff; there's little risk and in the long run it pays a damned sight more.'"[1]

— Emmett Dedmon, *Fabulous Chicago*

Chicago would never again witness an era as frenzied and dramatic as the years between the Great Fire and the end of the Levee. Up to a dozen newspapers exploited the comic and tragic happenings that occurred almost daily. Elections were considered entertainment, and local politicians were more important to city residents than governors or presidents.[2] The most amazing and memorable of the political figures from this colorful era were Bathhouse John Coughlin and Michael "Hinky Dink" Kenna.

Talking about Coughlin and Kenna means talking about the First Ward. The original boundary of the First Ward began at the south bank of the Chicago River and extended south to Monroe Street. The west boundary was the south branch of the river, and the east was the shore of Lake Michigan. The north, east, and west boundaries of the First Ward remained the same throughout the years, but the south boundary was constantly changing. By

1890, the ward's southern boundary had moved to Twelfth Street, by 1901 to Twenty-second Street and by 1912 to Thirty-first Street.[3]

The First Ward had a split personality, with big business and financial interests in the north end and immigrants and prostitutes in the south. The ward was an incredible mixture of good and evil, legitimate business and degenerate vice, Prairie Avenue with millionaire mansions and Dearborn Street with rollicking houses of pleasure. There were saloonkeepers and ministers, gamblers and social workers, businessmen and crooks, politicians and reformers, society women and whores. This ward held the heart and soul of the city, and controlling the ward were Aldermen Coughlin and Kenna.[4]

In the south end of the ward, the vice and saloon operators such as Jim Colosimo provided unquestioning financial and voting support for Coughlin and Kenna because the wily pair ensured the protection of the vice operators from police interference. The political power of the two aldermen enabled them to select the district police captain who directed the uninterrupted operations of the vice district. In turn, the two aldermen ruled the Levee with an iron hand.

At the ward's north end, the business and financial leaders realized that the aldermen were the link to their needs for governmental services and privileges. Coughlin and Kenna held veto power in the city council over all building, zoning, and licensing matters within their ward. If a department store, hotel, or bank needed a city license or land rezoned or a driveway permit or an alley closed, Coughlin and Kenna determined if the request would be honored. So the businessmen provided financial support for the aldermen whenever it was asked.

The first of the pair to be elected alderman was Coughlin. He was born on August 15, 1860. The Coughlin family lived in a frame house at Harrison and Franklin streets in a vice-filled area on the south edge of downtown. Through the racing and gambling connections of his brother, John Coughlin obtained a position as a rubber in a Turkish bathhouse on Clark Street. He soon moved to a better situation at the bathhouse in the Palmer House, considered the finest in the city. After he had saved sufficient money, he purchased his own bathhouse at 143 E. Madison Street. Shortly afterwards he opened a second bathhouse in the basement of the Brevoort Hotel. These bathhouses were heavily patronized by gamblers, racetrack men, and politicians.

Through his bathhouses, Coughlin became acquainted with Chesterfield Joe Macklin, the Democrat political boss in the First Ward. Their friendship resulted in Macklin naming Coughlin to the post of precinct captain in the Democratic ward organization. Macklin was pleased with the voting support that Coughlin was able to develop and moved the aspiring politician into the position of president of the First Ward Democratic Club.

Coughlin patiently served Macklin and waited for an opportunity for advancement. That time occurred in 1892 during a bitter fight within the ward's Democratic Party ranks over the candidacy for the aldermanic position. Macklin, realizing that he could not win, seized the initiative and maneuvered Coughlin into the opening.

In those early days, each ward had two aldermen elected in alternate years for two-year terms. These aldermen made up a thoroughly corrupt legislative group; graft and bribery were everyday occurrences. Even though the pay was only three dollars per meeting, many of the aldermen managed to develop significant wealth. Some owned large homes in wealthy neighborhoods, others enjoyed second homes outside the city, and a few even had country estates complete with riding stables.

During his initial bid for alderman, the reform newspapers strongly opposed John Coughlin and endorsed the bid of the independent Republican candidate. The papers pointed out that Coughlin was supported by the ward's vice operators and could be expected to favor them if elected. On election day, a burly team of Coughlin followers worked diligently at the polling places to ensure that only the "right" people voted. The turnout was embarrassingly low, but Coughlin won. The date was April 5, 1892. Amazingly, the rotund and mustached bathhouse owner held that office uninterrupted for the next forty-six years—longer than any other alderman in the history of the Chicago city council.

Chicago historians Lloyd Wendt and Herman Kogan described Coughlin's attire as he entered the city council chambers to take his seat for the first time:

> Coughlin had donned a coat of delicate gray with trousers to match. His waistcoat was a darkish green, checked with white, his racing colors. His shoes were a bright tan and he wore a shirt of brown silk. The ends of his waxed mustache jutted out like those of a grand vizier, and his closely cropped hair thrust up like that of a Prussian general.[5]

In 1893 Carter Harrison was elected mayor without the help of Coughlin, who had unfortunately thrown his lot with the opposition. When Harrison took office, he showed his strong displeasure with Coughlin and the First Ward Democratic Organization for their lack of support on election day. Acting under Harrison's orders, police raided gambling houses in the First Ward. The vice operators began to doubt the ability of Alderman Coughlin to protect them. Seeking assistance, Coughlin turned to saloon owner and fellow member of the First Ward Democratic Organization, the politically wise Michael Kenna.

Kenna had been born on a cold winter's day in 1858 in a rough frame shanty on DeKoven Street near Conley's Patch. During his youth Kenna's boyfriends hung the nickname Hinky Dink on the diminutive lad. His formal schooling ended when he was twelve. He began hawking newspapers on State Street. Moving from one lowly occupation to another, by age twenty-four he had saved sufficient money to open a small saloon at 120 W. Van Buren Street in the heart of downtown. The place was really small, slightly larger than eight feet by ten feet. Kenna poured drinks into dirty shot glasses from a gallon jug of whiskey. The sign in the window read "Hinky Dink's Place." To add to his income, Kenna opened a gambling room on the second floor. At five feet, one inch tall he was forced to develop a stern demeanor to prevent patrons from brawling.

Michael Kenna and John Coughlin were decidedly a mismatched pair. As Wendt and Kogan pointed out:

> Their differences were vast. Coughlin was bluff and hearty; Kenna was the glummest little man in the ward organization. Coughlin was the accomplished backslapper; Kenna cared little for gay companionship and was aloof almost to the point of snobbery. Coughlin laughed at everyone's jokes, asserted his friendship for every man and sought votes in his bathhouse precinct by knocking on doors and personally extolling the multifold attributes of the party candidates; Kenna spoke sparingly, rarely smiled, counted only a picked few as his friends, and organized the saloon hangers-on as a corps of assistance precinct captains to make door-to-door calls and offer promises of free beer and lunch. Coughlin was all sound and fury; Kenna was silence and action.[6]

However, both Coughlin and Kenna were wise and cunning and were natural-born politicians who agreed that the name of the game of life was to make money and gain power. Coughlin had become alderman first, but Kenna soon joined him. They realized that in unity there was strength, and they remained together throughout their careers.

Having worked together in the Democratic ward organization, it was natural for Coughlin to seek Kenna's counsel in the problems caused by the police raids instigated by the mayor. Kenna proposed a twofold plan. Coughlin should offer strong support for Harrison's planned run for the U.S. Senate, and when he was in the mayor's good graces, take maximum advantage of the number of visitors expected for the World's Columbian Exposition of 1893. To show his pleasure over Kenna's assistance and to cement their relationship, Alderman Coughlin made Kenna the committeeman of the First Ward, a position with responsibility for all patronage, neighborhood city services, and backroom political dealing in the ward. He also became the collector for protection money and graft payments.

As directed by Kenna, Coughlin met with the mayor and offered his support in Harrison's planned senate run. Harrison accepted and overnight the heat went off on the gambling joints and brothels in the First Ward.

Kenna next went to work to improve an old protection system that had been set up years earlier by gambling boss Michael Cassius McDonald. The madams, gamblers, and saloonkeepers obtained protection from police harassment and raids by paying a fee to a collector. A portion of the money collected was used for a defense fund to provide bail and court representation for anyone who was arrested in a vice raid. The majority of the money was split among the aldermen and the district police captain. Isaac Gitelson "Ike" Bloom, the owner of Freiberg's Dance Hall, was put in charge of collections, and James Colosimo became one of the collectors. This new role added to the relationship between Colosimo and Coughlin and Kenna—a relationship that was to continue to the day Colosimo's body was placed in his casket.

In 1895 Kenna told Coughlin that he would like to run for the second aldermanship in the First Ward. Explaining this action to reporters, Kenna remarked: "It's this way. I didn't want an office, but the boys kept coming to me and asking me to run, more for a joke, I thought, than anything else, and so I finally consented, after considering this matter carefully to make this run."[7]

Solidly backed by Coughlin, Kenna easily won the nomination for Democratic candidate for alderman by acclamation of the assembled precinct captains at a rowdy ward meeting. Winning the election was not as easy. In his first run for alderman Kenna was defeated.

Realizing that a large financial chest would be needed to ensure the outcomes of future elections, Coughlin and Kenna decided to hold a fundraising ball. The event was a resounding success, and Coughlin secured reelection with the new income. In 1897, the pair schemed to use their political power to secure two objectives: push Kenna into the aldermanic post and Carter Henry Harrison Jr. into the mayor's office. The Civic Federation took great offense at Kenna's candidacy. The federation used all of the vitriolic language against the little man's candidacy they could. They publicly declared Kenna as unfit to serve.[8]

A stormy election campaign followed, but when the votes were counted on April 6, 1897, Harrison and Kenna were winners. The Levee erupted in glee; now the lid would be off and the brothels could run without police interference. Informal parades snaked their way to dangerous bonfires while fireworks discharged continuously. Copious amounts of beer and whiskey were consumed while prostitutes and gamblers linked arms with bums and drunks. It was a long night of revelry and hijinks.

Kenna celebrated his election by opening a new saloon—Working-man's Exchange. The exchange offered a giant stein of beer for five cents. In 1904, Kenna boasted he had once sold twelve thousand glasses of beer in a week.[9] The saloon grew to be one of the city's most famous with entrances on Clark and Van Buren streets, a thirty-foot walnut bar, a huge table filled with free lunch items, and a reputation for serving the largest steins in the city.

The city council during this era was a sad conglomeration of uneducated and unethical men with backgrounds in ward politics but not in civic govern-ment. They stood for two things—making as much money as they could and getting reelected every two years. Ninth Ward Alderman Nathan T. Brenner described this lack of integrity: "There are only three aldermen in the entire sixty-eight who are not able and willing to steal a red-hot stove." A slightly milder view was held by the Civic Federation, which estimated that no less than fifty-seven of the sixty-eight aldermen were thieves and grafters. Their small three-dollar-per-meeting stipend was augmented by twelve thousand to thirty thousand dollars a year in graft, plus special bonuses occurring when-ever a transit or utility franchise was up for vote.[10] Coughlin and Kenna proudly took their seats in the front row among this band of thieves. Each year their power grew until they were the bosses of the council.

For Coughlin and Kenna the increase in vice activity in the First Ward due to the toleration of these activities by Mayor Harrison led to a unique problem. The vice area grew so large that it extended beyond the south boundary of the First Ward. Saloons and brothels in the Second Ward would not be beholden to Coughlin and Kenna. The vice operators would look to the Second Ward aldermen for their protection. This situation was intolera-ble. It endangered the unified influence over the Levee that Coughlin and Kenna enjoyed. The Second Ward alderman, Democrat Charles F. Gunther, owner of the largest candy manufacturing company in Chicago, was not inclined to cooperate with Coughlin and Kenna either in sharing protection money or changing his ward's northern boundaries. For the First Ward alder-men the solution was clear—Gunther had to go.

To the great pleasure of the two aldermen, political newcomer William Hale Thompson had decided to run for alderman of the Second Ward on the Republican ticket. On election day in April 1900, instead of the usual loan to Gunther of Democrat "voters" from the flop houses in the First Ward, Coughlin and Kenna held back. Gunther lost, and Thompson became alder-man with a big debt to the canny pair who explained to the freshman alderman that he could repay them by introducing a bill in the city council to revise the southern boundaries of the First Ward so as to include the entire Levee Dis-trict. Thompson cooperated fully, and with the political muscle of Coughlin and Kenna the ordinance moving the First Ward's south boundary further south was passed on January 7, 1901. The entire Levee was back under control of Coughlin and Kenna.[11]

For almost fifty years the two men held their power in the First Ward. Not only did they collect the protection money from the vice operators and the bribes from the selling of permits of all types, they reaped sizable graft from public contracts and traction franchises. They named judges, mayors, and governors.[12] They controlled an army of city jobs. Attacked repeatedly by reformers, crusaders, newspaper publishers, ministers, clergymen, and business leaders the pair only grew bolder. Republicans tried again and again to unseat them but failed. To show his disdain for this criticism, Coughlin enlarged his wardrobe to include more colorful outfits, including a mountain-green dress suit, silk hat, red vest, and patent-leather shoes. In the background Kenna quietly manipulated ward and council politics while ensuring the flow of payments from the brothels and gambling dens of the ward.

Not content with being sartorially outrageous, Coughlin also wrote poetry and songs.[13] Bathhouse John's most famous ballad was titled "Dear Midnight of Love." He premiered this song to a packed Chicago Opera House on the night of October 8, 1900. A carefully selected young girl backed by a chorus of fifty male and female singers in formal dress and the Cook County Democratic Marching Club band took the stage and the words of the song filled the theater:

> *Dear Midnight of Love,*
> *Why did we meet?*
> *Dear Midnight of Love,*
> *Your face is so sweet.*
> *Pure as the angels above,*
> *Surely again we shall speak,*
> *Loving only as doves,*
> *Dear Midnight of Love.*[14]

There were three verses of a similar nature. The crowd roared and demanded endless encores and even brought Coughlin himself to the stage for a speech. Mayor Harrison took bows from his box. Pandemonium reigned. Finally the curtain descended. The song was published with the cover showing a majestic photo of Bathhouse John himself in full dress clothes flanked by white doves.

It was Coughlin's finest moment, but dark clouds loomed on the horizon. There was steadily mounting criticism and growing public pressure against the Levee, considered by many to be a festering sore on the city's reputation. The blue-blooded wives of many of the city's most influential businessmen found the district to be repugnant and distressing, and, as usual, the press and the pulpit were outraged. A war between the libertines and the reformers was steadily building over the concept of a segregated vice district. Fighting the reformers were Aldermen Bathhouse John Coughlin and Michael "Hinky Dink" Kenna and their staunch ally, Big Jim Colosimo.

Chapter Seven

THE LEVEE

"Pick a Baby, Boys, Don't Get Stuck to Your Seats"

1893—1911

If virtue would allure like sin,
How easily might goodness win various
If right went laughing by like wrong,
The devil would lose half his throng.[1]

— Paul James Duff,
Side Lights on Darkest Chicago

The success of the World's Columbian Exposition of 1893 brought money to Chicago's businessmen, fame to Chicago's reputation, and prostitutes to Chicago's streets. Sensing big money and willing gentlemen, loose women from American and European cities headed to Chicago in 1892 and 1893. How many of these scarlet ladies arrived was never clear; the reformers counted high and the police counted low. In 1867 the estimate was that there were thirteen thousand prostitutes in Chicago. By 1900, the figure had risen to ten thousand.

The majority of Chicago's prostitutes worked in red-light districts that were called levees. The name "levee" was coined in the 1800s by gamblers who rode steamboats up and down the Mississippi. Each of the major riverfront towns had a bawdy area featuring rough saloons and low-class whores along the docks. The gamblers called these levees. By the 1850s this term was used in Chicago to designate an area along the north bank of the Chicago

River where low-down whorehouses and disreputable dives operated along the dark streets near the warehouses and loading docks.

After the Civil War, Chicago had four vice districts called levees—two in the south end of downtown and one each on the Near West Side and on the Near North Side. The west and north districts lost their nickname over the years, but the two south-side levees retained the moniker. At the turn of the century, both south-side levees were only a few blocks from the city's business and financial center. Each of these levees was treated as a segregated vice district. In a segregated vice district the laws of Illinois and Chicago concerning prostitution were not enforced, and saloons were allowed to operate all night. The city fathers had decided that it was better to have vice under control and that eradication was impossible and not good business.

Custom House Place, the most famous of the red-light districts, was only a few blocks south of the business district.

While Carter Harrison was mayor, he chose to continue the practice of having segregated vice districts. Open and notorious resorts outside of the segregated vice districts were harassed and raided by the police.

This decision by the mayor would spark a debate that raged for many years. On one side were the city fathers and the major businessmen who considered prostitution an important attraction for traveling commercial men and male visitors to the city. On the other were the ministers and clergymen, later joined by the reformers and crusaders, who were outraged by the immorality and decadence of the prostitutes and red-light districts. No compromise could be found, and the battle ebbed and rose for fifty years.

In 1903, pressured by real estate interests, Mayor Carter Harrison Jr. was forced to move the vice areas further from downtown. Because both areas were in the First Ward, the mayor talked this matter over with Alderman Coughlin. Bathhouse John found a way to satisfy the businessmen while keeping the vice in his ward. He convinced the resort operators to relocate, en masse, to Twenty-second Street. The new vice district was bounded by Twenty-second Street on the south, Archer Avenue on the north, Wabash Avenue on the east, and Armour Avenue on the west. Now called the Levee, with a capital *L*, by the press, police, and public, this area boasted the largest concentration of vice activity in any city in the United States.[2] The few madams that had remained behind either closed up shop or fled into the Levee after raids directed by State's Attorney John J. Healy.

Male visitors to Chicago had no trouble finding a good time. The hackney drivers in the taxi stands, the coppers on corner duty, the doormen and bellboys at the hotels, and the kid at the corner newsstand knew the directions to the Levee. Most of these self-appointed guides knew the names of the more famous madams and the addresses of their bordellos. So did the touts who made a living by steering customers to specific resorts. Haunting the train depots, the hotel lobbies, and even the downtown sidewalks, these streetwise hucksters quickly sized up potential customers and whispered friendly advice into their not-so-innocent ears. Cheap paper booklets containing the names and addresses of the resorts were given away on street corners and cigar stands. Even a gaudy weekly newspaper was available that contained suggestive gossip and advertisements about the madams, the sporting ladies, and the pimps.[3]

The Levee had everything a man seeking action might desire, from fancy bordellos to bawdy resorts to dirty crib shacks. In addition, there were gambling joints, saloons, dance halls, seamy theaters with burlesque acts, barrelhouse joints, voodoo doctors, peep shows, obscene book and magazine stores, rigged auctions, opium dens, and drug stores selling condoms, fake elixirs, homemade nostrums, and useless salves for dealing with certain types of infections.[4] Peep shows were offered to the youngest of boys. The Palace of Illusion operated by Harry Thurston had a Negro chorus line performing obscene dances.[5]

The Levee's teeming streets and refuse-strewn alleys housed blacksmith shops, all-night oyster bars, livery stables, pawnshops, Chinese laundries, flop houses, barbershops in basements of tenement buildings, tintype picture galleries, second-hand and third-hand stores, cheap restaurants, undertakers, hot tamale stands, air-rifle shooting galleries, "fooey" lawyers, bail-bondsmen, and countless newsstands. Walking vendors from preteens to the aged and infirm filled the blocks hawking pencils, shoelaces, candies, and a variety of junk.[6]

The heart of the Levee was Freiberg's Dance Hall at 20 E. Twenty-second Street near Wabash Avenue. Gents could purchase drinks for the house ladies and dance with them until the early hours of the morning. The dancing included the most popular steps of the day such as the bunny hug, turkey trot, grizzly bear, castle walk, shimmy, and foxtrot. The house ladies were encouraged to take their customers next door to a seedy hotel for a quick interlude. Most of the ladies' earnings went to the management. The dance hall operated with unwritten rules. No overt sexual acts were permitted on the premises, and fights were swiftly dealt with by club-swinging bouncers and bartenders.

Freiberg's was owned and operated by notorious and menacing Ike Bloom with Bathhouse John Coughlin as a silent partner. Ike Bloom provided the link between Coughlin and the Levee operators, and the money followed the link. Decisions as to whether a resort could open and the weekly protection fee were made in the dance hall's private office. Sol Friedman, Ike Bloom's brother-in-law, operated a nearby store where Levee operators had been told to purchase the clothing for their prostitutes and the whiskey and supplies for their resorts. The fire insurance for the saloons and bordellos was obtained from Coughlin's insurance agency.

Because of its notorious popularity, Freiberg's frequently was targeted by the crusaders and reformers on their inspection tours of the Levee. Bloom welcomed these parties and bought them rounds of lemonade. He gave them a table at the edge of the dance floor even if he had to push regular customers to the back row. Bloom said, "When they asks for the center of the dance floor to kneel down and pray, and sing 'Washed in the Blood of the Lamb,' I give it to 'em. I even give 'em my jazz band too, which plays their accompaniment and plays it mighty damn well."[7] Bloom was convinced that the publicity resulting from their speeches and sermons brought in additional business.

An unwritten agreement between resort operators and nearby property owners set the eastern boundary of the Levee at the L tracks behind Wabash Avenue. This agreement was reached because a few blocks east of the Levee were the magnificent mansions of Prairie Avenue where many of the city's wealthiest families lived in luxury and grandeur. Over time, the increasing number of resorts caused the boundary to weaken. In 1903, Prairie Avenue's longtime residents decided to fight back. Lawyer Louis J. Behan was hired by vigilance committees in the First Ward and Second Ward to bring legal action against prostitutes who moved too far east. Behan secured indictments against keepers of several resorts. When the cases went to court, charges against twenty-three of the twenty-four defendants were dismissed. The remaining trial involved a charge against Ike Bloom. On the eve of his court day, Bloom took the witnesses against him to dinner at Freiberg's and bought them many drinks and large steaks with all the trimmings. Bloom then instructed them how to testify the following day. The next morning Bloom was turned loose.

The crown jewel of the resorts on Dearborn Street was the Everleigh Club, which was opened in 1900 by Ada and Minna Everleigh. Competing with the Everleigh sisters were Vic Shaw, who had been the queen of the madams until the arrival of the Everleigh sisters, and Georgie Spencer. Both madams offered high-class prostitutes in luxurious surroundings. Shaw's bordello at 2014 S. Dearborn Street featured Gladys Martin, who was Vic's biggest moneymaker. Nearby were other upscale houses, including French Emma's, Casino, Utopia, and Sappho.[8]

Also on Dearborn Street was a dive operated by "Blubber Bob" Gray, who weighed three hundred pounds, and his wife, Therese. The customers were seated on crude wooden benches while most unattractive whores wearing transparent shifts walked back and forth across the parlor. Therese would literally shout at the men, "Pick a baby, boys! Don't get stuck to your seats."[9]

One discreet house catered to prominent out-of-town businessmen.

These customers notified the madam in advance of their arrival dates. The madam would arrange for women to meet the specific eccentricities of the clients. This resort offered periodic wine dinners with notices sent out to a selected list of Chicago businessmen. The working girls, called "inmates" in the press, wore gauzy slip-overs while serving the guests at the dinner table.[10]

Many of the bordellos featured special services. An expensive resort offered wealthy patrons the opportunity to view catfights between two whores in a boxing ring. The Jap House, with a large Japanese lantern over the front doorway, had Oriental girls with reputed unique charms. The House of All Nations had two front doors: one for two-dollar visits and the other charging five dollars. Unknown to any uninformed visitors, the same girls covered both entrances. The madam at the House of All Nations maintained that her girls were direct imports from Poland, Bohemia, Sweden, and other countries, but the truth was that they were first-generation descendants of immigrants from those countries. The California bordello featured speed of service. Patrons were quickly moved by the madam from the front door to their choice of a girl, to brief seclusion, and to the door. The regular charge was one dollar, but when business was slow the price dropped to seventy-five cents.[11] Other colorful establishments were the Little Green House, the Bucket of Blood, and French Emma's with an all-mirrored bedroom.

High-class Negro prostitutes could be found at Black May's, which was open only to white men. If a customer had enough money he could witness a "circus" that featured the most depraved acts imaginable. Across from Black May's was a low-cost brothel offering Chinese and Japanese women.

Each of the better brothels had a "perfessor" who played the piano. Some of these talented pianists were paid as much as ten dollars a week plus tips. Police reporters would sit for hours listening to the music and telling stories, all the while downing free drinks. These piano players developed a unique style of music, which eventually would be called ragtime.

Two detectives at the Twenty-second Street police station dutifully registered the girls in the resorts. A file was kept with their names and identification. The girls were instructed by the madams on what to say in their interviews with the detectives. They were told to claim that they were from out of town, had led immoral lives before being hired at the resort, and were of legal age. The police enumeration records at the station in the Levee listed eleven hundred girls working in resorts in 1909—a gross undercount.[12]

The public display of vice in the Levee was staggering. At all hours of the day and night women in their underclothes could be seen at windows making vulgar hand signs. In the warm weather with the windows open the ladies made vile suggestions to passing men. Some women in open kimonos stood in doorways of resorts beckoning men inside. Touts on the sidewalk extolled the vices and beauty of the women inside. Bright white lights on signs above the doorways blazed with the names of the bordellos.

Saturday nights in the Levee had a carnival atmosphere. The tinkle of piano music came from the doorways and windows. Carriages and hackneys arrived in an unending stream from early in the evening until the morning hours. Well-attired Gold Coast gentlemen, having earlier had cocktails at their clubs, entered the better houses in groups. Blue-collar workers swung from the steps of the horse cars and headed into the garishly lit streets. Pimps, cadets, and touts graphically explained the wares available in their respective houses. Meanwhile, young lads in their early teens came to gawk at the beckoning women in the windows and began their sex education.

Enjoying the pleasures of the Levee were students and teachers, lawyers and judges, doctors and ministers. There were members of the city council, county board of commissioners, state legislature, and U.S. Congress. Out-of-towners felt comfortable visiting the Levee because they saw the tall-helmeted patrolmen at each corner. The wealthy patronized upscale bordellos, while those with less than a dollar visited the street cribs.[13]

The lowest of the Levee dives were around Armour Avenue and Nineteenth Street in a "Bedbug Row" of filthy cribs. Crib houses contained one prostitute in a tiny, dirty room or shed—frequently with a dirt floor. There was a cot with a dirty mattress, a dirty towel, and a water basin. Many of the girls were Negroes who charged twenty-five cents a customer. Others were has-beens or alcoholics who could no longer get employment at an upscale resort. It was next to this area that Big Jim Colosimo opened his first whorehouse.

Underneath all the showy glitz and racy entertainment, the driving force behind the Levee was money. While the madams were the visible operators of the resorts, the actual owners were often tough and shady characters.

The Levee had become very important to Kenna and Coughlin and the First Ward Democratic Party. The protection money and fees provided a large and continuing source of income. The financial kitty of the two aldermen allowed them to serve as powerful rulers, not only in their ward, but also in the city council. Using their war chest the aldermen could place a desirable mayor into office or prevent an opponent getting elected.[14]

Chapter Eight

"If Christ Came to Chicago"

Rev. William T. Stead

1893–1894

Said Christ our Lord, "I will go and see
How the men, My brothers, believe in Me."
But still, wherever His steps they led
The Lord in sorrow bent down his head,
From under heavy foundation stones
The Son of Mary heard bitter groans.
"Have ye founded your thrones and altars then,
On the bodies and souls of living men?
And think ye that building shall endure
Which shelters the noble and crushes the poor"?[1]

— William Stead,
If Christ Came to Chicago

O n October 28, 1893, the same day that Mayor Carter Harrison was assassinated by a crazed gunman, a stout man with a carefully tended beard alighted from a train at a downtown station. His clothes were of the heavy woolen variety popular in the British Isles. The man, Rev. William T. Stead, would ignite a reform movement in Chicago that would besiege the Levee.[2] The son of a Congregational minister, he was a dedicated reformer and a fire-breathing journalist. In England, where he was the publisher of the *Review of Reviews* and former editor of the *Pall Mall Gazette*, his editorials caused prime ministers to listen and parliament to react.[3]

Many months earlier, a director of the World's Columbian Exposition had read an article about reform that Stead had written. The director convinced the other board members to invite the Englishman to Chicago. The fair had raised the city's prominence but also the level of vice and corruption. The board wanted the fair to show the world that Chicago was a great city, but the image that the city was getting was not what the board members had hoped. They decided that Reverend Stead should come and assess what needed to be done to clean up the city. A little late, he arrived on the day the fair ended.[4]

Stead promptly set about to investigate the city's social conditions. He dined with the wealthy in the massive homes on Prairie Avenue. He had tea with society ladies. He spoke with civic leaders, important dignitaries, and wealthy businessmen. But he didn't stop there. He repeatedly visited with the lower classes and spoke with bums, madams, prostitutes, and crooked and honest cops. He interviewed aldermen who freely admitted their part in city hall boodling. He visited police stations, bordellos, and crib houses. During the aftermath of a blizzard, he worked for three subfreezing days with snow-removal laborers.[5] He visited "Hinky Dink's" Workingman's Exchange on State Street and Mary Hastings's brothel on Custom House Place.

What Stead found in Chicago brought him sadness and despair. It caused him to bemoan the path the city was following. He resolved to restore Chicago to its true role as the shaper of the American destiny. Only one month after his arrival in Chicago, Stead convened a conference of religious and civic leaders in the Central Music Hall. His announced purpose was "to consider whether, if Christ visited Chicago, he would find anything he would wish to have altered."[6] In his talks at two mass meetings at the music hall he decried the flagrant vice, crime, and poverty conditions, the indifference of the leading businessmen, and the pernicious political corruption that he had found. He was sharply critical of the wealthy business leaders of whom he said: "Who then are the disreputable? Those who are dowered by society with all the gifts and opportunities, and who have wealth, leisure, and talent, and live entirely self-indulgently, these are much more disreputable in the eyes of God and man than the worst harlot on Fourth Avenue."[7] He named millionaire businessmen Marshall Field, Philip Armour, and George Pullman as Chicago's Holy Trinity at the heart of the problems. He spoke of their greed and disregard and indifference to the plight of the poor workers who toiled at their companies.

Stead was moved to write a book about what he had found in Chicago. Even though the work was four hundred pages long, it took him only two months to complete the manuscript. On February 24, 1894, Stead published *If Christ Came to Chicago*, a startling book that rocked the city to its foundations. It became a best seller in the United States and Europe, selling more than three hundred thousand copies.[8]

The fame of the book rested almost entirely on a detailed exposé of Chicago's dirty linen. Stead explicitly linked corruption and vice to Field, Pullman, and Mayor Harrison. He attacked commercialized vice, lax tax collections, inept newspapers, boodling aldermen, greedy capitalists, political corruption, and crooked cops. He asserted that sixty-six of the city's sixty-eight aldermen were grafting and most of the police force was accepting vice payoffs. He declared that police officers were collecting from fifteen to a hundred dollars a week from the madams.[9]

Stead believed that the underlying reason why corruption and vice flourished in the city was the general indifference of the city fathers, the law-abiding citizens, and even the ministers and religious leaders. He said that the people had replaced the religion of the church with the same opportunistic philosophy as that of the dominant political engine in Chicago, the Democratic Party. Mincing no words, Stead described this situation in blunt terms:

> "We have asserted in its baldest and plainest form the working principle on which the smart man of Chicago acts. Everything that is not illegal is assumed by him to be right . . . so long as it is permitted by law or so long as they can evade the law by any subterfuge, they consider that they are doing perfectly all right. They believe in the state, they have ceased to believe in God."[10]

The book contained a two-color map with the location and names of the brothels, gambling joints, and saloons in the Custom House Place vice district at Harrison and Dearborn streets in Coughlin and Kenna's First Ward. In this one precinct, Stead found thirty-seven houses of prostitution. The book listed the owners, tenants, and taxpayers of "property used for immoral purposes."[11]

Stead noted that there were more than four hundred brothels operating in Chicago. He decried the fact that many of these whorehouses were in buildings owned by prominent citizens who profited handsomely from the rents.[12] He was against licensing of prostitution but felt little could be done to end the age-old problem. He favored going after the worst places under public nuisance actions.[13]

Stead estimated there were ten thousand prostitutes in Chicago. He said high number was the result of the low wages paid by the city's most prominent department stores. He cited a case involving the head of a dressmaking section in one of the stores who also was the manager of a house of ill-fame. He said she found the combination of the two positions "very convenient, as she recruited in one establishment by day for assistants in the other at night."[14]

Stead reported that his research into the brothels revealed the twin roots of prostitution. Carrie Watson, a smart and cynical madam of a longtime Clark Street brothel, had told Stead that women turned to prostitution because of poverty on the part of the woman and passion on the part of the man. Watson had explained to Stead that stenographers in offices and clerks in stores did not earn enough to buy clothes or support their families. As a result, some of them entered the immoral life and discovered that it was an easy way to make a living.[15]

Stead met with the colorful madam Vina Fields. He described Fields as a Negro woman who ran one of the largest resorts in the city. He said Madam Fields had "over sixty girls in the house during the fair, all Negro, but all for white men." Fields told Stead that she believed prostitution was caused by misery from unhappy homes, cruel parents, and bad husbands.[16]

Stead portrayed madams such as Kitty Plant and Mary Hastings as the most disreputable of their profession. He found the obscene performances at Plant's bordello were "unnatural and worse than bestial." He reported that Hastings ran a fetid house at 144 Custom House Place in an alley between Dearborn and Clark streets. He said Hastings boasted of employing girls who had been thrown out of other houses for fighting or stealing and that "no client could suggest an act too disgusting to be performed in her establishment."[17]

Reverend Stead lashed out at the white slave traffic that brought in girls via an "underground railway" from far-off cities. He cited the case of an eighteen-year-old girl from New York who appeared in a house on South Clark Street. When her parents followed her to the city and notified the police of their daughter's disappearance, her keepers secretly sent the girl to Council Bluffs, Iowa, and a woman from a resort in Council Bluffs appeared in the Chicago brothel.[18]

The minister argued that the segregated vice districts were supported by the large wholesale houses and downtown businesses that claimed vice provided entertainment for their "out-of-town cousins." The merchants said that when visiting businessmen and salesmen came to Chicago they wanted to see the theaters, enjoy the vice resorts, and go to the gambling houses.[19]

Believing that "all roads lead to city hall," Stead ended his chapter on vice in Chicago by stating:

> When the police and the large wholesale houses and country cousins are in collusion to support unnatural crimes which the good people of Chicago fondly imagined existed only in the corruption of the later Roman Empire it is obvious that the moral reformer has a very uphill task before him.[20]

If Christ Came to Chicago left a stain on the city's honor that would take many years to remove. On the positive side, the book served as the genesis of a reform movement aimed at ending the city's worst vice conditions.[21] Stead so aroused the city's conscience that the Civic Federation, one of the city's early reform groups, was organized.[22] Stead's actions constituted the first significant move in the closing of the Levee.

Chapter Nine

THE SISTERS EVERLEIGH

Two Southern Ladies, or So They Say

1900–1912

If it weren't for the married men we couldn't have carried on at all and if it weren't for the cheating women we could have made another million.[1]

— Ada and Minna Everleigh

A da and Minna Everleigh were the most famous madams in the Levee. They were good friends with Big Jim, Hinky Dink, and Bathhouse John. While all five essentially were in the same game—making money from the sale of women—the two sisters were very special and definitely unique. They operated the Everleigh Club, which the Chicago Vice Commission called "the most famous and luxurious house of prostitution in the country."[2]

The Everleigh Club was in the heart of the loud and boisterous Levee. Men shouted at the loose women in the windows of the resorts, and the women answered back with suggestive offers. Drunks stumbled into the gutters. Fistfights broke out. Jack-rollers lurked in dark alleys waiting to mug some hapless individual and grab his wallet.[3] But all was serene at 2131–2133 S. Dearborn Street. As gentlemen callers stepped from their carriages they encountered a quiet scene of sophistication and gentility. A uniformed police officer was stationed nearby to maintain decorum, quiet the drunks, and discourage footpads. Gentlemen mounted the stone steps and rang the bell.

Immediately a liveried Negro servant would open the tall, thick, wooden doors. Once inside the receiving parlor, the patrons beheld the most opulent, most fashionable, most notorious bordello of its day.[4] No Parisian brothel was equal to the Everleigh Club in the magnificence of its appointments, the style and taste of the evening-gowned hostesses, and the quality of its food and wines.[5]

Every evening four classically trained, professional musicians playing the violin, cello, piano, and harp provided a pleasant backdrop. Between their sets, the piano was played by the stylish, yet refined Van Venderpool who received fifty dollars a week and his meals, plus tips. Van's first set each night began at ten o'clock, and often his last notes would sound around seven in the morning.

Patrons who stayed overnight usually presented a sizable gratuity to the ladies who had provided them with a pleasing and memorable time. A mulatto maid provided freshly pressed clothes followed by a waiter with a lavish breakfast. In the corridor, another maid would discreetly present a bill. Checks, cash, and for many of the gentleman callers, credit were acceptable. Local and out-of-town checks were returned from the bank with a rubber stamp on the back inking the words "Utopia Novelty Company, Inc."[6]

Many, if not most, of the stories that the sisters told of their earlier lives to eager reporters and writers were partially or completely false. Ada and Minna Everleigh were born in Greene County, Virginia, in 1864 and 1866, respectively.[7] They were of Irish stock. They grew up in Louisville, Kentucky.

According to the sisters' colorful personal accounts they married two brothers and lived for a while in Kentucky.[8] After deciding that married life was not for them they left the town and their husbands behind. The sisters said they found work as actresses in a traveling repertory company until they received news that their father had died and left them an estate of thirty-five thousand dollars. In 1898, drawn by the Trans-Mississippi Exposition, they moved to Omaha, Nebraska. Using their inheritance, they opened a brothel and furnished it with beautiful young girls. In the winter of 1899, after making a sizable profit from the men attending the fair, Ada and Minna moved to Chicago to open their very special brothel.[9] A much more believable and likely account is that they began their working lives as prostitutes and later became madams.[10]

When the sisters arrived in Chicago they learned that ex-madam Lizzie Allen was interested in selling her bordello at 2131 and 2133 S. Dearborn Street. Allen had purchased the property during the World's Columbian Exposition for use as a house of prostitution. After the fair she sold the furnishings and gave a lease to Essie Hawkins, who continued to operate the resort. The premises consisted of two three-story, stone buildings joined together along a common wall. The Everleigh sisters purchased the entire property from Allen. Madam Hawkins moved out to operate at a different location in the Levee. The sisters moved into separate apartments, one in 2131 and the other in 2133.

Minna was a natural charmer with a strong personality supported by red hair and gray-blue eyes. She was dark and slender, volatile and effusive. Her suite had marble walls and Persian rugs. There was a book-filled library, a fifteen-thousand-dollar gold-plated piano, and a bronze statute of Cupid. Her huge canopy bed dressed in pink silk had specially built springs and mattresses. During business hours, Minna tended to the libidinous desires of the patrons of the club.

Ada was blonde, tall, and cold.[11] She decorated her apartment in a refined and subdued style. She rarely came down to the public rooms. It was her job to manage the business side of the club. Ada had no objection to staying in the background and allowing her sister to be the life of the party on the first floor.[12]

The buildings were remodeled to create fourteen extremely well-furnished and soundproofed rooms with exotic names, including Silver, Gold, Rose, Chinese, Music, Egyptian, Oriental, Japanese, and Moorish. Several parlors contained fountains that sprayed the air with a perfume linked to the character of the room. There was even a room in the basement designed to replicate the sleeping compartment of a cross-country train. In addition, there was a library, an art gallery, and a formal dining room. Mahogany staircases led from the two entry halls to the upper floors. The most popular room with the patrons over the years was the Gold Room with its golden draperies, gilded chairs and even a gold-rimmed goldfish bowl. The walls of the room were trimmed in gold leaf. There were gold statutes and four six-hundred-dollar gold spittoons. To maintain the room's luster the gold leaf was redone each year, and the gilded door handles were polished daily.

On February 1, 1900, the day the sisters opened the Everleigh Club, the temperature was eight below zero. The weather did not discourage the invited guests who were more than generous in their spending. The sisters reported that they collected one thousand dollars on opening night. Ada was left with an eight-hundred-dollar profit after operating costs of two hundred dollars for the two four-piece orchestras, the colored staff, and sundries.

Only two weeks after the club opened, on the night of February 14, 1900, Coughlin greeted the sisters at the First Ward Democratic Club ball. As Jim Colosimo, Victoria Moresco, and their entourage looked on from their nearby seats, Minna and Ada arrived after midnight and sat in the first balcony along the railing. A courtly bow from Coughlin and a gift of bottles of wine welcomed the sisters to Chicago. They shared a glass of champagne with Jim and Victoria, but then left before the wild bacchanalia really got started.

More than five hundred beautiful and talented young ladies worked at the club during its eleven years of operation. At least twenty-five of these talented young ladies were on the premises each evening. Many were of unusual beauty, and others were especially skillful in the arts and practices of seduction and debauchery. Of equal importance to the millionaires, dignitaries, and famous personages who visited the club was the extreme discretion and secrecy required and provided by Ada and Minna.

The sisters did not hire very young girls or amateurs. The women who were taken on were the finest available. They were experienced, professional, and usually had a sizable following of admirers. It was rumored that some men corresponded with their favorite girls and traveled long distances to spend a single night with them.[13] Ada and Minna gave the girls detailed instructions on etiquette and demeanor, along with orders that if the instructions were not followed their employment would be terminated. Rule number one was that the girls were ladies and must behave as such at all times. The girls were told to speak with proper diction and to never use language that was rude or uncouth.

Ada Everleigh explained to a writer how the girls were selected: "They must have worked somewhere else before coming here. We do not like amateurs. Inexperienced girls and young widows are too prone to accept offers of marriage and leave. We always have a waiting list. To get in a girl must have a pretty face and figure, must be in perfect health, must look well in evening clothes. If she is addicted to drugs, or to drink, we do not want her. There is no problem keeping the Club filled."[14]

The charges were the highest in Chicago—fifty dollars for a brief sojourn, two hundred dollars for overnight, twenty dollars a bottle for the least costly champagne. The cost of a private dinner for two was one hundred dollars, not including wines and champagne. The girls received a quarter of the fees but made more than that from their tips, which the sisters graciously allowed them to keep intact.

Each night, the sisters had their evening meal together at eight o'clock. Minna enjoyed chicken, and Ada favored vegetables. If there was company, a rare and honored privilege, the guests would be served wine, soup, salad, entrees, brandy, and after the meal fruits, pecans, bonbons, and liqueurs. Many brands of imported champagne and fine French wines were maintained in the cellar.

Ada and Minna had many friends among the wealthy and politically well connected. Their closest associate from the vice field was Big Jim Colosimo, who frequently visited their establishment.[15] On some Sunday nights when the club was closed to the public, Colosimo prepared a grand spaghetti dinner for the sisters, and sometimes a few of the working girls received permission from Ada and Minna to join the party.[16]

The Everleigh sisters strenuously avoided all publicity in newspapers and magazines. Despite this aversion to reporters, the club was known across the

United States and in Europe. One example of their fame took place in March 1902 when Prussian Prince Frederick Henry came to America for a visit. After being shown New York, he traveled by train to Chicago. He appeared at all the correct places and visited with all the important dignitaries. He attended a banquet, a choral concert, and a ball. He visited Lincoln Park and the Germania Club near North Avenue and Clark Street. During his stay he asked that he be taken to the Everleigh Club, which he said he had heard about in Europe. A stupendous and lavish party was held in the club in his honor with many important guests from Chicago's elite. Repeated toasts to Prince Henry and to the king of Prussia led to the first recorded occurrence of nobility drinking champagne from a hostess's slipper. Despite the promotional value of such an event, neither Ada nor Minna ever discussed Prince Henry's visit to their establishment.

Scandalous events may have taken place in the club, but they were locked forever behind the massive doors and within the intense secrecy of the sisters. The most famous event alleged to have taken place in the club never did. For more than a hundred years stories have persisted that in 1905 Marshall Field Jr. was shot at the club and later moved secretly to his home at 1919 S. Prairie Avenue. He did in fact die from a gunshot wound on November 27, 1906. Despite the more colorful version, Field committed suicide in his bedroom on Prairie Avenue.[17]

Time magazine, although not around in 1900, once called the Everleigh Club the most luxurious bordello the United States had ever seen. The refinement of the club was in sharp contrast to the uncouth orgies of the First Ward Balls, which their friends Coughlin and Kenna were conducting annually and at which Big Jim Colosimo and an entourage of friends were always in attendance.

Chapter Ten

FIRST WARD BALL

Revelry, Debauchery, and Drunken Celebration

1896–1908

A real description of the 1907 ball is simply unprintable. You must stop them from putting another on this year. You must stop this disgrace to Chicago. You must stop it in the name of the young men who will be ruined there.

> — Arthur Farwell, president of the
> Chicago Law and Order League,
> speaking to Mayor Fred A. Busse

The Tribune *wishes to announce that it will print a list of every respectable person who attends the First Ward Ball next Monday night. Every effort will be made to make the "among those present" as complete as possible.*[1]

> — *Chicago Tribune*

The two most spectacular demonstrations of the debauched nature of the Levee were the gilded resort run by the Everleigh Sisters and the annual decadence commonly known as the First Ward Ball. These two attractions brought nationwide notoriety to Chicago.

The history of the First Ward Ball began with a benefit party held annually for Lame Jimmy, a well-liked musician who played piano and fiddle in madam Carrie Watson's resort. Lame Jimmy had one leg and walked with a single crutch. Out of sympathy for his infirmity, Watson and her girls threw a benefit Christmas party each year for Jimmy. The first such affair was held in 1880 at a bawdy dance hall, the most disreputable establishment in the Levee.

Admission was one dollar, and the revelry went on until dawn. Each year thereafter madams, prostitutes, pimps, gamblers, vice operators, hoodlums, politicians, police, and Levee hangers-on visited Freiberg's to give a small financial gift for Lame Jimmy and stayed to drink beer and whiskey. Madam Watson called the party a time when joy "reigned unrefined." Unfortunately, in 1895, a wild shooting took place between two drunken coppers at the benefit. The incident was featured in the local newspapers and brought strong objections from the reformers and crusaders. The mayor vetoed any further benefit parties for Lame Jimmy.[2]

The following year, Bathhouse John Coughlin and Hinky Dink Kenna were determining how much cash they would need for campaigning during the upcoming First Ward aldermanic election. Their capital was low because the pesky vice crusaders had forced Mayor George B. Swift to clamp down on vice.[3] Thinking of Lame Jimmy's benefits, the aldermen decided to hold a similar but much larger fund-raiser. For the site they picked the Seventh Regiment Armory at 3300 S. Wentworth Avenue. Soon everyone associated with the First Ward organization was hustling tickets and shaking down proprietors of saloons, brothels, and gambling joints for contributions. The workers on the lowest level in the Levee—prostitutes, cadets, gamblers, pickpockets—were forced to purchase fifty-cent tickets, and saloon owners, gambling house operators, and madams had to pay even more. Crooked politicians and underworld figures realized that it was in their best interest to attend. The whiskey distributors and the beer brewers reluctantly agreed to provide their products at heavily discounted prices.[4]

Alderman Coughlin sent out word that there would be drinking, dancing, and a magnificent formal march. The madams and their ladies, the gamblers and their table men, and the saloon owners and their bartenders quickly got into the mood by fashioning elaborate costumes and extravagant outfits. Held just before Christmas in December 1896, the first ball was a smashing success.[5] Kenna called it a "lollapalooza." With the profits at twenty-five thousand dollars they agreed that an annual affair would be a most worthwhile idea.

Following the initial spectacle, word of the debauchery and libertine behavior spread from coast to coast. Businessmen from New York, Boston, Pittsburgh, Kansas City, St. Louis, and San Francisco developed a "need" to visit Chicago during the scheduled times of future balls. Each year ten thousand to fifteen thousand people attended. Many more stood in the street gawking or protesting. Many of Chicago's leaders in politics and business filled the first tier of boxes sitting next to the city's most famous madams. In the early years Mayor Carter Harrison made an annual appearance and drank a glass or two of champagne. At one of the balls he told *Tribune* reporter Arthur Sears Henning that he always left the ball before the brothel keepers arrived.[6]

In succeeding years, to accommodate the growing number of attendees, the ball was moved first to the First Regiment Armory at Sixteenth Street and Michigan Avenue and eventually to the Coliseum at 1500 S. Wabash Avenue. These highly profitable and unarguably astounding events were unlike anything seen before in Chicago. One reformer provided this description:

> In the vast hall, where the annual round-up of the unsavory and vicious had to take place, there assembled a crowd of pimps and prostitutes that could not be gathered together, at one time and in one place, in any other city of the habitable globe, not even in Paris, noted for its demi-monde and their revelries; or is it reasonable to suppose for a moment that Sodom and Gomorrah, in the zenith of their notoriety, could have produced an outpouring more to the taste of his Satanic Majesty.[7]

The ball that was held on February 14, 1900, was especially lusty and colorful. Crowds overflowed the sidewalk and street in front of the armory as an endless line of carriages brought revelers to the event. Before the evening was over there had been drinking, skylarking, merrymaking, fighting, semi-nudity, and sexual assaults. For the first time, madams Ada and Minna Everleigh attended. Accompanied by a full retinue of ladies, entertainers, and patrons from their club, the sisters entered their reserved box just before midnight. They said that they had dropped by to pay their respects to their two aldermanic patrons. They watched the festivities but remained aloof from the raucous fray.

To set the stage for the grand march, the dance floor was cleared. Aldermen from other wards, assorted police officials of all ranks, state legislators, judges, and mayors from nearby towns moved back to watch the promised spectacle. The Honorable John Coughlin, alderman of the First Ward, attired in a new, finely tailored, green dress tailcoat, mauve vest, lavender trousers and tie, pink gloves, yellow shoes, and a shiny black top hat, and the Honorable Michael Kenna in more subdued finery, led the grand march. A seemingly endless lines of patrons, twenty-six abreast, streamed to the center floor to the blasting diapason of two complete bands. They repeatedly marched up and down the hall with the thousands of spectators screaming, whooping, and hollering.[8]

The next morning and afternoon the newspapers ran stories describing the events in detail and strongly worded editorials disparaging the abbreviated costumes and the "blur of tobacco smoke, red slippers, and cosmetics."[9] The wire services provided colorful and descriptive copy for out-of-town papers. The reformers, church leaders, and crusaders raised the loudest possible protests. Undisturbed, Kenna and Coughlin counted their profits.[10]

The ball on March 29, 1902, was titled "Veiled Prophets" by John Coughlin. The attendees were beside themselves with excitement because word had spread that Bathhouse John was expected to enter the main floor riding an elephant. When the trumpets blared and the drums thundered, an elephant appeared with a rider on top wearing a splendid green outfit. From a distance he could have been Coughlin, but he actually was a circus handler. Two huge beasts named Venus and Gypsy, rented from Ringling Brothers' winter circus quarters in Baraboo, Wisconsin, were the biggest spectacle of the long and boozy night.

The fifteen thousand revelers gathered for the annual First Ward Ball in the Coliseum on December 22, 1903, and found the grand march to be more spectacular than ever. At midnight Coughlin led two thousand gaily garbed participants in an intricate march coiling back and forth around the hall. He showed amazing dexterity as he switched from marching forward to backward thirty times to the delight of the crowd who cheered lustily each time he spun around.

Planning for subsequent balls began in the late summer of each year. Early in the 1900s the planning committee composed of Coughlin and Kenna and assorted precinct captains, bail-bondsmen, gamblers, saloonkeepers, and resort operators was enlarged to include Big Jim Colosimo.[11]

Each year the crowd swelled with every level of society well represented: hooligans, drunks, footpads, pickpockets, burglars, confidence men, bucket-shop promoters, madams, pimps, gamblers, saloonkeepers, precinct captains, aldermen, political leaders, elected officials, police officers of all ranks, state representatives, business leaders, bluebloods, voyeurs, newspapermen, court clerks, city attorneys, judges, lawyers, neighborhood residents, and adventurers from as far away as the east and west coasts, Canada, and Europe. "If a great disaster had befallen the Coliseum last night there would not have been a second-story worker, a dip or pug ugly, porch climber, dope fiend, or scarlet woman remaining in Chicago," mused a *Tribune* reporter after one ball. His story described the three long bars where seventy-five kegs of beer were emptied while two hundred waiters served thirty-five thousand quarts of beer and ten thousand quarts of champagne.[12]

Reporting on the tenth annual ball held on December 9, 1907, the *Record-Herald* stated:

> Scarlet women, Levee resort owners and salon keepers gave the real zest to the caucus. The dance did not start until midnight properly, these people being busy until that time gathering their own funds. In the fear that the table facilities would be insufficient, five bars were provided. Any individual who could be relied upon to buy wine with sufficient rapidity was provided with a free table. As the night waned, carrying bottles in by two's

and three's proved inadequate and it became necessary to hustle them in by the case. Men and women in maudlin stupor snored and gasped under tables and over chairs. Less stupefied couples on the floor tried valiantly to go through the dances the musicians wearily were grinding out. Everywhere men and women dropped exhausted from the excesses of debauchery and drinking. The bleak glimmer of dawn in the east appeared before the masquerade and fancy dress ball staggered to a finish.[13]

While the rowdiness and obscenity at the balls continued, the tolerance of much of the city for this event was fast waning. What the man in the street once saw as amusing was now considered a tasteless, bad joke. Ministers, reformers, and crusaders vocalized a growing dissent as acceptance of the public debauchery rapidly diminished. More concerns were raised, more sermons were delivered, and more strident demands for a halt to the event were publicized. Even some aldermen began to take an opposing position.

On September 28, 1908, a committee of Presbyterian ministers met to discuss bringing pressure on the city council to withhold a permit for the "annual insult to the people of the city and a carnival of crime." Rev. Duncan C. Milner, who chaired the meeting, said, "The annual ball of the First Ward Democratic Club is worthy of pagan Rome in its worst days."[14] Other reformers proposed various measures to dissuade Kenna and Coughlin from holding another "orgy." One group said that they would place cameramen in front of the hall to photograph any businessman that dared attend. Another urged public listing of the names of the "respectable" attendees. A third said they would have special officers of the Anti-Cigarette League and the Chicago Law and Order League inside the ball to make arrests for any violations of city ordinances. The *Tribune* joined in stating that the paper would print the name of every "respectable person" who attended the ball.

The indomitable Lucy Page Gaston—teacher, writer, lecturer, member of the Woman's Christian Temperance Union, and founder and head of the Anti-Cigarette League of America—took particularly strong opposition to the ball: "We know all about these orgies and will do all in our power to have the decent element of Chicago put a stop to this form of degeneracy . . . every ball of the past has left its trail of ruined boys and girls and broken homes. I know that the popularity and political strength of the attendees is gauged by the number of empty champagne bottles that cover the tables and floors."[15]

A particularly vocal opponent was Arthur Burrage Farwell, president of the Law and Order League. He had held distinguished positions during his long career as a civic reformer. His family had arrived by ship in Boston in 1636. His father had been a U.S. Senator. Burrage was a classic reformer of great and dedicated fervor. He resided in the Hyde Park neighborhood and had a vested interest in keeping the district "dry." He was steadfast and strong, and woe betide the villain when Arthur Burrage Farwell was on his trail.[16] Farwell, who had fought unsuccessfully for three years to end the ball, exclaimed at one meeting, "Last year a police official told a friend of mine [at the ball] to keep a sharp lookout for the fillings in his teeth; he was liable to have the clothes stolen from his back."[17] Farwell was determined to end the balls.

The rector of the Grace Episcopal Church went to court to file for an injunction to prevent the ball from being held. On December 11, 1908, Superior Court Judge Albert G. Barnes dismissed the petition deeming that the case was not a proper one to be heard in a court of equity.

Regardless of the protests and declamations, Coughlin and Kenna pushed ahead with their plans. On December 13, 1908, the night before the eleventh ball, a dynamite bomb exploded in a small one-story building at the southeast end of the Coliseum Annex. No one was injured, but workmen readying the hall were knocked down and dozens of windows were broken. In spite of the bombing, the two sponsors of the ball held a meeting at First Ward headquarters at 440 S. State Street. They gave a pep talk to the floor managers, ushers, and bouncers with strict instructions that no one who gets a "load on" before they get to the hall should be let in. The alderman added, "Preachers may come if they will behave themselves and conform to the rules laid down for other people."[18]

Despite the protests and the bombing, the eleventh ball was held. Even though Police Inspector John Wheeler and a force of three hundred uniformed officers stood ready to keep the peace, a problem arose almost immediately. Nearly two thousand persons arrived before the doors were opened and tried to push their way into the hall. One hundred fifty ushers wearing evening clothes worked to force the early arrivals into something resembling entry lines. The crowd was so large that the trolley cars could not move down Wabash Avenue. Coughlin, in a smart new black ensemble instead of his traditional fancy green outfit, arrived by automobile, observed the jam-up and quickly got the cashiers in place and the doors open. The revelers streamed in—knocking chairs, tables, plants, and each other to the floor.

Coughlin moved back and forth from the hall to the sidewalk trying to maintain order. Standing outside was *Record-Herald* cartoonist Wincey King and photographer Lyman L. Atwell with his 4x5 Speed Graphic camera. Coughlin spotted Atwell as he was about to take a photograph using flash powder. Coughlin and some of his followers rushed toward Atwell and struck him, knocking him down. King also was knocked to the sidewalk. Atwell was kicked and his camera was broken. Nearby police officers took no action. One officer responded to Atwell's plea to disperse the attackers with a coarse, "Go chase yourself!"

The entire night was a mob scene. Twelve thousand persons managed to elbow, push, and fight their way into the giant hall as thousands more milled about the streets around the building seeking a way to get into the night of debauchery. As the stroke of twelve neared, the most important madams with their retinues began to fill the reserved boxes after waiters and bouncers roughly ejected those usurpers who had improperly occupied the boxes. City Attorney John R. Caverly joined Alderman Kenna in his box. The Everleigh sisters had a box of their own, and nearby in another box was Big Jim Colosimo and his closest associates.

At midnight, three bands struck up a martial air and the grand march began. His hair in a well-oiled pompadour and his brown mustache razor trimmed, John Coughlin, wearing evening clothes, a lavender necktie, and a red sash across his chest, took the arms of the Everleigh sisters. They were followed by the most sumptuous whores from the Everleigh Club wearing their finest, gaudiest, and gayest attire. The crowd let out a lusty cheer when some working girls wearing a bathing suit costume that was currently in vogue at some resorts joined the hundreds in the march. One crude woman was dressed as a nun.

On the sidelines boisterous drunks shouted and hooted. Those closest to the marchers reached out to grab the women as they passed. Waiters pushed through the thick crowds and lost most of their drinks on the way to the boxes. The stench of spilled beers, ten-cent cigars and cheap perfume hung above the dancers as the bolder men engaged in carnal behavior with drunken prostitutes. When revelers grew too boisterous or disagreeably drunk they were subdued by a combination of strong waiters, First Ward heavies, and uniformed police officers and given the bum's rush out into the crowded streets. As the night wore on women slumped to the floor. Some had fainted; some were drunk. Their limp bodies with clothing wildly askew were hoisted into the arms of red-faced men who pushed and yelled trying to get to the exit doors. Sometimes the crowds were so thickly packed that hapless women were passed overhead from hand to hand. Slowly the party wound to a close as the sun came up over Wabash Avenue.

The Law and Order League's Arthur Burrage Farwell, who had attended as a very unofficial observer, exclaimed the next day in outrage, "I doubt that any city in the world at any time ever permitted such a disgraceful orgy." The *Record-Herald* trumpeted, "VICE DEFIES DECENCY."[19]

On December 16, 1908, *Record-Herald* photographer Atwell appeared before Municipal Judge Dicker and obtained a warrant for the arrest of Coughlin on a charge of assault and battery. On December 22, 1908, the case of the City of Chicago against John Coughlin was heard by a jury before Criminal Court Judge Newcomer. Concerning the attack by Coughlin, Atwell testified: "He spied me with the camera and came toward me at a run or a good trot. He first knocked King down and then he jumped on me. He hit me in the face and I lifted my camera to shield myself. Then he hit me in the body five or six times."[20]

Coughlin took the stand and swore that he never struck anyone. He said he saw Atwell preparing to take a flash picture and remembered the dynamite explosion of the night before. Coughlin said he was greatly concerned that if Atwell took a flash photo the crowd would think a bomb had gone off and would go into a panic. Coughlin testified that he said to Atwell, "For heaven's sake, don't shoot! People will be killed." Six witnesses swore that Coughlin had told the truth. The jury was out for fifty minutes before they returned a not guilty verdict.

Late in 1909, the two First Ward aldermen announced that they would hold a twelfth annual ball. Frustrated and angered but not defeated from ten years of failure, the reformers pushed harder. Civic leaders solicited the support of Catholic priests who had a special influence with the two Catholic aldermen. Roman Catholic Bishop Alexander J. McGavick and Rev. Maximilian Kotecki raised their voices in protest, and the Young Men's Association of Saints Peter and Paul Church sent a letter of resolutions to the city council protesting the ball. The association's letter scorned the ball as the annual flaunting of Chicago's vicious elements while collecting illegal tribute from them for the profits of a few politicians. It recalled that in the past years this saturnalia provided the opportunity for vicious and unfortunate men and women of the red-light district to display their degradation in public to the great injury to morals of others attending the ball out of ignorance or curiosity. The association appealed to the mayor, the city council, and the chief of police to enforce the laws that they had sworn to uphold.

The association's resolutions went to the city council where a floor flight took place between the aldermen who wanted the letter read and Aldermen Coughlin and Kenna who wanted it "filed." The proponents won, and for ten minutes the two aldermen from the First Ward were publicly castigated by the reading into the record of the resolutions. Mortified, Kenna hid under his desk during the reading.[21]

Speaking with reporters, Mayor Fred A. Busse surprisingly announced that unnamed reformers had threatened to blow up his home with a bomb and to slug him on the street unless he refused a dance permit and stopped the ball. The reporters learned that Busse was indignant that Coughlin and Kenna broke promises made in 1908 that that year's ball would be the last. Meanwhile incorruptible Police Chief LeRoy T. Steward, who strongly opposed the ball, stated that he would detail sufficient police officers to the ball to ensure that every relevant ordinance and statute on the books would be enforced. He issued an order stating that there would be:

No drunkenness.
No tights or immodestly short skirts.
No evil language or actions.
No disorder whatever.
No minors allowed, especially girls.
No known criminals or suspicious characters.

The public chuckled at these rules aimed at eliminating the activities the ball featured.

Finally, yielding to the many pressures, Mayor Busse called a meeting in his office with Coughlin, Arthur Farwell, and Rev. E. A. Bell, head of the Midnight Mission. There were many charges and rebuttals with Bell telling Coughlin, "You are leading yourself and others to damnation." To which Coughlin responded, "You make your living off the women in the red-light district." Bell charged Coughlin with "being like Satan at the head of the hosts of the damned leading the grand march of vice and degeneracy." [22] No resolution of the problem was reached during the meeting, but Mayor Busse was convinced that the ball should not be held. He began to work behind the scenes. Several days later, caving in to a direct request from Busse to stop the event, Coughlin announced that in deference to public opinion the ball would not be held.

In an attempt to make some campaign money, Coughlin said that in place of the ball an alcohol-free concert would be offered that would be "remarkably fine" and a "great treat for women and children." He added that arrangements were still in progress but a military band and soloists of great note would appear. The concert was held, but it was an economic failure and was never repeated. Coughlin said he had gracefully "bowed to the goody-good people of Chicago."[23] Many years later reporting on vice and corruption in Chicago, the *Illinois Crime Survey* described the yearly ritual as "the annual underworld orgy, given by Alderman Michael Kenna ('Hinky Dink') and Alderman John Coughlin ('Bathhouse John'), bosses of the First Ward, for the purpose of retaining control of prostitutes and criminals of the First Ward Levee for political purposes and for political funds."[24]

Chapter Eleven

PIMP TO VICE LORD

Big Jim on the Rise

1902–1912

"Who's your daddy?" Ask a Chicago mobster that clichéd question and there can only be one honest answer: Big Jim Colosimo . . . the George Washington of organized crime in the Windy City—a sort of grandfather of the godfathers.[1]

— Lawrence Binda, *The Big Bad Book of Jim: Rogues, Rascals and Rapscallions Named James, Jim and Jimmy*

The successor to Mike McDonald as kingpin of the underworld and the founder of the criminal dynasty which ruled Chicago during the Thompson regimes and much of the 1930s was Big Jim Colosimo.[2]

— Emmett Dedmon, *Fabulous Chicago*

Big Jim Colosimo had reached manhood. He was reasonably literate and spoke English and Italian. He pomaded his thick, black heroic mustache and jet-black hair. Handsome with broad shoulders, he was a loud-spoken extrovert with a winning manner and was talented in the art of making friends. He was also cunning, strong-willed, unscrupulous, and very capable with his fists. All this made him an imposing figure who commanded respect wherever he went.[3]

Jim's first entry into adult criminality began in the late 1890s when he became a partner with several Italians who were sending Black Hand letters to local Italian businessmen. However, he soon gave up the vicious practice of extorting money from fellow Italian immigrants for the relatively safe business of commercial vice. Starting small, Jim became the manager of a small band of streetwalkers who plied their sordid trade along the sidewalks in the south end of downtown. Before too long, problems with the police prompted Jim to end his career as a pimp. He began to look for a more secure and more profitable approach to the vice field.

One day, through fate or by calculated design, Jim met Victoria Moresco, an unmarried Italian immigrant running a brothel at the western edge of the Levee. Jim turned on the charm, and Victoria liked what he had to offer. A fellow Italian immigrant, Jim would be acceptable to her father and family, and he could help her run her business. He had political connections in the First Ward that gave him clout and immunity to arrest. Jim's other qualifications were not bad either. He was handsome, personable, and lusty.

Victoria was the daughter of Paul and Mary Moresco. Her parents had been born in Italy, Paul in 1853 and Mary in 1857. They had married in Italy in 1878. Paul was a cemetery monument maker, and Mary stayed at home to raise the family. Victoria, one of eighteen children, was born in Italy in 1882. Her father's salary was low, and the family lived in poverty. In the hopes of obtaining a better job and decent living conditions, Paul and Mary gathered their surviving children and immigrated to New York City in the mid-1880s. They moved to Chicago in 1891. The entire family was jammed into a few rooms in an overcrowded tenement apartment building at 526 Division Street on the Near North Side. As Victoria grew up on the hard streets of this Italian slum she put on weight but built character. While not an attractive woman, Victoria was physically strong and had street smarts.

In the late 1890s, Victoria became the madam of a one-story brothel near Bedbug Row, a strip of twenty-five-cent crib houses, known for low-cost, low-class prostitutes, in the 2000 block of Armour Avenue. Why a young woman from the Italian neighborhood north of the Chicago River moved to the South Side Levee and entered the sex business is something that Victoria never revealed. But she had the moxie and talent to keep the brothel open, and that made her an attractive partner for Big Jim.

On July 22, 1902, Justice of the Peace John C. Murphy married Jim and Victoria at city hall. Colosimo listed his age as twenty-three and Victoria said she was twenty.[4] Little is known of their home life, but many years later Victoria mentioned to a newspaperman that some evenings she read to Jim from the classics while they listened to Italian opera music on the phonograph.

Jim learned the business side of prostitution from his wife and soon took over the operation of her brothel at Armour Avenue and Archer Street. He renamed the resort "the New Brighton." When he had enough money to open another brothel, he placed it next door at 2031 Armour Avenue. To honor his bride Colosimo named the resort the Victoria, and his wife took over the operation of this new bordello. As the customers waited their turns with the girls, they were entertained by "music professor" Izzy "the Rat" Buchowsky banging out ragtime tunes on a battered upright piano.

Big Jim and Victoria Moresco began their joint operation in the early 1900s. Their whorehouses were neither the bottom nor the top of the prostitution ladder, but they frequently had new girls and consistently enjoyed a steady stream of lusty male customers. The Colosimo-Moresco brothels developed a good reputation; there were no panel rooms and no drugging of clients' drinks.

Colosimo moved carefully, adding one operation at a time. After the Victoria came a bordello at Twenty-second and Dearborn streets named the Saratoga. In the months that followed, Jim took over several of the crib shacks in Bedbug Row. Jim got 60 percent of the earnings of each working girl, the customary amount at the time. In addition, the girls had to pay for their clothing and any needed services.

Protected by Jim's connections, Jim and Victoria were quick to expand their operation. Soon the couple was operating a string of four houses. Two of the resorts were one-dollar houses and two were two-dollar houses.[5] Jim discovered that some nights he had more customers in the one-dollar houses than the two-dollar houses and other times it was the reverse. To better service the need on any particular night, Colosimo ran the girls from the less busy houses down the dirt alley behind the buildings to the busier resorts. The customers never knew the difference.

With the pimps and touts at his brothels, Colosimo now controlled another fifty voters. Jim added these potential votes to those of the Italians in the tenements around the apartment where he lived and the street sweepers in the newly established trade union that he controlled, and these numbers convinced Coughlin to make Colosimo a precinct captain. Precinct captains were the backbone of the political organizations in Chicago. They registered the citizens in their precinct and made sure that they all voted correctly on election day. The precinct captains engaged in many types of voting fraud, from filling in blank ballots to intimidating and beating supporters of other candidates. To ensure the cover-up of the voting irregularities they paid off elections judges and clerks.

Hinky Dink and Bathhouse John were happy with Big Jim's work and found another way to take advantage of the young Italian American's industry and muscle. For several years Ike Bloom had been the collector of protection payments for the aldermen from the Levee bawdy houses, gambling joints and saloons in the First Ward. Believing that Big Jim could bring in more money each month than Bloom, Bathhouse John and Hinky Dink replaced Ike as their collector with Big Jim. As Colosimo began to move up the ladder of success, Bloom went into a decline. Bloom continued to run Freiberg's and in his later years went to work for Colosimo, but he never again held a leadership role in the Levee.

When Coughlin and Kenna decided to raise the protection fees, several saloon owners and brothel operators grumbled that they were not going along with the increase. Colosimo responded with a forceful example of the danger in not paying up. He visited one of the leading objectors, Georgie Spencer. Operating a brothel on South Dearborn Street two doors down from the Everleigh Club, Spencer was the toughest and meanest madam in the Levee. Once, during a raid, it required six uniformed officers to put Georgie, kicking and screaming, into the wagon. When Georgie told Jim that she would not pay the increase, Colosimo put on a set of brass knuckles and knocked down the most formidable of the whorehouse madams. As she lay moaning on the floor, Jim took three hundred dollars from her purse.[6] The other recalcitrant operators quickly fell into line.

Bathhouse John and Hinky Dink were happy with their new "muscle." Colosimo collected one hundred to three hundred dollars a month from each brothel, depending on its size, twenty-five dollars a day from each gambling joint, and fifty dollars a week from each saloonkeeper who wanted to remain open after the 1 a.m. closing hour.[7] This money was divided between Big Jim, the two aldermen, and the district police captain.

Coughlin and Kenna also gave Jim the authority to determine the issuance of new saloon licenses. With Colosimo as the middleman, the aldermen didn't need to get their hands dirty by actually taking the necessary bribes from the applicants. Colosimo acted as their not-so-discreet front man.[8]

A decisive event that fueled Colosimo's rise took place in April 1909. Roy Jones and George Little, former partners and powerful bosses in the Levee, decided to part ways due to a serious disagreement and lawsuit over the division of profits from their dives.[9] With the dissolution of the powerful Jones-Little combine the newspapers said that "wily Italians" from "sunny Italy" grabbed a number of choice operations in the Levee. Jim Colosimo, one of the wily Italians, took several of the businesses.

Colosimo's new role as collector of the payoffs from the brothel operators and his relationship with Coughlin and Kenna gave him authority over the brothels, saloons, and gambling houses in the First Ward.[10] He calculatingly used his power to become the first Italian in Chicago's history to take full advantage of a crime-politics connection.[11]

By 1911, Colosimo's domain was growing larger. From his office in the combination restaurant, saloon, hotel, and brothel he owned at 2001–2003

Archer Avenue, Jim controlled billiard parlors, saloons, restaurants, and a string of brothels, including the New Brighton at 2001 Archer Avenue, the Saratoga on Dearborn Street, the Victoria on Armour Avenue, the resort at 2119 Armour Avenue and another on the Far South Side at 113 W. Ninety-fifth Street. These operations were managed for Colosimo by Johnny Torrio, Joe Aducci, Sam Hare, Roxy Vanille, and Joe "Jew Kid" Grabiner.[12] Other members of Colosimo's gang were Billy Leathers, "Big Ed" Weiss, Blubber Bob Gray, "Dago Frank" Lewis, "Chicken Harry" Cullett, John "Jakie" Adler, Mac Fitzpatrick, Mike Carrozzo, W. E. Frazier, and Joe Moresco, Victoria Moresco's brother.[13]

Although the immigrant Italians were in the minority in the First Ward, Jim fashioned them into an effective voting bloc that exerted an influence in local politics far beyond its numerical strength. He organized social and athletic clubs for the Democratic Party organization but always remained in the background and never ran for a political office. He wisely allowed Irish politicians to hold the elected offices. He was interested only in money and power.[14]

Jack Lait, *Chicago American* organized-crime reporter, knew Big Jim personally. Lait wrote, "It so chanced that my early reporting nights threw me in with the birth of modern gangsterism, the commercial racketeering system, which ante-dated Prohibition." Lait said Big Jim was the first in the country to put all of the pieces together. "Jim had foreseen that the essential components of an organized vice business were force, political drag with the payoff, organization with brains and efficiency, merciless management at the top and monopoly so the take would be all the traffic would bear, and a variety of fields for the same reasons that prompt a trust company to accumulate a wide-range investment portfolio."[15]

At his peak in 1914, Big Jim controlled, directly or indirectly, more than one hundred resorts and businesses. He had acquired an interest in several gambling joints and opium parlors.[16] The newspapers estimated that his income from his vice operations was over a half million a year. Underworld gossip whispered that he also controlled the sale of Italian national lottery tickets in Chicago and the distribution of a portion of the grapes from the produce markets to Sicilian households where the fruit was fermented into wine for illegal resale to Italian immigrants.[17] He had developed a crime syndicate and ran this operation until his murder in 1920 when it was immediately taken over by his deputy Johnny Torrio. Many years later, *Time* magazine compared the potency and organization of Colosimo's operation with Al Capone's mob."[18]

Chapter Twelve

FAMILY AND BUSINESS

The Other Side of Big Jim

1902–1912

He owned the biggest cars in town, had uniformed servants, wore a dia-mond ring on every finger, diamond studs in his shirts, diamond cufflinks, had diamonds in his belt and suspender buckles, carried diamonds in bags and often toyed with them.[1]

— Norman Mark, *Mayors, Madams, and Madmen*

As he succeeded in business and developed a steady income, Big Jim began to bring his family from Italy to Chicago. First to arrive was brother Frank in 1902. Frank had trouble adjusting to Chicago's noisy and hectic life. It was not like his hometown of Petilia Policastro, a village over the mountain from Colosimi where Jim was born. Frank made several trips back and forth between Italy and the United States. Each time he entered, Frank told the immigration inspectors at Ellis Island that he intended to per-manently reside in America. Finally, Frank made up his mind. He returned permanently to Italy and married a woman in Petilia Policastro. He did make one last visit to Chicago. In September 1920 he was required to appear in Cir-cuit Court in connection with the probate of Jim's estate.[2]

Next was Big Jim's father, Luigi. In 1903, he sailed in steerage from Naples on the SS *California*. On the ship's manifest, Luigi stated that his home residence was P. Policastro, Italy, and that he was going to Chicago where his cousin Gennaro Colosimo lived.[3] Luigi told the purser that he was carrying twenty-nine dollars. After nineteen days, the ship reached New York Harbor on August 25. When Luigi arrived in Chicago he moved into Jim's new home where he lived until after Jim's death. Luigi never learned English and did not become a citizen. Jim used his father as a trusted confident and advisor. Over the years Jim placed real estate and businesses in his father's name. Some said that when necessary, Luigi sailed back to Italy carrying money for his son to move it out of reach of the government.

Next to come to Chicago was Jim's sister Bettina, who reached New York on May 5, 1899. Later brother Frank came to visit. While they enjoyed living in Jim's home, they found life to be very different from that in Colosimi and Petilia Policastro, the sleepy Italian towns they had left in Italy. Both returned home. Only Luigi remained at his son's side.

In the early 1900s, Jim entered the legitimate business field with the Coliseum Billiard and Pool Room Parlor at 239 E. Twenty-second Street. The poolroom had its own phone with number 1549, a rarity in those days. In 1905, Jim advertised the poolroom on the front cover of the *World's Annual Sporting Records*, a locally printed sports information booklet. The cover featured an ad for the poolroom and a large photograph of a sporty, handsome-looking James Colosimo with a short handlebar mustache and a striped bow tie.[4] To help out Victoria Moresco's younger brother Joseph who was selling newspapers at Clark and Washington streets, Jim gave the young man a job at the poolroom. As business increased Big Jim hired John, another of Victoria's brothers. A few years later, Big Jim turned over the poolroom to the two brothers.

In 1904, Jim opened a hotel and saloon at 2001–2005 S. Archer Avenue.[5] This enterprise prospered. By 1908, *L'Italia*, an Italian language newspaper in Chicago, published an article reporting that the Colosimo Hotel and Buffet had been renovated completely and was now considered the most elegant on the South Side. The paper stated, "Italians who desire wines and liquors of the finest brands will find them at Signor Colosimo's."[6] This business was the forerunner of Colosimo's famous café on Wabash Avenue. The last listing of the Archer Avenue establishment was in the 1912 *City Directory*, the year that Jim opened his new restaurant on south Wabash Avenue.[7]

Jim and Victoria lived in the red-light district in a rented apartment on Twenty-first Street. In 1909, he decided to move from the Levee. With a reported income of fifty thousand dollars a year from his brothel operations Jim felt that he could afford a better style of living. After securing a ten-thousand-dollar mortgage, Jim purchased a house at 3156 S. Vernon Avenue on July 24, 1909. The house was two miles south of the Levee. Jim bought the property in his father's name; then Luigi transferred the deed to his son. Jim, Victoria, Luigi, and brother Frank moved into the spacious, nine-room, two-story brownstone. In 1914, during one of those rare moments when the state's attorney actually was enforcing laws in the Levee, Jim transferred ownership to Victoria to forestall the placing of any court judgments against the property. When Jim obtained a divorce from Victoria in February 1920, he transferred the property from Victoria back to Luigi.[8]

The neighborhood around the Colosimo home on Vernon Avenue was quiet and genteel. The streets were shaded by leafy trees. Jim had several servants, including two chauffeurs in livery. His motor car was the biggest and best. The location was outside the Levee but close enough so that it was only a short ride to his office at the restaurant.

Jim filled the home with imported objects of art and costly furniture. He purchased lacquered chinoiserie clocks and cabinets, morocco-bound books, valuable paintings, marble sculptures, and bronze statues, many of these items from Italy. He added heavy, ornate furniture, thick Persian rugs, and elaborate chandeliers and gilded light fixtures. He even bought an entire rare coin collection for display in the parlor. Although he didn't know it at the time, 3156 S. Vernon was to be his last home.[9]

The 1910 U.S. Census showed Jim, Victoria, Luigi, and Frank living in the Vernon Avenue home. Jim's employment was listed as saloon proprietor, and Luigi was shown as living on his own income. Victoria and Frank were described as not working.[10]

In 1911, Jim again placed an ad on the front page of the current *World's Annual Sporting Records*. This time there was no photo and the advertisement simply stated "James Colosimo 2001–3 Archer Ave. Chicago, Illinois."[11]

In 1912 Jim began his third and most successful legitimate business venture. He rented space at 2126 and 2128 S. Wabash Avenue in a dirty, musty building that had been occupied by a small restaurant.[12] He remodeled the premises and opened a saloon and an Italian restaurant. Over time Colosimo's Café became a highly visible front, which obscured his criminal and vice activities. More importantly, the restaurant became one of his major interests, and he lavished time and money on its operations. Some members of his gang believed their boss should have kept his focus on his vice operations. Their thinking proved to be valid.

As Jim built his vice syndicate he thought he had all of the bases covered. He had no problem with other vice operators. He was in solid with Coughlin and Kenna; he was serving as their collector of protection money. The police were under control thanks to payoffs to them of a portion of the collection money. What could go wrong? A farm boy from Indiana named Clifford Roe was about to create major problems for Jim—investigations, raids, arrests, and possible felony prosecution for him and his henchmen. And Roe could not be bought.

Part Two

CHICAGO—CITY OF VICE AND CORRUPTION

Chapter Thirteen

FIGHTING VICE
AND CORRUPTION

Crooked Coppers and Dishonest Politicians

1901–1910

The City Hall gang went into office on the promise that the town was to be open, an' they've kept it open. Course they've got to put up a little bluff when the reformers get after 'em, but I know, and the push knows that Chi is going to be "right" for the likes o' you an' me as long as the gang is in power.

— Josiah Flynt, "In the World of Graft"

A crucial part of running a vice operation in the early 1900s was gaining an understanding of the local political and police system. Jim learned how the system operated from the two political giants of the First Ward—Coughlin and Kenna, who had virtually written the book. The pair had a keen understanding of human nature. They knew that gambling, whoring, and drinking had been practiced continuously since the city was founded, and they utilized this situation to their advantage by secretly protecting the vice operators from arrest while collecting fees for this service. The aldermen set the rates that vice operators had to pay to remain in business. Each week, a collector picked up the protection money and turned it over to the two political leaders, who gave the police a share of the collection and controlled the appointment of the district police commander—thus obtaining his cooperation.

Jim first learned of this corrupt system when he was a teenager living near the Levee. With his knowledge of the system he started building his vice operations in 1902. But he still had to learn how to deal with a new problem—the rising tide of criticism of vice and corruption.

Starting in 1894 with the publication of Reverend Stead's *If Christ Came to Chicago*, attacks on vice and corruption began to occur more frequently during the early 1900s. Josiah Flynt, an investigative reporter for *McClure's Magazine*, wrote in 1901 that Chicago was an "open" town. He said, "the police department consents to the city's being 'open,' and has an understanding to this effect with the other Powers that Rule. . . . Naturally, the chief of the force cannot admit this openly."[2]

To quiet these attacks, on April 30, 1901, newly reelected Mayor Carter Harrison Jr. appointed a new chief of police, Francis O'Neill. Chief O'Neill, whose honesty rendered him powerless over a corrupt department, attempted unsuccessfully to bring the Levee under control. Frustrated by the helplessness of Chief O'Neill, Louis J. Behan, who was head of a "vigilance group," entered the fight against prostitution in 1903. Starting with the First Ward, Behan obtained a warrant signed by Police Magistrate John K. Prindiville against Ike Bloom for operating Freiberg's Dance Hall after 1 a.m.[3] Soon Behan obtained other warrants, and more arrests were made. However, Kenna and Coughlin controlled the courts so the cases went nowhere, despite the best efforts of Behan and his group.

The same year, the city council's investigating committee attempted to bring pressure on the open vice conditions in the Levee. The committee conducted investigations and held public hearings, which revealed that police officers in the Levee area were forcing prostitutes to pay a tribute or be hounded and arrested. Alderman Herrmann, committee chairman, turned over the results of the investigation to State's Attorney Charles S. Deneen and Police Chief O'Neill. Deneen took no meaningful action, but O'Neill transferred five police officers from the Levee District to outlying police stations. When the newspaper clamor died down and the reformers relaxed, the corrupt Levee system returned to its old evil ways.

In 1905 Chief O'Neill told reporters that large cities like Chicago needed more police officers to cope with crime conditions in their community. He compared his city with New York, saying that in Chicago the police had a much larger area to patrol. Furthermore, O'Neill said, New York with four million inhabitants had one officer for each 500 persons, while Chicago with two million inhabitants had one officer for each 869 persons.[4] He neglected to point out that, in addition, his officers were inefficient and ineffective.

Chief O'Neill may have been correct, but the citizens were tired of empty promises. On April 7, 1907, Fred A. Busse was elected reform mayor of Chicago. Mayor Busse promptly announced that he was going to strictly enforce the vice ordinances. His first move was to replace O'Neill with Capt.

George M. Shippy. Once in office Chief Shippy assigned Capt. Stephen Wood to handle vice enforcement in the Levee. Fortunately for the vice operators, Wood's policy of law enforcement for the Levee was basically live and let live. Conditions worsened. Naked women appeared in resort windows. Solicitation for prostitution occurred openly, saloons stayed open on Sundays, and automatic pianos played loudly day and night. When questioned about the open prostitution in the Levee, Captain Wood blustered that he was responsible for many new controls. He listed:

All prostitution in the First Ward had been moved into the Levee.
Inmates of the resorts were registered at the district station.
Unless prior police consent was obtained no recruits (youngest girls) were permitted to work in the resorts.
The practice of prostitutes roping prospective customers into the bordellos had been ended.[5]

Captain Wood did not mention that his rules had no effect on the brothels and bordellos. Basically, everything was under control and running smoothly for the madams.

The *Record-Herald* was determined to prove that vice remained rampant in the Levee. In the late morning hours of September 20, 1908, the newspaper sent reporters to the most notorious dives. All were open and running noisily, ignoring the ordinance requiring a one o'clock closing and the numerous ordinances dealing with the suppression of vice. Many of the places had large numbers of women in the back rooms, others had pianos playing from midnight to daylight, and all were filled with loud, drunken customers.

In the front-page exposé that followed, the *Record-Herald* listed Ike Bloom's joint at Twenty-second Street and Wabash Avenue among the dance halls, saloons, and resorts where the laws were being flouted with impunity. The newspaper stated that police officers on the streets took no notice of the music, laughter, and bright lights after closing hours, let alone the workings of the fallen women. The paper angrily charged that vice operators contributed five hundred dollars each month for protection, which was contributed to "certain politicians and others whose word is law."[6]

This new round of publicity by the newspapers and the ensuing public indignation got Chief Shippy's attention. He promised that this time he would remove and replace every officer from the Levee District. However, logistics, seniority, and other problems stymied his plan. Only 56 of 114 officers were transferred. Captain Wood was among them, and Capt. Edward McCann was placed in charge of the Twenty-second District.

Captain McCann initially appeared to cooperate with the state's attorney in working to dismantle the white slave traffic that was bringing girls into the district. But when an investigation by police officers working under the state's attorney found two girls being held against their will in a vice resort on South Dearborn Street, McCann defended the brothel operators. He said that the practice of holding girls at a resort until they paid their debts to the madam for clothing and food was necessary because if the girls were allowed to escape the payment of their debts, the brothels would go out of business.[7]

In mid-1908, McCann was promoted to inspector and given command over several districts, including the Levee. An investigation by the state's attorney found evidence that McCann was protecting the madams in their white slave practices of holding girls in the brothels against their will. In the greatest police scandal up to that time, McCann was indicted in July 1909. The grand jury uncovered an elaborate system of police graft and protection involving McCann and other police officers. After a headline-making trial, McCann was convicted of accepting bribes from resort keepers. On January 31, 1910, Criminal Courts Judge Barnes sentenced McCann to one to five years in the state penitentiary at Joliet. McCann, claiming that the resort owners had set him up because he was too strict, demanded a new trial. The Illinois Supreme Court denied his request, but that didn't stop Gov. Charles S. Deneen, who had earlier been State's Attorney of Cook County, from granting McCann a full pardon. McCann stridently professed his innocence until he died.[8]

Nearing the end of his days in the chief's office, a more pragmatic Shippy embraced the concept of segregated vice. Offering a very unappetizing option to the reformers and the public, he said: "We can drive out every occupant of the Twenty-second Street District Station in forty-eight hours. But do you want us to drive them into the lake, as has been suggested? Do you want them driven to the resident districts? What do you want done with them? Isn't it better to keep them corralled in one spot with their names and histories tabulated?"[9]

In August 1909 Mayor Busse, bowing to public pressure, decided to replace the virtually worthless Shippy with Col. LeRoy T. Steward, a stern disciplinarian with a military background. Chief Steward took his turn at dealing with Chicago's vice problem.

Throughout this tumultuous period, Colosimo ran his brothels without police interference. Neither the newspapers nor the state's attorney ever mentioned Colosimo's resorts. In more than three dozen raids by the city police and the state's attorney, no Colosimo brothel was hit. His immunity, which began as a precinct captain and grew as his relationship increased with Kenna and Coughlin, served as a shield for his vice activities.

At this time the community at large was becoming more aware and more disturbed over the vice and corruption in the Levee. A mass meeting of the members of the Church Federation was held on January 31, 1910, to discuss the serious problems of the growing social evil. This meeting and the passions it aroused led to startling reform actions. Coughlin, Kenna, and Colosimo may not have realized the danger because the money was rolling in, but dark storm clouds were forming over their heads.

Chapter Fourteen

WHITE SLAVERY
Wayman and Clifford Wage War

1908–1909

> *Damned, debased, deceitful,*
> *Lustful, lewd and lost;*
> *Making Damsels into dregs,*
> *Reckoning not the cost.*[1]
>
> — Clem Yore, "The Maquereau,"
> *Songs of the Underworld*

> *But when the remnants of her beauty fails, the human devil will let go her*
> *chains and cast her out—a hopeless, pitiless, despised leper, to be spurned*
> and loathed until she is—
> > *"Mad from life's history*
> > *Glad to death's mystery,*
> > *Swift to be hurled*
> > *Anywhere—anywhere*
> > *Out of the world!"*[2]
>
> — William Burgess, description of a prostitute,
> *The World's Social Evil*

While Chicago's prostitution problem was bad enough, there was a corollary practice called white slavery that was even worse. White slavery was the transportation of women from one state to another through cajolery and lies and the placement of these women in houses of prostitution. While girls were never kidnapped off the streets of their hometowns, they were induced through flattery, money, promises of good jobs, or other equally bogus offerings to go to another city far from their homes where they ended up against their will in brothels. In many case, these women whose ages ranged from fifteen to twenty-five were initially held captive in the resorts by physical force or intimidation. The girls who were not willing to begin serving as prostitutes voluntarily were raped and made to undergo repeated acts of sexual violence until they submitted.

White slavery was needed in the Levee because of the demands of regular customers of the resorts for new girls. While local girls were recruited whenever possible, the supply was not sufficient to meet the demand of so many brothels and their customers. Another problem was the limited lifetime of working girls. After five years of servicing the unending flow of men at the better resorts the girls were turned out by the madams and ended up in the lower-class establishments. After ten more years in the lower-class whorehouses and crib shacks the diseased and physically depleted women ended their destructive careers as streetwalkers or hangers-on in saloons where they tried to induce men to go in the back room or at least buy them a drink.

Jim Colosimo, with his string of brothels, was always in need of new girls. Rather than leave this critical recruitment process to happenstance he turned to Maurice Van Bever, a well-known white slaver and brothel operator. For many years, Maurice and his wife, Julia, had been running resorts in the Levee. They had purchased a luxurious home with the income from their girls. Each day the pair would ride through downtown in their fancy brougham driven by a top-hatted coachman in gold-buttoned livery. Big Jim and Maurice agreed to begin a white-slave operation to supply their own bagnios and provide fresh girls to other Levee vice operators. The new partners planned to charge madams ten to three hundred dollars for a girl. They found field agents in New York, St. Louis, and Milwaukee.[3] Before their partnership was ended by a criminal prosecution, they were responsible for bringing several hundred young girls to Chicago to work in the resorts.[4]

Because Colosimo wanted more young girls, he agreed to purchase them at one hundred dollars each from pimp and resort operator Harry Guzik. Aided by his pandering wife, Alma, the slimy Guzik toured small towns in Illinois, Wisconsin, and Iowa seeking young ladies interested in improving their income and seeing the big city. After a lot of drinking and some sex with both of the Guziks, the girls would be invited to come to Chicago all expenses paid. Those who arrived were quickly broken in the trade and delivered to Big Jim's whorehouses.[5] For the new girls, Colosimo charged his customers ten dollars a trick from which he gave five dollars to the Guziks until one hundred dollars had been paid. He also paid for the Guziks travel expenses.[6]

For a number of years, this vice-supply program operated without a serious hitch, but in 1906 a new name began to be heard in the Levee—Clifford

Roe. Roe was soon to become the most important figure in Chicago in the fight against white slavery and prostitution. Every brothel operator, every madam, every officer in the Twenty-second Street police station became aware of this young man who had made ending white slavery in the Levee his life's work. Even Colosimo found that Roe was a force to be reckoned with.

Clifford G. Roe was born in 1875 on an Indiana farm. His parents brought him to when he was three years old. After his early schooling in Chicago, Roe received a bachelor's and a law degree from the University of Michigan. After graduation, Roe returned to Chicago to look for work. He was short and slight but had a walk of peculiar springiness. He was a hard charger with a thirst for seeing his name in print. He found a position in a small law firm, but his interests were in the criminal law. In 1906, he managed to be appointed as the youngest prosecutor in the Cook County State's Attorney's office.

The rookie prosecutor was assigned to the lowly Harrison Street police court. After observing the unending streams of young women who were brought into court on prostitution charges, Roe grew determined to bring an end to this sordid practice. In February 1907 he was greatly moved by a case involving a sorry prostitute known as Agnes Taylor who had been sold into a resort on Armour Avenue. On his own time Roe began to visit churches and clubs to tell them the story of Agnes Taylor's pitiful life and tried to interest them in joining the battle against white slavery. In February 1908, responding to his fervent pleas for help, five hundred Protestant ministers held a meeting to discuss the white-slavery question. Roe addressed the ministers and urged them to take action. They formed the Illinois Vigilance Association and began to fight against prostitution and white slavery.

At the same time, Assistant State's Attorney Roe continued his fight in the courtroom against the pimps, procurers, and madams. He tried more than a hundred cases and won all of them. Because of his success, State's Attorney Healey assigned Roe to full-time investigation of the white-slave problem.

While pursuing his investigation, Roe visited civic associations and urged them to develop a unified organization to take action. Because of his efforts, a civic committee was formed, which succeeded in having a pandering statute passed by the Illinois General Assembly and signed by the governor in July 1908. Roe later was able to have an amendment added making illegal the common practice of madams holding their girls at the brothels for indebtedness until all monies owned the madam had been taken from their meager pay.

In September 1909 the B'nai B'rith, Commercial Club, and other downtown businessmen's organizations lured Roe from the state's attorney's office to start a private organization to battle white slavery. His sponsors pledged fifty thousand dollars. Roe announced that his slogan would be "Protect the girl!"

His task was to investigate white slavery in the Levee and prepare white slavery cases to give to the county prosecutors and assist them in the trials.[7] One of his targets was Big Jim Colosimo, the vice lord Roe had heard so much about.

At the end of the first year, Roe reported that his office had investigated 348 cases and assisted in obtaining 54 convictions for white slavery. Roe claimed he had restored hundreds of girls from the resorts to their relatives and driven from Chicago one thousand undesirable men who were involved in the prostitution trade. He boasted, "Chicago was the first great American city to look the vice situation squarely in the face and make a determined, businesslike fight."[8] Interestingly, Roe later revealed that the first half-year of the organization's efforts was financed by the *Chicago Tribune*, the major beneficiary of numerous stories and interviews concerning his fight against white slavery.

Another procurer of women for the Levee resorts was Emma Duval who was known as "French Em." She had an arrangement with a white-slave ring that obtained girls directly from Ellis Island in New York. The girls were shipped to Blue Island, Illinois, where they were placed in a series of interconnected frame buildings with boarded-over windows and locked doors. These immigrant girls, most of whom could not speak English, were from Italy, France, and England. At the Blue Island barracks, they were stripped naked, held captive, and displayed to various resort owners from the Levee and cities in the Middle West. One of the larger purchasers of these immigrant girls was Jim Colosimo, representing his own and several other Levee resorts. After eight years of plying her vicious traffic in women, Duval was arrested by immigration inspectors and burly, red-haired Secret Service agent William C. Dannenberg. Several years later Dannenberg was selected to head the Chicago Police Morals Division and became another Colosimo nemesis. Duval was released on bond and immediately fled the country. No prosecutions followed because while the inspectors had her books, Duval had concealed the names of the white-slave purchasers in an unbreakable code. As a result, Colosimo and the other vice operators were able to avoid white-slavery indictments.[9]

Next, federal investigators traced a shipment of twelve girls from St. Louis to Chicago and from there to brothels owned by Colosimo and the Van Bevers. The Colosimo resorts were managed by Johnny Torrio and Sam Hare. The government made no arrests because they lacked jurisdiction; the federal White Slave Act had not yet been passed. This investigation led Roe to his most sensational case. One morning Roe told several police reporters, "We have obtained positive evidence that agents who obtained women for the Colosimo resorts not only plied their trade in St. Louis but conducted traffic between New York and Chicago. We have girls for witnesses who were held in the Colosimo resorts: the Saratoga and the Victoria. We have evidence that one of the girls was beaten cruelly in one of the resorts. Besides Sam Hare, manager of the Victoria, John Torrio, manager of the Saratoga, and Joe Bovo, one of the field agents of the [Colosimo] organization, we have evidence against others of the [Colosimo] gang who we are looking for."[10] This case substantiated that Torrio was working as a manager of a Colosimo resort as early as 1909.

Roe gave his evidence to the state's attorney. Two of the girls, Pearly Henderson and Hazel Elbe, admitted that they had been taken by Joe Bovo from St. Louis to Chicago to work in the Colosimo and Van Bever resorts. The police arrested Bovo, Torrio, Hare, and Maurice and Julia Van Bever for pandering. Torrio was identified as manager of the Saratoga and Hare as manager of the Victoria; apparently Victoria Colosimo had retired from operating her namesake whorehouse. The sensational story ran on the front pages of the Chicago newspapers. The reporters wrote that Colosimo was involved in the case but had not been arrested because no direct evidence had been found linking him to the allegations.

Joe Bovo was defended in court by Colosimo's friend and attorney Rocco De Stefano. Despite some back-of-the-scene attempts by Levee interests to get the two women to change their testimony, they stood fast and the case went to trial. On December 3, 1909, Bovo was found guilty with sentencing delayed until after the other trials. Three days later, Torrio and Hare stood trial before Municipal Court Judge Henry M. Walker. The state's case began to dissolve when Bovo, who had agreed to testify for the state, said that Hare and Torrio did not know he had brought the two girls from out of state. After some legal maneuvering, charges against Hare and Torrio were dismissed for insufficient evidence.[11] On December 24, 1909 Bovo pled guilty and was convicted of pandering. He received a six-month jail sentence and a three-hundred-dollar fine. Lurking in the background of this case was De Stefano, who presumably had arranged the strategy for Hare, Torrio, and Bovo. Before the trials, De Stefano had reached an agreement with the prosecutors in which Bovo would testify against the others in return for a lighter sentence. De Stefano did not say what Bovo would testify about.

Next to be tried were the scapegoats for Torrio and Hare, Maurice and Julia Van Bever. They were convicted of pandering and sentenced to one year in jail plus a fine of one thousand dollars each. This conviction ended Maurice Van Bever's career as a Levee vice operator. Because he had been a partner with Colosimo in running several brothels, his conviction resulted in an organizational vacancy that allowed Torrio to move up in the Colosimo vice organization. To the insiders it appeared that Colosimo had decided he no longer needed Van Bever as a partner.

Roe had taken a courageous stand against Coughlin and Kenna, Colosimo, the vice operators, and the police captain in the Levee. While Roe never got Colosimo jailed, he caused serious problems for his vice operations. Colosimo agreed that Roe had been a nuisance, but given that Big Jim was making six hundred thousand dollars a year he could afford a few bumps along the way.[12]

Responding to pressures from Chicago citizens and organizations to end the practice of luring girls from one state to another for prostitution President Taft sent a message to Congress supporting the passage of a statute providing for the prosecution of panderers engaging in the interstate commerce of women for immoral purposes. This brought about the passage of the federal White Slave Act, informally known as the Mann Act. The law was passed on June 26, 1910, making it a federal offense to bring women across a state line for sexual purposes. White slavery as a common practice in Chicago and around the country was over.

Chapter Fifteen

MARCHERS AND HYMNS

Gypsy Smith Comes to Town

1907–1909

I may have been guilty of colossal blunders, but, thank God, I haven't made the blunder of sitting on an easy chair and criticizing those who were seeking to do good in the world.[1]

— Gypsy Smith, speech at the Seventh Street Armory

By 1905 missionaries were coming from all over to rescue the fallen women of the Levee. When they arrived, they preached on corners and prayed in the resorts. They raised an infernal ruckus and provided no end of local amusement. Adding to the din, ministers in churches across the city raised a chorus against the segregated vice district with fiery sermons.[2]

An extraordinary scene began to develop in the Levee. Redemptorists, zealots, crusaders, reformers, and evangelists—local and out-of-town—found their way to the wretched streets with expurgation in mind. One group of three women could be heard nightly singing as they moved from corner to corner urging the resort customers to end their sinful ways and return to the Christ Jesus. Known by Levee loafers as the "Midnight Trio" they briefly became a local institution until one member chose to desert her husband and take off for California with a character of highly uncertain character whom she had met in the Levee.[3]

Tired of the corruption and vice in their city and the endless Sunday sermons in their churches, the voters surprised themselves by electing a reform candidate as mayor. Fred A. Busse, a Republican and former state treasurer, was sworn in as the new mayor in April 1907. While Busse was thought of as an honest man he had another side. He was considered by friends to be a gay blade and man-about-town with close associates who were gamblers and gangsters. One of his friends, Barney Bertsche, had engaged in a gun battle in front of city hall. During the wild affray Bertsche shot and killed a detective and wounded two other persons. Thanks to his connection with the mayor, Bertsche managed to avoid jail.

Within a few days of being sworn in, Mayor Busse began to implement his campaign promises. He appointed George M. Shippy as chief of police with orders to clean up the Levee. Shippy got off to a poor start when he appointed the laissez-faire, do-nothing Stephen Wood as supervising captain of several districts, one of which included the Levee. The negative reaction to this blunder forced Shippy to replace Wood with veteran Capt. Edward McCann. McCann had a good reputation for honesty. He took office with a plan for controlling the Levee. The plan specified that:

No children were to allowed in the Levee.
No solicitation by prostitutes was allowed on the streets.
No rapping on the windows to solicit customers was allowed by ladies
   in the brothels.
All prostitutes were to register at the district station, and,
All prostitutes in the resorts were to have periodic medical
   examinations.

McCann demanded that his officers enforce the new rules. The press and the reformers considered McCann's proposal to be a novel approach to an age-old problem and decided to give him a grace period. The results were disappointing—nothing changed.

Into this environment came a young criminal lawyer named John E. W. Wayman. He announced his candidacy for the Republican nomination as State's Attorney of Cook County. While thought to be personally honest, Wayman was suspected of being supported by the United Societies for Local Self Government, an organization of saloonkeepers and persons with vested interests in maintaining the status quo. Personally, Wayman was a "wet." He favored liberal laws for the sale of beer and alcohol and opposed Sunday closing ordinances. As the election neared, Wayman was opposed by the "drys" and many religious organizations. But with a variety of constituencies on his side, including the Irish and German communities that favored allowing saloons to be open on Sunday, Wayman won the Republican nomination against former State's Attorney John J. Healy who had held that position from 1904 to 1908. With the momentum now in his favor, Wayman went on to win the state's attorney's office in the regular election.

Newly elected State's Attorney Wayman began his term in office besieged by the reformers who wanted the Levee closed. Agreeing to look into the matter, Wayman dispatched investigators to determine the conditions in the red-light districts. When his men returned with accounts of sin and sex, Wayman ordered raids and arrests. In court, the assistant state's attorneys began to vigorously prosecute madams, whores, and miscreants of all sorts.[4]

Despite Wayman's actions, reporters found conditions in the Levee unchanged. Realizing that more support was needed, Ernest A. Bell, secretary of the Illinois Vigilance Association, added his voice to the clamor. Bell warned that men and youths from Chicago and from out-of-town were being irresistibly drawn to the Levee, if only by curiosity. Bell reported that the red-light district was in full operation illuminated by signs with blazing lights and booming with a raucous blend of music, laughter, fighting, and caterwauling. Visiting Shriners in their red fezzes, Spanish-American war veterans in their brown military hats, and sharply dressed buyers and salesmen in town for the latest displays of goods and products were drawn to what everyone considered the place to find a good time. These visitors joined the cattlemen who had traveled to Chicago with their boxcar loads of livestock and the butter-and-egg men who had brought their wares to the market—all on their way to the Levee with fresh money in their pockets.[5]

Not only had Captain McCann's novel restrictions failed, but he learned that he was in serious trouble. Vice operators in the red-light district west of downtown, which came under McCann's area of responsibility, had provided Wayman with information on police corruption. In July 1909 McCann was indicted on five counts of bribery and five counts of malfeasance as an officer. The charges resulted from reported graft paid to McCann by West Side vice-district resort owners. Wayman charged that McCann had been "buncoing" the reformers by claiming to be restricting vice while he was receiving graft from the resorts.[6] McCann denied the charges and pleaded that the vice operators were out to get him for his tough control policies.

Because of the serious charges against McCann, Mayor Busse decided that Chief Shippy, McCann's boss, apparently was not the man to accomplish control of prostitution in Chicago. In August, the mayor replaced the failing Shippy with LeRoy T. Steward. Beginning his new assignment, Steward moved quickly to take the high road on vice enforcement. He announced new regulations to purge the city of undesirable elements and control the vice areas. The new rules included:

No soliciting on streets, in saloons, or from doorways or windows.

No signs, lights, or colors on resorts indicative of the character of
    premises.

No "exhibition shows."

No persons between three and eighteen allowed in the vice districts.

No males allowed to loiter around the resorts.

No males allowed to own or conduct resorts.

No swinging doors on saloons.

No resorts within two blocks of a school, hospital, church or public
    institution.

No resorts located on streets with streetcar lines.

No women without male escorts in saloons.[7]

A final rule required the police to arrest as vagrants any men who sub-
sisted on the income of working girls of resorts.[8] The reformers noted quickly
that while Steward had a better list of rules than McCann none of them explicitly stated that there would be no prostitution.

Whether Chief Steward's policies were being implemented as he claimed
was a matter of debate. Five days after the new orders were sent to the district
captains the *Chicago American* reported that nothing had changed in the Levee
and none of the new directives were being observed. Confusing the issue, the
Tribune, which had supported Busse's election, reported that many changes
were occurring in the vice district in response to the chief's orders.[9] The citizens were left to wonder which account was correct.

In October while the debate was still raging on whether Steward's new
orders were reducing prostitution, Rodney Smith, a noted clergyman and
well-known reformer from England, arrived by train from the East Coast.[10]
Reverend Smith, known popularly as Gypsy Smith (sometimes Gipsy Smith),
claimed that he was in Chicago to tackle the problems of the Levee. The day
after his arrival Smith announced that he would hold a series of prayer meetings in the Seventh Regiment Armory. On October 11, thousands of
Chicagoans flocked to the Armory. In the colorful and dramatic rhetoric for
which he was known, Smith said that the souls of the helpless working girls of
the vice districts must be saved now. Smith, always a firebrand, screamed at the
men and women that they professed to be Christians yet were too timid, "to
speak above a whisper." He said his listeners had become "hard-hearted." He
criticized the throngs for their failure to bring their friends and neighbors to
the meetings. He pointed into the crowd and shouted: "It's just this sort of
people who are killing me. Yes, actually killing me. You go into the inquiry
room here and leave professing to be Christians, but what have you done to
show me you are Christians?" Smith demanded that the attendees "follow in

the footsteps of the Christ" and make the descent into the underworld of vice and crime. He energized his listeners; they became inflamed with his passion. Thousands of the attendees rose to their feet and pledged to walk with him through the Levee.[11]

On the early evening of October 12, 1909, Smith and twelve thousand enthusiastic followers marched into the Levee. Smith's announced intention was to reclaim the vice district for Christianity.[12] The Levee crowds were awestruck. The resort owners looked on with dismay. The following day Smith rejoiced in the success of his endeavor, but said he did not believe that his job was finished. He held more prayer meetings. Night after night Gypsy Smith rose to new heights of oratory in demanding his followers join him in a second massive march to the Levee. In mounting religious fervor, thousands of praying, singing supporters again promised to follow him.

Reverend Smith heard that the police might oppose the second march. He contacted W. A. Peterson, treasurer of the Laymen's Evangelical Association, and the two men hurried to meet with Chief Steward at police headquarters. Smith explained that he was planning a peaceful and prayerful march. Somewhat reluctantly, Steward consented to issue a permit if certain conditions designed to prevent disorder problems were observed. Smith agreed with the provisions. Later the same day, Chief Steward admitted that he did not favor the march but did not want to appear to be "interposing the slightest bar to religious activity of any legitimate character." Steward and his deputies quickly drew up a plan to place a strong police presence in the Levee on the night of the march.[13]

Each evening Smith continued his pleadings for his listeners to join the march. "If the people [in the Levee] don't want to come to church, we must bring the church to the people," preached Smith. At one meeting, he revealed that some girls who worked in the Levee had sent letters to him. He read aloud from one letter: "I am lost and I know it, but I could go back to my father's farm in Idaho and nobody would know I was lost unless I told them. I have tried to kill myself, but I haven't the courage. Do I have to tell everybody at home I have had this trouble? I am eighteen. Maisie."[14]

Many of the listeners wept unashamedly. By the end of the week fifteen thousand men and women had pledged to accompany Smith on his second march through the Levee.

October 18, 1909, was the day of the next march. That evening, Smith, dressed all in black, addressed a huge assemblage in the Seventh Regiment armory. He treated them to one of his hell-and-brimstone sermons. "A man who visits the red-light district at night has no right to associate with decent people in the daylight," shouted the evangelist, "No! Not even if he sits on the throne of a millionaire!"[15] As he finished speaking, the throng filed out of the armory and formed into a long, snaking column. Ahead of them was a platoon of mounted police officers followed by a Salvation Army brass band with blaring horns and thumping drums. Next came Smith accompanied by fifty-nine local ministers. Twenty thousand marchers carrying torch lights entered the Levee at Twenty-second Street and Wabash Avenue. As the band began to play "Onward Christian Soldiers" the marchers lustily joined in. Some carried banners reading "God Is Love" and "Jesus Shows the Way."

Turning west on Twenty-second Street where the onlookers were five deep, the marchers sang "Where Is My Wandering Boy Tonight." At Dearborn Street they turned north. When they reached the Everleigh Club, Gypsy Smith and the other ministers fell to their knees on the hard paving blocks. They prayed and sang. Along the curbs and standing in front of the resorts were hundreds of men and boys watching the most extraordinary spectacle in the history of the Levee. The prayers and singing lasted two hours. A ragtag band of onlookers, drunks, young teenagers, loafers, and persons opposing the march straggled at the end. The antagonists taunted the marchers with hostile remarks.[16]

As Smith and his followers continued their walk through the streets of the Levee, the exterior lights of the resorts and saloons were extinguished. Curtains and drapes were drawn over the windows. The customers left and the doors were locked behind them. After the march was over the Levee reopened for business. Discussing the events the next day, the vice operators agreed that late the previous evening their sordid business had boomed due to the crowds that had been attracted by the commotion. Even Chief Steward who had watched the march with his captains said he had been told that several saloons reported the most business in months. The *Chicago American* reported a grim picture:

> The chill, cold wind that whirred the dust and papers and dead leaves through the streets of the Levee districts, north, west and south, today was a fitting accompaniment to the scenes along its route, for today is accounting day, the end of the time of grace, and tonight the new regime goes into effect. They are ready for it among the red-lights. South, where the greatest Levee of the city stretches itself along Dearborn Street and Armour Avenue and Wabash Avenue for three blocks and straggles off into the neighboring streets, there was uneasy activity. Deep gloom pervades all "red-light" districts of the city. Resort proprietors freely forecast "business ruin."[17]

Pushed into action by the march, Chief Steward held a meeting with Inspector John Wheeler, who was in charge of the area that included the Levee, and Captain Cudmore, who was directly responsible as district captain.

Steward demanded that the vice ordinances be enforced in the Levee. The chief then met with the press. He told the reporters: "Go see for yourself. We are doing the work. Go and look at the results."[18]

Within a few days, changes were in fact occurring in the Levee. Raids and arrests were being made in record numbers. The brilliant, flashing electric lights on the fronts of the resorts were dark, and the only male workers in the brothels were the porters. No male proprietors, touts, or bartenders were visible. Hastily erected solid partitions without convenience doors now separated saloons from houses of prostitution. The noise and racket were gone and, except for a few pianos played by women, no music could be heard in the streets. The gaudy signs and name plates were down. Any connecting doors that had existed between the resorts and the saloons were nailed shut. Uniformed officers and detectives from the district patrolled the sidewalks and actually made arrests for violations of city ordinances and state laws. Inspector Wheeler and Captain Cudmore walked through the streets of the Twenty-second Street area at 1 a.m. to ensure the enforcement of the Sunday liquor ordinance. They found the Levee to be quiet. Where hundreds of cars and carriages had been cruising down Dearborn Street a week earlier, now less than a dozen could be seen. Aldermen Kenna and Coughlin were nowhere to be seen. As a matter of fact, neither was Jim Colosimo.

Mayor Busse was pleased. He said Steward "is at the head of the police department and I will stand back of him." Chief Steward reported that he was satisfied with the way in which his orders were being carried out.[19]

One example of the crackdown occurred late in the evening on October 13, 1909. White slaver Maurice Van Bever was arrested for pandering by patrolman Dever who was working with anti-vice crusader Clifford Roe. Roe had earlier secured a warrant for Van Bever based on a confession from a Richard Tyler, who had been arrested for pandering in the Mollie Hart case. Tyler admitted to being part of a white slave gang that in the previous six months had procured twelve women for Van Bever's resorts at 2100 and 2101 Armour Avenue.

By the morning of October 15, 1909, matters had grown so desperate in the Levee and the city's other vice districts, that some prostitutes left the resorts and began soliciting on the streets of downtown and nearby residential neighborhoods. Special orders were quickly given to the police in all districts to be on the lookout for such women. Detectives Starek and Grace arrested an eighteen-year-old woman whom they had seen accost several men on a downtown street. When her young husband ran up to protest he was thrown into the patrol wagon with his wife.

Joining the fight, the Baptist Ministers' Conference made an extensive investigation into the problem of segregated vice districts. On December 28,

1909, they sent a report to Busse, Steward and the members of the city council. The report blamed these officials and their predecessors for the vice districts, which the conference stoutly maintained had been "outgrown" in other American cities. Speaking for the conference, Dr. M. P. Boynton said, "It is an unspeakable shame that such houses are allowed to so adorn themselves with lights, gay colors, leaded glass canopies and other insignia and boldly declare their character to every passerby."[20]

Dr. Boynton claimed that candidates for mayor, in order to ensure their election, made deals with the politicians who controlled the Levee. He added that the Levee prostitution could be stamped out entirely with an order from the mayor. Their statement was true and such an order was soon to be coming.

Chapter Sixteen

THE BATTLE FOR THE LEVEE CONTINUES

Reformers and Crusaders on the March

1910

Heighohoe! Come, ye buyers!
We have chattels here to sell!
We are known as law defiers,
Walking on the brink of hell.
Here is one! See how she quivers!
Young and beautiful, and fair.
While ye bid, her fine form shivers
In an uttermost despair.
Ha! Here comes a well drest Madam
Seeking chattels for her trade.
Buy, ye fallen sons of Adam!
Low the price to you is made.
Madam gets her! Fifteen? Yes, sir!
Cheap for such a likely thing.
Take her to your "House" and dress her—
Feelings to the Devil fling.[1]

— Revs. F. M. Lehman and N. K. Clarkson,
The White Slave Hell

B y 1910, Chicago's population had jumped to 2,185,284, making it both the fastest-growing and second-largest city in the United States.[2] The city had 7,200 licensed saloons, 4,000 establishments where beer and liquor were sold by special permit, and thousands of dance halls, cheap theaters, gambling dens, poolrooms, bowling alleys, penny arcades, brothels, and houses of prostitution. In the sex fields alone there were 25,000 women and 10,000 men engaged in the prostitution business.[3]

Pressure to force city officials to take action concerning the vice situation continued. Protests against the "social evil" now were being made by many groups, including the Immigrants' Protective Association, the Society for Social Hygiene, the Chicago Law and Order League, the Chicago Midnight Mission, the Juvenile Protective Association, and the Chicago Federation of Churches—to name a few. The problem was that their actions were not producing meaningful results because there was no coordination and little cooperation among the groups. The anti-vice crusaders began to recognize this lack of unity and took measures to combine their actions.

The first major unified accomplishment was the coming together of six hundred Protestant church congregations under the auspices of the Federal Council of Churches and the Central YMCA. On January 31, 1910, at a mass meeting of clergymen and church workers, Dr. Herbert L. Willett fiercely denounced the Chicago police as predators and exploiters of vice. He introduced a resolution censuring the police charging that it was useless to expect any significant results in the correction of this evil while the police tolerated this unlawful business and even maintained a silent partnership by sharing in the spoils of the traffic in women. Willett said that a vice commission was needed to examine the problem, and the attendees unanimously passed a resolution calling on the mayor to form a vice commission.[4]

On March 5, 1910, representatives from the Federal Council of Churches and the Central YMCA visited Mayor Fred A. Busse. They presented the resolution from the mass meeting and a petition demanding an investigation of conditions in the Levee. Much to everyone's surprise, Busse agreed. Soon afterward he created the Chicago Vice Commission with thirty members. Of the formation of the commission, Busse said: "These [vice issues] are the most perplexing questions with which modern civilization is confronted. Since Chicago has been a city we have drifted with regards to these questions. In this we have not differed from other American cities."[5]

Busse named clergymen and representatives from important civic institutions as commissioners. Dean Sumner from Saints Peter and Paul Church was chosen as the first chairman, and U.S. District Attorney Edwin W. Simms, who had been active prosecuting white-slavery cases, was named secretary. Other commissioners included millionaire and philanthropist Julius Rosenwald, Chief Justice Harry Olson of the Municipal Court, and Professor Graham Taylor, head of Chicago Common. The commissioners selected George J. Kneeland, former head of field work for a civic vice investigating committee in New York, to head a team of investigators. The commissioners agreed that their role was to investigate prostitution and white slavery in Chicago and recommend methods for coping with these problems.[6]

In April 1910 the elections for city council were held. The First Ward race had not been affected by the movement toward vice reform. Coughlin was running for reelection against Republican John Townsend, the choice of the reformers and local newspapers. On his way to vote on election day, Coughlin said with a smile, "It's all my way; Townsend thinks he is running and he has a big surprise in store when the votes are counted." Kenna, though not up for reelection, was busy that day in the saloons and flop houses rounding up voters for Coughlin.[7] Bathhouse John won with his usual large plurality.

After the election, other aldermen showed that they were taking note of the movement toward reform. Goaded by Mayor Busse, the city council enacted an ordinance on July 1, 1910, that formalized the municipal vice commission. The aldermen begrudgingly appropriated five thousand dollars for its operations and later added five thousand dollars more. The ordinance charged the commission with the investigation of vice conditions throughout the city. Ironically, two of the "yes" votes in the city council favoring creation of the commission were made by Aldermen Coughlin and Kenna.

The police department began to be affected by the vice-reform movement. On August 24 in a surprise move Chief Steward transferred most of the personnel from the Twenty-second Street station to other districts throughout the city. A total of two lieutenants, three sergeants, and twenty-eight patrolmen and vice officers were relocated. Captain Cudmore, the do-nothing commander of the Twenty-second Street station, was transferred to the Warren Avenue District, and Captain Halpin was moved into command.[8]

The association of brewers in the city was alarmed by the growing opposition to alcohol being served in houses of ill repute. They worried that the anti-vice movement might become an anti-alcohol movement. On April 30, the brewers notified Steward that they supported his order that prohibited the sale of beer and liquor in disorderly houses. "Let us put our own house in order" was the slogan adopted by the brewers. Percy Andreas, head of the Chicago Consolidated Brewing and Malting Company, said, "Separate the disorderly house from the saloon and make a license an asset to be prized and safeguarded."[9]

One of the most steadfast and vocal of the reformers to attack the Levee was a local minister, Rev. F. M. Lehman. He was determined to save as many girls as possible from the vice dens and stop the white-slave trade. Working with Rev. N. K. Clarkson, he wrote a book called *The White Slave Hell, or With Christ at Midnight in the Slums of Chicago*. He began to exert pressure on Captain Halpin and the vice operators in the Levee. Lehman also fought to end the tacit support of the Levee by the organized church. The truth was that the majority of members of the Catholic Church were Irish, German, and Polish immigrants and their families. They were opposed to alcohol restrictions and were silent on matters of prostitution and gambling. The hierarchy of the Catholic Church seemed disinclined to enter the battle against vice. Lehman said that he had little sympathy for corrupt officials in Chicago, but until the organized church moved from its lethargy there was no point in crying out against corrupt political government. He hoped for a new Gypsy Smith–type march in the Levee led by the organized church in Chicago. He exhorted the silent church members to march "with flashing eye and fire-baptized zeal into the Red-light Districts and drives the nefarious trafficker in girls back to the gates of hell."[10]

The leaders of the reform movement held firmly to the belief that the elected officials had the duty and obligation under Illinois law to suppress commercialized vice. These leaders were determined to make the officials fulfill their sworn obligations. The combined efforts of the ministers and the civic associations were moving the mayor and police department to take action. The battle to close the Levee was being fought in earnest. Slowly, these dedicated members of the community were changing the quarter-century-long culture of segregated vice districts in Chicago. Even the city fathers were beginning to think that a reputation for having a colorful, lusty Levee was not beneficial to the economic success of the world's fourth-largest city.

Chapter Seventeen

REPORT OF THE VICE COMMISSION

Lots and Lots of Vice in Chicago

1911

Disorderly houses are prohibited and persons connected therewith or fre-
quenting the same are subject to a penalty of not less than $200.
    Saloons—Must be closed from 1 a.m. to 5 a.m. and persons other than
employees most not remain in the same at such time. Doors must be locked,
shades and screens removed so that an unobstructed view of the inside may
be had from without under penalty of $20 to $100.[1]

                          — Penal Ordinance of Chicago, 1914

Alderman Charles E. Merriam announced in January 1911 that he would run for the Chicago Republican mayoral nomination. The reformers and good-government types were elated. They believed that Merriam, a candidate of unquestioned honesty and dedication to good government, had an excellent chance at becoming the next mayor given the rising tide of public opinion rising against vice and corruption. Former mayor Edward F. Dunne responded by saying he would file for the Democratic nomination.[2]

    Meanwhile, incumbent mayor Busse announced that he would not run for reelection. After serving three terms as mayor, Carter Harrison Jr. had moved to California. To regain their political power in Chicago, several influential politicians, including Alderman Hinky Dink Kenna, reached out for Harrison and induced him to run in the Democratic primary against Dunne. The First Ward organization went to work to get Harrison on the ballot. When the ballot position was secured, Coughlin proudly declared that two thousand of fourteen thousand citywide residence affidavits filed for the nomination of "Our Carter" were the work of his precinct captains. He denounced as a vicious lie the rumor that the signatures had been collected from saloons customers and flophouse denizens at a cost of fifty cents apiece.

In the gritty world of city council politics Kenna was up for reelection and was fighting hard to retain his First Ward position on the city council. An anti-Kenna opposition group sprang up calling itself the First Ward Regular Democratic Organization. They immediately went on record stating that they would field a strong opponent against Kenna in the February 28 primaries. The new group named Col. Leopold Moss, who had been a member of the late Gov. John P. Altgeld's staff, as their candidate.

Moss, wealthy owner of the Marshall Ventilated Mattress Company, lived downtown in the Great Northern Hotel. The morning after his candidacy was announced Moss received a letter stating, "If you value your life you had better withdraw." Moss, a former cowboy and self-made businessman, was not so easily deterred. Ignoring the threat, he minced no words in his attack on the corrupt methods that were used to keep Kenna and Coughlin in office. Moss's platform included these planks:

- End the vice trust of graft and crime.
- Destroy the nefarious alliance between the Republican and Democratic leaders that has enabled the vice trust to exist.
- Protect business enterprises in the ward from the blackmailing operations of men who fostered vice that they may live upon its profits.[3]

The turnout for the primaries was record-breaking on both sides of the ticket. Democratic candidate Carter Harrison and Republican candidate Charles E. Merriam won their parties' mayoral nominations and began to square off for the big fight. A lopsided vote in the primary for Harrison in the First Ward was engineered by Kenna, Coughlin, and Colosimo. The three schemers intended to work equally as hard in the regular election to push Harrison into office. They believed it was crucial to elect Harrison, who would allow the vice activities in the First Ward to continue. In the First Ward aldermanic primary, Kenna won easily over Moss as was anticipated by the city-hall insiders.

Fueled by the preelection rhetoric of the candidates, new reform organizations appeared almost overnight hoping to ride the wave of anti-vice sentiment. The first was a strange band called the Affiliated Civic League. Attorney Percival Steele, the group's founder, described the league as "unlike any other organization in the country." He said the league was going to develop information on corruption and vice in the First Ward because "all graft and vice in Chicago radiate to the First Ward where the strings attached to certain forms of crime draw the price of protection." Steele said the league would give its findings to public officials to aid them in arresting and punishing offenders. Steele chose an unusual partner—reformed confidence man and gambler Harry Brolaski. Assistant Chief of Police Herman F. Schuettler scoffed at the idea of a self-confessed lawbreaker turning reformer. Schuettler said: "I have no time for his kind. I don't want to see him, for he is not of the square." Brolaski began making disclosures on downtown gambling. His statements so infuriated Chief Steward that he said if Brolaski came into his office he would "kick him out." During its short tenure the league had almost no impact on corruption or vice in the First Ward but frequently provided juicy vice stories for the Chicago papers.[4]

Next on the scene was the International Reform Association headed by Rev. A. S. Gregg. He said he had toured the South and West Side vice districts in February 1911. He reported that the conditions he found would not be tolerated in any other city on the continent. Gregg said the First Ward was the center of vice and crime in Chicago and for the public good the police and their corrupt political partners in that ward needed to be replaced.[5] Neither Gregg nor the association accomplished anything tangible, and both gradually faded from view.

Despite the valiant efforts by Republican Party workers, reform-minded voters, and several newspapers to get Alderman Merriam elected mayor, Carter Harrison Jr. won his fourth term as mayor on April 4, 1911, with a solid 17,132-vote plurality. A vote-fraud attempt had taken place when an employee of Kenna's Workingman's Exchange transported eight loafers and drunks who had already voted in the First Ward to have them vote again in the Eighteenth Ward. This typical First Ward tactic was foiled by agents of candidate Merriam, but that exposure did little to overcome the Harrison juggernaut.[6] And, as expected in the First Ward city council race, Kenna returned to office as co-alderman with Coughlin.

The bad guys had decisively won a round in the fight between decency and corruption. The word on the street was that the police would not interfere with gambling and vice operations. Gamblers and madams and prostitutes from all over the country began heading toward Chicago, as if there were not enough on the scene already. The reformers hung their heads in dejection, but as unlikely as it seemed, a landmark event was about to occur that would decisively energize the vice-reform campaign.

On the day after the election and one year after being appointed, the commissioners of the Chicago Vice Commission released their long-awaited study, *The Social Evil in Chicago*. The report made headlines and spawned newspaper columns and editorials, ultimately proving so popular that thirty thousand copies were printed. The 368-page report was the most extensive and exhaustive ever made of the vice problem of a major city in America.

The commission members had met eighty-eight times during the year, with some meetings lasting twelve hours. On hearing some interviews, several commissioners experienced revulsion from the depravity described. They wrestled with the question of whether to recommend that the city keep segregated vice districts or risk dispersing vice throughout the city. Ultimately, the commissioners rejected the concept of segregated vice districts and proclaimed them illegal, immoral, and detrimental to the city. The commissioners believed that segregated vice districts ensured and perpetuated governmental corruption. The commissioners concluded that the segregated district approach to vice operations was unreliable, intolerable, and futile.[7]

The vice commission investigators, hard at work since July 1910, had labored untiringly day and night and sometimes seven days a week. Actually visiting every known house of prostitution in the city and countless vice apartments and shady saloons, the valiant investigators even inspected three Lake Michigan excursion boats looking for hanky-panky. The investigators found 1,020 locations where prostitution existed and 4,194 women engaged in whoring. They estimated that men visited the resorts five million times a year.

The investigators calculated from the daily books kept by the keepers of the resorts and from interviews with madams and working girls of houses of prostitution that the annual gross from the vice trade was thirty million dollars.[8] The vice operators made fifteen million dollars a year, minus their operating costs, with the other half of the money going to the politicians and the police.[9] The investigators found that the income of the Everleigh sisters was one hundred thousand dollars a year, which the Everleigh Club's unofficial biographer Charles Washburn later said was low by twenty thousand dollars.[10]

The investigators reported that Coughlin and Kenna, through their collector, Jim Colosimo, were charging madams a fee of one hundred dollars per month for each floor of a building they used for their operations. Saloons paid fifty dollars each month to stay open after the required 1 a.m. closing hour. Not satisfied with their booty, the two aldermen required each saloon and vice establishment in the First Ward to purchase their fire, theft, and personal injury insurance from Coughlin's insurance agency. Regular payments were required from designated vendors that serviced the saloons, brothels, and gambling dens with alcoholic beverages, food, linens, and sundries.[11] The aldermen had perfected a system that Big Jim Colosimo, and later Johnny Torrio and Al Capone, would use as a primary income source for their organized-crime syndicate.

The report explained how the resorts recruited girls from the ranks of saleswomen, store clerks, domestic help, waitresses, and factory workers. Regarding why women turned to prostitution, the report stated:

> Is it any wonder that a tempted girl who receives only six dollars per week working with her hands, sells her body for twenty-five dollars per week when she learns there is a demand for it and men are willing to pay the price? Which employer wins the half starved child to his side in this unequal battle?[12]

The study even described the dangers to "youths of tender age" who were working as newsboys, delivery boys, and messengers. The investigators reported that these boys were debauched by coming into contact with the working girls in the houses.[13]

The commissioners made six recommendations. The first and by far the most important was that "local government had to achieve immediate, consistent, and persistent repression of prostitution with the ultimate ideal of absolute annihilation." The other recommendations were:

- Eliminate segregated vice districts by wiping them out of existence.
- Appoint a morals commission.
- Establish a morals court.
- Close certain downtown hotels and massage parlors.
- Appoint a morals squad of women police officers to visit and care for girls and women affected by the implementation of the commission's recommendations.[14]

In their closing statement, the commissioners said:

> There must be a constant repression of this curse on human society. . . . We believe that Chicago has a public conscience which when aroused cannot be easily stilled. . . . We may enact laws; we may appoint commissions; we may base civic administrations for their handling of the problem; but the problem will remain as long as the public conscience is dead to the issue or is indifferent to its solution. The law is only as powerful as the public opinion which supports it.[15]

The operators of the vice dens in the Levee determined quickly that the commission report could not to be ignored. To head off any meaningful action by reformers, the Levee operators formed an informal group led by Jim Colosimo and Ike Bloom, operator of Freiberg's Dance Hall. The pair met repeatedly with other Levee vice figures, including Minna and Ada Everleigh, to plot a course of action to derail the growing momentum of public opinion against the Levee. The two sisters wisely and correctly counseled that this time the opposition was stronger than ever before and that even the power of Coughlin and Kenna might not be able to withstand the movement to end the segregated vice district.[16]

Despite the newspaper editorials that action should be taken on the commission's recommendations, Professor Herbert L. Willett, pastor of the Memorial Church of Christ, bemoaned that little would be done. Willett sounded a gloomy prospect when he opined that the report of the vice commission would never be acted upon by Mayor Harrison's administration. Willett maintained that graft was responsible for more crime and vice in Chicago than any other single factor. He said, "The root of the white slave traffic is graft and it extends from the owner of the property to the policeman on the beat."[17]

Mayor Harrison sagely turned this hot potato over to the city council. A majority of the aldermen, hoping the matter would fade with time, passed a resolution placing the vice commission report and its explicit information containing names and addresses "on file." A handful of aldermen was incensed that the vice commission report was filed without being used as a tool for prosecution. Alderman McInerney shouted, "Let them take it to the grand jury or anywhere that it belongs, I do not care whom it hits; let them take their medicine, be it poor man or public official." McInerney was not alone. "Let's publish the whole thing, if it is something that the grand jury should take up that can follow later," seconded Alderman Egan.[18]

Interestingly, two members of the vice commission, Municipal Court Chief Justice Harry Olson and commission Chairman Dean Sumner, spoke against opening the sections of the commission's name and address files containing explicit information. Olson warned that the report contained enough explosive material to shock the nation from one end to the other if disclosed. He advised the aldermen that they were playing with fire, citing that the report revealed the identities of two hundred members of the police force, public officials, and others involved in the vice rackets and contained evidence against members of respectable society who earned rental income from illegitimate enterprises. Sumner objected to the release of the report on the grounds that the owners of the vice properties were no more guilty than the mayor, the chief of police, and other officials who allowed such conditions to exist.[19] Despite the posturing pro and con the city council firmly placed the report, including the explicit section that listed names and addresses, under lock and key in a basement vault at city hall from which it never returned.

Mayor Harrison had long held an unwavering belief that segregating vice was the only practical answer to controlling prostitution in a large city. Well aware of the growing public criticism of the segregated vice district and support of the report of the vice commission, he devised a strategy aimed at appeasing the reformers while convincing the public that he was controlling vice. He promised a series of attacks not on the Levee but on other vice activities. He said he would:

> Close the brothels on south Michigan Avenue.
> Eliminate white slavery in Chicago.
> End street-walking and street solicitation.
> Shut the brothels and saloons where men were drugged and robbed.
> Stop public advertising of prostitution.

Hoping for his share of the anti-vice publicity, State's Attorney Wayman ordered a grand jury investigation into the evil cabal known through the newspapers as the Levee vice trust. Information was provided by Harry Brolaski of the Affiliated Civic League. He named Kenna and Coughlin as co-heads of the vice trust. The grand jury returned indictments, but they were later dismissed when the court learned that the grand jury had inappropriately heard evidence outside of their chambers. Suspicion grew in the public's mind that Wayman's grand jury theatrics were motivated more by political reasons than by the findings of his investigators. Stung by negative comments in the newspapers, Wayman became more aggressive. He ordered the detectives and investigators working in his office to make raids throughout the Levee. Wayman took a strong public position stating the segregated vice district had to be closed.

Ignoring Wayman and confident in his political power, Mayor Harrison appointed Capt. John McWeeney as chief of police, replacing Steward. McWeeney clearly understood his assignment. Instead of an attack on the vice districts he announced he was going to declare war on bombers, Black Handers, and labor sluggers. He arrived at 7:40 a.m. for his first day of work. He told the sleepy-eyed city hall reporters, "Paid reformers would receive little attention from me. Vice is an old as history and to advertise it is only to encourage it. . . . I am not treating vice separately—as for instance, only one district—but vice as a whole." None of the reporters and few of the public missed the message that vice in Chicago was going to continue unabated.[20]

Chapter Eighteen

EVERLEIGH CLUB CLOSES

Mayor Harrison Finally Takes Action

1911

Although the shuttering of the Everleigh emporium of love was inevitable, as well as the hop joints and the red-lighted cathouses which comprised the rest of Chicago's Levee, at least Minna and Ada come though it all as the two most famous madams the world has ever known, and they will live on in print for generations to come.[1]

— Ray Hibbeler, *Upstairs at the Everleigh Club*

As 1910 ended, many more individuals, groups, and organizations were becoming concerned about the segregated vice districts in Chicago. Arthur Burrage Farwell, the Hyde Park reformer and president of the Chicago Law and Order League, was vigorously working to end the houses of ill-fame and the disorderly saloons in the First Ward. Clergymen and reformers pressured Mayor Carter Harrison Jr. to reverse his long-standing support for an open city. A new group, the millionaire owners of the luxury residences along Prairie and Michigan avenues, had become distraught about the encroachment of streetwalkers and prostitutes working out of small neighborhood apartments, an overflow from the Twenty-second Street red-light district. Responding quickly to the millionaires' complaints, Harrison issued an order to the police to begin a crackdown on vice along Michigan Avenue from Twelfth to Thirty-first streets. Harrison's move bought him a little time because it reduced the pressure from the powerful Prairie Avenue property owners, but it did not quiet the crusaders or reformers who wanted an end to the Levee.

In 1911 the most famous segregated vice district in Chicago was the Levee. In the Levee the most famous brothel was the magnificent Everleigh Club, with its gilded parlors and unusual bedrooms. Not only were Chicagoans aware of this extravagant and lavish bordello, but wealthy and influential persons from around the world were well familiar with what was considered the finest whorehouse in the United States. Because of the stature and visibility that the club enjoyed, this high-class brothel became a lightning rod for protests and complaints from everyone interested in ridding the city of its horrible vice reputation. Reformers, crusaders, clergymen, critics, and wives of the city's civic leaders saw it as a virtual lighthouse for the sinners. The club's fame that fed its popularity proved to be its downfall.

In addition to the pressures to close the club's doors, Minna and Ada Everleigh had another problem. Almost from the day they opened for business, they had been dealing with jealous operators of other Levee resorts. Envious of the amount of money being made and the freedom from arrest enjoyed by the sisters, madam Vic Shaw had continuously conspired against them. In addition to Shaw schemes, harassment came from the resort immediately south of the Everleigh Club operated by brothers Big Ed and Louis Weiss. They were aided by Big Ed's girlfriend, Aimee Leslie, who managed the resort to the north of the club. The touts for the two resorts began a dedicated effort to snare drunken customers and out-of-towners that weren't sure of where they were going away from the Everleigh Club and into their houses of prostitution. Meanwhile, the other resort operators were engaged in spreading rumors meant to embarrass the Everleigh sisters.

Minna and Ada were able to deal with these troubles. They considered them to be part of operating the city's most renowned bordello. They were shielded from newspaper criticism through the intercession of wealthy and powerful customers and city officials who had received sizable contributions to their election campaigns. The sisters had contributed generously to special funds for fighting reformers and law and order candidates for public office. Lastly, they had the protection of the mayor, with whom they had a secret funding arrangement.[2]

The Everleighs knew from the start that the First Ward was controlled by Michael Kenna and that they had to either cooperate with his protection-payment plan or close. It was clear to Minna and Ada that despite the influence of their blue-chip clients, the real power in the Levee was in the hands of John Coughlin and Kenna. Years later, Minna admitted that there was a third power, Big Jim Colosimo. At the time the club had opened Ike Bloom was the collector responsible to Kenna for the vice payoffs, but the Everleigh sisters had a particular dislike for the disreputable Bloom and refused to deal with him. When their friend Big Jim Colosimo replaced Bloom as the Levee collection manager, the sisters were pleased. Minna later revealed that Big Jim had plenty to say about what went on in the Levee and that over a ten-year period she and her sister had given one hundred thousand dollars in payoffs to Colosimo to be shared with Coughlin and Kenna.[3]

But as with all good things there had to be an end. The city fathers, those men who gave orders to the mayor, decided that the city had to clean up its act. A reputation for being the nation's vice capital was not a solid foundation on which to build a growing and prosperous city. While Harrison was pondering on how to resolve this tricky dilemma the answer jumped into his hands. The proverbial straw that broke the camel's back and doomed the club was not the efforts of the reformers or the newspaper editorials or the in-fighting from the other madams and operators, it was an advertising brochure. A lavishly illustrated booklet, six inches long and four inches high, called the *Everleigh Club, Illustrated,* that extolled the beauty and ostentation of the Everleigh Club had been distributed widely by the sisters. Minna had come up with the idea to print an attractive advertising piece. The thirty-one-page booklet contained one exterior photo of the two buildings and twenty-nine interior photographs showing the entry hall, the ornate staircases, the decorated parlors, and the lavish and theme-related bedrooms. The booklet brashly urged visitors to see the city's two greatest attractions, the stockyards and the Everleigh Club. Thousands of copies made their way across the United States and to England and Europe.

During a business trip that Mayor Harrison made to St. Louis, a man showed the mayor one of the booklets and asked if it truly represented the city. Embarrassed, the mayor decided that the club had violated his rule against advertising for prostitution and made the decision that he had to take action. While this may have been the *causa belli*, the underlying reason was the decision made by the city fathers that the club had to go. The gossips in city hall said the days were numbered for the club whose owners went to France for annual visits, for the club that was immune from police interference, for the club that had the largest income of any resort in the Levee, and for the club whose notoriety extended throughout the United States and Western Europe.

The newspapers caught wind of the story and began to report the existence of Minna's advertising booklet. In an interview Harrison was quoted by the *Chicago Record-Herald*, "The Everleigh Club has been advertised far and wide."[4] According to Mayor Harrison, the reputation of the city of Chicago was at stake. He first threatened to close the club, but his warning had little effect. The sisters kept the club in full operation. The patrons continued to come, believing that the club was immune. The mayor then told Chief John

McWeeney that he must close the club. McWeeney confidentially advised Minna and Ada of Harrison's order. Still assuming that their connections would overcome the mayor's order, the sisters continued operations. Chief McWeeney took no action. When Harrison learned that the club was still running, he decided on a bolder and stronger measure.

At 11 a.m., Tuesday, October 24, 1911, Harrison announced publicly to a group of reporters assembled in his office that the Everleigh Club was to be closed immediately. The mayor said: "I am absolutely opposed to using such a place as a show house from one end of the United States to the other. They must close their doors and will not be allowed to reopen while I am in power. A place of the character of this resort has absolutely no place in a civilized community."[5] He added, "If there are any other places like it, they will be regulated also, regulated out of business." Harrison, who had long believed in the necessity of segregated vice districts and whose principal supporters were John Coughlin and Kenna, had reversed his own politics.

The mayor's written order that the Everleigh Club at 2121 Dearborn Street be shut down was sent that morning to Chief McWeeney's office. At 2 p.m., McWeeney sent the clearly worded directive to Inspector John Wheeler at the Harrison Street station, whose command included the Twenty-second Street District Station. Strangely, the order mysteriously languished on Wheeler's desk for hours before it was sent to the Twenty-second Street District Station, where once again it sat in a message box. The actual closing of the club didn't occur until a reporter woke McWeeney late Tuesday evening to tell the sleepy chief that the club was in full operation. McWeeney personally phoned the surprised desk sergeant at the Twenty-second Street station and told him to shut the club at once. At 1 a.m., Wednesday morning, the police finally closed the club.

As the clock had been ticking down on Tuesday evening, the Everleigh Club was going strong with all of the lights ablaze, the orchestra playing gaily, and the girls in their finest gowns. The Everleigh sisters, having been tipped off by McWeeney, were holding one last night of celebration. Minna and Ada had notified many of their best customers who immediately rushed to the club. Reporters learning of the order joined the club regulars for one last visit. Laughter, music, champagne, fine wines, gourmet dinners, and general merriment reigned. As midnight passed, it seemed to the revelers that the closing had been rescinded; but, at 1 a.m. Wednesday, several squads of uniformed police from the district arrived at the front door. The officer in charge apologetically explained that the order came from downtown and could not be ignored. He had no choice; the place had to close. The patrons got their hats and coats, entered their carriages, and were driven away. At 1:30 a.m. the lights went out. Two police officers took up a post at the front door. Assuming the closing to be a temporary measure the sisters offered no opposition, no bitter comments. They shut the doors and planned a vacation.[6]

After the sisters closed the club, they had the furniture covered and took a train to the East Coast and later an ocean liner to Europe. Their hand-picked girls moved to other resorts in the Levee and bordellos in far away states. Levee old-timers guessed incorrectly that the heat would be off after a few weeks or months and the sisters would return and the Everleigh Club would open again.

In August 1912, the Everleigh sisters did return to Chicago after a six-month vacation in Europe. They purchased a fine home on the Near West Side and began to make moves to reopen their Club. The noxious Ike Bloom offered to act as their go-between with the politicians and suggested that a contribution of forty thousand dollars would allow them to reopen. He told the sisters that the money would be consolidated with contributions from other madams for a fund to pay off politicians at city hall and the state capital in Springfield. Bloom said the payment would be used not only to reopen the club, but also to protect the other resorts in the Levee from police raids. The sisters, who never liked or trusted Bloom, contacted their close friend and confidant Jim Colosimo. Colosimo, who was quietly behind the proposal all along, advised that they should meet with Bloom and work it out. Bloom and Colosimo urged the sisters to pay their share. Reading the daily newspapers filled with stories about the resolve of the reformers, the sisters wisely refused. They sold the furniture and permanently retired from the business that had rewarded them with one million dollars in capital, two hundred thousand dollars in jewelry, twenty-five thousand dollars in unpaid IOUs, and an unrivaled place in Chicago's history.

The closing of the Everleigh Club marked the beginning of the end for the Levee. As if the shuttering of the club were not enough misfortune for the Levee, more troubles came from an overseas critic. Lena Wallis, a leader among the English suffragettes, visited Chicago and walked through the Levee with a number of deaconesses. After viewing the South Side vice district, she told a meeting of Methodist ministers that she had come into contact with many of the evil conditions in the big cities of England, but "nothing exists there which compares with the flagrant flaunting of vice in Chicago."[7]

Chapter Nineteen

GANGSTER FROM NEW YORK

Johnny Torrio Arrives

1905–1912

Each morning he ate light breakfast, kissed his wife goodbye at the door, and drove to his richly appointed office at the Four Deuces. That his job consisted of buying and selling women, corrupting public officials and private business executives, checking gambling receipts, arranging beer and liquor shipments, conferring with strong-arm goons and murderers—all this and more—mattered little. When the day's work was done he drove back to his apartment, back to his wife.[1]

— Hank Messick, *The Private Lives of Public Enemies*

The story must back up for a moment to bring Johnny Torrio onto the scene. Torrio was a man of contradictions. He abstained from alcohol, did not gamble, and never had a personal relationship with a woman except his wife. He never swore and did not like others to swear in his presence. In business dealings he was dependable and trustworthy. Yet he provided liquor, girls, and gambling for all comers. He was a stone-cold killer and responsible for ordering numerous murders. After Colosimo's murder, he took over and expanded his former boss's vice organization. He was the most complex character in the crime world of Chicago in the early twentieth century.

Torrio's demeanor was that of the ascetic. His dark eyes constantly surveyed those around him, and his dispassionate face displayed little emotion. His clothing matched his temperament. His suits were dark, his shirts were white, his ties conservative, and his only jewelry was a wedding ring.

Torrio was the first out-of-town hoodlum hired by Big Jim Colosimo. He rose through the ranks to become Colosimo's first deputy, and after Colosimo's murder he became head of his former boss's criminal enterprise. His role in the underworld was lasting and brutal.

John Torrio was born in Irsina, Italy, on January 20, 1882. Giovanni Torrio was the second child of Thomas Torrio and Maria Carlucci. Thomas Torrio died in an accident not long after Johnny was born, and Maria took her son to the United States. They arrived in New York Harbor in April 1884 and moved in with Maria's brother, Dominic Carlucci, who lived in New York City.[2] When Johnny was four years old, his mother married Salvatore Caputo, the owner of a small grocery store on James Street near the East River. In the back room of his stepfather's grocery was a blind pig. At age seven, young Johnny was given work by his stepfather as waiter, cleaning boy, and runner for the bootleg liquor store. Torrio learned at an early age that Caputo avoided paying city, state, and federal taxes and license fees. He discovered that more money could be made from an illegal business than in a legitimate store. Torrio's formal education was spotty at best, but while working at the blind pig he sporadically attended Catholic and public elementary schools.[3]

As a teenager Torrio formed a gang of Italian immigrant children who lived in the tough and crime-filled James Street area in lower Manhattan. Initially, the nascent James Street gang limited their activities to petty thefts and muggings, but they soon added the shaking down of local Italian merchants. The gang was a source of income and provided Torrio with thugs he could use to aid local politicians at election time in getting out the right vote. This relationship with the politicians gave Torrio standing in the neighborhood and some protection from the police.[4]

During the elections in 1905, Torrio used the James Street gang to assist the Five Points gang in supporting the incumbent mayor, George B. McClellan, and the slate of Tammany Hall candidates. The two gangs intimidated voters, beat the opponent's political workers, and turned in fraudulent ballots. Their efforts were not in vain; Mayor McClellan won another term by a slim margin.

Two large and powerful rival gangs were operating in lower Manhattan, Paul Kelly's gang and Monk Eastman's gang. Eastman was a rough and crude hoodlum. Kelly was the opposite; he spoke well, dressed conservatively, and enjoyed fine music. Torrio joined forces with Kelly, who took a liking to the young mobster. From Kelly, Torrio learned how to be a proper gentleman, a serious businessman, and a successful gang leader. Torrio also learned the wastefulness and foolhardiness of violent rivalries between gangs. These lessons stayed with Torrio throughout his life and enabled him to build a multimillion-dollar criminal empire in Chicago during Prohibition.

At the same time, Frankie Yale was running a gang whose headquarters were at the Harvard Inn at Coney Island in Brooklyn. Torrio knew that Yale was one of the toughest of the Brooklyn gang leaders. They became associates and exchanged favors of a criminal nature. In 1920 Torrio called on Yale to perform a very deadly mission that dramatically changed the vice picture in Chicago.

By the time he was nineteen Torrio was using the alias of J. T. McCarthy and working as a manager for amateur boxers. There was considerable betting on the outcome of amateur matches because New York, in a foolhardy attempt to end fixed fights, had banned professional boxing. Gamblers, promoters, and fixers turned their full attention to amateur fights. Soon the same problem of fixed fights emerged in the amateur bouts. Torrio entered his fighters in the amateur card. He called the shots with his fighters and told them when to take dives. Torrio used his profits from betting on the bouts to buy real estate.[5] He managed a saloon at James and Water streets and turned a vacant building into a pool hall and a boarding house into a brothel.[6] When Torrio moved to Brooklyn he opened a saloon, He also formed the John Torrio Social Association, a front that served as a hangout for his gangland buddies.[7]

Torrio occasionally traveled to other cities to promote fights or attend boxing matches. His first visit to Chicago was to attend some fights in 1905.[8] Two years later, when professional prizefighters Johnny Conlon and Kid Murphy were scheduled to box in Dolton, Illinois, Torrio came to Chicago again. A Chicago newspaper reporter writing about the proposed match described Torrio as "an eastern sporting man." Torrio let it be known that he "liked" Conlon and was interested in taking wagers up to one thousand dollars. Presumably, Torrio had inside information concerning the likely outcome of the bout. The press wrote that Torrio would have no trouble in securing takers because the locals favored Murphy.[9] At the last moment, officials scrapped the fight, leaving the backers of Conlon and Murphy scrambling for a new site. Unfortunately for Torrio, the match could not be rescheduled, and he returned to Brooklyn.

During Torrio's visits to Chicago, he met Colosimo. Big Jim persuaded Torrio to leave Brooklyn and join his vice ring. Sensing an opportunity, Torrio moved to Chicago. He wrote to New York and offered to sell his share of the Harvard Inn to his business partner in Brooklyn. In 1909 Colosimo placed Torrio in charge of the Saratoga, one of Big Jim's brothels in the Levee.[10] Even though Torrio was now based in Chicago, he kept his gang contacts alive in New York and on occasion engaged in criminal ventures with Kelly and Yale.[11]

In August 1911, Torrio became involved in another kind of sporting event. A wrestling match was scheduled between Frank Gotch and George "Hack the Russian Lion" Hackenschmidt. Torrio offered to wager five hundred dollars on Gotch at even odds and hinted that there was money available for larger bets. The match took place in the Chicago White Sox Baseball Park on

September 4 with Gotch the winner. In a newspaper article, Torrio was referred to as a "South Side sporting man," indicating that the press now viewed him as a Chicagoan.[12]

Around this time, Black Hand extortionists were demanding money from Colosimo. Assigned by Colosimo to resolve this problem, Torrio became involved in a multiple murder.

The Black Hand story began at the turn of the century when small groups of Italian criminals in New York and Chicago began to commit extortions in the Italian immigrant community. These hoodlums sent notes to Italian businessmen written in Italian containing drawings of a black hand or the words *mano nera*. These so-called Black Hand letters were designed to generate fear in the recent arrivals, many of whom could not speak English and did not trust American law enforcement. If the recipient of a letter did not pay off, the written threats were followed by beatings, bombings, and murders. These incidents began to occur with more frequency as many criminals copied this criminal activity.[13] Many accounts have suggested incorrectly that the Black Hand was a single organization that grew to become the organized crime syndicate in America.[14]

On the night of November 22, 1911, police responded to a report of a shooting in the long, dark underpass below the Rock Island Railroad tracks near 2047 Archer Road. Rushing to the scene in a horse-drawn patrol wagon, the police found two men shot dead and a third dying from gunshot wounds. The dead were identified as two Chicago hoodlums named Pasquale Damico and Francisco Denello. In the autopsy Damico was found to have been shot nine times in the back and Denello shot once in the head and once in the side. The wounded man, Stefano Denello, brother of Francisco, had dragged himself a block from the shooting scene where he was discovered crawling under the sidewalk by a police officer. Rushed to nearby People's Hospital with bullet wounds in his head and side, he refused to tell detectives the circumstances of the shooting. He asked the Colosimo be brought to his bedside, but when the police brought Colosimo to the hospital room, Stefano "erfused to talk to him."[15]

In December, Stefano was moved to Cook County Hospital where he continued to refuse to cooperate with police. No further record can be found about him.[16] Capt. Patrick Harding of the Twenty-second Street station told reporters, "This city is rid of a bad gang. It is my belief that the three men were lured to the scene of the shooting by men who they blackmailed or were attempting to obtain money from through Black Hand letters. The Denello brothers and Damico have done most of the Black Hand work in this police district." The names Torrio and Colosimo were not mentioned in the police and newspaper reports.[17]

The most likely explanation of this multiple shooting was the the gang was blackmailing Colosimo with Black Hand letters and Torrio was dispatched to bring closure to the problem.

After the shooting, Torrio started to work at improving the operation and income of the Saratoga brothel. This whorehouse was a two-story, ramshackle structure in which over-used prostitutes charged one dollar a trick. Located on Dearborn Street two doors away from the Everleigh Club, the tout in front of the Saratoga was able to corral sufficient numbers of men who were taking a look at the Everleigh Club to make the brothel a profitable operation. Applying his business sense, Torrio dressed his whores in gingham rompers with sashes tied in large bows at the back. The girls wore silk bows in their hair and high-heeled shoes on their feet. While Torrio didn't have high-class prostitutes, he did have whores who could give the illusion of being little girls. The gimmick worked, and the business prospered.[18]

Torrio needed a constant supply of prostitutes to work in the Saratoga. To obtain them, he became involved with a white-slave ring operated by panderer Maurice Van Bever and his wife, Julia. Torrio got the girls he needed, but the relationship with the Van Bevers created serious legal problems for him.

The first problem began in 1909 when federal agents investigating the white-slave traffic in the Midwest traced twelve girls who had been moved from St. Louis to Chicago and placed in resorts owned by Van Bever and Colosimo. Colosimo's resorts were managed by Johnny Torrio and Sam Hare. Chicago police arrested Torrio, Hare, and Van Bever. When Torrio was on trial for pandering, the pimp who had transported the girls to Chicago testified that Torrio did not know the girls had come from out of state. The case was dismissed.[*]

Torrio's second problem came in 1911. Agents from the newly formed Bureau of Investigation of the U.S. Justice Department (later named the Federal Bureau of Investigation) visited a whorehouse in Bridgeport, Connecticut, on a tip that some of the working girls had been shipped across state lines. One of the prostitutes told the agents she had been transported from Chicago to Bridgeport by Torrio and Van Bever who were acting as agents for Colosimo. The girl agreed to testify against the trio. For safekeeping the federal agents placed the girl temporarily in the Bridgeport city jail. The Cook County state's attorney was notified by the agents and began preparing indictments charging transporting a woman across state lines for prostitution.

Meanwhile Torrio learned of the investigation from his informants in the Chicago police and called on his New York gang friend Frankie Yale for assistance. Yale, through his contacts on the East Coast, was able to locate where the agents had temporarily hidden the girl. Late one afternoon, a car containing two men claiming to be federal agents arrived at the jail. They persuaded the jailers that the girl was in danger. They said she needed to be moved to

---

[*] A full account of this incident is presented in Chapter 14, "White Slavery."

another location for her protection. The gulled jailers turned the girl over to the two men; the following day her lifeless body with twelve bullet holes was found in a graveyard near Bridgeport. The jailers later identified pictures of two members of the James Street gang that Torrio had led in New York as the bogus federal officers. No legal action was taken against the kidnappers of the girl. Without her testimony the planned indictments in Chicago were scrapped. Colosimo and Torrio were suspected by federal agents of being involved in the girl's murder. The two Chicago vice operators were taken into custody by the agents and brought to the federal building for questioning. Torrio and Colosimo repeatedly denied having knowledge or involvement in the kidnapping and murder; they were released without charge.

Torrio soon took over management of Colosimo's saloon and resort at 2001 S. Archer Avenue and the brothel at 2118 S. Armour Avenue. Torrio placed Roxy Vanille, a cousin from New York City, in charge of the Armour Avenue brothel.

In 1915, thirty-three-year-old John Torrio married Anna Theodosia Jacobs in Covington, Kentucky. On their license Torrio listed his occupation as "saloonkeeper" and Jacobs listed hers as "cashier." John was thirty years old, and Anna was twenty-five. She had come from a town that was not far from the vice and gambling hotspots of Newport, Kentucky. Nothing is known of how Torrio and Anna met, but they fell deeply and lastingly in love. Torrio brought his new wife to Chicago where they lived for many years until he fled to New York in the mid-twenties after almost dying from gunshot wounds sustained during the Beer Wars.

When Torrio arrived in Chicago he lived in the Levee at 101 W. Twenty-first Street.[19] After their marriage the couple moved to a modest apartment nearby on Nineteenth Street and Archer Avenue. Later they moved many miles south of the Levee to a four-room flat in a two-story building at 417 E. Sixty-fourth Street.[20] Still later he moved to 7011 S. Clyde Avenue.

Torrio remained with Anna until he died. He usually had dinner at home. In the evening, the couple listened to phonograph recordings because Torrio enjoyed classical music and could follow a score. Occasionally, the couple attended a play or a concert. Anna said of her husband, "My married life has been like one long, unclouded honeymoon. He has done everything to make me happy. I have had love, home, and contentment."[21]

By the end of 1914, Torrio had become Big Jim's second-in-command. He was in charge of Colosimo's resorts in the Levee. In addition, he was managing the gambling joints, roadhouses and resorts in the far south and west suburbs. He enlarged Colosimo's gambling ventures by convincing cigar-store owners to rent their back rooms for use as handbooks.[22] He ran the operation in an efficient and profitable manner. A steady stream of money was coming in from the resorts, saloons, and gambling joints.

Chapter Twenty

STATE'S ATTORNEY WAYMAN'S RAIDS

The End of the Segregated Vice District

1912

There is, and for many years, has been a connection between the police department and various criminal classes in the City of Chicago (and) a bi-partisan political combination or ring exists, by and through which the connection between the police department and the criminal classes . . . is fostered and maintained.[1]

— Civil Service Commission, Final Report
on the Police Department

As 1911 began, two big issues were facing the reformers; one was the segregated vice districts, and the other was prostitution in Chicago, mainly in the brothel-filled Levee. The segregated vice districts, of which the Levee was the largest, were a product of the ingenuity of the vice bosses and the city fathers. The idea had been to contain prostitution and all-night saloons to specific geographical districts where those interested could be serviced but which would keep vice and seedy dives out of the rest of the city, more or less. The plan called for little or no enforcement against vice and saloon violations within the segregated vice areas. The resorts and dives would operate unmolested, the police and the politicians would get their payoffs, and persons looking for vice would know where to find it. With the exception of the reformers, clergymen, and newspapers, most city residents were satisfied with this arrangement.

The reformers chose to tackle one problem at a time. They decided to focus on forcing the city fathers to end the concept of segregated vice districts and leave until later the brothels and prostitutes operating in the city.

The city council had ignored and buried the Chicago Vice Commission report on *The Social Evil in Chicago*. While the report made front-page news when it was issued in 1911, and thousands of residents read its findings on vice in Chicago—it sputtered and died. A new champion was needed to head the battle against vice. Stepping up to become the new leader was the Chicago Committee of Fifteen. The committee adopted a strong platform in opposition to the segregated vice districts. Founded in 1908 this private organization had been working on issues relating to pandering and white slavery. While the committee never achieved the visibility of the vice commission, it accomplished something far more important. The committee gave the information that had been developed by its investigators to the state's attorney. This information was used to obtain the warrants that brought about the end of the segregated vice districts.[2]

For two years the Civil Service Commission had been conducting field investigations into corruption between politicians and police officers. The commission found strong evidence of payoffs to the police for vice protection.[3] The commission reported that their investigators determined there were as many as twenty thousand prostitutes in Chicago, of whom two thousand were working in the Third Precinct of the First Ward—more commonly known as the Levee.

In January 1912 the commission opened hearings into corruption in the police department. Inspector John Wheeler, who was responsible for the Twenty-second Street District Station, was called to testify. Attempting to protect himself, Wheeler passed the blame to his bosses, claiming he had never received an order from the mayor or the chief to close up the Levee. While seemingly uninterested in closing the Levee during the period that he was responsible for the policing of the red light district, his familiarity with the Levee was apparent from his testimony on the district's streets and the activity conducted there: "Bedbug Row ran from Sixteenth Street to Twentieth Street. The resorts around Sixteenth and Seventeenth Street featured Negro prostitutes and were considered the lowest dives in the Levee. The center of the red light district was from Twentieth Street to Twenty-second Street. Radiating outward were brothels and low-life saloons along Dearborn Street, Armour Avenue and Wabash Avenue from Sixteenth Street south to Twenty-fourth Street."[4]

At the end of the hearing, the commission discharged Wheeler from the police department on grounds of corruption.

During the summer, Chicagoans read a new book titled *The Vice Bondage of a Great City* by Robert O. Harlan of the Young People's Civic League. Harlan painted a vivid portrait of the Levee and described the vice trust that operated there. He said it was a secret organization with powerful bosses in charge and brothel operators, police officers, and politicians as shareholders. The lifeblood of the organization was a protection and graft system that provided a sizable income for the members of the trust. The trust bosses kept the major share, and the remainder was distributed to the politicians and the police. Harlan wrote that police inspectors, captains, lieutenants, sergeants, and patrolmen received payoff money.[5] Harlan listed specific dollar amounts that he said were the monthly graft payments from the vice joints to the bosses:[6]

House of prostitution	
Dollar houses	$20
Five-dollar house, per inmate	$35
Ten-dollar houses, per inmate	$40
High-class houses	$500 to $1,000
Assignation hotels	$25 to $500
Saloons with women hustlers	$100
Infamous dance halls	$50
All-night saloons	$50
Handbooks and poolrooms	50% of profit
Massage parlors	$100
Streetwalkers	$20 to $50
Laundries doing work for the "houses"	50% of profit
Stores selling clothing to prostitutes	66% of profit

By August, the outcry created by Harlan's book forced Mayor Carter Harrison to take action. He ordered the police to close five resorts that were named in a letter he had received from the Committee of Fifteen. Several leaders of the vice trust were arrested in the raids. Chief John McWeeney solemnly announced he had evidence implicating Jim Colosimo, Ed Weiss, Blubber Bob Gray, Jew Kid Grabiner, and others in the harboring of girls for immoral purposes.[7] Despite the "evidence," Colosimo was not arrested, and the "evidence" did not result in successful prosecutions.

One of the many speakers challenging the segregated vice districts was the renowned Rev. Dwight L. Moody, who had founded a mission that became the Moody Bible Institute. He bemoaned, "If the Angel Gabriel came to Chicago he would lose his character within a week."[8] The Civic Welfare League, composed of civic and church organizations that were active in social reform, announced that it would hold a march with two major themes:

A protest against the red-light districts, lawless saloons and other elements that were contributing to the moral decay of the city, and,

A demand that State's Attorney Wayman, Mayor Harrison and Chief
McWeeney enforce the vice laws.

The much-ballyhooed parade was on September 28, 1912. More than ten
thousand marchers stepped off from Eighteenth Street and Michigan Avenue
and headed for downtown. Rain began to fall and continued throughout the
day. Leading the march were Rev. Elmer Williams of Grace Methodist
Church riding a high-spirited horse and Brig. Gen. Ramsey D. Potts of the
Salvation Army with a large contingent of his uniformed soldiers and a thirty-
piece brass and drum band. Next came dozens of other bands and drum-and-
bugle corps interspersed between scores of floats from churches, religious
organizations, anti-saloon committees, temperance groups, Boy Scout troops,
and men's clubs. The marchers were joined by hundreds of automobiles filled
with horn-tooting, sign-waving supporters. The drenched but enthusiastic
marchers passed the reviewing stand in front of the Auditorium Hotel at Congress Street and Michigan Avenue.[9] A loud and clear message was being sent
to the city fathers that the citizens of Chicago would no longer tolerate segregated vice districts.

Emboldened by the success of the march, the Civic Welfare League
decided to hold an evening assembly in Orchestra Hall. The meeting brought
together all of the organizations that were members of the league. A substantial crowd assembled to listen to speakers decrying the social evils of Chicago.
The audience unanimously passed resolutions urging vice enforcement action
by the police and state's attorney. The resolutions strongly condemned State's
Attorney John Wayman, Mayor Harrison, and Chief McWeeney for failing to
enforce the vice laws. The state's attorney was singled out for his repeated failure to take action in this matter.

Next, the Law and Order League headed by Arthur Burrage Farwell
jumped in to the fight with a new tactic that gave a serious scare to Wayman.
The league won a civil action forcing the closing of a disorderly house at 2132
S. Armour Avenue down the street from several of Colosimo's brothels. The
case was appealed to the Illinois Supreme Court, which upheld the trial court's
decision. A weapon had been discovered that did not need cooperation from
the police or the state's attorney. The league was also planning a novel attack
against the state's attorney himself.

This groundbreaking success of using the civil code to close a whorehouse moved Municipal Court Chief Justice Harry Olson to hurriedly meet
with State's Attorney Wayman. Judge Olson warned Wayman, "If you don't
close the red-light districts of Chicago, the counsel of the Law and Order

League will go before the Supreme Court and get your attorney's license taken away."[10]

Wayman had long been ignoring the problems of the Levee because he was secretly preparing to run for governor of Illinois in 1913. To assist him in his run for higher office, Wayman had obtained the backing of the United Societies for Local Self Government, an association of saloonkeepers, brewers, and operators of alcohol-related businesses. The United Societies stood for a "wet" Chicago and opposed alcoholic beverage controls over resorts and saloons in the Levee. To keep the support of the organization, Wayman ignored the Levee and found other targets for investigation and indictment. In the fall of 1912, the United Societies changed their position and decided not to support Wayman for governor. Without the financial and elective advantage of the United Societies, Wayman decided to win public approval by riding the wave of anti-vice sentiment. He began to court the Committee of Fifteen.[11] On the last day of September Wayman issued a statement:

> Disorderly houses have been running in segregated districts for a good many years under public supervision. . . . If the hour has arrived for the abolition of such segregated districts it needs no public meeting or prayer to bring it about.[12]

Sensing that his political opponent was capturing public opinion, on October 1, Mayor Harrison announced that he was going to clean up the segregated vice districts. Even though he stalled on taking action in the Levee, Harrison did order the police to shut down the red-light districts on the West Side and North Side. Regarding the Levee, Harrison said, "(later) we'll take a whirl at the segregated district and dispose of it, if the people want it."[13] The behind-the-scenes power of Kenna, Coughlin, and Colosimo was deterring Wayman from moving on the Levee.

Disregarding the mayor's rhetoric and stalling, State's Attorney Wayman began his move against the Levee. In a remarkable statement on Wednesday, October 3, Wayman declared his previous position on vice was based on the fact that that his two predecessors—Charles S. Deneen and John J. Healy—did not interfere with the resorts in the segregated districts. Believing that this policy had public approval he had adopted it as his own. Wayman said he had changed his mind over the past few months as civic groups and church organizations had clearly demonstrated the problem of the social evil in Chicago. As a result he was now going to prosecute every house of ill fame in the Levee for violation of the prostitution statutes.[14] He did not mention that Carl Waldron, head of the Committee of Fifteen, was about to bring charges of corruption against the state's attorney's office. Nor did he mention that

church associations were demanding a special grand jury with a special prosecutor to look into the entire vice mess.[15]

Wayman's plan was implemented on Friday morning. Wayman directed
First Assistant State's Attorney Thomas Marshall to quietly obtain warrants
charging violation of the state prostitution statue against 135 divekeepers in
the Levee. Municipal Court Judge Jacob Hopkins issued the warrants, which
were suppressed until they could be served. Leading the list were longtime
Levee bosses: James Colosimo at 2108 Armour Avenue, Ed Weiss at 2030–32
Armour Avenue, Harry Guzik at 2115 Dearborn Street and 2033 Armour
Avenue, Jakie Adler at 201 Dearborn Street, Jew Kid Grabiner at 2107
Armour Avenue and 2014–16 Dearborn Street, and madam Van Bever, wife of
Maurice Van Bever, at 2031 Armour Avenue.[16]

The state's attorney announced that within the week warrants would follow against the owners and agents of property in which houses of ill fame were
allowed to operate. After his statement Wayman held a meeting in his office
with Chief McWeeney. When the chief left the Criminal Courts Building he
was visibly angry. Pressed by reporters for a statement, McWeeney refused to
comment.[17]

The first raids began late on Friday evening as state's attorney's investigators entered the Levee and began to make arrests. The state's attorney's men
were disliked by district police personnel in the Levee. As soon as the district
officers learned of the warrants, they tipped off the major vice operators. A
mad scene broke out when state's attorney's squad cars containing scores of
raiders raced down Twenty-second Street as madams, prostitutes, pimps,
saloonkeepers, and cab drivers hurriedly made their exits. A crowd of jeering
onlookers assembled and added to the ruckus. Most of the major operators,
including Big Jim, managed to escape before the raids. About 340 people were
in the resorts. Everyone was arrested. They were taken to the Twenty-second
Street station where bondsmen on retainer from the vice trust posted bonds
for the operators, madams, and prostitutes.[18] The citizens had to find their
own way out of jail.

Sgt. Stephen H. Berry of the state's attorney's office provided a description
of that wild night. Sgt. Berry, accompanied by Detectives Oakey and Murphy,
began their raids at Vic Shaw's long-running brothel at 214 S. Dearborn
Street. Fifty patrons were arrested while a large crowd, attracted by the clanging gongs from the patrol wagons, watched from the street. Sergeant Berry
next moved to 2114 Armour Avenue. Some patrons at that resort, described by
Berry and his men as "lowbrows," objected to their arrest, but after several
were knocked to the floor the resistance ended. Berry remembered that
wealthy men appealed to him to let them go because an arrest would lead to a
divorce or cause their reputations to be blasted. One patron took out his

checkbook and asked Berry to name the amount while another presented his watch and diamond ring. Their entreaties were in vain. All customers were roughly shoved into the wagons along with the madam and her girls.

On Saturday morning, Wayman opened a new front. Beginning his attack on the owners of property that housed vice activities, he secured capiases for Harrison B. Riley, president, and Justin M. Dall, secretary, of the Chicago Title and Trust Company—the city's largest and most famous trust insurance firm. The court papers issued by Municipal Judge William N. Cottrell charged the two men with renting out property for disorderly purposes. The title and trust company was cited in a summons stating that the firm leased property at 1905 Armour Avenue to A. Marcovitz for immoral purposes.[19] These moves caught the attention of the city's leading businessmen who began to urge Mayor Harrison to "close that damn Levee and take the heat off."

Worried that he was being overshadowed by Wayman, Mayor Harrison offered a new answer to the problem of the social evil. Stalling yet again, he declared that the question of segregated vice districts should be put to a public referendum so that the citizens' opinions could be determined. The mayor stated that if the public opposed the segregated districts he would act promptly.[20] The city council debated the referendum and soundly rejected it. Looking for a face-saving action, Harrison appointed nine aldermen to a committee chaired by Alderman Charles E. Merriam to study the elimination of vice versus the segregation of vice.[21] The reporters had heard all this many times before and knew it meant sweeping the problem under the rug.

Trying to develop an emergency strategy to hold off the inevitable, the Levee bosses met in Colosimo's Café on Saturday morning after the first night of raids. They decided to try to blunt the state's attorney's offensive. Because the raids had been based on information provided by the Committee of Fifteen, the vice bosses ridiculed the committee by announcing their own Levee Committee of Fifteen. The leaders of the Levee Committee were Jim Colosimo, Roy Jones, Blubber Bob Gray, John Jordan, Ed Weiss, and Ike Bloom—all well-known vice operators. They attempted to raise forty thousand dollars by collecting money throughout the red-light district from saloon owners, resort operators, and madams, including the Everleigh Sisters.

Realizing that the two First Ward aldermen could no longer protect them from the strength of the new anti-vice campaign, they hoped to buy enough legislators in Springfield to pass a state bill protecting the segregated vice district. The committee implemented an interim scheme designed to quickly bring pressure on the city fathers to sway them into a more tolerant posture regarding vice. Early Saturday afternoon, the madams and operators of all the resorts were told that their girls had a job to do:

Put on their loudest clothing and paint their faces elaborately.
Visit residential areas, ring doorbells and request lodging.
Rent rooms in respectable neighborhoods.
Not accost men but be on the sidewalk as much as possible.
Frequent the respectable cafes and make a big show of their
    presence.[22]

The prostitutes took their instructions very seriously. Saturday afternoon, they began to parade down Michigan Avenue from Randolph Street downtown to the Hyde Park neighborhood on the South Side. Wearing heavy makeup and garish clothing with large floppy hats, they rang doorbells of homes and apartments and asked to rent rooms. They were careful not to break any laws or get arrested. The respectable housewives in the apartments found this vulgar display very offensive.[23] The unprecedented spectacle lasted for two days when the Levee Committee called it off. Word had been received that the city hall politicians thought the idea was a bad advertisement for the city. The Levee's short-term counterattack failed, and their long-term strategy failed as well—no bill protecting the segregated vice districts was ever introduced in the state legislature.

The raids continued on Saturday night. Sgt. Stephen Berry from the state's attorney's office expected the Levee to be deserted but found it was not. Resorts that had been raided on Friday were back in business. Berry's first raid on Saturday was at 2111 S. Dearborn Street where Sluggy Gilhooley and others tried to rush through the front door but were stopped by Patrolman Lynch. Sergeant Berry punched several and sent them crashing to the floor. Gilhooley took three punches to the jaw before he dropped. Spitting out teeth as he rose, Gilhooley rushed the sergeant. Berry hit him with an uppercut that caused Gilhooley to bite off half his tongue. Gilhooley didn't get up.[24]

Even on the Lord's Day the assault continued. Calling a news conference, State's Attorney Wayman announced that as soon as ownership information could be obtained from the county recorder's office, he would move against the property owners, "irrespective of who or what the persons are," he added for emphasis. On Monday, Wayman gave the county recorder a list of addresses where prostitution was taking place in the segregated vice districts and asked for the names of the property owners. He asked the county treasurer for the tax receipts for the properties.[25] The downtown businessmen heard him clearly and increased their pressure on the mayor to end the segregated vice districts. Wayman vowed that he would use his police power to have his detectives keep the Levee as tight as a drum until his term of office ended on December 2, 1912.[26]

A third night of raids by the state's attorney's detectives took place on Sunday night, October 7. Seven resorts were raided and fifty-one men and women arrested. Alerted by the front page stories in the newspapers for the two previous days, three thousand persons thronged the Levee to watch the colorful activities. As the whores were being pushed and shoved into patrol wagons, the ladies waved handkerchiefs at the crowds who cheered during particularly amusing incidents.[27]

On Monday the newspapers reported that several crusaders had managed to get into trouble in the Levee during the raids. After a Sunday evening meeting at Hull House to discuss the social problems facing the girls who were being arrested and who were soon going to be out of work some of the attendees unwisely decided to go to the Levee and observe the conditions on a first-hand basis. The group included Arthur Burrage Farwell, head of the Law and Order League; Lucy Page Gaston, head of the Anti-Cigarette League; Rev. Joseph H. Chandler, president of the Chicago Federation of Churches; Dr. Anne R. Ranes, superintendent of the Citizen's League; Col. and Mrs. Aldrich of the Law and Order League; and Mrs. Katherine L. Wolff, president of the Woman's Anti-Vice Crusade. They went to Phyllis Adam's resort at 2111 S. Dearborn Street. As soon as they got inside, Detectives Lynch and Shea burst through the door shouting, "Get your clothes, girls, the place is pinched!" Farwell tried to tell the detectives that his party was investigating vice conditions. "That's what they all say," responded Lynch, "Hand that con to the sergeant. You'll have to wait for the wagon." Fortunately, Sergeant Berry arrived at the last moment and, recognizing Farwell, released the group over Lynch's strong objections.[28]

Several weeks later, on October 28, social activist Kate J. Adams, who had worked for four years in the Levee area and spoken with many prostitutes, testified before a city council hearing. She described in specific detail what went on in the Levee. She named James Colosimo as the leader of the vice trust and said he owned brothels at 113 W. Nineteenth Street and 2000 and 2106 S. Armour Avenue. She identified the members of Colosimo's gang: Andy Craig, Joe Aducci, Sam Hare, Ed Little, Roy Jones, Blubber Bob Gray, John Jordan, and Ed and Louis Weiss. Adams said other members of the vice trust were Ike Bloom, operator of Freiberg's Dance Hall on Twenty-second Street; Solly Friedman, who transacted business for Bloom; Jakie Adler and Harry Hopkins, operators of the Silver Dollar Saloon and resort on South Dearborn Street; Jew Kid Grabiner; Ed Weiss, assisted by his nephew Louis; Harry and Jack Cusick; and "Dago Frank" Lewis. Adams claimed that these men had continuously operated vice dens in the Levee for many years. Adams said that the trust collected from two hundred resorts, gambling joints and disreputable saloons in the Levee and turned over part of this money to the police and political leaders of the ward.[29] Adams had provided the council with a full and specific description of the vice problem in the Levee.

In late October, Mayor Harrison finally was forced by the nonstop state's attorney's raids and by the crusaders and reformers with their relentless marches, church sermons, and newspaper editorials, to give way on the segregated vice issue. He removed his powerful political support for the segregated vice districts and sent out word that segregated vice districts were no longer to be tolerated in Chicago.

While the concept of segregated vice was through, the brothels, all-night saloons, and gambling joints continued to operate on a more discreet level. The blazing lights and electric signs announcing the names of the joints were dimmed. This had happened before, but this time the lights never came back on. By November the vice operators had to place cappers and touts at various corners throughout the Levee area to direct potential clients to the resorts.

Because the resorts were still operating, Attorney Wayman angrily dispatched his investigators and detectives to make a second series of raids that started on November 19, 1912. Once again state's attorney's squads swarmed into the Levee. The screams of the women, the clanging of the wagon bells, and the shouts of onlookers were heard throughout the night. Colosimo's brothel was one of the first to be hit. Twenty working girls of Big Jim's resorts were arrested. The protective shield provided by the two aldermen had failed. Colosimo, who had been tipped off, was not present during the raids.

In mid-November, Mayor Harrison told Chief McWeeney that "the South Side red-light district must be closed and kept closed until further notice." McWeeney gave the same message to Capt. Michael F. Ryan, who was in command of the Twenty-second Street District. Never before in the history of the Levee had such an order been issued. Ryan sent his officers to make raids in the Levee. They arrested twenty women in resorts operated by Colosimo, Ferdinand Buxbaum, and Big Ed Weiss.[30]

Ending the tumultuous year, Wayman announced that he would not run for reelection but would try for the governorship in 1913. The Democrats seized the opportunity and got their candidate, Maclay Hoyne, elected State's Attorney of Cook County in December 1912. In his inaugural remarks, Hoyne insisted that during his tenure the state's attorney's office would function as a law office not a police agency. On matters relating to saloons and prostitution, he was going to leave those areas to the mayor, police department, and city council.[31] Political pressure was not dead after all.

Sociologist Walter Reckless summed up the changes in the Levee when he wrote in *Vice in Chicago:* "The brilliant lights no longer radiate; the echoes of music, boisterousness, and hilarity no longer resound. Solicitation by women at the windows of modern protected resorts is taboo. Carousing patrons are discouraged and the cadets no longer loaf about the premises."[32]

Chapter Twenty-One

MORALS SQUAD

Equally Disliked by Everyone

1913–1914

Let the politicians keep their hands off the police department and we will
have the best and most efficient police protection in the world in a few years
. . . an organized vice trust backed by powerful politicians is responsible for
the demoralization of the police department.[1]

— Maj. John V. Clinnin, speaking before
the Irish Fellowship Club

As 1913 began, the concept of tolerance of the segregated vice district
was finished, and the reformers were pleased. Michael Kenna, playing
along, arranged for the replacement of the captain of the Twenty-
second Street District Station with Capt. Michael F. Ryan. However, since he
worked for Kenna, Ryan was not expected to close the Levee joints and he
didn't. Even the earlier shutdown of some resorts by Mayor Carter Harrison
was mitigated by the inaction of Ryan. The vice merchants continued as
before but without the brazen public displays of the past twenty years. The
segregated vice district may have been gone, but the resorts, whorehouses, and
all-night dives remained. The only difference was the absence of flashing electric lights and blazing signs advertising the resort names.

Just when the Levee bosses thought they could resume operations—minus
the lights and signs—Mayor Harrison made a move in 1913 that would forever
change the Levee. He set in motion a chain of events that would end in a
bloody gun battle and cause the closing of the Levee. Based on the Civil Service
Commission investigations of the police in 1911 and 1912, Harrison decided to

reorganize the police department. The investigations had exposed the gross inefficiency of the department and the lack of integrity of many of the officers, so Mayor Harrison drew up a reorganization plan to build a better and more honest department. Integral to his plan was the creation of a second deputy superintendent responsible for personnel and equipment matters and citizens' complaints against police officers. Less noticed but far more significant, the plan established a morals division under the new deputy superintendent.

The Civil Service Commission dutifully held an examination for the second deputy superintendent position, and within a few weeks Commissioner John J. Flynn announced that Metellius L. C. Funkhouser headed the list. The forty-nine-year-old Funkhouser was working as an insurance agent. He had fought in the Spanish-American War and held the rank of major in the First Infantry Division of the Illinois National Guard. He lived in Evanston, a suburb bordering Chicago on the north. Newspaper interviews reported that Funkhouser was uncompromisingly incorruptible and that he would rigorously enforce the vice laws.[2] The Levee bosses smirked; they had ridden through many a reformer before and they would do it again—they thought.

On March 13, 1913, Mayor Harrison appointed Funkhouser to the position of second deputy superintendent with the directives to divorce the police from politics, seek out corruption in the police department, and attack prostitution and gambling throughout the city. Funkhouser selected U.S. Secret Service agent William C. Dannenberg to be chief investigator in charge of the newly created morals squad. The old-time police reporters remembered him as the federal investigator whose work in 1905 resulted in the smashing of the Colosimo–Van Bever white-slave ring. Once in office, Dannenberg recruited and hired a group of private detectives he knew personally—men he believed had integrity and competence. These men were sworn in as city police officers giving them the same authority and powers as regular officers.

The district captains quickly understood that the morals squad meant trouble for them and for the aldermen's graft and protection system. To impede the success of Dannenberg's unit, the captains decided to provide only lip-service cooperation to Dannenberg and his investigators. The street-level officers joined in by creating a tip-off system to warn brothel operators, saloonkeepers, and gambling-house owners when morals squad investigators were heading for their neighborhood. Captain Ryan of the Twenty-second Street District Station summed up the views of many of the members of the police force when he told the press, "We don't need no Dannenbergs around here. He uses stool pigeons, and I won't stand for it."[3]

Within a week of being sworn in, Funkhouser sent Dannenberg and his investigators to make a citywide investigation on vice in Chicago. The investigators submitted a detailed report listing the resorts, dives, and gambling houses in the city's three major vice districts.[4] Speaking for the madams, gambling house operators, and saloonkeepers, Johnny Torrio told the press: "They're running us into a hole. I'm getting tired of payin' dough to get a chance to run, and havin' these guys bustin' me and my friends every day or so. We got to take a couple of them into an alley and kick 'em up some. So's the others will wise up to the fact that they're not wanted around here."[5]

Between March and October 1913, Deputy Superintendent Funkhouser sent seven reports to Chief McWeeney that described wide-open vice conditions in several police districts.[6] The reports showed that vice laws and city ordinances were not being enforced by the district officers. The district captains disputed the validity of the reports. Not distracted by the captains' self-serving condemnation of the findings in the vice reports, Mayor Harrison added five regular police officers to work with Funkhouser's investigators. He also ordered the closing of Roy Jones's café at Twenty-first Street and Wabash Avenue and Maxim's café at 2107 Wabash Avenue, two longstanding vice joints in the Levee. The identification of these two locations had been made during colorful hearings of a state senate vice commission, which had been meeting in the LaSalle Hotel. The commission, which was supposed to be focusing on smut songs and obscene dances in saloons, had described the two dives as among the worst in the vice district.[7]

Meanwhile, Clifford W. Barnes of the Committee of Fifteen was continuing in his crusade against vice in Chicago. Barnes announced that if Mayor Harrison, Police Chief McWeeney and Health Commissioner Dr. George B. Young did not close down the vice resorts, the committee would. In a letter sent to the three officials Barnes charged the "lid was decidedly off" in Chicago. The letter named sixty-two vice joints, the keepers of these resorts, and the owners of the buildings in which the resorts were located. Chief McWeeney expressed surprise at the information but said that an investigation would start immediately.[8]

After waiting several weeks for McWeeney to take action, Harrison discreetly surveyed the Levee on his own. After his secret tour, the mayor announced that he was revoking the licenses of seventeen saloons connected to resorts in the Levee. The mayor's action forced the Twenty-second Street District Station police to go through the Levee and shut down the resorts whose licenses had been revoked. Most significant was the closing of the New Brighton, the saloon and brothel at 2001 Archer Avenue operated for Colosimo by John Torrio.[9] This was the first time a resort owned by Colosimo was closed.

On July 8, 1913, a second letter from the Committee of Fifteen to Harrison listed the names of twenty-two Levee resorts where immoral conditions existed. Some of these locations were places that supposedly had been closed by the mayor's license revocations. In addition, committee president Barnes said ordinance violations were observed taking place in these premises in the presence of uniformed police officers.[10]

Giving up his futile attempts at running a department that was really controlled by the aldermen, Chief McWeeney turned in his resignation on October 24, 1913. He told his friends that he was leaving because Harrison had given the special vice control powers to Second Deputy Superintendent Funkhouser. Undeterred by the former chief's comments, Harrison appointed James Gleason to the vacant position. Gleason was thought to be an honest man and more favorably disposed toward Funkhouser than his predecessor. Encouraged by the change in administration, Funkhouser gave a green light to Dannenberg and his morals squad to begin raiding Levee resorts.

Until this time no matter who was in charge, the Levee always had flourished. Neither the mayor nor the state's attorney had ever successfully closed the resorts. The reason was simple: only one person controlled what went on in the Levee. That person was the captain of the Twenty-second Street District Station, who took his orders not from the chief but from the two aldermen of the First Ward. To show his contempt for the morals squad, Captain Ryan had his officers circulate Dannenberg's picture to the madams and operators of the resorts. Not deterred by Captain Ryan's disdain, the raiders began to hit resorts in the Levee.

By January 1914, Dannenberg's squad had made repeated raids and arrests in Levee bordellos. An attack was made directly against Funkhouser and Dannenberg in an attempt to interfere with their vice control actions. Both were named in a bill in circuit court to prevent the city from paying the salaries of the two officials based on an allegation in the filing that they were in office illegally. The bill charged that Funkhouser and Dannenberg were civilians, not sworn regular police officers, and therefore not entitled to hold positions in the police department. The complaint was filed by Joseph Kucharski who listed himself as a "taxpayer" and a retired grocer. Dannenberg asked: "Who is Kucharski? I never heard of the man. Probably a tool of somebody." The police reporters suspected that Kucharski was fronting for a group of disgruntled captains. Funkhouser had no illusions about what was happening. He claimed that "certain elements" were doing everything they could to discredit him. The restraining order moved slowly through the legal process and ultimately was denied.[11]

Undaunted by the civil filing against their bosses and by lack of cooperation from district officers, Funkhouser's men continued their nightly raids in the vice areas and particularly attacked resorts operated by the vice trust. Among these was the Rhinegold Saloon and Café, 1930 Dearborn Street. That raid, on January 8, 1914, netted ten women and seven men, including

John Torrio, who was operating the resort for Big Jim Colosimo.[12] Clearly the raiders were not impressed with the influence of Colosimo.

Greatly disturbed by the actions of Dannenberg and his investigators, the Levee bosses held a meeting at Colosimo's café. Colosimo sat at the head of the table and ran the meeting. After heated discussion they all agreed that Dannenberg had to be stopped. To stop him they worked up a plan of action. They would first offer Dannenberg a sizable bribe. If the bribe attempt failed, they would escalate their fight and, if necessary, murder Dannenberg.

Point man in the bribe scheme was Harry L. Cullett. Known as "Chicken Harry," he had been a Chicago police detective with a long and unsavory history of involvement with vice figures. The previous September, when Cullett was about to be charged in connection with an investigation of vice in the West Side vice district, he resigned from the department. Cullett was contacted by a representative of the vice bosses to carry out the first stage of their plan to bring Dannenberg under control. As directed by the vice bosses, in mid-January 1914 Cullett contacted Dannenberg through intermediaries with the proposition that Dannenberg would receive a large amount of money each month if he would allow the Levee to operate and stop the nightly raids. Dannenberg feigned agreement with the proposal but immediately reported this contact to Funkhouser who decided that Dannenberg should appear to go along with Cullett in order to trap him in a crime.

A face-to-face meeting between Cullett and Dannenberg was arranged for late February. The meeting was called off by Cullett because he was uncomfortable with the location. A second meeting was scheduled. Before leaving his office to go to this meeting, Dannenberg was thoroughly searched by members of his squad so that they could later testify in court that he had no money on his person. At about 8:30 p.m. on February 26, Dannenberg arrived at the Central Drug Store at the corner of Sheridan Road and Wilson Avenue on Chicago's North Side. At 8:45 p.m. a taxi arrived, and Cullett got out. Dannenberg and Cullett walked slowly back and forth along Sheridan for several minutes so Cullett could be certain that they were not being followed. Fortunately, Cullett did not see Dannenberg's investigators and two *Tribune* reporters who were hiding in nearby bushes and doorways.

The pair turned into a dark alley behind the drug store where Cullett told Dannenberg that he would be paid twenty-two hundred dollars a month if he allowed the Levee to operate. Cullett said to make it appear to the public that Dannenberg was continuing his attack on vice resorts he would be given a list of "fall houses" to be used for sham raids. Each day Dannenberg would be provided with the name of one resort that he could raid and arrest two women for prostitution. When Dannenberg agreed to the arrangement, Cullett passed five hundred dollars as down payment with the promise of one thousand dollars more by March.

Acting on a secret signal from Dannenberg the investigators from the morals squad ran from their cover and placed Cullett under arrest. He was taken to the Sheffield District Station and charged with bribery. At a hastily called news conference, Dannenberg described the incident and said Cullett had named the Levee operators who provided the bribe money. Cullett, Dannenberg said, listed the men behind the bribe money as Johnny Torrio, "Polack Ben" Kelley, Beck Moriarity, and the Marshall brothers.

Almost at once, the influence and power of Kenna and Coughlin could be felt in the behind-the-scene moves intended to put "the fix" in the Cullett case. The original charge against the former police officer was dismissed because Municipal Court Judge Flake contended that it did not contain specific details of Cullett's actions. A second filing against Cullett collapsed when the judge held that the evidence did not warrant prosecution. The state filed a *nolle prosequi* (no prosecution) on the case, and Cullett was freed. [13] Due to the exercise of raw political power by Aldermen Kenna and Coughlin the case against Cullett fell through, but because of Dannenberg's honesty, the bribe attempt by the vice trust had failed. The raids by the morals squad continued unabated.

The vice trust decided to move to its fallback plan—violence. Their first action was directed at a suspected stool pigeon for the morals squad. On April 7, Isaac Henagow walked into Roy Jones's saloon and ordered a beer. The Levee bosses suspected that Henagow was a secret informant for the morals squad. Shortly after Henagow began to drink a glass of beer, James Franche walked in. Known as "Duffy the Goat," Franche was a member of the Colosimo gang. He pulled out a pistol and shot Henagow through the heart. When the patrol wagon from the Twenty-second Street station arrived Henagow was dead. Later the same month, a sergeant attached to the morals squad was stabbed to death while investigating the Henagow murder. The Levee bosses were making their countermoves against Dannenberg and Funkhouser.

In June, Funkhouser responded to these outrages by increasing the pressure on the Levee. In one month the morals squad raided thirty-two Levee resorts and made 214 arrests. The raids showed that although the segregated vice district policy had ended several years earlier, vice resorts were continuing to operate throughout the Levee. [14]

Meanwhile, to escape the heat of the summer and the heat of the problems being caused by Funkhouser and Dannenberg, seven aldermen announced that they would embark on a two-month visit to Canada and Europe seeking information that would help the city deal with the social evil. Their itinerary included Toronto, Montreal, Liverpool, Manchester, Paris, Antwerp, Frankfort, Munich, Vienna, Budapest, Dresden, Berlin, Hamburg, Copenhagen, and Stockholm. Apparently they had a great trip and were hosted lavishly both on and off the record, but they learned little about social evils that they didn't already know.[15]

On July 13, while his morals squads were hitting three Levee vice dens, Funkhouser personally led a raid at Jordan's Café. Jordan's had a reputation for being the spot where lighthearted parties from the Gold Coast and north suburbs went on slumming expeditions. Many of the society women caught in the raid begged the arresting officers to let them go. One woman offered her two diamond rings. Another pleaded that her family would be disgraced. The stoic Funkhouser locked up the entire crowd.[16]

On July 15, Funkhouser announced that there would be a campaign of "moral lightning" raids, meaning that the location of each raid would be a complete surprise without the usual tip-offs from the district police. He said: "You can't catch Indians by blowing a bugle. Hereafter, the work of this department will be carried out in absolute secrecy." Funkhouser could not have imagined what dreadful results this new attack would bring.[17]

On July 18, the *Tribune* ran an expose that maintained that Captain Ryan of the Twenty-second Street District Station could not be forced by the chief of police to raid vice resorts in the Levee. The article stated that Ryan had been put into his position by the local political boss-vice lord combine. Responding to the article, Chief Gleason announced a deodorizing of what he called the "has-been tenderloin." The chief said arrests would be made in the Levee of slummers, idlers, sightseers, pseudo vice investigators, and "near evangelists" who make soapbox speeches, attract crowds, and take up collections.[18]

The battle between Funkhouser and Dannenberg on one side and the Levee vice leaders and the police from the Twenty-second Street District Station on the other was nearing its tragic climax. Across the city, police officers had observed the animosity grow between the Twenty-second Street District Station "regulars" and Funkhouser's "green cops." As the raiders tore into the Levee night after night, the regulars began to lose their credibility with the resort operators in the vice district. The raids were making a mockery of the protection money that was being paid to the police to prevent such events.

For the Levee vice bosses, the mounting number of raids was the last straw. Once again they convened in Colosimo's Café. By this time, Dannenberg's detectives had netted more than two thousand panderers, prostitutes, and customers. The bosses agreed that the raids had to be stopped. Bribery had failed. Murdering Henegow and a police sergeant had failed. It appeared to the vice bosses that Mayor Harrison and Chief Gleason were solidly behind

Funkhouser and Dannenberg. The conspirators decided to murder
Funkhouser, Dannenberg, and members of the morals division. John Torrio
was placed in charge of this final attack. Torrio contacted for his cousin Roxy
Vanille,[*] a former member of one of the tough New York street gangs.[19]
Vanille was to be the agent provocateur.

---

[*] Numerous spellings for this name have been found in old newspaper clippings. For simplicity, only
Vanille is used in this book.

Chapter Twenty-Two

THE SHOOTING OF SERGEANT BIRNS

Colosimo's Plan Goes Sour

1914

This whole nasty affair can be placed at the door of politics. Nearly every great wave of so-called "reform" in the police department runs back to politics.[1]

— Capt. Michael Ryan, 22nd Street District Station

An event that might have ended the tragedy before it took place occurred in April 1914. The saloon operated by Roy Jones had been closed because of a raid. With no bar to tend, Jones began to drink heavily in various Levee saloons. Late one evening after having consumed a large amount of alcohol, Jones unwittingly revealed to a secret police informer that Jim Colosimo and Maurice Van Bever had formed a plan to kill Funkhouser and Dannenberg.

Before this conversation, Isaac Henagow, an informer for the morals squad, had been murdered and an investigator from the squad had been knifed to death while looking into the murder. And now the owner of the bar where the Henagow murder had taken place was drunkenly muttering about a plot to kill Funkhouser and Dannenberg. In hindsight it is easy to see "danger" spelled in big red letters. There was no indication that this story was ever acted on by the deputy superintendent or the inspector. Whether this disregard of a potential early warning signal was due to Jones's drunkenness and unreliability, or the failure of the information getting to the correct official, is not known.

On July 3, disgusted with Captain Ryan's lack of enforcement action in the Levee, Chief Gleason issued an order directing the district police to close Colosimo's café and other saloons and resorts. Ryan ignored the order. Upon learning that the chief was starting to clamp down, Colosimo brought together his henchmen at his restaurant to implement the final step in their plan to stop the raids. Among those at the dinner meeting were Twenty-second Street station Detectives Ed Murphy and Johnny Howe, white slaver Maurice Van Bever, and Johnny Torrio. The plan was hatched and agreed to.

On Thursday, July 16, three cops from the Twenty-second Street station were warned by a fellow officer "not to hang around the Levee tonight because something is going to happen." That evening Dannenberg and Detectives Amort, Merrill, Sampson, and Humpf of the morals squad left their office at headquarters and headed toward the North Side—ostensibly to raid joints in the East Chicago Avenue District. Around 9 p.m. the squad doubled back and quietly moved into the Levee. Near the site of their first planned raid, Dannenberg left the others and walked to a drug store at Prairie Avenue and Twenty-second Street. His men were going to conduct a raid and then rendezvous with him at the drug store. The four detectives, all in civilian clothes, walked west from Prairie Avenue to the Turf, at 28–30 Twenty-second Street.

The Turf was a whorehouse operated by Jakey Woolframe on the first floor of a building on the alley between State Street and Armour Avenue. The raiders moved into the Turf and arrested three women and one man. The officers called for a patrol wagon from the Twenty-second Street District Station. With everything under control Detectives Sampson and Humpf left to rejoin Dannenberg and prepare for the next raid. When the horse-drawn patrol wagon arrived at the Turf with its gong sounding loudly, a crowd gathered. After the prisoners were removed, Detectives Amort and Merrill remained inside the resort hoping that the crowd outside would disperse.[2] The detectives did not know that Colosimo and Torrio had been alerted by their police tipsters at the district station of the location of the raid.

When less than a dozen men remained in front of the resort, Detectives Merrill and Amort left the building and walked east on Twenty-second Street toward Prairie Avenue. The crowd followed and began to grow in numbers. Angry men yelled vicious taunts and made ugly comments. By the time the detectives reached Wabash Avenue the crowd had swelled to thirty men. Behind the crowd was a slow-moving red sedan driven by Torrio. With him were his cousin Roxy Vanille and a Colosimo hood named Mac Fitzpatrick.

At this time only one hundred yards away on the south side of Twenty-second Street were Sgt. Stanley J. Birns and his partner, Detective John C.

Sloop from the nearby Twenty-second Street station. Both were in civilian dress. Later investigation indicated that Sloop was an agent of one of the Levee bosses. Birns and Sloop had been sent from the station to a nearby street to search for a wanted criminal. In the investigation that followed no explanation was given why the Twenty-second Street District Station detectives were on Twenty-second Street instead of where they had been assigned to go.

At 9:35 p.m. Merrill and Amort walked past Swan's Billiard Hall on the north side of Twenty-second Street, halfway between Wabash Avenue and Michigan Avenue. A brick flew through the air at the detectives. The missile had been thrown by a big man in a light gray suit. The crowd grew ugly. One of the detectives drew his revolver in an attempt to intimidate the hecklers. Amort and Merrill saw the man in the gray suit who had thrown the brick step from the crowd and move behind an elderly woman. Suddenly, the man stepped away from the woman and fired three shots at the detectives. One shot hit Merrill in the right hip. Although wounded, Merrill fired four shots at the man. The man fired twice more at the detectives and slipped back into the crowd.[3]

Hearing the shooting from the other side of the street, Birns and Sloop pulled out their guns and ran toward the crowd. Sloop later claimed he saw two men firing revolvers. Neither Birns nor Sloop recognized the men as police. Birns and Sloop thought that the two men were firing at them. Sloop took shelter behind a steel lamp post and Birns standing exposed on the sidewalk fired twice. Now Merrill and Amort, thinking they were under heavy attack, dodged into the doorway of the poolroom and began to shoot directly at Birns and Sloop.[4]

Firing their revolvers, Birns and Sloop charged across Twenty-second Street toward Merrill and Amort both of whom were returning fire. Bullets hit Birns in the heart and lungs. He spun around and dropped into the gutter. Merrill was shot again and went down. Sloop picked up Birns's gun and tried to take a stand.

Thinking that he and his partner had walked into a trap, Merrill jumped on the back of a passing motorcycle and yelled to the driver, "Drive for God's sake, get out of this!" Sloop fired at the motorcycle. The driver lost control of the heavy machine and both riders fell into the street. Sloop, still firing the two revolvers, fell to the street with a bullet in his left leg.[5] Merrill, bleeding from his wounds, rose and staggered to a car driven by Edith Milward, who took him to Mercy Hospital.

Hearing the commotion, a uniformed officer on patrol came running to the scene. He encountered a wounded man who had been shot in the foot. The officer was about to arrest the man, but the victim claimed he was only a spectator hit by a random shot. A person standing nearby vouched for this story and the officer turned the man loose. The wounded man was later found to be Roxy Vanille.

Also attracted by the noise and the crowd, Twenty-second Street District Station Sgt. Edward P. O'Grady ran to the scene. He saw Torrio and Fitzpatrick helping the wounded Vanille into the back of Torrio's red sedan. The pair told the sergeant they knew nothing of what had gone on and were taking this injured man to a hospital. The sergeant allowed them to drive away.

The Twenty-second Street District Station received several frantic phone calls reporting a shooting. From all directions beat officers, detectives, and sergeants raced to the bloody scene. Wagon and ambulance gongs filled the air. The crowd grew into the hundreds, and reporters and photographers began to arrive. From witnesses the police obtained a description of the mystery man in gray who had fired the first shots. He was said to have been a white male, twenty-five to thirty years old, five feet ten inches tall, about two hundred pounds, smooth shaven, and good looking with dark hair. He was wearing a straw hat and a gray suit.[6] None of the witnesses knew his identity. Detectives from the district station and from headquarters began to search the Levee for this man.

Sergeant Birns was carried around the corner to the office of Dr. Melbourne Mabee on Michigan Avenue. Mabee said when he examined Birns the officer was already dead from gunshot wounds in his left shoulder and left abdomen.[7]

In the melee two bystanders had been wounded. Twenty-year-old James Carroll, a fireman for the Chicago and Northwestern Railroad, was shot in the groin and seriously wounded. He was taken to Mercy Hospital in critical condition. Another man, Frank Langon, was hit by a bullet in the right foot. He later told police that he had hurried home after the shooting before discovering the seriousness of his wound. Information about Langon was obtained from records at St. Anthony's Hospital that showed that he was treated that evening at the hospital and released.

Captain Ryan, who coincidentally had been talking with Colosimo and friends on a corner only a few blocks from the shooting, told the press that the two detectives from the morals squad "are green cops looking for someone to pick on them. They saw the plainclothes men coming and they got scared and let loose."[8]

As the miserable night passed into the next morning, the highest officials in the police department were summoned from their homes to meet at the Cottage Grove Avenue station. At the meeting were Police Chief James Gleason, First Deputy Superintendent Herman F. Schuettler, Second Deputy Superintendent Funkhouser, Civil Service Commissioner Elton Lower, Lt. Edward Grady, and Morals Inspector William Dannenberg.

Noticeably missing was Capt. Michael Ryan of the Twenty-second Street District Station. The meeting lasted until 5 a.m. As he left, Lieutenant Grady announced that the shooting was caused by a failure of the detectives to recognize each other. Chief Gleason, barely suppressing his anger at the fact that Amort and Merrill were engaged in arrests and raids while still on probation, said that the shooting was the result of sending inexperienced men into the vice district.[9]

On Friday morning, the day after the shooting, Coroner Peter M. Hoffman solemnly announced he was empanelling six high-school principals as a coroner's jury to determine exactly what happened and where to place the blame.[10] That afternoon Hoffman convened an inquest over the body of Birns. Relatives of the dead and wounded, police officials, reporters, and spectators jammed the back room of the Western Casket Company, 47 E. Twenty-second Street. As Funkhouser began to give his testimony one of the spectators shouted "stool pigeons, sneaking —!" He was immediately grabbed by two police officers and rushed outside. Funkhouser testified that, "There were about thirty shots fired in all, of which the police fired twenty-five." He added, "I am sure that people in the crowd took part in the shooting."[11]

The most dramatic moment in the inquest came when Dannenberg identified two bullets that had been removed from the body of Birns as .22-caliber specials, the type used by all members of the police department.[12] Birns's family and friends gasped and cried at this news. Coroner's physician Joseph Spring testified that the bullet removed from the wounded spectator named Carroll was not of the same type, which indicated that a non-police gun was also involved.[13]

The tragedy made banner headlines across the front pages of all Chicago newspapers. New editions were replated repeatedly throughout the first night, the morning after the shooting, and for days thereafter to keep up with the breaking story lines. News articles, photographs of the dead and wounded, diagrams of the shooting scene, rumors, sob-sister stories, editorials, and anonymous revelations concerning the shooting and the vice trust filled the front and inside pages of the papers. Commenting for the press, police officials robustly criticized or loyally supported the actions of the morals squad detectives—depending on which side of the fence the officials were sitting. The *Tribune*, which had editorially supported Dannenberg's raids all along, reported that in the spring the vice conditions in the Levee had returned to the level that had existed before State's Attorney Wayman had closed the segregated vice district two years earlier. "Several weeks ago signs of a gradual removal of the police lid on the redlights became noticeable to the public," the paper stated, "Many of the longstanding resorts and saloons had turned on their lights again and run all night.[14]

On Saturday, July 18, the *Daily News* ran on page one a box summary of the amazing number of stories covered in that day in their own paper on the shooting and its aftermath:

DEVELOPMENTS OF THE DAY IN POLICE LEVEE SCANDAL
Sweeping investigation of police, vice and crime promised by civil service commission at the request of Chief Gleason
  State's Attorney Hoyne declares police stories of Levee battle are false.
  Promises to "clean up" the district independent of police.
  Big police shakeup promised.
  Capt. Michael Ryan, commander of the 22nd Street District Station requests of Chief Gleason that he be transferred.
  Chief Gleason demands 1,000 more patrolmen in order that the municipality be policed adequately.
  Relentless search for the mysterious "man in gray," suspected cohort of the "Levee barons" is prosecuted without success.
  Police officials seek the connecting link between Levee kings and the tragedy itself.
  Political backers of the segregated section scurry to cover as municipal and other forces seek to expose them.
  Mayor expected to be called home.
  Funkhouser promises a new and exhaustive report on vice.[15]

Mayor Harrison, vacationing at his summer home on Huron Mountain in Michigan, was wise enough to stay far away from Chicago and the accusations and charges that were developing from the shooting. He sent a brief, innocuous message to his office stating that the Civil Service Commission should determine whether an investigation similar to one they had undertaken regarding police corruption in 1911 was necessary.[16]

Numerous inquiries were launched to search for the facts of the bizarre incident. The investigations uncovered the vice trust's secret plans to get rid of Dannenberg. The investigators found that the Levee bosses learned that Dannenberg was with the raiding party when it left headquarters on the night of the shooting and dispatched the hit team headed by Vanille to kill Dannenberg; but the scheme had failed because he was not with the detectives from the morals squad when the shooting began.[17]

A witness to the shooting, Mrs. Tillie Sykes, went to the Cottage Grove station to give a statement. Mrs. Sykes, owner of a restaurant at 97 E. Twenty-second Street, said she was standing in front of the restaurant when the shooting took place. She saw a crowd moving down the street followed by three automobiles. Mrs. Sykes told the police that she saw a man in gray walk past her. The man drew a revolver from his pocket. "Then," she said, "the shooting began in earnest."[18]

The hunt for the mysterious "man in gray" heated up considerably when the police, using a variety of means, obtained confidential information that the "man in gray" was Roxy Vanille and that he had been hired by the Levee bosses to kill Dannenberg. Their informants told the detectives that Vanille had fired the shots that brought on the battle between the two groups of detectives and that the bullet hit Merrill.[19] The detectives also learned that Vanille was shot in the foot by one of the detectives from the morals squad during the fray. He had been hustled into a motor car belonging to Torrio and taken to a hospital. The *Daily American* reported:

> "Roxy" Vanille, also known as "Yellow" Vanille, owner of a disreputable house at 2119 Armour Avenue, was not seen in any of his usual haunts. Vanille was a cousin of John Turrio [Torrio] who newspapers termed "business manager" for Big Jim Colosimo's café on Wabash Avenue just north of 22nd Street.[20]

State's Attorney Hoyne assigned a large number of assistant state's attorneys and investigators to the case. They learned that Vanille had been driven to the scene of the shooting by Torrio. This car, along with a crowd of rowdies from Levee dives, had slowly followed the two morals squad detectives as they left the scene of their raid. After the melee, Torrio sped off with the injured Vanille in the car. The investigators uncovered information indicating that the car had stopped briefly at Colosimo's café and left to go to a nearby hospital for medical treatment for Vanille. At the emergency room, doctors told Vanille that the wound was not serious. Torrio then drove Vanille to St. Anthony's Hospital, which had a doctor friendly to the vice interests on the staff. With Torrio standing in the emergency room, the doctor operated on Vanille to remove the bullet. Vanille was admitted to the hospital.

With the operation over and the patient in good shape, Torrio decided it was time to leave town. He drove his red automobile to Porter Lamp Burke's roadhouse at Cedar Lake, Indiana. Other Levee characters also decided to go to Burke's roadhouse. John Jordan, Jakie Adler, Harry Hopkins and "Saffo the Greek" joined Torrio at Cedar Lake. Also hurrying to the roadhouse was Jordan's wife, longtime madam Georgie Spencer. She brought five thousand dollars in cash from a secret kitty to facilitate the escape of anyone the police might charge with the murder of Birns. The investigators thought it interesting that all of these mobsters went to the one hideout.

All throughout the month of July, the police staged an intense crackdown on vice in the Levee. As the pressure grew on the vice trust, the *Tribune* reported a conversation between Colosimo and Torrio:

> Johnny Torrio and "Big Jim" Colosimo talked matters over yesterday; and they admitted to each other that "things look bad." They can't rely on the "Dink" to pull the inside wire at City Hall, and as "Big Jim" said himself, they're "getting the hook from both ends." Johnny Torrio, during his talk with "Big Jim," said the only hope of the "district" was to cut away from the "Bath" and "Dink," but if they did that they wouldn't have a prop to stand on.[21]

The *Tribune* added that Colosimo had recently paid forty thousand dollars to redecorate his café but was now willing to sell the whole business for ten thousand dollars.[22] On July 26, Big Jim transferred several items of real estate from his name to his wife, Victoria. The transferred property included the residence at 3156 S. Vernon Avenue, the restaurant and saloon at 2120–2128 S. Wabash Avenue, and parcels of land at Wentworth Avenue and Twenty-fifth Place and State Street and Seventy-eighth Street. The grossly underestimated worth of all the properties was given as nineteen thousand dollars. Colosimo had made the transfer to move his property beyond the reach of any judgments that the city or county might obtain against him.

Edward J. Fleming, secretary to State's Attorney Maclay Hoyne, announced that Vanille was being sought by the state's attorney's office.[23] The front page of the *Daily News* proclaimed "Call Rocco Vanille the 'Man in Gray.'"[24] Chief Gleason removed Captain Ryan from his command on the grounds that Ryan was either corrupt or incompetent. The chief also ordered detectives to obtain summons for the Levee vice kings. The state's attorney's office issued summons for five resort and saloon owners under the guise of violating the 1 a.m. Sunday closing ordinance. One of those named was Jim Colosimo.[25]

Chapter Twenty-Three

COLOSIMO
IN A CELL

State's Attorney Hoyne Has His Day

1914

A power in the vice district and a power in the secret council of Sicilian societies. More than once men suspected in connection with gunfights in Little Italy have been traced to the neighborhood of Colosimo's old resort.[1]

— *Chicago Tribune*

On Monday, July 20, State's Attorney Maclay Hoyne ordered the arrest of Jim Colosimo in connection with the Levee shooting of Sergeant Birns. It was early afternoon when state's attorney's detectives entered Colosimo's café and walked directly to Colosimo. Big Jim greeted them warily and looked them over, but he did not remember ever seeing them before. They asked Colosimo a series of point-blank questions related to the shooting. Colosimo refused to cooperate, saying, "Lay off, fellas." As astonished waiters and bartenders looked on, the detectives arrested Colosimo, placed him between two of them in the back seat of an automobile, and drove off.[2] The king of the Levee and the brains behind the powerful organization of red-light bosses had been publicly humiliated.

Colosimo was driven to the Hyde Park District Station, far out of reach of his political power. He was questioned for seven hours by State's Attorney Hoyne and his investigators. When the interrogation was over, Hoyne came out of the back room and told the reporters, "Colosimo wouldn't talk much and what he did tell wasn't true."[3]

Colosimo was transported to the Twenty-second Street station, finger-printed, and booked. This was the first time that James Colosimo had ever been formally arrested.[4] Placed in a locked cell, he was held without bond for a half day before the state's attorney gave permission for his release on bond.

The newspapers, recognizing the public's interest in Big Jim Colosimo, tried to outdo each other with bold headlines, revealing stories, and secret interviews. He was repeatedly referred to as the owner and operator of Colosimo's Café at 2128 S. Wabash Avenue. The restaurant and its fittings were depicted in colorful detail.

The *American*, in an exclusive sidebar story, provided a detailed examination of the operations of the Levee. The paper said an unnamed city investigator had given exclusively to the *American* an inside look at the organization and operations in the vice district. The investigator revealed that the Levee was divided into three sections, each ruled by a vice overlord. The first section was along Armour Avenue between Archer and Twenty-second Street. The dives in this section were protected by and paid tribute to John Torrio, identified as the proprietor of the New Brighton resort at the corner of Archer and Armour Avenue. Torrio was described as the "right hand man of Big Jim Colosimo who wore the sparkling crown as king of the red-light district." The second section, along Dearborn Street between Twentieth and Twenty-second streets, was under the control of Jakie Adler, and the third section in the area around Twenty-first and State streets was managed by the three Marshall brothers.[5] Playing catch up, the *Daily News* agreed with the *American* on Torrio's high status in the Levee and added that he was one of the "Big Five of the South Side Badlands."[6]

Not wanting to lose circulation to the *American*, which was published by William Randolph Hearst, the *Tribune*, published by Robert R. McCormick, began a lengthy series written by "Officer 666," purportedly a disgusted police official. Officer 666 reported that:

> When the city politicians decided to close Custom House Place and move the red-light district to 22nd and State Street, Roy Jones, George Little, Frank Wing and Ed Weiss became the "Big Four," the heads of the new segregated Levee.
>
> At this time, a new man appeared named Jim Colosimo. He took up residence in a house on Archer Avenue and after being tested to determine if he could be trusted he was given the opportunity to become the most powerful factor in the 22nd Street District Station aside from the political bosses.
>
> Rules were laid down that each resort would pay a "tax" of from ten to two hundred dollars a week depending upon the nature and amount of

• *The earliest known photo of James Colosimo shows "Big Jim" on the cover of an advertising booklet (above left).*

• *Jim was twenty-seven in 1905 and had married Victoria Moresco (top right) two years earlier.*

• *John Torrio, (right center) became manager of Big Jim's vice empire and later would order his murder after Colosimo married singer Dale Winter (above right) and began neglecting business.*

• *Corrupt Mayor William Hale "Big Bill" Thompson (left) enabled gangsters to turn Chicago into the nation's most wide-open city.*

• *Big Jim's hometown of Colosimi, Italy (above), lies in the pine forests of a mountainous region of southern Calabria.*

• *At right and below are front and rear views of the two-story house at 78 Fontana (now Vico Il Europa) where Vincenzo Colosimo was born on February 6, 1878. Vincenzo came to America in 1891 and settled in Chicago, where he assimilated into into his new land and changed his name to Jim Colosimo.*

• *The Levee (above and left) the largest and most famous of Chicago's segregated red-light districts, opened in the late 1890s and reached its peak in 1913. In 1914, raiders from the state's attorney's office virtually shut down the district.*

• *John J. "Bathhouse John" Coughlin and Michael "Hinky Dink" Kenna (below left and right) were longtime First Ward aldermen and rulers of the Levee.*

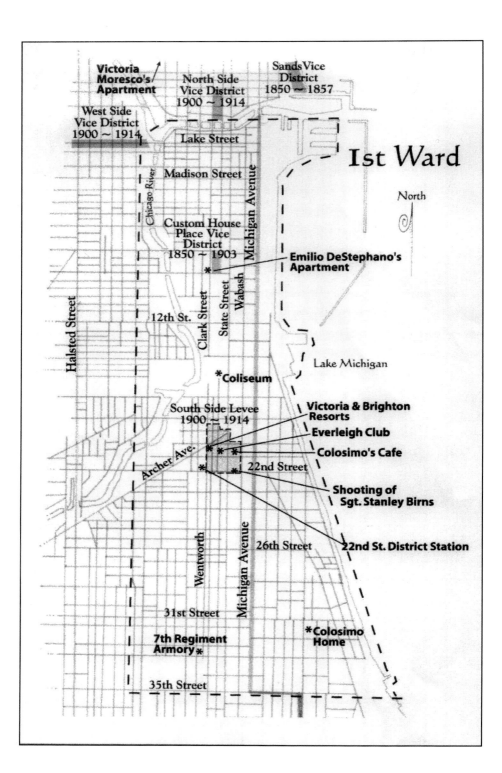

Victoria
Moresco's
Apartment

North Side
Vice District
1900 ~ 1914

Sands Vice
District
1850 ~ 1857

West Side
Vice District
1900 ~ 1914

Lake Street

1st Ward

Chicago River

Madison Street

Michigan Avenue

North

Custom House
Place Vice
District
1850 ~ 1903

Emilio DeStephano's
Apartment

Clark Street

State Street

Wabash

12th St.

Lake Michigan

Halsted Street

*Coliseum

South Side Levee
1900 ~ 1914

Victoria & Brighton
Resorts

Everleigh Club

Colosimo's Cafe

Archer Ave.

22nd Street

Shooting of
Sgt. Stanley Birns

Wentworth

Michigan Avenue

26th Street

22nd St. District Station

31st Street

7th Regiment
Armory *

*Colosimo
Home

35th Street

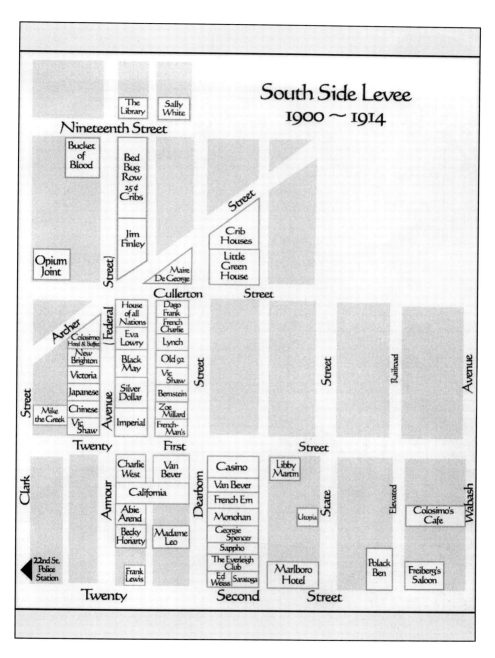

South Side Levee
1900 ~ 1914

The Library

Sally White

Nineteenth Street

Bucket of Blood

Bed Bug Row 25¢ Cribs

Jim Finley

Opium Joint

Street

Maire De George

Crib Houses

Little Green House

Street

Cullerton Street

Archer

Colosimo Hotel & Buffet

New Brighton

Victoria

Japanese

Mike the Greek

Chinese

Vic Shaw

(Federal)

House of all Nations

Eva Lowry

Black May

Silver Dollar

Imperial

Avenue

Dago Frank

French Charlie

Lynch

Old 92

Vic Shaw

Bernstein

Zoe Millard

French-Man's

Street

Street

Railroad

Avenue

Clark

Street

Twenty

First

Street

Charlie West

Van Bever

California

Amour

Abie Arend

Becky Horiarty

Madame Leo

Frank Lewis

Dearborn

Casino

Van Bever

French Em

Monohan

Georgie Spencer

Sappho

The Everleigh Club

Ed Weiss

Saratoga

Libby Martin

Utopia

Marlboro Hotel

State

Street

Elevated

Polack Ben

Colosimo's Cafe

Freiberg's Saloon

Wabash

22nd St. Police Station

Twenty

Second

Street

• *Chicago's First Ward (left) was the center of the city's business, commercial, and enter-tainment districts and home of the Levee (above), the best-known red-light district in America in the early 1900s.*

Maps produced by Lynda Wallis

• Sisters Ada and Minna Everleigh (top right and right) ran the popular Everleigh Club at 2131-2133 S. Dearborn Street. The opulent resort offered high-class prostitutes in luxurious surroundings.

- *Victoria Shaw (top right) was queen of the madams before the Everleighs arrived.*
- *Located at 2014 S. Dearborn, Vic Shaw's brothel (above left), with its complement of hostesses (above), was a big competitor of the Everleigh Sisters.*
- *Freiberg's Dance Hall at 20 E. 22nd Street (left) was the Levee's most infamous night spot and was operated by the menacing Isaac Gitelson "Ike" Bloom (top center).*

• *Chicago life as described by Rev. William T. Stead (above) in his best-seller* If Christ Came to Chicago *rocked the city to its foundations and sparked a reform movement that would besiege the Levee.*

• *Reformer Rev. Rodney "Gypsy" Smith (right) attracted thousands of Chicagoans to a series of prayer meetings and led 12,000 enthusiastic marchers down Dearborn Street in the heart of the Levee on the night of October 12, 1909 (below, in a political cartoon).*

• *Evangelist Rev. Ernest A. Bell (above, at center) raises his arm in prayer as he preaches in the Levee.*

• *In the drawing at left, a female missionary talks with a lady of the Levee in a brothel while several crusaders watch from a doorway and patrons act nonchalant.*

• *Missionaries kneel in prayer (below) on Dearborn Street in the Levee as resort patrons and passersby watch.*

- *The Paris resort at 2100 S. Dearborn Street (above) was owned by white-slaver Maurice Van Bever.*
- *Crusader Clifford Roe (right) led the fight against pandering and the white slave racket.*
- *Col. LeRoy T. Steward (far right) was Chicago's police chief from 1909 to 1911.*
- *Chicago police officers of the 1900s stand outside their district police station (below).*
- *The Levee in the daytime was filled with drunks, bums, and idlers passing the time on the curb.*

PHOTOS FROM THE AUTHOR'S COLLECTION

• In 1914, Colosimo held a banquet (above) at his restaurant for close associates, including several civic and political leaders and members of the police department.

• After Sgt. Stanley Birns (right) was fatally shot, likely by fellow officers, in the Levee in April 1914, Big Jim Colosimo was arrested as a conspirator and his restaurant closed down for three months.

• Colosimo and defense attorney Charles E. Epstein (below left) prepare a defense in connection with Birns's shooting.

• Outgoing State's Attorney John E. Wayman turns over the office key to his successor, Maclay Hoyne (below right, in bow tie). Both men attacked the brothels and Colosimo.

• Pictured above at Big Jim Colosimo's home at 3156 Vernon Avenue are (from left) Colosimo, his father Luigi, and John Torrio, who would become one of Chicago's top crime bosses.

• At right are the two buildings of Colosimo's Café: 2126 (top) and 2128 S. Wabash Avenue. The popular restaurant offered fine dining in posh surroundings as well as a dance floor and stage (below).

• *Colosimo became smitten with singer Dale Winter (top left) and began an affair with her before divorcing wife Victoria. Big Jim and the beautiful entertainer were married April 17, 1920, on the steps of Indiana's West Baden Springs Hotel (left).*

• *Lafe Prow (below left, with sons William and Robert) and his wife, Betty, were witnesses at Colosimo's wedding, and the guest list included such notables as English theater magnate Charles Cochran, opera conductor Giacomo Spandoni, and former Assistant U.S. District Attorney Francis Borrelli.*

Chicago Daily Tribune.

WEDNESDAY, MAY 12, 1920

COLOSIMO, VICE KING, SLAIN

BANKERS HOPE TO CLAMP LID ON SPENDING ORGY

NEW MEXICAN RULERS SEEK FAVOR OF U.S.

STATE ATTORNEY OF MINNEAPOLIS INDS. DOUGE NE!

SHOT DOWN IN HIS OWN CAFE; SLAYER FLEES

Unl. Witness to the Crime Is Gone

THE CHICAGO DAILY JOURNAL

SEVENTY-SEVENTH YEAR—NO. 21

WEDNESDAY, MAY 12, 1920

PRICE TWO CENTS

10 TH-LAST EDITION

COLOSIMO KILLING

ORDER BUNTE FIRM ARRESTS FOR SUGAR PROFIT

AS ENRIGHT DEATH SEQUEL

MURDERED CAFE OWNER AND HIS BRIDE

Newspapers trumpeted Colosimo's demise.

THE CHICAGO DAILY NEWS. FINAL EDITION

SPORTS ON PAGE 21

TWO CENTS 43TH YEAR—113.

TUESDAY, MAY 11, 1920.

★ HOME EDITION

JIM COLOSIMO IS MURDERED

TO-DAY'S BASEBALL GAMES

REBELS GATHERING AT THE MEXICAN BORDER

LEGLESS LOCHINVAR FREE

KING OF LEVEE SHOT IN RESTAURANT.

WIN WAR BY AUDACITY, WILSON TOLD NAVY

EXTRA

SLAYING OF COLOSIMO INVOLVED IN MYSTERY OF THE UNDERWORLD

Corpse Found in Room of Levee King's Cafe on Wabash Avenue Near 22d Street, Many Times Subject of Inquiries

Several Suspects Taken Into Custody from Their Haunts in the Old Levee District and Hundreds of Curious Persons Gather Round Restaurant.

SHERMAN HAILED AS NEXT COMMITTEEMAN

BOX SCORE

Lowden Forces Claim Votes to Displace Thompson on National Body.

ELECTION SET FOR JUNE

• *Big Jim Colosimo lies in a pool of blood (above) on the tiled floor of his café as Officer James R. Mescall and another policeman guard his body.*

• *A reenactment (left) shows how Big Jim's murder may have occurred. Note the bullet hole in the glass of the door at left.*

• *A bevy of police vehicles and a sizable crowd gather in front of Colosimo's Café (below) shortly after the murder.*

• Brooklyn gang leader Frankie Yale (above left), was probably the killer of Big Jim Colosimo, presumably carrying out the execution May 11, 1920, at the request of longtime pal John Torrio.

• Chicago's first vice lord was interred in the family mausoleum (above right) at Oak Woods Cemetery.

• Nearly a decade after his murder, Liberty magazine (right) ran an extensive article with photos on Colosimo.

Underworld KING

The scene outside Jim Colosimo's café after his body was found in its lobby. Police are keeping the sidewalk clear.

P. & A. photos

and beck of his superiors. No longer did he have to sleep in hallways and rear rooms of saloons; no longer did he count his pennies in his calloused palms as he stared through bakery windows.

He formed his companions into a labor union, too; and soon he was being interviewed by organized workers' chieftains as well as politicians. He selected Dago Mike Carrozzo as his right bower. Mike was to be blamed long years later for the murder of Mossy Enright, another notorious gangster. Jim and Mike ruled their subjects and their boundaries with brass knuckles and knife and gun.

JIM expanded. Soon he was friendly with Tony D'Andrea, head of the Unione Siciliani after Mike Merlo died. He was friendly with Diamond Joe Esposito, one of Senator Deneen's followers. Tony and Joe later expired when some pal pulled a trigger.

Jim expanded further. He did not now wear the white garb of a white wing, but his wide shoulders fitted tightly into the box coats that bespoke the maquereau. Victoria Moresco ran a night-life resort, and soon she was Jim's girl. He married her on July 22, 1902. They were childless till the end—when Jim cast her off for another and a younger woman, as we shall see.

Jim lived for years along these lines, enjoying political power and police preference and waxing financially fat. He spread his activities into Burnham and other towns near the great growing iron and steel areas of the South Side.

Johnny Torrio steps into the picture. Gambling and crooked enterprises of all sorts engaged him and Colosimo; their partnership brought them wealth and power and amusement. In February, 1914, Maria Caputa, Torrio's mother, and old Luigi Colosimo opened a restaurant and bar at 2126 South Wabash Avenue. Jim ran it, and it was to become nationally famous as Colosimo's Café.

Around the corner was Ike Bloom's notorious dance hall. Near by was Polack Ben's place. Friberg ran another joint until he amalgamated with Ike. The district

[CONTINUED ON NEXT PAGE]

Dale Winter, the second Mrs. Jim Colosimo; and above, her husband, Jim, bearing the mark of changes due to her refining influence, but with the shadow of the underworld still clinging to him.

business of the establishment. The collectors brought the money to Colosimo's house and the money was split three ways between the police, the political bosses and the "Big Four" plus Colosimo.

Any saloon or resort that did not pay was raided by the police who chopped up the places with fire axes. Captain Michael Ryan was transferred into the district and became Alderman Kenna's right hand man.

When Major Funkhouser was made 2nd Deputy Superintendent an orchestrated campaign of law suits, verbal attacks and hostile articles in a weekly publication began. All of this was the work of Colosimo.

None of this stopped Funkhouser and Dannenberg in their raids.

The Colosimo/Torrio gang had moved into action the night of the shooting between the two groups of police officers.

When Roxy Vanille was shot, he was carried by Johnny Torrio to Torrio's waiting auto and driven to St. Anthony de Padua Hospital. He was placed under the care of Dr. Hillman, a nightly regular at Colosimo's Café.[7]

In response to the *Tribune's* series, the *American* treated Chicagoans to an eight-column headline, "COLOSIMO IN CELL DEFIES POLICE," and for the first time, Colosimo's photo ran on the front page of a Chicago newspaper. In the picture, Colosimo appeared as a swarthy, round-faced man with a short, bushy, black mustache and dark bushy eyebrows. He had on a white suit, white shirt with a high collar, and a striped tie.[8]

On the morning of Tuesday, July 21, well-known defense attorney Charles E. Erbstein appeared in police court at the Twenty-second Street police station. Erbstein filed a habeas corpus petition demanding that the police and the state's attorney bring James Colosimo before a judge. Looking rumpled after a night in the lockup, Big Jim was brought into the courtroom. He displayed an easy manner and an engaging smile as he stood with Erbstein before Judge Kersten. Colosimo had been arrested on a subpoena charging that he had operated Colosimo's Café in violation of the 1 a.m. closing ordinance. Judge Kersten granted the writ and directed his personal bailiff to immediately serve notice on State's Attorney Hoyne and Police Chief Gleason that the writ had been granted. Colosimo was released by the judge, but Big Jim was not to be allowed to leave the courtroom.

In a surprise move by the state's attorney, Colosimo was arrested in court and charged with conspiracy to obstruct justice and concealment of witnesses of importance to the investigation of the shooting. Judge Kersten ordered Colosimo held on five thousand dollars bond.[9] Briefly Colosimo was again taken into custody, but he was soon released on a bond provided by Auron Andrews, a professional bondsman who regularly appeared in court when Levee characters had been arrested. Erbstein and a disturbed Colosimo walked out of the police station. As reporters and photographers swarmed around, the pair got into a waiting car and was driven away.

On the day after Colosimo's arrest the *American* ran a long article that described the vice lord's personal life in great detail. The story reported:

> Big Jim was a good mixer at parties.
>
> He made a practice of going to the opera every night of the season and sometimes taking twenty to thirty of his countrymen with him. After the opera Colosimo went back stage into the stars' dressing rooms and talked with the singers about his version of the night's performance.
>
> People across the country thought of him as a patron of the Wagnerian ring-cycle. He reportedly went to Europe to see new operatic productions.
>
> Enrico Caruso and other famous singers often visited with Big Jim at his restaurant.
>
> His friends included people from high society, the stage and various professions.
>
> He enthusiastically attended big-name boxing matches and went to major fights across the country.[10]

On July 21, Hoyne, trying for more headlines, disclosed that he had new evidence. He said the evidence proved that Roxy Vanille was the man in gray who had fired the first shot in the deadly police duel and was the pivotal man in the plot to kill Inspector Dannenberg. Hoyne said Vanille was under guard at Wesley Hospital where he was being treated for a shattered ankle caused by a pistol shot. Going into Vanille's criminal history, Hoyne said, "Only a short time ago he was freed from the penitentiary in Billings, Montana, after he killed a man there."[11] According to Hoyne, Vanille's release, after serving eight years of a fifty-year sentence, was secured by the leaders of Chicago's commercialized vice so they could use him to slay Dannenberg. After arriving in Chicago, Vanille had been placed in charge of a shabby resort owned by Colosimo at 2110 Armour Avenue. Hoyne said that on the night of the shooting Vanille was wounded and was placed in an automobile by John Torrio and Saffo the Greek. At the emergency room, a doctor removed the bullet from Vanille's foot and handed the slug to Torrio.[12]

State's Attorney Hoyne said he was going to appear before the grand jury to seek indictments against Colosimo for conspiracy to kill Dannenberg's officers and for conspiracy to obstruct justice for planning to hide Torrio and Vanille after the shooting of Birns. Hoyne said he also was going to seek an indictment against Torrio for conspiracy for using his auto to rush Vanille away from the scene of the incident and keep him hidden from the police.

Hoyne indicated that he was furious with Colosimo for "sealing his lips" about the shooting. Supporting his theory that Colosimo was involved in the entire affair, Hoyne said his investigators had learned that Torrio started out in his automobile from Colosimo's café before to the shooting and returned to the cafe with the wounded Vanille in his auto immediately after the fracas. Hoyne thundered, "If Colosimo is going to try to bluff us out, we are going to give him the works and good and proper, too."

Hoyne related for the reporters what he claimed was the true account of what had taken placed on the fateful night of July 16:

> A half-hour before the raid at the Turf, word passed through the informal communication network in the Levee that Funkhouser's men were going to hit the district.
>
> John Torrio, Charley Malbaum and Saffo the Greek were sitting in Torrio's automobile in front of his house of prostitution at 2002 Armour Avenue. Torrio went into his resort and called several Levee operators including: Mike the Goose, Dago Frank, and Roxy Vanille.
>
> In a short while Mike the Goose and Roxy Vanille arrived at Torrio's resort. Vanille was given a revolver and he hurried off on foot in the direction of the Turf located two blocks to the south. Torrio drove his car to the Turf and parked nearby.
>
> Torrio watched as the two morals squad detectives walked away from the building where they had made their raid. They were followed by a crowd composed mostly of Levee hoodlums who had been told to assault the detectives when they got under the "L" tracks that crossed over 22nd Street.
>
> As the throng neared this point the sluggers saw Captain Michael Ryan, Detective Bill Schubert and Jim Colosimo on the corner near Freiberg's dance hall. Because of the presence of the police captain, the sluggers allowed the detectives to continue walking.
>
> After the detectives passed the intersection the crowd grew more vicious the officers drew their guns fearing violence was about to occur.
>
> At that moment 22nd Street District Station detectives Birns and Sloop appeared on the other side of the street and the shooting started. Several Levee hoodlums also were firing.
>
> When Vanille fell wounded he was dragged into Torrio's car by Torrio and Saffo and hurried to the hospital. At the hospital Vanille said his name was Frank Langon.[13]

The mystery of who Frank Langon was had been solved. Once this "victim" had left the scene the detectives had never been able to locate him because there was no such person. The true name of the man shot in the foot that night was Roxy Vanille.

Mayor Harrison, not wanting to appear neutral in a matter involving the killing of a police sergeant and certainly not wanting to be upstaged by his political enemy State's Attorney Hoyne, ordered the police to close Colosimo's Café.

Chapter Twenty-Four

THE LEVEE CLOSES

They Said It Couldn't Be Done

1914

These conditions was in the First Ward before you and I were born and they'll be there after we're dead.

— Alderman Michael Kenna,
testifying before the grand jury

After the shooting of Sgt. Stanley J. Birns the enraged public was demanding that the Levee be shut down. Still on vacation in Michigan, Mayor Carter Harrison needed to pacify the voters. Without waiting for approval from the aldermen of the First Ward, Harrison ordered Chief James Gleason to put a captain who was free of any compromising influences in charge of the Twenty-second Street District Station.

While it was tough to identify a captain who was not tainted by corruption, Gleason found one—Capt. Max Nootbar. This burly German American had a big sandy mustache, a bald head, and the most unusual background of any commander in the department. A graduate of Heidelberg University, a criminal psychologist, a cowboy, and a world traveler, he had been a U.S. consular secretary in Hamburg. He was tough as nails and a stickler for discipline. Nootbar admitted that his more worldly philosophy on prostitution had evolved from his travels in Europe where segregated vice was the preferred method of control, but he said that this would not interfere with the strict performance of his duties. With a hand-picked team of sergeants, detectives, and patrolmen transferred at his request into the Twenty-second Street District, Nootbar promised to clean up the Levee in thirty days.[1]

Nootbar told the press: "I am under no obligation to Aldermen Kenna and Coughlin. I don't owe them anything, and I don't need anything they have."[2] One of Nootbar's first acts was to remove the photograph of Freiberg's Dance Hall operator Ike Bloom that had long hung on the wall of Michael F. Ryan's office in the station house. Nootbar threw the photo into the garbage can. The officers in the station got the message.

Meanwhile, Sergeant Birns was buried in St. Adelbert's Cemetery in Norwood Park. While his body had lain in state in his home at 1848 N. Western Avenue, thousands came to pay their respects or watch the activity. The crowd, lured by the sensational media coverage of the shooting, spilled over the sidewalk and delayed the Western Avenue traffic. An eight-column headline appeared in the *American*, "COLOSIMO MUST TELL ALL." After serving a subpoena on Colosimo, State's Attorney Maclay Hoyne said Big Jim would be given one chance to testify to all he knew about the vice district and the shooting or be charged with perjury.[3]

The state's attorney began bringing witnesses before the grand jury with the intention of indicting Colosimo and Torrio.[4] The first witness was Detective Amort; then Inspector William C. Dannenberg, Chief Gleason, and Dr. Gilman. Upon leaving the grand jury room Dr. Gilman admitted to reporters he had testified that soon after the shooting he had treated Vanille's foot wound in a house on East Twentieth Street near Wabash Avenue.[5]

Colosimo decided to quickly get his own version of the incident into public print. Talking openly about the shooting for the first time, Big Jim told a *Daily News* reporter that he was standing on Twenty-second Street near Freiberg's Dance Hall talking with Captain Ryan and others when the shooting took place. Colosimo claimed, without explaining how he knew, that Vanille had been four hundred feet from the scene of the shooting when a bullet hit him in the toe. Colosimo blamed county-level politics for the investigation of him and the vice district. He said that some time ago, Alderman Michael Kenna had announced that he would not support County Judge Owens for reelection. Now, according to Colosimo, Owens had seized the opportunity to get back at Kenna by spreading stories that linked Colosimo to the shooting. "Anyone can see through it," Colosimo explained.[6]

The word on Twenty-second Street was that Colosimo was feeling very gloomy over the problems caused by the shooting and was seriously thinking of selling his restaurant. Privately, Colosimo and Torrio were meeting almost nightly in the closed café. Some evenings they were joined by Roy Jones and Ben Pollack. The state's attorney's investigators had been searching without success for Torrio and Saffo the Greek. Defense attorney Robert E. Cantwell offered to surrender them.[7]

On July 23, Hoyne obtained warrants from Municipal Court Judge

Williams charging Vanille with murder and Vanille, Torrio, Saffo, Jew Kid Grabiner, Maurice Van Bever, and others with conspiracy to commit murder. State's attorney's investigators arrested saloon owner Jakie Adler and white slaver Van Bever, who were wanted in connection with the shooting. Van Bever was alleged to have been an insider in the plot to get rid of Dannenberg, while Adler was to said to have baited the morals squad detectives from his car as he followed the crowd.[8]

Meanwhile, the Civil Service Commission was continuing its yearlong hearings on vice and corruption in the Twenty-second Street District Station. The commission disclosed that it intended to bring charges against Captain Ryan and other ranking officers of the Twenty-second Street District Station. On July 25 Ryan resigned for "medical reasons" but actually to avoid being fired by the commission. Patrolmen from the Twenty-second Street District Station had testified before the commission that Ryan directed them not to arrest or harass most of the proprietors in the Levee. Other patrolmen said that their superiors ordered the officers to ignore violations of the law at Colosimo's restaurant, Freiberg's Dance Hall, Roy Jones's saloon, and John Jordan's café.[9] Undaunted by Ryan's resignation the commission charged the three shift lieutenants from the Twenty-second Street station, Michael T. Morrisey, James J. McMahon, and James P. Allman, with inefficiency, incapacity and neglect of duty. Gleason suspended the lieutenants.

Still vacationing in Michigan and attempting by long-distance phone to bring the situation under control, Mayor Harrison advised Chief Gleason that Freiberg's was to be closed. Consequently, early Sunday morning, the unthinkable happened. Ike Bloom, wanting to avoid more trouble for Kenna, closed Freiberg's promptly at 1 a.m. for the first time in twelve years.[10] Additionally, the liquor license was revoked for Roy Jones's saloon, and Chief Gleason said he would ask for the revocation of the liquor licenses for Colosimo cafe and Jordan's cafe.[11]

Harrison, interviewed by an enterprising reporter while packing his bags for return to Chicago from his summer home in Huron Mountain, Michigan, said: "I believe commercialized vice is as much of a crime as highway robbery or burglary. The idea of segregation is all wrong. It is as if we segregated all burglars and furnished them with certain districts within which they might rob and burgle. My ideas of the vice question have been wrong."[12]

Harrison had changed his views by 100 percent. The power of pubic opinion had persuaded him that it was no longer politically safe to hold the position that segregated vice districts were acceptable.

On July 30, Harrison returned to his office and immediately met with Chief Gleason. The mayor announced that he was revoking the liquor licenses for the resort named the New Brighton Café at 2001 Archer Avenue operated by Johnny Torrio.[13] Of course, Torrio had only been fronting for Big Jim, the longtime owner of the New Brighton.

The month ended with ex-Captain Ryan testifying at the Civil Service Commission hearings against his former lieutenants Morrisey, McMahon, and Allman, charged by the commission with inefficiency and neglect of duty for failing to drive vice from the Levee. Ryan spent most of his time on the witness stand trying to vindicate himself of the charge that he had allowed the Levee to run wide-open. He made no attempt to protect his former loyal subordinates. Instead he testified that he had made every effort to eradicate vice in his district, certainly a bald-faced lie.[14] The ex-captain was a sorry example of the results of the segregated vice district and the pay-for-protection plan of Aldermen Kenna and Coughlin.

Survey, a national weekly magazine, had its own explanation of what had been going on in Chicago. The magazine said that the problem of the shoot-out in the Levee had been created several years earlier when the city council passed an ordinance creating the position of Second Deputy Superintendent of Police with two qualifications: one, that he be a civilian, and two, that he have responsibility for a citywide morals squad. The first requirement turned the regular officers against the deputy superintendent, and the second resulted in the vice bosses bringing all the power they could muster against the holder of the new office. The article concluded that the mayor faced, on one side, the political influence of the two powerful First Ward aldermen and, on the other, the many forces demanding elimination of the Levee. Confronted with a Hobson's choice, the mayor made a sudden conversion to vice reform and the closing of the Levee.[15]

The Italian newspaper *L'Italia* carried a negative story on the events. The paper told how Deputy Superintendent Funkhouser was moving to close Colosimo's Café for violating the closing-hour ordinance because policewomen had purchased beer in the café after 1 a.m. on a Sunday morning. The paper added that Johnny Torrio, who worked for Colosimo, had thought it expedient to leave Chicago in the wake of the Sergeant Birns killing. The paper said that Torrio had been taken into custody in New York but was released when the police found that there was no outstanding warrant for his arrest.[16] It was a blow to Big Jim Colosimo that the newspaper of his homeland, which had reported positive stories about him and his restaurants, had seemingly turned against him.

In late August, Mayor Harrison revoked the licenses of Colosimo's, Freiberg's, and several other saloons. The vaunted power of Kenna as political boss of the Levee was being challenged, but on September 16, in a very *sotto voce* action, Assistant City Prosecutor Marshall Solberg appeared before Municipal Judge Rooney and withdrew the two pending cases in which Colosimo was charged with selling liquor in his saloon after the 1 a.m.

closing hour. Solberg explained the evidence was lacking, but he could rein-state the cases at a later date. "Could," but didn't.

In the criminal court, the charges against Colosimo, Torrio, and the others were dismissed. Duffy the Goat Franche stood trial for the murder of Henagow. He was found guilty and sentenced to hang, but he obtained a new trial on technicalities. In the second trial, the jurors accepted Franche's claims of self-defense and found him not guilty. The two political strongmen in the First Ward, coupled with the corruptive power of the vice trust headed by Big Jim Colosimo, were able to thwart justice again.

County Judge Owens weakened the political strength of Kenna and Coughlin by ordering seven hundred names removed from the election registration books of the First Ward. The majority of names were supposed tenants of old Levee hotels, which existed primarily for purposes of prostitution and providing flops and addresses for the voters Kenna and Coughlin paid on election days. However, among the expunged voters were James Colosimo, Maurice and Julia Van Bever, Sol Friedman, and Ike Bloom.

The rescinded liquor licenses had effectively closed most of the operations in the Levee. By the end of 1914 detectives under Inspector Dannenberg's directions had conducted numerous raids on the last few resorts. While a few resorts and dive joints continued to operate clandestinely for a dozen years, one by one they eventually closed. The ladies of the Levee finally had fallen victim to the combined forces of the Committee of Fifteen, State's Attorney Wayman, Mayor Harrison, Deputy Superintendent Funkhouser, Inspector Dannenberg, and Captain Nootbar. The girls moved into other sections of the city or left town, and the Levee neighborhood slowly decayed into a broken-down slum.

In spite of his great success Dannenberg was coming under fire. In recent months Deputy Superintendent Funkhouser and Inspector Dannenberg had been feuding. Funkhouser complained that that Dannenberg would not obey orders. The difficulties between the two strong-minded men reached such a state that Funkhouser sent a letter to the Civil Service Commission accusing Dannenberg of subordination. Dannenberg got the message but declined to resign. Funkhouser told the press he was reluctantly going to have to press charges against Dannenberg. Appearing at an informal hearing called at his request before the civil service board on December 19, 1914, Dannenberg discussed the matter with the commissioners, and they cleared him of the charges of insubordination. The board agreed that there had been frictional differences between the two men but there were insufficient grounds for dismissal. Dannenberg walked out of the hearing and submitted his written resignation, which he had prepared in advance, to Chief Gleason. Gleason accepted the resignation, and the greatest vice raider the Levee had ever known left the police department.

Chapter Twenty-Five

OUT IN THE COUNTY

Fun and Games in Burnham

1914–1915[1]

The United States had become an increasingly mobile society. The automobile linked together city and suburb, making the locations on the fringe of the expanding city easily accessible from downtown. The taxicab driver could now serve the same purpose of the cadet-roper who formerly canvassed the train stations and amusement parks in search of prostitutes and male customers. The move to the suburbs simply meant that the social evils were even more decentralized than before and that much harder to suppress.[1]

— Richard Lindberg, *To Serve and Collect*

As the segregated vice district ended and the Levee began to fade, Big Jim Colosimo provided the impetus and financing for new vice resorts in the far south suburbs and unincorporated territories. To achieve his objectives Colosimo utilized some of his best men—Johnny Torrio, Jew Kid Grabiner, Joe Frazer, Jake Guzik, Ike Bloom, Maurice Van Bever, and Jakie Adler—as his agents.[2] This expansion program was made possible because of a great technological advance.

In 1900 there were 8,000 registered automobiles in the United States. By 1910 there were 468,500, and by 1915 there were 2,445,666. This development radically changed the cultural and social life of the community. People began to travel greater distances, going directly from their door to wherever they wanted to go. Automobiles also enabled persons seeking adult recreation to go "out in the county" to get a drink, gamble a couple of bucks, find a little sex, and generally have a good time.³ One beneficiary of this unique use of the automobile was a small incorporated village named Burnham at the far south end of Cook County.

Burnham, Illinois, was eighteen miles south of Chicago's downtown at the extreme southern edge of Cook County and flat against the Indiana border. Less than one mile square, its low-income inhabitants lived in inexpensive frame houses amidst a handful of shabby saloons and small stores. In 1907, the village's three hundred residents voted to incorporate their community. The next year, twenty-year-old Johnny Patton, a local resident who had worked as a bartender in the town's saloons since he was fourteen, was elected village president. Patton, elected only because no one else wanted the job, had the dubious honor of being the youngest mayor in Cook County. He held the position until 1935 while administering a community that attracted what he termed "pleasure-loving people." Local residents swore by the mayor, whom they called "a grand little fella." They claimed that he had "done a heap of good here . . . helps everyone who needs it [and] has a nice home and three pretty children." This was a good report card for the man who ran "the liveliest town on the south shore of Lake Michigan."⁴

Johnny Patton frankly admitted that he didn't smoke, drink, swear, gamble, spit, or chew. His conduct most of the time was polite and gentlemanly, especially when being observed by reporters or investigators. A banty guy with a narrow face, Patton was full of fun and always ready with an Irish joke. He was a stylish dresser and usually wore a white shirt and a bow tie. In summer he sported a straw boater and the rest of the year a smart gray cap. Because of his age and youthful appearance the newspapers always referred to him as the "boy mayor."

Some people said Patton was as crooked as a dog's hind leg. His town was a rough-and-tumble place where people were beaten and sometimes killed if they got out of line. To provide order Patton selected a police force that was corrupt, unprofessional, and completely under his control. Patton changed Burnham from a sleepy, economically depressed, blue-collar town to a money-making, honky-tonk sin city. That change was facilitated by a meeting of the minds between Patton and Johnny Torrio.

Torrio had observed that cars were fast replacing horse-drawn carriages in the Levee and suggested to Colosimo that they take advantage of this development by opening resorts out of the purview of the bothersome reporters and reformers that focused their actions and concerns on Chicago. Colosimo agreed with the idea. Putting his money where his mouth was, Colosimo provided money, managers, and muscle. The first step in Torrio's plan took him to the pint-sized town of Burnham, where he talked to the operator of a local bar about the prospect of opening a restaurant in the town.

The bartender suggested that Torrio speak with Mayor Patton. The two men met and after some discussion Patton made a devil's deal with Torrio and never looked back.

On that first day Patton showed Torrio the old Arrowhead Inn at 13822 Entra Avenue. The property was a dilapidated, wooden, two-story building that straddled the Illinois-Indiana line. Torrio purchased the property for fifteen thousand dollars. He hired carpenters to add a bar on the first floor and divide the second floor into small bedrooms.[5] When the construction was finished, Torrio arrived at the Arrowhead with girls from his Levee resorts. He put them to work as good-time girls on the first floor and quickie whores on the second. Torrio made Patton the manager, installed the village's police chief as bartender, and hired the village trustees to be waiters.

The new Arrowhead Inn was in operation by late 1913, based on the pleadings in a lawsuit filed by the United Breweries Company. The company claimed that fifteen hundred dollars was owed to them by the Arrowhead Inn in Burnham, which they said was owned by Colosimo. The breweries charged that Colosimo and Torrio had fraudulently concealed the property to prevent United from collecting their bill. The matter was settled out of court, but the lawsuit proved that Colosimo was financially involved in the early 1910s in the expansion of vice to the suburbs.[6]

The Arrowhead Inn was Cook County's first one-stop restaurant-saloon-whorehouse, and it became a virtual gold mine. In its first month the income was more than nine thousand dollars. The Arrowhead operated twenty-four hours a day, seven days a week. At its peak ninety girls worked three eight-hour shifts. On the first floor the girls worked as friendly drinking and dance partners for any men who were interested. On the second floor, the same girls made their dubious charms available for short-term rentals in the tiny bedrooms. Soon the profits were ten thousand dollars monthly, divided half to Colosimo and half to Torrio after they gave Patton his payoff.[7]

Spurred on by the success of the Arrowhead, Torrio opened the Burnham Inn, which for a time he personally managed. In the following months, Torrio added the Barn and the Coney Island Café to his stable of resorts in Burnham. Torrio became the power behind the mayor.

Torrio realized that there was no reason to limit his expansion to Burnham. Colosimo agreed. Over the next few years, Torrio opened places in Chicago Heights, Stickney, Posen, Blue Island, and other towns.[8] These roadhouses, resorts, and gambling parlors provided a local oasis for residents in south and west suburban towns. They were used by Chicago residents whenever the heat was on and the vice joints in Chicago were down. To avoid surprise raids, Torrio made deals with local gas-station operators, café owners, and roadside vendors to make a fast phone call if sheriff's deputies or other enforcement types were seen in the area. This early warning arrangement for vice and gambling joints "out in the county" endured through decades of use by the Chicago crime syndicate.

As the state's attorney and the mayor shut down resorts in the Levee, the now-unemployed working girls relocated to the houses that Torrio and Colosimo were running in the suburbs. By the time State's Attorney Hoyne and Twenty-second District Captain Nootbar closed the Levee, Torrio was operating a dozen roadhouses in the far south and west ends of Cook County. These Torrio-Colosimo vice operations triggered fifty years of gambling and prostitution in suburban Cook County, thanks to the laughingly easy corruptibility of the elected one-term county sheriffs and small-town mayors.[9] These suburban vice operations continued throughout Colosimo's life.*

By the summer of 1915, Torrio had added a string of down-and-dirty brothels in Burnham. Basically crib houses, they were in a seedy strip known as the "craw." Girls were two dollars a visit and beer was a dollar a quart. Soon, Torrio had two hundred girls working in shifts around the clock. Mayor Patton obliged Torrio in every possible way, enacting no curfew ordinances or liquor restrictions. The roadhouses in Burnham ran twenty-four hours a day, seven days a week.[10] In the bigger establishments there were bands and orchestras. Jazz musicians played for the out-of-town visitors and whores. Milton "Mezz" Mezzrow, who became a well-known white jazz musician, was one of the "big-name" entertainers who appeared at the roadhouses. In the early morning hours lachrymose whores would request Mezz to play sad songs like "The Curse of an Aching Heart."[11]

Even though Patton was now considered a member of the Colosimo gang, Big Jim deemed it best to have a proven underling protecting his interests in the far south suburb. Frank Hitchcock, who had served as a manager for Colosimo in the Levee, was installed as unofficial deputy mayor under Patton and became co-manager with Patton of the Arrowhead Inn. The inn was across the street from a similar roadhouse operated by Ike Bloom.[12] Jakie Adler, a longtime Levee resort operator, opened a so-called hotel in the midst of the craw.

On the night of February 7, 1916, in Burnham, a mysterious fire destroyed one of the roadhouses that functioned mostly as a whorehouse. According to the *Tribune* the roadhouse was operated by Torrio. At the height of the fire men and women jumped from second-floor windows and Torrio was said to have broken his ankle as he leaped from the porch. The patrons

---

* The vice joints continued to operate long after Colosimo was murdered. Finally, in 1962 a reform sheriff was elected in Cook County who appointed an incorruptible chief of police. This chief shut down the county for good. Full disclosure: the sheriff was Richard B. Ogilvie, and the chief was the author of this book.

and employees ran from the burning building. When the fire engines arrived, the frantic and dazed employees failed to tell the firemen that not everyone had escaped. In checking the ruins the firemen found the body of Laura "Happy Irish Rose" Clarke. Because it could not be determined whether Clarke had died before or during the fire, Coroner Peter Hoffman ordered an investigation. Detective George Scrivner kept reporters from questioning the girls who had worked in the resort. He explained, "The girls have been drinking and are in no condition to give intelligent answers to questions." The mystery of Clarke's death went unsolved.[13] No one in Burnham was interested in pursuing the matter.

In June 1916, Sheriff John E. Traeger was pushed into getting tough with Burnham. The Republican National Convention was coming to Chicago, and the crusaders and ministers were seizing the opportunity to advise Traeger that this wide-open patch of sin and damnation in south Cook County was going to give Chicago a bad name. Pressured into action by the ministers and newspaper exposés of wild nights in Burnham, a reluctant Traeger, who undoubtedly had been paid handsomely and regularly, began a drive against the roadhouses in the far south end of the county. Traeger roared a public warning to Patton that unless the big roadhouses were cleaned up, dire action would be taken. As a result of this get-tough campaign, the Burnham Inn and the Arrowhead Inn, for the first time, closed their doors at midnight on Saturday night and remained closed on Sunday. This imposed closure lasted a few weeks, and then the lid came off again when the noisy ministers and nosy newspapermen were gone.

The sheriff should have included the Burnham Inn as a target of his clean-up campaign. This roadhouse was the scene of many riotous parties that lasted until the early hours of the morning. Many nights the drinking turned to arguments, the arguments to fights, and the fights to shootings. "Dandy Joe" Hogarty, owner of the H&H cigar store, a mobster hangout at 50 Twenty-second Street, could have testified to this unpleasant practice.

On November 23, 1916, Dandy Joe was drinking with friends in the Burnham Inn. After midnight, Tom Enright and his tough stockyards gang entered the inn. The two groups joined tables and were enjoying the liquor and loose women when a dispute arose. Enright's gang fired their guns at Hogarty, who died shortly after he hit the floor. Most customers ran from the roadhouse, jumped into their cars, and fled. Manager Frank Hitchcock, who later claimed he had unfortunately stepped out when the shooting began, waited for the town's cops. The police arrested two of Hogarty's party who were still at the scene even though they denied seeing anything. No one from Enright's party was ever located. A waiter named Kid Conley had been shot through the wrist. He lamented, "If it was raining soup, I'd be there with a fork." Patton arrived soon after the shooting and expressed annoyance over the incident, possibly due to his role in operating the inn.[14]

On October 15, 1917, Colosimo and Torrio purchased the Speedway Inn in Burnham. Torrio placed Jew Kid Grabiner in charge. The Speedway became the third large roadhouse being operated by Torrio for Colosimo in Burnham. Nearby were Torrio-Colosimo gambling joints with nickel-and-dime slot machines[15] and two-dollar resorts where the girls' share was eighty cents a trick. Colosimo gang members served as managers in these locations.

Year in and year out the whoring and partying in the roadhouses in Burnham continued unabated. Sheriff Traeger, a consummate political hack, and his corrupt deputies helped to maintain the status quo. An attempt to oust the crooked and corrupt Mayor Patton by independent candidate Merle E. Wilson was defeated by a large turnout from the roadhouses, gambling joints, and vice resorts.

A new era in vice and gambling activities had begun far from the big-city reformers where only the town police chief or the sheriff needed to be bought.

Chapter Twenty-Six

CHIEF HEALEY
HAS TROUBLES

Colosimo's Vice Operations Continue;
Big Bill Thompson Becomes Mayor

1914–1917

*Jim Colosimo who, with little or no fear of the consequences, was isolated in
a sense of invulnerability because of his close ties with the law, the government of Chicago, the political powers. He, pimp and crime boss, operated in
safety on deceit and manipulation by those who were elected to public office.
He helped make the city's politics contemptible by control of thousands of
votes.*[1]

— Stephen Longstreet, *Chicago, 1860–1919*

By 1914 the concept of segregated vice districts in Chicago was finished,
and the notorious Levee was closing. Many resorts had closed. Other
resorts were dimming their lights and quieting their touts but discreetly remaining open. Because the visible signs of prostitution were gone,
the clergy and the reformers moved to other targets. The police made few vice
raids, and the payoff system continued. Some ladies of the Levee stayed in the
resorts that were operating under Colosimo's mantle of protection, while others moved to Colosimo's roadhouses and brothels out in the county. A number
of prostitutes began working from rented flats, getting their customers from
taxi drivers. The remainder hung around saloons and hotel lobbies. Superintendent Samuel P. Thrasher of the Committee of Fifteen boasted that of the
one hundred resorts running three years earlier there now were only forty.[2]
The *Survey*, a national magazine, reported that open commercialized vice in
Chicago had been greatly reduced and its profits whittled away.[3]

Big Jim Colosimo had made a fortune during the golden years of the Levee. Forced to close most of his brothels in the Levee, he was able to continue vice operations at the New Brighton, the Saratoga and the Victoria due to his longtime relationship with the First Ward aldermen. He opened new places in the county and increased his holdings in gambling parlors and opium dens in the city. Meanwhile, he was operating two restaurants: the Brighton at Armour and Archer streets and Colosimo's Café on Wabash Avenue.[4]

Due to its distance from downtown and the Levee, Colosimo managed to open a new resort on the Far South Side at 113 W. Ninety-fifth Street with Joe Aducci as manager. Aducci was a precinct captain for Colosimo's good friend Nineteenth Ward Republican Committeeman Joseph "Diamond Joe" Esposito.[5]

With the Levee closing, the *Chicago Examiner* looked to other sensational stories to boost newsstand sales. In July 1914, the paper carried a page-one story with new revelations about the Everleigh sisters and their contacts with the Levee bosses. Chief Judge Harry Olson said to *Examiner* reporters that he had learned from Minna Everleigh that the sisters had paid Coughlin and Kenna more than one hundred thousand dollars during a twelve-year period for their whiskey, taxicabs, groceries, and insurance. Olson said that Colosimo's people had threatened to kill Minna if she disclosed that information. The story caused a brief flurry of threats of sweeping investigations, but nothing came of the disclosures.[6] Not to be outdone by a Hearst paper, later in July the *Tribune* exposed three organized vice rings still operating in the Levee. The newspaper reported that the most powerful was the Colosimo-Torrio-Van Bever ring with Big Jim as its leader.[7]

Colosimo's Café was still closed due to Mayor Carter Harrison's license-revocation order following the Levee shootout. In order to reopen, Colosimo arranged for one of his waiters, Paul Bergamini, to apply in his name for a liquor license on October 27, 1914. Colosimo had spent a large sum of money remodeling and redecorating the café and wanted to quickly get back in business.

On January 28, 1915, in what the press viewed as a peace offering to Coughlin and Kenna to repay the damage to their income and reputation caused by the raids and closings in the Levee, Harrison reissued the liquor license for Colosimo's Café, or "spaghetti palace," as it was called in the *Tribune*, which missed no opportunity to attack Big Jim. Explaining his turn-around concerning the establishment owned by the vice lord behind the tragic events in the Levee, Harrison said the city counsel's office could not locate any witnesses willing to testify that the restaurant had engaged in illegal activity, while many respected citizens were willing to swear to the good conduct in the café. On reopening night, the band played "Oh, How She Could Yacki, Hacki,

Wacki, Wo" to a full house of patrons dancing the turkey trot, the bunny hug, and the castle walk. Colosimo sat at a back table and watched over the service by his waiters in their neatly pressed dinner coats.

The next year brought another mayoral race to Chicago. Because Carter Harrison said he would not seek another term, William Hale Thompson, the Republican alderman of the Second Ward, announced his intention of running for the city's highest office. Thompson, who came from a moneyed family in Boston, had spent several years in Wyoming starting at age fifteen. He had worked on ranches, ridden horses, and herded cattle before deciding to live in Chicago. Six feet tall and an excellent sportsman, he lived in the Hotel Metropole on south Michigan Avenue and frequently paid social visits to the Levee. Thompson originally possessed scant interest in politics, but due to teasing by a social friend who had been a Second Ward alderman, he had run for alderman and gotten the political bug. Running for his first term as alderman, Thompson was pitted against the powerful and rich reformer Democrat Charles Gunther. With strong help from the Coughlin-Kenna election machine Thompson had beat Gunther. Even so it was a close race— 2,516 to 2,113.[8]

During Thompson's service as Second Ward Alderman he did not involve himself in the nitty-gritty of politics and seldom attended council meetings. The political bosses did not think Thompson was very smart, but they agreed he knew how to win over the public in his speeches. He promised every group he spoke before whatever he thought the group wanted. He promised the prohibitionists he would support the state's blue laws and told the "wets" he would oppose blue laws. He told the Negroes that he would provide jobs. He told the Irish that he was dead against the English.

In late 1914, "Big Bill" Thompson decided to run for mayor. Because he did not have the political machine connections necessary to win a mayoral race, Thompson chose two allies to obtain campaign funds and voting power. Big Jim Colosimo and the bosses of the newly developing labor unions paved the way for Thompson's election. During Thompson's several campaigns for the mayor's office these two new allies—labor unions and the crime syndicate—formed a criminal partnership that lasted for more than fifty years. It was the beginning of crime-syndicate-dominated unions in Chicago.[9]

But it was Thompson's pandering to the blacks on the South Side that put him in office in his first run. This voting bloc, for self-serving reasons, continued to support Mayor Thompson during his many years in office.

On April 26, 1915, in the general mayoral election, Republican William Hale Thompson beat Democrat Robert Sweitzer by 139,480 votes—the greatest plurality of any candidate for public office in the history of Chicago. Based on Colosimo's assistance during the election campaign, Thompson realized that Colosimo could provide money and muscle not just at election time but throughout the year.[10] A discreet relationship developed between the two men that allowed Big Jim for the first time to have direct access to the mayor's office. This direct connection to the mayor gave Big Jim new power and prestige, which translated into an increase in income from his vice dens, gambling joints, and saloons.[11] Big Jim maintained this link with Thompson for the remaining years of his life, although he continued to work closely with his longtime friends Coughlin and Kenna.[12]

In the late summer of 1919, the very "wet" Mayor Thompson learned that reformers were trying to convince State's Attorney Maclay Hoyne to bring charges of malfeasance against him for failure to close the saloons at Saturday midnight and all day on Sunday. Trying to avoid an indictment, Thompson hurriedly ordered the police to close the saloons from midnight Saturday through Sunday.[13] This move satisfied the reformers but upset many persons of German and Irish descent who wanted to buy beer on Sunday. To avoid alienating a large percent of the city's population Thompson instructed his corporation counsel to study the issue seeking to find a Solomon-like solution. Spurred on by the urging of his boss, Corporation Counsel Samuel Ettelson wrote an opinion that customers could remain in saloons and resorts on Saturday nights and Sundays, but the bartenders could not sell them alcoholic drinks. Thompson took Ettelson's advice, and the police did not make drinking arrests after Saturday midnight or Sunday. Beer and alcoholic beverages were sold in coffee cups and other innocent-looking containers. The lid was off again.[14]

Thompson had a clear and simple position on drinking and morals. He was a "wet" and kept a mistress. Demonstrating his personal convictions, he soon began to dismantle the office of Second Deputy Superintendent and the morals squad.[15] He ordered his police chief to transfer the officers on the morals squad back to their previous police assignments. In November he replaced the relatively honest Chief James Gleason with Capt. Charles C. Healey. Healey's claim to fame was that he had been the commander of the traffic division.[16] After his swearing in, Healey vowed to rid Chicago of all crime—a lofty promise, which during his term in office he failed to do in every respect. He said the first step was to "close every poolroom in the city," which he labeled as "crime factories." As expected, Healey adhered to Thompson's "wet" policy. Not only the pool halls but everything else stayed open.[17] It was clear to all that Healey was not going to be a vice fighter.

The Vice Committee of the Illinois Senate released their long-awaited final report after conducting years of investigations and hearings into vice problems in Illinois. While the report included other cities in Illinois, the emphasis was strictly on Chicago. Downstaters who clearly controlled the senate had little love for Chicago. The committee reported that segregation of vice as a system of municipal regulation was a bad idea that increased immorality and materially lessened community respect for law and order. Unfortunately, this finding came two years after the end of the segregated vice-district concept in Chicago. The committee found that the major cause of women entering prostitution was poverty driven by the substandard wages of two to six dollars a week for work in department stores and factories. The report stated that thousands of girls were driven into prostitution because of the "sheer inability to keep body and soul together" on the low wages received by them.[18] A police sergeant who had worked the city streets for many years testified, "You can take a dozen contributory causes, you can say it is fondness of dress, hasty marriages, divorces, Greek restaurants, Greek cafes, and so forth, but, if you sift it right down, it is poverty."[19]

Along with Mayor Thompson and Chief Healey, State's Attorney Hoyne had little interest in vice fighting. His office opened a major investigation into graft in the police department. One day, Hoyne's investigators walked into police headquarters and, before anyone could get a legal order to stop them, removed a wide variety of books and records. Seriously worried about this invasion of city property, Thompson immediately responded by placing police officers on guard at city hall to prevent further seizures. Thompson complained bitterly that Hoyne had overstepped his office and predicted that the raid on police headquarters would cost the state's attorney fifty thousand votes at election time. Not deterred by Hoyne's politically motivated actions, Thompson continued in his program aimed at eliminating the pesky vice squad and the unwanted office of Second Deputy Superintendent by discharging Morals Inspector Francis D. Hanna. The *Tribune* bluntly publicized its irritation with the dueling between the mayor and state's attorney over securing popular support by editorializing "A Plague on Both of Your Houses."[20]

"Who got the money?" publicly asked State's Attorney Hoyne concerning the discovery by his investigators of a private club that served as a graft collection tool for ex-Mayor Harrison's campaign fund. An investigation had found that the Sportsman's Club, a Republican organization, was used to shake down saloon owners, brothel keepers, slot machine manufacturers and distributors, gambling house operators, and prominent citizens. Each member paid $100 for a life membership. Club solicitors had suggested to potential members that Mayor Thompson was personally interested in the club, meaning that members could expect to obtain special favors from the mayor's office.

An assistant state's attorney and a team of investigators raided the club's offices and grabbed all the books and records. Looking through the books, the state's attorney's men found that among the club's life members were a slot machine manufacturer, saloon owners, gambling operators, and such notables

as James Colosimo, Mayor William Thompson, Police Chief Charles C.
Healey, his buddy, Police Capt. Morgan Collins, and William H. Luthardt,
Healey's secretary. Hoyne announced that between $100,000 and $140,000
had been collected by the club's solicitors, yet the club had numerous debts
and unpaid court judgments. In fact, Hoyne said, the club existed only on
paper; there were no meetings and no activities. Hoyne presented evidence to
the grand jury showing that the club, known to local politicians as "Mayor
Thompson's club," was merely a "blind for getting gambling graft and shaking
down prominent citizens."[21]

While the investigation of municipal graft was in progress, Rev. W. H.
Pierce described Chicago's First Ward as, "The most unsanitary, intemperate,
illiterate, uncivic and immoral ward in the world" on October 5, 1916, in an
address at the Rock River Conference of the Methodist Episcopal Church.
The clergyman based his remarks on a survey conducted by thirty social workers who had scoured the infamous ward. Pierce said that among the most evil
establishments in the ward were Colosimo's Café, Alderman Kenna's Workingman's Exchange and Freiberg's Dance Hall operated by Ike Bloom. Pierce
said: "There are 852 saloons—one to every sixty persons. There are thirty-
three dance halls, nearly all of them connected with saloons; 99 poolrooms; 25
billiard halls; 32 theaters; 22 movies and burlesque shows; 20 bowling alleys;
10 museums and arcades. We counted a total of 1,117 destructive forces and
53 constructive forces."[22]

On October 23, 1916, "CHIEF HEALEY INDICTED" screamed the
headlines across the front pages of the Chicago newspapers. Healey had been
indicted on findings of malfeasance and conspiracy by the Cook County grand
jury. The charges included permitting saloons to be open on Sunday and to
sell liquor after 1 a.m., and allowing slot machines, gambling joints, brothels,
and street prostitutes to operate. Also indicted were Healey's secretary,
William Luthardt, and Charles T. Essig, downtown gambler and organizer of
the Sportsman's Club.[23]

Standing by his appointee, Mayor Thompson scoffed at the indictments.
He said, "The chief has a clean bill of health as far as I am concerned."
Thompson announced that he would not suspend Healey pending his trial.
He lashed out at State's Attorney Hoyne for publicity-motivated actions and
roundly criticized the indictments.[24]

Showing little fear of the mayor's unsubstantiated statements, Hoyne
pledged that he would urge the grand jury to continue investigating graft in
city hall and in the police department.[25] The state's attorney then announced
he had uncovered new and more disturbing problems involving Healey. On
January 8, 1917 state's attorney's investigators arrested four men in a raid on a
so-called payoff office in a building on Dearborn Street. The men were Police

Lt. Augustus M. White, well-known fixer Tom Costello, brothel operator Mike "de Pike" Heitler, and bail bondsman W. R. "Billy" Skidmore. When the raiders entered the room, the four men were dividing money collected from vice and gambling resorts into several piles. Unknown to the counters, the money included marked bills that had been added to the protection money.

The raid was the culmination of a supersecret, yearlong, undercover investigation conducted personally by Edward J. Fleming, secretary to State's Attorney Hoyne. Fixer Costello, for personal reasons, had agreed to work with Fleming in what today would be termed a sting operation. After the arrests Costello and White were grilled hard by the state's attorney's investigators. Both confessed that they were part of a graft and corruption ring that protected saloons, gambling, and vice resorts in the West Side red-light district along Lake Street. Costello admitted that he was head of the ring and said the members included Heitler and Skidmore. City hall insiders whispered that in return for their testimony Costello and White had received promises of immunity from prosecution.[26]

Colosimo soon learned he also was to be named in this investigation. Costello told Fleming that he personally had collected protection money from Colosimo and delivered it to Police Chief Healey's home. The seized records from the raid showed that Colosimo had paid one hundred dollars a month in protection money from October 1915 to December 1916. The records also showed that Torrio had paid three hundred dollars a month from June 1916 through September 1916. Hoyne said that Healey "has been nailed hard and fast as head of the vice-graft ring which levied tribute on the underworld of the West Side." In a subsequent indictment Healey was charged with accepting graft from Costello to protect the vice operations of Colosimo, Torrio, and others.[27] Costello's most significant revelations were those that described his personal contact and involvement with former Chief Healey. Costello said that he had gone to Healey's home with protection money on the average of three times a week during the past year. These visits continued during the period that he worked undercover with Fleming. When Fleming learned about the visits, he had his investigators place Healey's home under surveillance. They had watched as Costello made his visits. For good measure, Fleming had placed a tap on the chief's phone. Fleming had done his work well. After the case had been well tried in the newspapers, Healey resigned in disgrace in December.

State's Attorney Hoyne was riding high in public opinion and newspaper editorials due to his shutting the Levee *and* indicting Chief Healey. He had developed a reputation for being a vice scourge.[28] When election time came in November 1916, Hoyne easily won reelection to state's attorney for a second term.

Mayor Thompson began scrambling to rebuild his tarred reputation. On January 11, 1917, he appointed fifty-five-year-old Herman F. Schuettler as Chicago's police chief. After working as a conductor on the Larrabee Street horse-car line, Schuettler became a Chicago patrolman in June 1882. Through thirty-four years of service, he advanced from patrolman to first deputy superintendent. Schuettler had a reputation for being very strict in his enforcement of the vice laws. These actions frequently caused problems for his superiors, especially when he suppressed lawlessness that they had ignored. Ben Hecht, writing for the *Daily News*, reported that "Wooden Shoes" Schuettler "was a tall, bulky, implacable enemy of crime, honest as the day and courageous as the lion."[29]

Thompson, trying desperately to take back the initiative, directed his new chief to "clean out immediately the corruption in all ranks of the department." Thompson told Schuettler: "Your authority over the department is absolute and complete and there are no curbs, limitations or restrictions, except as imposed by law, upon your power or purpose to administer impartially the police system of this city to the best of your ability and for the lawful protection of the people. No person is authorized to come to you as representing me, to ask for any favor or prestige from the police department, nor shall I grant any myself."[30]

Due to a wide variety of legal maneuvers designed to delay the case, the Healey trial did not get under way until December 1917. Healey predicted, "The production of evidence will establish my innocence so firmly that there will not be a shadow of doubt."

During the trial, Costello testified that he gave $13,900 in protection money to the chief over a fourteen-month period. Costello also revealed on the witness stand that Johnny Torrio was the operator of a chain of resorts in the Levee. Costello said that Torrio had been referred to him by Captain Smith, who at that time headed the Twenty-second Street District Station. In their first meeting, Torrio told Costello that Smith had said that Costello was on friendly terms with Chief Healey and the Committee of Fifteen. Torrio told Costello that he wanted protection from police interference for his own places and those of several others. Costello explained that arrangements were made for Torrio to give protection money to Costello for Healey. Subsequently, Torrio gave Costello six envelopes each month containing money for Healey. The money in five of the envelopes came from resorts and saloons in the First Ward. Torrio told Costello that the sixth envelope would be empty because he couldn't be expected to collect money from other resorts and also pay for protection for his places. Costello testified that after three payments Chief Healey told Costello to stop accepting the payments from Torrio because there were too many complaints against the establishments involved.

Healey had told Costello that they were "too raw," and he could no longer shield the places from police raids. Costello told Torrio what Healey had said, and the payments stopped.[31]

Continuing his testimony, Costello admitted that he had known Jim Colosimo for about a year. Costello said he met Colosimo through a Levee character named Sam Rothschild. One day in October 1915, Costello had a visit from Rothschild, who said he had been sent by Colosimo. Rothschild said that Colosimo had been paying graft to the police from the local district, but they were unable to protect him when heat came down from headquarters. In addition to stopping the "heat from downtown," Colosimo wanted the police-women who had been watching his place removed and the district officers to go easy on him. Costello testified that he had discussed this matter with Chief Healey who agreed to take money from Colosimo. Costello began collecting one hundred dollars a month from Colosimo for Healey.[32]

The heads of the Republican Party in Chicago were very concerned with the trial. They were planning to run Thompson for reelection, but if his police chief was convicted, voters might shift to the other candidate. To the dismay of the Republicans, State's Attorney Hoyne announced that he was going to run for mayor in the next election. The Republican political bosses in the aptly described smoke-filled room decided that it was crucial to the Republican strategy that Healey be found not guilty.

The famous defense attorney Clarence Darrow was retained to represent Healey. Throughout the trial Hoyne's assistant state's attorneys fought hard. Among their evidence were fourteen hundred wiretap conversations between Chief Healey and Costello and others. Darrow countered by saying his client was old, weary, and feeble and, "I wouldn't make him chief of police. This man is a child in the hands of Costello."[33] Darrow's fiery eloquence and courtroom legerdemain were able to make the difference.[34]

After an eight-week trial the jury found Healey not guilty. The jury felt that the fixer Costello was not truthful, and they disregarded his entire testimony. The jury did not even believe the conversations in the wiretaps. Hoyne said he would proceed sometime later with the remaining indictments, but he never took action on these matters again.[35]

Part Three

CHICAGO—CITY OF FALLEN DREAMS

Chapter Twenty-Seven

METAMORPHOSIS OF BIG JIM

Vice Lord to Restaurateur

1917

The most important criminal in Chicago during the decade which followed Wayman's raids on the South Side was Big Jim Colosimo, who ruled the underworld for a longer period than any other one man in the history of the city. He was one of the few vice moguls who made more money after the Levee was closed than before. His receipts from the innumerable immoral enterprises which he either owned or controlled were conservatively estimated at fifty thousand dollars a month for some eight years.[1]

— Herbert Asbury, *Gem of the Prairie*

Long before Colosimo, a dictator in the Everleigh days, came into power he was noted for popularizing quaint expressions. "Betsy," meaning a revolver, was one of these, and his "Remember the Maine," which meant to watch your step, were picked up far and wide.[2]

— Charles Washburn, *Come into My Parlor*

After years of hard work in the Levee, Colosimo had transcended the role of vice lord. Colosimo now had the largest and strongest group of hoodlums, racketeers, and gangsters in Chicago. The gang was multi-ethnic with Italian, Irish, Jewish, and Greek members.[3] His interests in syndicated prostitution, saloons, gambling, and roadhouses were so vast that a few years later Torrio and Al Capone would use Colosimo's organization and operations as the foundation on which they would build the Chicago Outfit.[4]

But Jim made a decision to seek something more. It may have been a need for social acceptance or his boundless energy driving him to new horizons. He began to straddle two worlds—the underworld and the upper crust.

Jim had developed a full life in the underworld, the Italian immigrant community, and in the battleground of ward politics. He had been a friend to many of the famed madams of the district. He knew Minna and Ada Everleigh personally. The sisters called on him when they had problems with the police or with the protection-payoff plan. He enjoyed cooking Italian food. On Sunday evenings he sometimes arrived at the Everleigh Club with his arms full of groceries for a spaghetti dinner for the sisters and some of their close friends. He would take over the kitchen and cook the entire meal.[5]

Colosimo was a colorful and respected figure. Some of the immigrants in the Italian community assumed that he was the head of the Mafia in Chicago. They were wrong; he was not. Jim was born on mainland Italy, not Sicily, which automatically excluded him as a Mafia member. Whether the Sicilian Mafia even existed in Chicago is debatable.[6] While not a sinister *mafioso*, he was a *padrone* in the South Side Italian community.

Each year large numbers of young Italian immigrants arrived in Chicago. Few could speak English. Colosimo functioned as a padrone for many of these new arrivals. He acted as an employment agency and found jobs for these hardy and willing, but unskilled, workers in the construction business. The immigrants paid a finder's fee of from one dollar to fifteen dollars to Colosimo for their jobs. In some cases, even after starting their new jobs they continued to pay him a weekly or monthly fee out of their salaries. For those arrivals that did not have decent housing he found low-cost living accommodations and even arranged for a neighborhood grocery to provide food on credit. These greenhorns paid a higher cost for their rent and groceries, with part of the markup going to Colosimo. He connected these young wage earners with private Italian bankers who opened accounts from which they could send money back to their families in Italy. Naturally the private Italian bankers later showed their appreciation to Colosimo.[7]

Historian Humbert S. Nelli wrote in *Italians and Chicago, 1880–1930* that James Colosimo was the most powerful and influential Italian in city politics. Nelli said that Colosimo was very successful in his widespread and lucrative vice operations that were unequaled in any Italian community in the eastern United States, making six hundred thousand dollars a year from prostitution and gambling. Nelli said that Big Jim was the first Italian in Chicago to take full advantage of the link between vice and politics.

Despite Colosimo's political influence in the First Ward and the frequent references made by the newspapers and the politicians to the Italian vote in the ward, the Italians never constituted a majority of the voters in the ward.[8] Colosimo was able through shrewdness and cunning to weld this minority vote into the main electoral force. He never sought public office and found no problem with Irish politicians who helped to elect their own candidates to positions in city government. He could be counted on to provide money for their campaign funds and votes at election time. In return he received immunity from arrest and protection from vice crackdowns.

Now that he had successfully used his personality, drive, and muscle to become a vice lord, Jim wanted to move up the social ladder. Helping him become socially acceptable was his lifelong friend and personal attorney Rocco De Stefano. Both had lived in a neighborhood infested with crime, saloons, gambling, and prostitution. Both had grown up in the household of Rocco's parents, the highly ethical Emilio and very religious Emmanuela; but they chose different paths. Rocco studied diligently in school and in 1898 became a lawyer. Two years later he married Raffela, with whom he had three children. He developed social graces and social acceptance and became a leader in the Italian community, making many contributions to Italian organizations and charities. Jim chose a route that led him to crime and vice; but the influence of living in the De Stefano household and Rocco's guidance gave Jim excellent preparation for becoming a gentleman.

The first visible sign of Jim's moving above the vice and criminal world was his increased attention to his restaurant and nightclub. He spent considerable money to improve its appearance and allocated more time to be on the premises. Even though he supervised the entire operation, whenever he could Jim took time to personally greet patrons as they entered. He toned down his loud basso voice and hired a tutor to teach him to speak correct English.[9] He became accepted and recognized by wealthy patrons and by singers and conductors from the opera world. Through his interest in boxing, he developed friends not only in the boxing world but in the newspaper business—ranging from local sports reporters to New York columnists. If there was a big fight scheduled in an East Coast city, he would organize a party of friends, pay for their train ride, and rent hotel rooms and purchase ringside tickets for the entire group.

Colosimo began to dress better. Always an imposing figure, he now pomaded his black moustache and dark black hair. He wore two- and three-piece white suits in the summers and tasteful, checked suits in the winter. His attire was accented by gold cufflinks, watches, and rings. He augmented them with diamond rings, stickpins, buckles on his suspenders and garters, and a diamond horseshoe on his vest. He sometimes carried a small chamois bag of diamonds. He had a uniformed chauffeur and a big, shiny car.

From living in the De Stefano home many years earlier, Colosimo had developed an appreciation of opera. He attended as many performances of the Chicago Opera Company as he could and sometimes took as many as thirty associates with him. When a traveling opera company was playing in Chicago, many of the singers, musicians and even the maestro himself would dine at Colosimo's Café. Jim made trips to New York to attend the Metropolitan Opera and had numerous personal friends in the opera business, from singers to conductors to impresarios. Occasionally he made trips across the Atlantic Ocean to enjoy operatic production. in his homeland.

Jim also loved to gamble. Between 1910 and 1920 he made many trips to the casinos in West Baden Springs and French Lick, Indiana. These two tiny towns in Orange County at the bottom of the Hoosier state were home to more than a dozen casinos and gambling joints. The most notable were the plush casinos at the West Baden Springs Hotel and the French Lick Springs Hotel that attracted gamblers, sporting figures, racehorse owners, politicians, and entertainers from Chicago, Springfield, Louisville, and Cincinnati. He mingled easily with the gamblers and the other players at the tables of chance.

Jim's favorite was the West Baden Springs Hotel; it hosted the most popular casino in the area. The hotel was of the highest caliber, with every possible service and amenity, including electric lights in every room and a wide variety of sport and health activities. The casino occupied a large room in the center of the first floor with roulette, faro, craps, and stud and draw poker. The hotel had a one-of-a-kind, automated miniature racetrack in a tent adjacent to the main building with mechanical entrants, six numbered horses, and a mule named Orphan Boy. A crank and gear apparatus activated the race while the customers placed their bets. Gambling on the racehorses was run by the casino with the winner paying five to one, place paying two to one, and show even. The track provided a pleasant diversion from the gambling tables inside.

Connecting the West Baden Springs and French Lick Springs hotels was a tree-lined, one-mile road frequented by grifters and sharpies who offered the shell game and other attractive gambling diversions. Sometimes groups of gentlemen strolling along the shady walk between the two hotels would stop to watch the games and end up losing their ready cash. In the business districts of the two towns were several saloons where visitors could lose their money to crooked gamblers.[10]

When Jim visited the West Baden Springs Hotel to gamble, he usually brought along several male friends. On occasion he brought his wife, Victoria. Chicago Sgt. William Norton, who was not averse to taking a shot at the rolling dice himself, remembered that he once observed Victoria as she busied herself in a unique activity near the hotel—pistol shooting. She lined empty bottles in a row and would blow them apart, one after another. Norton said that, back in Chicago, Victoria had frequented shooting galleries at the amusement parks in the city and suburbs.

On one of his early trips to southern Indiana, Colosimo, accompanied by two men, knocked on the door of the home of Marcus Lafe Prow. Prow was the night manager of the West Baden Springs Hotel, who also handled convention bookings. Because night had fallen, Prow cautiously opened the door and suspiciously eyed the three men. Big Jim said hello and named a man in Chicago who was a mutual friend. Jim told Prow that the mutual friend had said that Prow could get persons into the hotel quietly and unannounced. Colosimo handed Prow an envelope containing a large sum of cash. Prow took the three men to the hotel's side entrance, and they all rode in the service elevator to the top floor. Prow put them in spacious rooms looking out on the formal gardens on the front of the hotel. He kept the rooms on either side vacant during Jim's stay. The mutual friend was the chief of police of Chicago, who knew Prow well because the chief had made arrangements at the hotel for police conventions. After Colosimo's first visit he always booked his reservations with Prow. Jim told friends, "Lafe made sure everything was done right." Prow would place him and his party on the top floor and ensure that no other guests were nearby. Jim would generously tip him at the end of each visit. [11]

During one visit, Jim discovered that Prow was having trouble getting his car to start. He purchased a more dependable car as a present. The pair developed a friendship that took them on fishing and camping trips together. Whenever Jim came to West Baden, he would have at least one dinner at Prow's home. One year at Christmas time, Jim was invited to the Prow family dinner. Jim came with a big toy truck and a scooter for Prow's two sons and left a large amount of money under his plate as a Christmas gift to the family. Despite the generosity on Jim's part, Prow's grandmother, who was over for the holiday, eyed Jim with great suspicion during the festive meal because she presumed he was a Chicago gangster. [12]

While Jim was moving upward in the social world, war had come to America. He registered for the draft on September 12, 1918. Although the war was a time of great sacrifice for American soldiers and their families, Colosimo made more money then ever before. The workers in the war factories throughout Chicago and Cook County and the servicemen from Great Lakes Naval Base and Fort Sheridan were drinking in Colosimo's saloons, gambling in his joints, and whoring in his resorts.

Overall, Colosimo was living a wonderful life. Everything was working out well for him except for one major issue involving two women—his wife and a lady friend, a problem that soon would be resolved with tragic consequences.

Chapter Twenty-Eight

COLOSIMO'S CAFÉ

Great Food, Fine Wine, and Gambling

1918–1919

Colosimo's 2132 Wabash Avenue / Table d'hote dinner between six and nine every evening, seventy-five cents / Italian Serenade Quartette Orchestra Public Dancing / Finest Restaurant in the United States.[1]

— Advertisement, *Chicago Tribune*

I saw several state legislators. There were a few I recognized as state senators of former years. I piped some men who are 'way up in the blue book. There were more prominent lawyers than I could count, the son of one owner of a department store in the Loop, half of the opera company and a score of the best known Loop-hounds.[2]

— Report by a detective sergeant of an investigation of Colosimo's Café

In the early 1900s Jim had opened a café at Armour and Archer. The restaurant did well and was highly regarded in the Italian community, but the brothels and crib houses next door were scaring away the type of clientele he craved. After some searching Colosimo found a another site for a restaurant at the northeast end of the Levee adjacent to the red-light district on the west side of Wabash Avenue, a half block south of Twenty-second Street. It was a dilapidated, run-down building, which for more than eighty years had been the site of a series of failed restaurants.[3] Jim rented the entire building. He had it cleaned, painted, and outfitted with new restaurant furnishings and equipment. By 1913 he was ready to open. He secured a listing in the *City Directory* as the operator of Colosimo's Café at 2128 S. Wabash Avenue.[4]

Several of the newspapers took Colosimo's efforts of gentrification seriously. In July 1914 a Chicago paper for the first time depicted Colosimo not as a vice lord but as the owner of a grand restaurant at 2128 S. Wabash Avenue. The article described the restaurant as lavish with a striped awning extending from the curb to the front door and matching awnings above the second- and third-floor windows.[5] At the same time, the *Tribune*, apparently not awed by the newly refined owner or by the lavishly redecorated restaurant, ran an article stating that Jim was "a power in the vice district and a power in the secret council of Sicilian societies. More than once men suspected in connection with gunfights in Little Italy have been traced to the neighborhood of Colosimo's old resort [Colosimo's Café]."[6]

After less than a year of operating the new restaurant, Jim decided to purchase the building. On February 4, 1914, George A. Gilbert and his wife, Carrie, conveyed the title for 2128 S. Wabash Avenue to Jim's father, Luigi, and Torrio's mother, Maria Caputo. The next day, Luigi sold his one-half interest in the property to his son. On the same day, Maria Caputo sold her half to her son. The full title was then transferred to family friend Mary Aducci and her husband, who later transferred a half interest to Rocco De Stefano. These legal transactions were fictions presumably made on the advice of lawyer De Stefano in order to hide the true owner, avoid civil judgments that might be filed against Colosimo, and to foil any attempts by the state's attorney to seize the property.

Along with purchasing the property, Jim opened a second dining room in the north end of the building. The new space had a dance floor with room for a band and singers to perform. He hired Antonio Caesarino, a well-respected Italian chef, to head the kitchen staff. Unhappily, the shooting of Birns took place in the Levee shortly after the restaurant's remodeling and grand opening. State's Attorney Hoyne was so convinced of Jim's culpability in the calamitous battle that on July 21, 1914, he ordered the arrest of Colosimo and the closing of the restaurant. Simultaneously the mayor revoked the liquor license. Rather than bring the matter into court, Colosimo, on the advice of De Stefano, accepted the revocation order.

Three months later, when the heat had died down, Colosimo's head waiter Paul Bergamini took out a new license in his name and Colosimo's Café reopened. For the rest of Jim's short life, the café operated without interruption despite liquor being sold after the 1 a.m. closing time every night and gambling taking place on the second floor whenever there were sporting men, and sometimes betting women, in the cafe.

The sidewalk in front of the restaurant was dark, with only a single streetlight, but a uniformed policeman from the Twenty-second Street District Station was stationed nearby to quiet disturbances and turn away drunks.

Colosimo's Café was divided into two rooms—one south at 2126 S. Wabash Avenue and a connected room to the north at 2128 S. Wabash Avenue. Inside the front door there was a small checkroom to the right for top hats, derbies, canes, camel-hair coats, and ladies' furs and wraps. To the left a tiny booth held a black candle-stick phone. The southernmost room was the original saloon and held a long, polished mahogany bar and highly decorated back bar with a fancy etched glass mirror. Usually used for more casual dining, the room was crowded with twenty-nine small tables covered by white cloths and lighted by rose and gold ceiling lamps that ran down the center of the room. The northernmost room was large and rectangular with forty-two tables crowded close together giving a sense of intimacy. The walls were covered in green velvet adorned with tapestries woven in Italy that were hung between gilded mirrors and paintings of pastoral scenes. Crystal chandeliers dropped from a ceiling that was painted to resemble a blue sky with fleecy clouds and lightly clad seraphim and cherubim. In front of a stage with a grand piano was a dance floor that could be lifted and lowered hydraulically. Up a flight of stairs was the second floor with a room used for high-stakes gambling.[7]

Jim was proud of the kitchen's old-country Italian cooking. One of the house specialties was spaghetti ala Caruso made with rich meat sauce and cheese-filled ravioli. Jim had imported thousands of bottles of strong red Italian wine and a variety of large cheese wheels. *Chicago Daily News* columnist Ben Hecht, a frequent diner who later would coauthor the play *The Front Page*, wrote that he particularly enjoyed the wide variety of imported cheese.[8]

The main room featured musical entertainment nightly. Initially, a small band played honky-tonk songs, and the show featured a comedian and a chorus line of scantily clad dancers. The music and dancing started in the early evening, but the real festivities did not begin until after midnight. Many nights the restaurant and nightclub ran until dawn. Jim would circulate through the dining room with a long, black cigar clenched between his teeth. He was especially cordial to the reporters and journalists who were attracted by free meals and drinks. The free-loading newspapermen repaying the favor spread the word of the Italian cuisine and the high-class entertainment. The reputation of what the *Tribune* had disparagingly called a "spaghetti joint" reached as far as Manhattan, and many visitors to Chicago headed to Colosimo's Café because of its fame as the best place in town for a good time and a fine meal.

One attraction of the café in its early years was the opportunity for slummers to mix in complete safety with criminals, madams, gamblers, and crooked politicians. For the men from the Gold Coast it was an opportunity to show their masculinity without any risk. For the society women the café afforded a place to be a bit naughty. As the restaurant became more fashionable, the brothel operators and madams were replaced by wealthy businessmen, city and county officials, state representatives, state senators, police captains, newspaper reporters, New York columnists, and visitors from across the United States and Europe.

In 1916 Colosimo raised the level of the entertainment to fit the more upscale clientele. The hotsy-totsy music, comedians with risqué jokes, and lightly clad dancers were dropped. Each night after the theater, the wealthy *haut monde* directed their chauffeured limousines to Colosimo's Café. Inside they enjoyed a fine Italian meal, lit their cigarettes and cigars, and sat back to enjoy a full orchestra with classy singers. The orchestra played prologues and arias from operas by Verdi and Puccini. This new type of show attracted the most renowned artists of the era, such as Italian opera singer Titta Ruffo, generally regarded as the greatest baritone of his generation.

One evening, Alderman John H. Lyle,[9] who ran unsuccessfully against Big Bill Thompson in the Republican mayoral primary in 1931, was treating the visiting attorney general of Arizona to dinner at Colosimo's Café. Because Lyle was an opera fan, Colosimo introduced the attorney general to Enrico Caruso, who happened to be in the café that evening. Caruso commented to Lyle, "You are very young. In Italy, our senators are older."[10]

By 1918 Colosimo's Café was one of the most important restaurants in Chicago. Famed *Tribune* columnist, sports writer, and frequent customer Ring W. Lardner in his column "In the Wake of the News," described how an unemployed but hopeful comedian believed that he would become a success if he could appear at Colosimo's Café.[11] In the story, the comedian secured a tryout for the floor show but was rejected.[12] In July 1919 when soprano Mabel Garrison sang selections from *Lucia di Lammermoor* at the Ravinia music theater, the "Society and Entertainment" column in the *Tribune* reported that her music "excites them all from Colosimo's to the Metropolitan Opera House."[13]

At the peak of its popularity the restaurant drew large crowds. The food was epicurean, the liquor aged and mellow, and the wines the best vintages of Italy and France. The music, dancing, and cabaret provided a sparkle throughout the rose-and-gold-hued room. Each night the restaurant was filled to capacity. Famous conductors and opera and classical music singers ate at Colosimo's whenever they were in town.[14] Customers included Clarence Darrow, criminal defense attorney; Marshall Field, department store owner; Potter Palmer, Prairie Avenue businessman and hotel owner; and scores of Lake Shore Drive millionaires, Gold Coast bluebloods, and North Shore socialites.

In his true-crime book on Chicago gangsters, *One Way Ride*, Chicago newspaperman and editor Walter Burns wrote a colorful paean describing the café:

> Millionaires sat down with the leaders of sawed-off shotgun vendettas. Women of society and courtesans ogled one another, surprised to discover how little difference there was to the naked eye between the Lake Shore Drive lady and the siren of 22nd Street. College boys and debutantes out for a lark danced with stick-up sheiks and their tipsy broads.
>
> All kinds of people. . . . The state's attorney and the chief of police gossiping over their chops. . . . The mayor and a judge of the Criminal Court with their heads together over steins of beer. . . . A banker stealing glances over his wife's shoulder at a madam of the half-world surrounded by her stable of bedizened beauties. . . . A group of young blades from the Gold Coast, bleary eyed and noisy, turning down highballs.
>
> Dago Mike Carrozzo and Vincent Cosmano sipping wine with the air of connoisseurs. . . . Bathhouse John Coughlin expositing on the beauty of his latest song to Hinky Dink Kenna. . . . Enrico Caruso, Titta Ruffo, Luisa Tetrazzini, and Amelita Galli-Curci fribbling gaily over spaghetti. . . . Mike de Pike Heitler, Monkey Face Charles Genkler, Loving Putty Anixter and Izzy the Rat Buchowsky guzzling hilariously. . . . Flo Ziegfeld, Morris Gest, George White, Julian Eltinge and George M. Cohan tippling sedately. . . . Gentleman Jim Corbett telling John McCormack how to put old John L. down for the count. . . . George Ade with a serious mien, and Ring Lardner looking abysmally solemn . . . Dean O'Banion, florist and gunman, with a gardenia in his buttonhole. . . . Angelo Genna of the bad Gennas, music lover and terrorist, catching the eye of the great Caruso across the tables and lifting a wineglass to his health. . . . Big Tim Murphy towering among his Italian gunmen, a picture of conviviality, his jovial, rubicund face all smiles. . . . All kinds of people.
>
> Among the tables strolled Big Jim Colosimo, proprietor and Bad Lands overlord, immaculate in his tuxedo, a powerfully built man as handsome as a brigand of romance, hair and drooping mustache as black as night, a face as hard and cold and white as marble, for all his show of geniality and great somber dark eyes that seemed to hint of tragic secrets.[15]

A special feature of Colosimo's Café that apparently was never investigated by the police and seemingly was unnoticed by the state's attorney was the gambling that took place on the second floor. This operation offered craps, card games, faro, and chuck-a-luck.[16] Colosimo served as banker for the gambling. Drawing from the one-thousand-dollar notes in his bulging billfold he made loans to known customers who had lost their cash at the tables.[17] In a divorce proceeding in Superior Court Judge Davis's courtroom in February 1920, a deposition from Lillian Swanson, a former maid in the employ of socialites Maj. Christopher R. Hoyme and his wife Mrs. Vera Bowker Hoyme, was filed. Miss Swanson stated that Mrs. Hoyme had told the maid an account of one night when she and seven others were shooting craps at 4 a.m. in Colosimo's. Many of the famous, wealthy, and powerful patrons who had dined on the first-floor found their way upstairs to the gambling tables.

Chapter Twenty-Nine

SINGING ANGEL

Dale Winter

1917–1919

Her repertoire included "Mighty Lak a Rose," "I Dreamt I Dwelled in Marble Halls," "O Sole Mio," "My Wild Irish Rose," "Drink to Me Only with Thine Eyes," and "Santa Lucia." She never sang popular songs, novelty songs or ragtime.[1]

— Chicago Herald and Examiner

Sipping their champagne, the crème de la crème of the city watched the Colosimo Café floor show with keen anticipation. They knew that the talented singers and attractive dancers were but a prelude. Drinking, gossiping and glancing about the room while an entertainer weaves between the tables and sings patrons' favorite songs for dollar tips, everyone waited. Then, the room darkened and a hush fell over the crowd. A single spotlight snapped on a beautiful, slender, young woman standing demurely next to the grand piano. She had poise, presence, and grace. The pale beauty of her face and neck and her lovely hands shimmered in the light. Softly the piano began and Dale Winter's mellifluous trill filled the room. No waiter was foolish enough to serve, no bus boy so stupid as to clear a table. No sounds from the dining room challenged Dale's sweet soprano. From wistful beauty to fortissimo Dale liberated her audience from the brassiness of the Levee and the bustle of the big city. The piano music ended. Dale's voice trailed off to thunderous applause. After one more song that lifted the patrons to a standing ovation, Dale Winter, demurely and graciously left the stage.

In November 1891, baby girl Dale B. Winters was born near Columbus, Ohio, to Franklin and Estelle Mae (Zeigler) Winters. Dale's father died when she was five, and soon after that her only sibling, eleven-year-old brother Clyde, passed away. Dale's mother married her first husband's younger brother, William B. Winters. In 1900, the family moved to Paulding, Ohio. William obtained work as a schoolteacher. Dale entered high school and sang in the glee club. After Dale's graduation the Winters moved back to Columbus. There, Dale began to pursue a musical career. When she was nineteen, the 1910 U.S. Census listed her occupation as "musician in opera house."

Estelle Winters, hoping to find opportunities for her daughter, took Dale to New York for audition calls. Producer George Lederer was putting together a road company of his hit operetta *Madame Sherr* that featured the popular song "Every Little Movement Has a Meaning All Its Own." Lederer selected Dale for the ingénue role. When rehearsals were finished and the touring company hit the road, Estelle went along to chaperone her daughter. The tour ended in San Francisco, so Dale and a friend developed a song-and-dance routine. The pair convinced a traveling vaudeville company to take them on the Orpheum circuit. Unfortunately, when the company went to Australia it fell flat. Dale and her mother were unexpectedly impecunious and stranded far from America. Kindly theatrical men loaned the abandoned pair money to sail back to San Francisco.[2] Along the way Dale dropped the "s" from her last name.

Finding no jobs available in California, Dale and her mother left to seek employment in the Midwest. In the summer of 1915, mother and daughter moved to Grand Rapids, Michigan. One day Dale met violinist Arthur Fabri, who was playing in the café of the Livingstone Hotel. Although they became good friends, in September Fabri left Grand Rapids for an offer of a job in Chicago with the house band at Colosimo's Café. Still seeking employment, Dale signed with an agent who promised her a role with a newly organized light-opera company that was forming in Chicago. When Estelle and her daughter got to Chicago they learned that the company had disbanded without giving a single performance.

One day Fabri was walking through the Loop looking for a new suit when he chanced to see his former acquaintance Dale. They stopped to talk, and Dale admitted to being broke. Fabri gave her money for some presentable clothes and arranged an audition for Dale at Colosimo's Café. At twenty-four Dale had developed into a very attractive woman with a peaches-and-cream complexion and wide blue eyes. When Fabri brought Dale to the restaurant, Jim came out of his office and personally auditioned her. He said he liked her beauty, charm, and voice. He offered thirty-five dollars a week. Fabri, knowing the sorry state of Dale's finances, interceded and convinced Jim that Dale was worth forty dollars a week. Dale began singing several nights a week in front of the four-piece orchestra led by Fabri. The violinist believed that Dale had a great natural tone and would profit from singing lessons, so he arranged for vocal training.

After several weeks of listening to Dale's singing at the café, Colosimo took a chance and featured her in the floor show at his Arrowhead Inn in Burnham. Dale sang lyric soprano in a show titled *From Grand Opera to Ragtime*. Sharing the bill with Dale were opera tenor Isadoro Prati, lyric tenor Frank Corlett, Parisian soubrette Mae Levene, and Kitty Hart, known as the queen of ragtime. Accompanying the singers was pianist Lester Hoetley. Other music was provided by George Bennett's Jazz Band. The show was a success, and Colosimo increased Dale's salary. She was now able to provide support for her mother and pay the rent on their apartment.

When the show at the Arrowhead Inn finished its run, Colosimo brought Dale back to the café. Big Jim began to take an interest in Dale and her career. He took over the payment for her singing lessons and convinced his close friend Cleofonte Campanini, conductor of the Chicago Opera Company, to find a scholarship for her to the Chicago Musical College. At the college she studied under Ruffo, Francesco Daddi, and Maestro Giacomo Spadoni, director of the Chicago Opera Company. Dale began to appear five nights a week at the café singing ballads and opera selections while wearing a stunning white gown.

In January 1917, Dale gave a special performance at the Garrick Theater. Rev. Dr. John P. Bushingham, pastor of the South Park Avenue Methodist Episcopal church, and his wife attended the show. They were so impressed with Dale that they asked her to sing at the church the following week. On Sunday evening, January 21, Dale sang "The Song of My Soul," "One Fine Day," and an aria from *Madame Butterfly*. The congregation loved her, but in the wee hours of Monday morning Bushingham was awakened by a phone call from a reporter for the *Chicago Herald*. The reporter informed the clergyman that Dale Winter was a cabaret singer at Colosimo's Café.

Reverend Bushingham said that he found that hard to believe because "she had the image of goodness written on her face. To every outward evidence she is a wonderful woman who we would receive into our congregation."[3]

Monday afternoon the *Herald* carried an exclusive story describing the nightclub singer's appearance at the church. The following week, Bushingham decided to give a sermon to his congregation in which he would discuss the message in John 8:7, "He that is without sin among you, let him first cast a stone at her."[4] Despite his plans certain members of the congregation indicated that they were adamant in their opposition to Dale's singing in their church.[5] Undaunted by the complaints from his flock, Pastor Bushingham planned to have Dale sing after the formal close of the service. He intended to conclude the service with the words, "The congregation is dismissed. All those desiring to remain for the concert will be welcome."[6]

When Dale learned of the concerns of the church congregation, she decided to cancel her appearance. She said: "Far be it from me to cause any of the elect to leave their comfortable pews to avoid hearing a cabaret singer. So I just said 'pooh, pooh' and forgot the whole incident." At the service, Bushingham sadly said, "Miss Winter, whose singing we enjoyed so much last Sunday who was to have been heard tonight, has begged to be excused." Later, Reverend Bushingham told a reporter, "Miss Winter can sing here any time in spite of hot weather or high water."[7]

Instead of appearing at the church, "the girl with the voice of an angel and the face of a goddess" entertained the crowd on that night at Colosimo's Café. Dale's mother explained to a reporter: "She's just the bravest girl in the world. She sings in a cabaret because she is brave enough—daughter enough—to assume a heavy indebtedness caused by months of illness from which I just recovered. She wouldn't have chosen a cabaret if better employment was offered. It didn't, so she accepted what was offered—and I am sure that's very much to her credit."[8]

According to Fabri, by this time he and Dale were dating seriously and planned to get married. Fabri noticed that Colosimo had begun to ask Fabri personal questions about Dale and was going out of his way to spend time with her. It was clear to the entertainers in the show that Colosimo was trying to edge Fabri out of the way. One day, Big Jim asked Fabri if he had seen "my girl." Until then Jim had always referred to Dale as "Fabri's girl." Fabri realized what was happening, and it broke his heart. There was nothing he could do to save his relationship with Dale that wouldn't cost both of them their jobs. Because the situation had become intolerable, a disconsolate Fabri enlisted in the army.[9]

Fabri completed his basic training with a Springfield rifle instead of his trusted violin. While at Camp Mills on Long Island awaiting orders for shipment to France, he obtained leave and returned to Colosimo's for one last chance at trying to win Dale. As Fabri entered the café, he encountered Colosimo's wife, Victoria. She greeted Fabri with, "So they're taking your girl away from you." She laughed sardonically, "Maybe they can fool you, but they can't fool me." Fabri turned, walked out of the restaurant, and never made another attempt to see Dale.[10]

As Jim became more interested in Dale, Victoria sensed the growing romantic attachment between her husband and the young entertainer. Victoria became very unhappy about the relationship. She learned that Jim gave an expensive fur coat to Dale only one day after he had given her a similar coat.

Reportedly, her display of Italian jealousy was a sight to behold. Like Fabri, she found the situation intolerable. She moved out of their house on Vernon Avenue and went to live with a relative in a west suburban town. She claimed that she wanted to be nearer to Mount Carmel Cemetery where her sister was buried. She may well have mourned her departed sister, but she had another reason for her almost daily visits to the cemetery—a monument worker she had met during an earlier visit.[11]

Because of Dale's beauty, many male customers at the café made proposals to her, most for dates and some for marriage. She turned them all away. Even when the offers came from wealthy North Shore bluebloods, Dale always responded with charming but definite "No." Many insiders, especially the reporters who hung out at Colosimo's, believed that Dale and Jim were having a serious romance. When confronted with questions about their relationship, both parties made evasions or denials.

As her singing improved, offers came from the East Coast to place Dale in Broadway productions. Morris Gest, famous producer and son-in-law of David Belasco, personally came to Chicago with an offer for her to sing in a big show he was producing. New York impresario Florenz Ziegfeld, who had launched the careers of Fanny Brice, W. C. Fields, and Eddie Cantor, arrived with a contract for her to appear on Broadway in his highly successful *Follies*. Local promoters and producers made numerous proposals to Dale. The young singer politely turned aside every offer.[12]

Newsman and editor Walter Burns, who personally knew Dale from his frequent visits to the café, wrote lyrically about her:

> Dale Winter sang nightly. A mystery girl with a Mona Lisa smile and a voice of gold, of a delicate lily-like beauty, gentle, quiet, modest. She looked out of place. Who was she? From where did she hail? By what unhappy chance had she been tossed as a professional entertainer into this maelstrom of drunken revelry?
>
> She suggested a nun. A dim religious cloister would have seemed her appropriate background. One could picture her in white purity counting her beads as a member of some holy sisterhood. She neither drank nor smoked. No indelicate word ever passed her lips. No whisper of scandal touched her. Rich roués sought to win her. Flowers, confections, notes appealing for clandestine appointments were her nightly routine. She remained always aloof, distinctly and beautifully in the scene but not of it, enveloped by an aura of innocence and protected, it might seem, by guardian angels.
>
> When, like a shining presence, she arose to sing, garbed in simple, shimmering white, a red rose across her bosom, a hush fell upon the

boisterous hubbub while her voice in the deep silence wove its spell of
dreams. Her song over, a shower of silver pieces clattered about her as
she stood with a cryptic smile and bowed to the clamor of applause. With
her work of the night ended, this Mona Lisa of the Red-lights went home
to her mother.[13]

In 1919, Dale was living with her mother, Estelle, in a rented apartment at
5716 South Parkway in Chicago. Discreetly, Colosimo was seeing her outside
of the café. He bought her fine clothes, expensive jewelry, and costly gifts
while providing her with all the money she needed. She enjoyed horseback
riding, so he bought them both expensive riding outfits and accompanied his
protégée on some of her rides on the bridle paths in Chicago's wooded parks.
He even arranged for a course in etiquette for her. Eventually, he began to
court her publicly. Johnny Torrio, a Roman Catholic, did not approve of such
an open show of infidelity. When Torrio learned that Colosimo planned to
divorce Victoria and marry Dale, he argued against the plan. When Colosimo
refused to listen, Torrio remarked, "Well, it's your funeral."[14]

Chapter Thirty

WARTIME PROHIBITION

1918–1919

Liquor is a menace to patriotism because it puts beer before country.[1]
— Wayne Wheeler, ardent prohibitionist

On April 6, 1917, Congress declared war on Germany. The prewar assistance to Great Britain and the battles of American troops in France created widespread shortages of critical items but substantially increased war-material manufacturing jobs in Chicago. Canny businessmen corralled large military contracts and attracted new workers to the city. Saloons, restaurants, nightclubs, gambling houses, and brothels operated at full capacity, many running around the clock. Because of the war, the police looked the other way. It was a boom time for vice.

Big Jim Colosimo was profiting handsomely from the rush of servicemen, war-plant employees, and others to his numerous business operations. The café was jammed each evening entertaining and serving the revelers until sunrise. In the midst of the euphoria, newly appointed First Deputy Superintendent Wesley H. Westbrook decided to attempt to enforce the city liquor ordinances. Early Sunday morning, April 29, 1917, Westbrook dispatched fifteen squads of detectives to check for violations in the saloon and nightclub areas. The raiders found plenty of infractions and made a total of sixty arrests. The detectives boldly marched into Colosimo's Café after hours. Colosimo and eleven of his restaurant staff were arrested. The police seized liquor that they found in a service bar. Colosimo was booked and released on bond. He claimed the seized liquor came from a storeroom, and the charges were dismissed.

In September, private investigators purchased intoxicating beverages after hours in Colosimo's Café and Freiberg's Dance Hall being operated by Ike Bloom. Sworn affidavits were turned over to Deputy Superintendent Westbrook stating that Colosimo's and Freiberg's sold intoxicants on Sunday, sold liquor between one and five in the morning, and sold liquor to soldiers in uniform. The reports also stated that waiters at Colosimo's brought women to tables to drink with male customers. Rumors spread across the Levee that Westbrook was going to recommend revocation of the liquor licenses for Colosimo's Café and Freiberg's. A few days later Westbrook did send a report to Chief Herman F. Schuettler recommending revocation of the licenses. Schuettler reviewed the findings, and on September 28, 1917, he dispatched a letter to Mayor Thompson recommending closing Colosimo's and Freiberg's.

On October 4, 1917, attorney William Marks, representing Colosimo and Bloom, rushed into court before Mayor Thompson could act on the recommendation for revocation. He asked Circuit Court Judges David and Cooper for a writ of prohibition to prevent the mayor from revoking the licenses. A ten-day continuance was granted on a motion by Assistant Corporation Counsel James W. Breen to allow him time to examine the petition. As a result of the court action, Mayor Thompson was served with a writ filed in Superior Court restraining him from revoking the licenses. As was expected, the case dragged on until it was forgotten.[2]

The newspapers created a clamor over the findings of failure to enforce the laws in the reports. City hall decided that to take the pressure off someone had to take the fall for failing to enforce the city regulations. Because most of the laxity occurred in the Levee, which was in the Twenty-second Street Police District, Capt. Max Nootbar was made the scapegoat. Nootbar would not be missed by the district police officers or by the saloon owners in the Levee. Schuettler filed charges with the Civil Service Commission against Nootbar for allowing the sale of alcoholic beverages after hours. Nootbar was replaced by Capt. John Alcock, who wisely posted detectives in Colosimo's and Freiberg's to prevent the sale of liquor on Sunday until the furor died down.

World War I provided additional ammunition for the arguments of the "drys" that the U.S. should prohibit the sale of alcoholic beverages. The prohibitionists charged that breweries and retailers of alcoholic beverages were working against America's efforts at fighting the war in Europe. Spokesmen for the "drys" maintained that grain, molasses, and other products were being diverted from the war effort and used for the production of alcoholic beverages. They accused factory workers who were engaged in military production of missing work or performing in a shoddy manner due to their consumption of alcohol.

Despite the outcry of the prohibitionists, the general feeling in Chicago was that city ordinances relating to liquor, beer, and wine should be ignored due to the pressure of the war. During the autumn of 1918, restaurants and saloons were running twenty-four hours a day and providing alcoholic beverages to soldiers, sailors, defense workers, and civilians in defiance of city ordinances and state and federal laws. Samuel P. Thrasher of the Committee of Fifteen said his investigators had found countless liquor violations throughout the Levee. At Colosimo's, investigators observed Big Jim acting as the greeter while sailors guzzled beer and whiskey long past 1 a.m. In September, the investigators again visited Colosimo's in the early hours of Sunday morning and observed seltzer highballs and gin rickeys being sold to servicemen, some of whom were intoxicated.

Spurred by findings of the Committee of Fifteen and by newspaper investigative reports, Lt. Hugh McCarthy, head of the police morals detail, sent squads to arrest the violators on September 14, 1918. The raiders busted joint after joint as sailors were found drinking and consorting with "evil" women. Still more raids followed as the district commanders, stirred into action from their seeming lethargy, sent out their own officers. In the wake of this police activity, Jim Colosimo closed his café at midnight on Saturday. Late partiers were shocked when they pulled up to Colosimo's early Sunday morning and found the doors locked.

On the national level, the prohibitionists had been pushing Congress to pass nationwide legislation prohibiting the manufacture and sale of alcoholic beverages. Congress remained unwilling to allow a vote on Prohibition even though, by the start of World War I, the majority of Americans were supporters of the Prohibition movement. Now, with the war creating new demands for grain to make bread for the armed forces and to send to starving populations devastated during the war, the "drys" convinced Congress to act.[3] Congress passed a temporary Wartime Prohibition measure intended to conserve grain for the army, America's allies, and the domestic population.[4] On November 21, 1918, the Wartime Prohibition Act was ratified forbidding the manufacture and sale of all intoxicating beverages of more than 2.75 percent alcohol content until demobilization was completed. The bill took effect on July 1, 1919, and was scheduled to run until the demobilization of U.S. fighting forces.

The armistice was signed on November 11, 1918. The Wartime Prohibition Act became law ten days after the war ended. Despite the cessation of hostilities, the Treasury Department moved resolutely ahead to implement the bill's provisions even though it seemed peculiar to most people with the war

over. In major East Coast and Midwest cities, as the result of the lack of public
support, there was little enforcement of the legislation by local police. On the
federal level Treasury agents were forcing the distillers and breweries to end
their production.

Chicago, locked in its own battle over the Prohibition question, held a
citywide referendum on the issue in May 1919. The "wets" triumphed with
400,000 votes to 150,000 for the "drys."[5] John Fitzpatrick, leader of the
Chicago Federation of Labor, suggested that one of the causes of the devastating race riot that occurred in Chicago in the summer of 1919 was "the denial
of beer and wine to the working class while the wealthy have their cellars
full."[6] Making a joke out of the Wartime Prohibition Act, Alderman Michael
Kenna, proprietor of the Workingman's Exchange that served the largest stein
of beer in town, announced that he was looking for a good spot in the Loop to
open an ice-cream parlor.[7]

The Wartime Prohibition controls and the likelihood of the passage of a
national Prohibition law moved Colosimo to develop and implement a small-
scale bootleg distribution operation that would provide not only his café but
also most of the Levee saloons with bootleg beer and alcohol.[8] His actions
were the beginning of the bootleg racket in Chicago. In the meantime, Torrio
continued to increase the number of vice dens across the county. He corrupted
the officials of Stickney, a town eight miles west of the Levee, in the same way
he had corrupted Johnny Patton in Burnham. As soon as he suborned the
Stickney officials, Torrio opened gambling joints and vice resorts in that town.
He then moved on to replicate this operation in other towns and unincorporated areas in Cook County. For himself, he created a vice emporium at 2222
S. Wabash Avenue, a block from Colosimo's Café. In this old four-story, brick
building he opened a saloon, a whorehouse, and a gambling operation called
the Four Deuces. Torrio added a small office from which he could transact his
own business. He had become a man to be reckoned with.

Colosimo was busy at work developing his small bootleg network, running
his restaurant, and courting Dale Winter. He completely missed the danger
signs from Torrio that would result in his death.

Chapter Thirty-One

EIGHTEENTH AMENDMENT

Liquor Sales Going Out, Bootleggers Coming In

1918–1920

It is here at last—dry America's first birthday. At one minute past twelve tomorrow morning a new nation will be born. Tonight John Barleycorn makes his last will and testament. Now for an era of clear thinking and clean living. The Anti-Saloon League wishes every man and woman and child a Happy Dry Year.[1]

— Anti-Saloon League press release

The Wartime Prohibition Act was the law of the land, but the saloons and resorts were openly selling beer and liquor in Chicago. Police Superintendent John J. Garrity admitted to the newspapers that almost 90 percent of the saloons in Chicago were violating the act openly. Illinois Attorney General Edward J. Brundage said that he would personally close every saloon in Chicago if necessary. "In one Loop bar near Monroe and LaSalle," Brundage said, "I saw them standing four deep behind the bar and men stumbling out so drunk that they fell over themselves."[2] Liquor and beer flowed at Colosimo's Café and all of Big Jim's resorts and roadhouses.

Prohibition had long been brewing in the United States. The national movement for Prohibition seems to have begun with a resolution passed by the fraternal order of the Sons of Temperance in 1856. Twenty years later, Congressman Henry Blair of New Hampshire introduced a Prohibition amendment to the Constitution. In the meantime, individual states were going "dry" on their own. By 1913, the "drys" claimed that more than 50 percent of

Americans were living in areas with some form of alcohol Prohibition. The Anti-Saloon League, the National Temperance Council, and numerous other groups were pushing hard for a national Prohibition. Congress, which for many years had looked at alcoholic beverages only as a source of tax revenue, was being won over by the prohibitionists. In 1915 and 1916 bills prohibiting the manufacture, sale, transportation, and importation of alcoholic beverages were debated in Congress but failed to pass. [3]

As the twentieth century began, tens of thousands of indignant women, seeing the damage wrought in the home by alcohol and alcoholism, took up the temperance banner. The clergy had always denounced alcohol from the pulpit, but now the church organizations were demanding action. When they were joined by the municipal reformers who were trying to reduce corruption and vice in the major cities, the goal of Prohibition became reachable. The anti-saloon leagues, the "drys," the women's crusades and the Temperance Union, the Prohibition Party, the church groups, and a host of other organizations formed a common bond—alcohol and beer had to go. The days were numbered for the sale of Demon Rum, as the clergymen called it.

In 1917, Congress was lobbied successfully by the leaders of the Prohibition movement. A resolution providing for an amendment to the Constitution that would prohibit the manufacture, sale, transportation, or importation of alcoholic beverages in the United States was passed and sent to the states for ratification. On January 8, 1918, Mississippi became the first state to ratify the resolution.

Chicago and Cook County were ignoring the national "dry" movement. One glaring example of this disregard was the town of Burnham where drinking, gambling, and whoring went on nonstop in Colosimo-controlled roadhouses and resorts. A spot-check by investigators from a civic organization found drunken men and loose women all over town. The investigators counted nineteen working girls in the State Line Inn, thirty-five in the Speedway Inn, and twenty-five at a resort called No. 12. All were reportedly having a good time. [4]

Temperance groups in Chicago, infuriated by the ongoing orgy in the far south suburbs, began pressuring the sheriff to act. Cook County Sheriff John E. Traeger claimed to be frustrated by the inability of his small force of deputies to control vice in the county roadhouses, gambling joints and brothels. [5] On May 18, 1918, Traeger changed his tactics. His new plan was to force Mayor Johnny Patton of Burnham and Mayor Paul M. Kamradt of West Hammond (later called Calumet City) from office. The sheriff had another new approach for dealing with the keepers and working girls of the resorts in the two towns. His intention was to have them interned as undesirable citizens and enemies of the government during the war years. He scheduled a meeting with the chairman of the State Council of Defense to propose the idea. The sheriff claimed that the worst places in Burnham were Big Jim Colosimo's Arrowhead Inn, Burnham Inn, and State Line Inn.[6] Nothing came of the sheriff's harebrained idea.

On July 19, 1918, a tip-off was flashed to the roadhouses and brothels of Burnham that a major raid was imminent. Within minutes the patrons, employees, and girls of the thirty-five resorts and saloons emptied wildly into the streets. They fled to their cars or went to their homes. Soon a raiding party of seventy-five federal agents, detectives, and deputy sheriffs arrived. The federal agents claimed that they were searching for goods stolen from railroad freight cars on sidings in the Calumet area. Information had been received that this loot was hidden in various locations in Burnham. As the raiders scurried from one saloon to another they collected Mayor Johnny Patton, who was found in one of Colosimo's roadhouses. He was taken by the federal agents for a long ride through back roads in Indiana while they plied him with questions concerning the thefts. The total recovery was five hundred pairs of trousers found in the shop of tailor Jacob Steinberg. The trousers were seized, and Steinberg was arrested. Patton was driven back to Burnham and released without charge. For his press interview, Patton demonstrated high indignation over the absurdity of the first "arrest" of his life.[7]

In October 1918, State's Attorney Maclay Hoyne announced that he would indict the mayors of Burnham, Cicero, and Burr Oak if Sheriff Traeger could secure appropriate evidence that these elected officials were negligent in enforcing the laws of their communities. Days and weeks passed; no one was indicted. Apparently Traeger had been unsuccessful in gathering evidence.[8]

Early in 1919, the Chicago Crime Commission was founded because of the efforts of Col. Henry Barrett Chamberlin, who appealed to the Chicago Association of Commerce to fund a private crime commission to deal with the growing problem of crime in Chicago. The association responded by giving strong support and financial assistance. Edwin W. Simms, former U.S. District Attorney and secretary of the 1910 Vice Commission of Chicago, was named as the commission's first president, and former police reporter Chamberlin was appointed executive director. The commission was composed of a board of distinguished local business executives.[9]

In its earliest days, the commission began its watchdog role on the problems of crime and corruption in Chicago. Because the commission initially directed its attention at improving the efficiency of the criminal justice agencies in Chicago, the organization did not examine the sordid role of Colosimo in his prostitution, gambling activities, and saloon activities. A statement was made by Simms showing that the commission was aware of the problems spawned by Colosimo and Torrio: "Modern crime, like modern business, is

tending toward centralization, organization, and commercialization. Ours is a
business nation. Our criminals apply business methods. The men and women
of evil have formed trusts."[10]

On January 29, 1919, Nebraska became the thirty-sixth state to ratify the
proposed Eighteenth Amendment to the Constitution. This was the magic
number the "drys" had been waiting for—the minimum required for an
amendment to the Constitution. The congressional resolution stated: "After
one year from the ratification of this article the manufacture, sale, or transportation of intoxicating liquors within, the importation thereof into, or the
exportation thereof from the United States and all territory subject to the
jurisdiction thereof for the beverage purposes is hereby prohibited."

Undaunted by the ratification of the amendment, Colosimo's Café continued to operate beyond the legal closing hours. An unusual incident took place
after 2 a.m. on the morning of February 6, 1919. A revolver slipped from the
hands of Police Sgt. Frank Johnson, fell to the floor, and discharged a slug into
the ankle of Sgt. William P. Kennedy. Both sergeants had been "visiting"
Colosimo's when the incident took place. The matter was investigated by the
police and then quietly dropped.

Chicago was holding mayoral and aldermanic elections in 1919. The
election was hotly contested. In the primary, Mayor Thompson was running
for reelection against popular Circuit Court Judge Harry Olson and reformer
Charles E. Merriam, a returning army captain and former alderman. For
Colosimo, whose complex vice empire depended strongly on a strict hands-
off policy by local police, it was important that he support the most likely
winner of the April mayoral race. The Democrats had split into factional
fighting, and none of their candidates seemed likely to win. Colosimo, a lifelong Democrat, decided to back Republican Thompson, whose wide-open
policies toward drinking and vice were well known, and provided financial
and manpower support.

The primary campaign was filled with wild charges and fiery oratory.
Regardless of the heat and finger-pointing of the campaign, Thompson won
handily in the primary with 124,000 votes to Olson's 84,000 and Merriam's
18,000.

In the general election Republican Thompson faced a split ticket—the
regular Democratic Party candidate Robert Sweitzer, Socialist John Collins,
Labor candidate John Fitzpatrick, and Independent Maclay Hoyne, the state's
attorney. The Democrats had been unable to control their own party.[11] On
April Fool's Day, Chicago's voters went to the polls and reelected Thompson.
He bested Sweitzer with 260,000 votes to 238,000.[12] On April 18, William
Hale Thompson was sworn in for his second term as mayor of Chicago. In the
same election, Michael Kenna also was reelected. By this time, no one could

even remember how many times Hinky Dink had been reelected as alderman of the First Ward.

The big question in the Levee was whether Colosimo's support for Republican Thompson had ruptured the working relationship with Democrats John Coughlin and Kenna. When the election dust settled, the longtime partnership between the three men was intact. Hinky Dink and Bathhouse John realized that the Democratic candidates for mayor did not have a chance and that Thompson was a believer in a wide-open town, so no damage was done.[13] It may well be that the aldermen realized that Colosimo was becoming more powerful and that it was best to remain in a partnership with him in the First Ward to ensure continuance of the protection money and campaign help that he provided.

Colosimo had attained a major objective through his support for Thompson. The mayor himself now was accessible to Big Jim. The vice lord's victory was partially overshadowed by a few bumps in the road that were just ahead. All of the troubles began in May.

In early May, Assistant Attorney General Franklin B. Dennison of Illinois held hearings on vice in Burnham, focusing on Colosimo's Arrowhead Inn. Based on information obtained at the hearings, Dennison concluded that a petition should be filed for an injunction to close the notorious resort. Dennison also was likely spurred on by the report of a *Tribune* reporter who visited the Arrowhead Inn on Easter Sunday morning at 5 a.m. The reporter found that bourbon, wine, and gin were being served in tiny china cups, and female entertainers were on hand to encourage the male drinkers. The publicity was good and bad for Colosimo. Good because it added to the reputation of his Burnham resorts; bad because he was continuing in his attempts to build a better public image.

The second problem took place after midnight on May 19. Marie Kerrigan, 627 W. Forty-sixth Street, was working as a cigarette girl at Colosimo's Café. She said she saw an intoxicated woman in the employee's dressing room. While she was trying to help the woman, a waiter grabbed Kerrigan and pulled her bodily out of the dressing room. "Mike the Greek" Potson appeared and struck her. Potson, who had been made co-owner of the café by Colosimo in 1918, dragged Kerrigan through the kitchen and out the rear door where he threw her into the alley.[14]

Kerrigan retained attorney Weldon Webster. After reviewing her charges, the attorney filed a suit against Colosimo and Potson in circuit court asking for five thousand dollars in damages for injuries. The suit alleged that Kerrigan had been assaulted by the manager and a waiter. Attorney Rocco De Stefano, representing Colosimo, responded that Kerrigan had never been employed by Colosimo's but was employed by an outsider who held the cigarette concession.

De Stefano pointed out that Colosimo was not present at the restaurant when the quarrel occurred and had played no part in the event.[15]

The story appeared in all the local newspapers. Kerrigan, who said she was nineteen, caught the sympathy of the readers when she claimed that she and her younger sister were the only support for her crippled father and mother. Kerrigan said she had been working for Samuel Wolf, a concessionaire who operated under the auspices of the so-called Tip Trust, a behind-the-scene cartel that ran concessions in various restaurants, hotels, and nightclubs. She said her salary was $13 a week. After several hearings De Stefano was able to get Colosimo removed from the suit. On November 30, the matter was closed with the payment of $125 to Kerrigan, who signed the closure agreement at an exotic nightclub called the Midnight Frolic, where she was working.[16]

Meanwhile Assistant Attorney General Dennison was continuing his vice investigation of Colosimo. When he learned of the Kerrigan incident, he decided to expand the hearings. Kerrigan met with Dennison and told him that the time she had worked at Colosimo's was "eight months of hell." She claimed that Colosimo's Café was open all night.[17] The public lost interest in the matter, and nothing came of Dennison's hearings.

The next and the biggest of the problems involved a newspaper reporter. The reporter worked for Colosimo's longtime nemesis, the powerful *Chicago Tribune*. Late on Saturday evening, May 17, *Tribune* reporter Morrow Krum, accompanied by a colleague, visited Burnham in connection with an investigation for the paper of vice conditions in the town. At their last stop, Colosimo's Arrowhead Inn, Krum ordered a dry gin fizz and his associate had Rhine wine. Krum then went into a phone booth to call in his story on activities he had observed. He told the city desk that the town was running wide open with drinks being sold on Sunday, accompanied by women and song. Unknown to Krum his phone conversation was overheard. As Krum and his partner left the roadhouse, they were accosted on the front porch by Colosimo and a crowd of eighteen waiters and men from town. Colosimo shouted, "You dirty rat, we heard you calling your office." Krum tried to move on but was slugged in the mouth by Colosimo. A short man who had been standing with the group punched Krum several times in the face and shouted, "You're damn lucky to get out of here alive, you rat." When Krum saw one of the men reaching toward his pocket as if for a gun, the reporter ran to his car.[18]

Going not to Burnham, where Patton controlled the machinery of justice, but to Oak Park where Justice Frank A. McKee was sitting, Krum filed complaints against Colosimo charging assault and battery and sale of intoxicating liquor on Sunday. A warrant was issued and Colosimo was arrested by a deputy sheriff. The case was heard in Oak Park by McKee, with Assistant State's Attorney John Owen as prosecutor. Krum was personally represented by former First Assistant U.S. District Attorney Joseph B. Fleming. The odds were against Colosimo beating this case. Despite strenuous efforts by defense attorney Harry Smitz, Colosimo was found guilty on both counts. He was fined $100 and $22.60 in costs for the assault and battery and $200 and costs for the liquor sale on Sunday. The *Tribune* labeled Colosimo "The Immune" in a headline referring to his protection from arrests and raids.[19]

Colosimo responded with a two-column advertisement in the newspapers proclaiming "Follow the Arrow to Colosimo's Arrowhead Inn. Featuring Syncopated Band—Grand Opera—Ballads—Ragtime. Serving chicken, fish and frog-leg dinners as well as 'a la Carte' at all Hours."[20]

This was the year in which the vice and gambling cabal of dive operators and politicians finally eliminated the "dangerous" position of second deputy superintendent. Maj. Metellius L. C. Funkhouser still held that office but had few responsibilities and a small staff. One of his duties was serving as the city's movie censor. In this role, he directed that scenes depicting the cruelty of Kaiser Wilhelm be removed from the movie *My Four Years in Germany*, a vitriolic anti-German film. The city council reacted strongly, charging that Funkhouser was pro-German—not a good assertion in view of the recent war. The heavily criticized censorship decision by Funkhouser and the pressure brought by a powerful group within the city council resulted in Acting Chief of Police John H. Alcock filing charges against Funkhouser and two of his aides. Funkhouser was brought before the politically controlled Civil Service Commission. The beleaguered deputy superintendent was supported by the newspapers and numerous individuals and organizations who believed that he was being forced out of his job by the city's vice and gambling interests. The commission ruled that Funkhouser should be discharged from his post and from the police department. To finish the matter, the city council voted to end the appropriation for the second deputy superintendent's office.[21] In the debate before the vote, Alderman Wallace said the results obtained through the efforts of the deputy superintendent's office were not sufficient to justify its existence and the money could be better spent on catching thieves, burglars, and crooks.

After the years of fighting vice and corruption, the second deputy superintendent and his morals squad that had been a constant threat to the brothel operators, saloon owners, and gambling house operators, as well as to the police captains in whose districts these dens were thriving, were no more.

At this time concern was being raised in the newspapers that private individuals had inappropriate influence in the affairs of the Chicago Police Department. On the police side, this alleged influence involved high-level administrators and district captains. Among those named as having a "large interest in police affairs" was Jim Colosimo, who was described as proprietor of a resort in Burnham and a cabaret at 2126 S. Wabash Avenue. The story went nowhere.

During the week of July 27–31, 1919, the most devastating race riot in Chicago's history took place. The rioting lasted for three days and left twenty-three blacks and fifteen whites dead and more than three hundred persons were injured. The ill-trained and ill-prepared Chicago police could not secure order, and the Illinois National Guard had to be called. Black workers in the Levee were beaten by white mobs, and the brothels were empty during the riots. Within a few days the fighting subsided and business in the Levee was back to normal.

A new protest against the wild activities in Burnham was raised by authorities in the state of Indiana. They protested the alcoholic excesses taking place in the town on their border. The authorities claimed that, on Sundays, a thousand persons from northern Indiana visited the various joints in Burnham. As the drunken Hoosiers returned to Indiana, large numbers were arrested on various charges. At one point, the jail in Lake County, Indiana, was so full that the inmates' feet were sticking out of the windows. Indiana officials asked State's Attorney Hoyne why the saloons in Cook County could sell alcoholic beverages seven days a week. The sheriff's office responded that their deputies had been working on the race riots but would "get right on it."[22]

With the Wartime Prohibition bill on the books and the National Prohibition Act a certainty, Torrio began to apply his business skills and natural intelligence to take full advantage of the work of the prohibitionists and Congress. Under Colosimo he had learned how to open and operate houses of prostitution and gambling joints. He realized that even though the sale of alcoholic beverages would be illegal, the demand for them would continue unabated. Torrio correctly reasoned that the same approach Colosimo had used to provide prostitution and gambling could be applied to providing the illegal beverages—bribery of public officials.

In 1919 Torrio made his first big move into the bootleg racket. The Stetson Brewery, owned by Joseph Stetson and his brothers, had challenged the legality of Illinois Attorney General Edward J. Brundage's ruling supporting the Wartime Prohibition Act. Torrio met secretly with Joe Stetson, and they discussed how to continue brewing and supplying beer despite Prohibition. They would simply bribe the police and local officials. This was the same formula that Torrio had learned from Colosimo to protect the vice dens, gambling joints, and bookie parlors. The two men decided to use intermediaries to purchase or lease city and county breweries at low-dollar prices resulting from the owners' desire to sell because of the Prohibition Act. Stetson and Torrio planned to place front men in charge of these companies, who in the event of raids, would be arrested in place of the true owners.[23] Their first move was the purchase in the spring of 1919 by Stetson and Torrio of the Manhattan Brewery at 3901 S. Emerald Avenue. Manhattan was sold to the pair by owner Charles Schaffner, who thought that it was time to leave what had been a highly profitable business.[24]

Stetson became Torrio's silent partner in many Chicago-area breweries.[25] He was a wealthy man who lived in quiet respectability in an expensively furnished home at 1218 Astor Street in the heart of North Side Gold Coast. Although the press was aware of Stetson's relationship with Torrio, this information was not printed. Some stories mentioned a mysterious wealthy backer, and others talked about a partner from the Gold Coast. No name was given.

In the fall, a sufficient number of states had ratified the amendment to make it law, and Congress acted swiftly. On October 28, 1919, the National Prohibition Act was passed into law with an effective date of January 17, 1920. While the Wartime Act had been almost totally ignored and lacked federal enforcement support, the National Prohibition Act was going to be different matter. Its passage marked the end of one era and the beginning of another, both for the country and for Big Jim Colosimo and Johnny Torrio.

Chapter Thirty-Two

DIVORCE AND SECOND MARRIAGE

This Time for Love

1920

I knew about the affairs with Dale Winter before we were divorced. I even talked to her about it and told her that I wouldn't stand for it—that Jim owed what he had to my working with him. She wouldn't admit the existence of any affair. Nevertheless, I heard many rumors and so I didn't interfere when Jim started proceedings for a divorce.[1]

— Victoria Moresco

Jim Colacimo (sic) was married there on the front steps of the hotel.[2]

— Charlie Barrett, assistant head waiter, West Baden Springs Hotel, *Memoir*

In 1919, when the U.S. Census taker appeared at Colosimo's comfortable home at 3156 S. Vernon Avenue, he was told that living in the house were Jim Colosimo; father Luigi, age seventy-three; sister Bettina, age thirty-five; and Victoria Moresco's sister Julie, age twenty. Jim's occupation was given as proprietor of a restaurant.[3] No mention was made of a wife. Later, Jim claimed that Victoria had moved out three years earlier.

At that time Dale Winter was residing in a rented apartment on the South Side with her mother. No one seemed to be able to learn the exact relationship between Dale and Jim, but all of the visible evidence pointed to a chaste friendship. No reporters hinted that Jim and Dale were engaging in premarital sex or that Dale was living at the Vernon address. Probably the most telling perspective on this question was that discarded wife Victoria, even at her most indignant and emotional moments, never suggested a sexual relationship between Jim and Dale. However, after Jim's death, Victoria's family and friends did offer some personal reflections on the troublesome relationship among the former brothel madam, the cabaret singer, and the vice lord.

Mrs. Nicholas Nardi, 224 Whiting Street, was a sister of Victoria Moresco. She gave her version of the split in the Colosimo-Victoria marriage. She said that in 1916 Victoria believed Jim was unfaithful to her, but the couple continued to live together. One day in January 1920, Victoria arrived at her sister's home in tears saying that she could no longer live with Jim because he was living with another woman. Soon Victoria collected her jewelry, which was worth forty-five thousand dollars, and her private banking account of thirty thousand dollars, and left to start a new life in Los Angeles. According to Mrs. Nardi, after Victoria moved out of 3156 Vernon Avenue, Dale moved in. Mrs. Nardi claimed that she had been told about Jim and Dale living together by her younger sister, who also was residing in the Colosimo home. The sister said the female entertainer was staying with Jim.[4]

Joseph Moresco, Victoria's brother, told of frequent quarrels between Victoria and Jim in the last months of their marriage. Moresco said that he was asked to be a peacemaker whenever they had fights. Jim would tell Joseph, "Go down to the house and talk to that sister of yours." In the period before the divorce, the quarrels became more frequent. Moresco said he advised his sister to "get a divorce if they couldn't get along together."[5]

Etta Potson, wife of Colosimo Café manager Mike Potson and a girlfriend of Victoria Moresco, sent a telegram from Long Beach, California, to her husband during the time the police were searching for Victoria after Jim's death.[6] In the telegram Etta stated that one of Victoria's sisters had died in 1917 while Victoria was still living with Jim. One day while visiting her sister's grave Victoria met a tombstone cutter who was working nearby. His name was Antonio "Tony" Villiano, and he was two years younger than Victoria. After that first meeting, Victoria began to bring fresh flowers to place on her sister's grave every week, and Villiano managed to find a reason to be working in the same area. When Victoria moved out of her husband's home, she moved near Mount Carmel cemetery to make the weekly visits easier. Villiano and Victoria began an affair and eventually moved to Los Angeles. When Victoria returned to Chicago from Los Angeles after Jim's death, attorney De Stefano asked Victoria whether she had married Villiano in California. She admitted knowing Villiano but said they were just friends. She broke into hysterical tears and vigorously denied that they had ever married.[7]

On February 3, 1920, Jim filed a bill of divorce in circuit court charging his wife with desertion. To fulfill the necessary legal requirements in Illinois for obtaining a divorce, the petition alleged that Victoria, without any cause, had left the domicile on September 1, 1917. Required notices of the divorce petition appeared in the classified sections of Chicago newspapers for four weeks. The hearing took place on March 29 before Circuit Court Judge John P. McGoorty. Colosimo's father, Luigi, and Victoria's sister June Chiavorotti were called by De Stefano to testify on Jim's behalf.[8] Colosimo declared that his wife had deserted him in 1917 because of her desire for finery and world-wide travel. He added that Victoria left him because he would not take her to Europe. McGoorty ruled in Colosimo's favor.

On March 31, 1920, McGoorty formerly dissolved the marriage between James Colosimo and Victoria Moresco after eighteen years.[9] Victoria received fifty thousand dollars for her troubles. Within two weeks, she traveled to California and married Tony Villiano.

One day after the divorce decree became final, the *Tribune* sent a reporter to Colosimo's Café to interview Big Jim. Their conversation appeared in the paper:

> Reporter: Are you going to marry Miss Winter?
>
> Colosimo: How can I marry Miss Winter when my decree was just signed today?
>
> Reporter: Miss Winter is wearing a most beautiful engagement ring.
>
> Colosimo: I can't stop that.
>
> Reporter: You have just returned from West Baden Springs. Miss Winter was there with you. You have reservations for this weekend. Who will be in the party?
>
> Colosimo: There will be Giacomo Spadoni, conductor of the grand opera, and Isadoro Prati, the tenor.
>
> Reporter: Why are you going back so soon?
>
> Colosimo: Well, you know it's the most wonderful place—golfing, horseback riding, the water, and—er—well—you know."
>
> Reporter: Will Miss Winter come along?
>
> Colosimo: She may follow—who knows. She has been studying under Ruffo, Spadoni and Prati. She may want to pursue her studies there.
>
> Reporter: But, why continue studying opera if she is to be married?
>
> Colosimo: Well, who knows? She may be planning an operatic career or concert tour."[10]

Finding little information in Jim's enigmatic responses, the reporter gave up. He sought out Winter and wrote that she was the queen of the cabarets. The results of his interview were:

Reporter: Who gave you that magnificent solitaire?
Miss Winter: A gentleman friend.
Reporter: You are going to marry soon?
Miss Winter: Every woman expects to marry and the sooner the better.
Reporter: Is Mr. Colosimo the fortunate man?
Miss Winter: There goes the overture, you must pardon me.

The article in the *Tribune* concluded, "She opened the show with the song, 'I Can't Wait Til Next Sunday Morning.'"[11]

Meanwhile, Colosimo's Café was operating with a packed house. The two dining rooms were filled each evening. Big Jim was spending more time on the floor of the restaurant. The café regulars had noticed marked improvements in Colosimo and the restaurant. He was dressing and acting more like a gentleman than a vice lord. He looked like a prosperous businessman, complete with sparkling diamonds on his shirt studs and on his many rings. The music in the restaurant had changed to classical. The food and wine had reached new gustatory heights. The regulars felt that these changes were the result of the relationship between Jim and Dale Winter.

Big Jim was spending more time with businessmen and professionals than with his mob friends and political associates. In opera season he was frequently seen in the Auditorium and Congress hotels with conductors and singers from the opera house. He bought drinks for his friends at the Auditorium bar. He would nod to the bartender who would promptly set out tall flute glasses for each person and pour expensive champagne. There was no check; the bill was paid by mail on a monthly basis. Many evenings he attended the opera and often brought associates to sit in his row of seats.

Jim's dream was to take Dale to Italy to study opera, but he had not been able to undertake this journey while he was married to Victoria. Quietly, he was turning securities into cash with the intention of purchasing a home on Lake Shore Drive for Dale and himself. He made plans for Potson to take over the full management of the café when the couple was traveling out of the country.

For his marriage to Dale Winter, Colosimo choose to return to the West Baden Springs Hotel. For him, there was no place grander in the entire Midwest. The hotel was reached by a long driveway off the highway. There were spacious grounds on all sides of the circular main building with its 708 guest rooms. The hotel was a virtual mecca for the wealthy set from Chicago. The dinner menu in the main dining room featured a choice of fried oysters in hot chili sauce, broiled tenderloin steak, grilled mutton cutlets, pork chops sauté, grilled ham, and eggs and omelets in any style. The dominant feature of the main building was a grand rotunda covered by a glass and steel dome 200 feet in diameter with an inner circumference of 600 feet.

The majestic dome rose 130 feet above the floor. The hotel bragged that it was the largest dome ever constructed.

A glass-enclosed veranda circled the front of the hotel. On the grounds there was a sunken garden, an opera house, a grand casino, a three-story natatorium with mineral springs, and large indoor and outdoor swimming pools. There were an eighteen-hole golf course, bowling alleys, billiard tables, and a one-third-mile-long, two-deck bicycle and pony track. The classy gambling casino on the main floor of the hotel attracted sportsmen and gamblers from throughout the Midwest. Almost every major gambler and important public official and politician in Chicago, including Gov. Len Small and Mayors Harrison and Thompson, visited the hotel and casino at one time or another.

The time for the wedding had come. Chauffeur Woolfson steered the gleaming Pierce-Arrow containing the two lovebirds to the county courthouse in Paoli, Indiana. The date was April 16, 1920, only two weeks after Colosimo's divorce was finalized. The couple asked for an application for a marriage license. Jim listed his correct age of forty-two. Dale, who was twenty-nine, gave her age as twenty-five. Dale wrote that she was a resident of Orange County, although the clerk knew she wasn't. Jim's longtime friend Marcus Lafe Prow signed as a witness and verified the information on the form as correct. The license was issued.

The next day was bright and sunny with the temperature in the midfifties. Jim and Dale were married on the front steps of the West Baden Springs Hotel. Isaiah Cassidy, a justice of the peace, performed the rites after tucking his trousers into his boots. The witnesses were Lafe Prow and Betty Parsons Prow, who had brought along their young sons, William and Robert.[12] Guests included English theater magnate and prizefight promoter Charles Cochran and his wife, circus proprietor Ed Ballard, opera conductor Giacomo Spadoni, tenor Isadoro Prati, and former Assistant U.S. District Attorney Francis Borrelli. Rocco De Stefano was there, along with a large contingent of Jim's friends.

As a remembrance of the wedding, Jim gave Dale a gold and diamond lavaliere and a diamond and emerald necklace with matching earrings. For the reception, he rented the grand ballroom and invited everyone at the hotel to attend. The Hagenbeck-Wallace Circus, which had its winter quarters in West Baden Springs, had been purchased by hotel owner Ed Ballard.[13] Colosimo asked Ballard to have circus acts perform on the hotel lawn for the entertainment of his guests. *Variety*, the show-business newspaper, carried an account of the wedding and the circus. The paper mentioned that a bear cub had bitten a guest on the leg during the performance.[14]

The couple spent their honeymoon at the hotel. During the day they rode horses along the hotel's wooded paths. Jim hired a professional photographer to take photographs of Dale in riding clothes atop a large black horse holding a long riding crop. The photographer took another of the couple in front of the artistic fountain at the hotel. Dale wore her new riding outfit and a matching hat. Jim wore a dark suit, white shirt, checked tie, and gray slouch cap. Jim sent eight-by-ten glossy prints to the Chicago newspapers. Evenings, Jim and Dale donned their fanciest attire for lavish meals in the dining room. After dinner they visited the casino. According to hotel guests, the newlyweds were clearly in the happy rapture of being newly married.

When they returned to Chicago, Dale moved into the Colosimo home on Vernon Avenue. Jim's family greeted her warmly and held a welcome-home party to honor the newlyweds. The first evening the couple went to Jim's café. As they entered, the employees and patrons stood up and sang a joyful welcome. The words of the song are lost, but the unspoken refrain was, "She's little Mrs. Big Jim now."[15]

In less than a month Dale would be a widow.

Chapter Thirty-Three

THE CLOCK
TICKS DOWN

The Street-Sweepers Union Returns with a Murder

1920

They'll hang you! You and Murphy will both swing![1]
— Mrs. Tom Enright shouting at Mike Carrozzo,
charged with the murder of her husband, *Chicago Tribune*

With Mayor Big Bill Thompson firmly established in office for four more years, Colosimo could be confident of his political connections and could run his resorts and the restaurant without fear of interference from the city police. He delegated his contacts with Thompson and other political bosses to Torrio, which put Torrio an elevated status. Colosimo made a small purchase in the beer-making business. He gave twenty-five thousand dollars to Torrio to give to panderer Jake Guzik to purchase an interest in a small brewery to provide beer for his resorts in Burnham and suburban towns.[2]

Unnoticed by almost everyone, a swarthy, thickset Italian with a long scar down the side of his cheek arrived in Chicago. Born in Brooklyn, New York, on January 17, 1899,[3] his name was Alphonse Capone. The fourth of nine children of an immigrant family from Naples, Italy, Capone grew up in the dirty, crime-infested streets and alleys of the New York Italian ghetto. A member of the James Street Boys gang and later the Five Points Gang, Capone

worked his way up the gangland ladder by committing a string of steadily esca-
lating crimes. While residing in an apartment in Brooklyn, he married Mary
Coughlin on December 30, 1918. In 1919 Capone got into a fight with a man
in a saloon in Brooklyn. Because Capone's vicious assault almost the killed the
man, Capone went on the lam. To provide a safe refuge for him, Torrio
brought the Brooklyn hoodlum to Chicago in late 1919 or early 1920.[4]
Capone used the name Al Brown.

Capone was given a two-bit job as a street tout for the whores at the Four
Deuces. His job, the lowest rung on the vice ladder, was to steer passing men
into the brothel on the upper floor of the club with promises of "fast ladies
inside." Crime historian John Landesco's inflated description of Capone's
position at this time was as a lieutenant of Colosimo.[5] A more accurate
account of Capone's rank was reported by famed Chicago newspaperman Bob
Casey. One night while Casey was in Colosimo's Café talking with Big Jim,
Casey asked, "What does Torrio do around here?" Colosimo answered, "Torrio is my bodyguard." Casey then asked, "What does Capone do?" Colosimo
answered, "He's Torrio's bodyguard."[6]

At 12:01 a.m., on January 17, 1920, the National Prohibition Act went
into effect. Reacting promptly to the implementation of Prohibition, the Loop
saloons and nightspots went dark while the owners decided whether to reopen
as restaurants serving "near beer" or close for good. Kenna announced he was
closing the Workingman's Exchange that he had operated for twenty-three
years. He said he would reopen as a candy store with soft drinks, sandwiches,
and cigars. The giant schooners of beer—called the largest and coolest in
town by Kenna—appeared doomed.[7] From that day on, while the Colosimo-
Torrio combine continued to reap a sizable profit from gambling and prostitution in the Levee and in southern Cook County, Torrio focused his attention
on various Prohibition rackets, ranging from ownership of breweries to beer
and liquor distribution.

A rash of serious crime was occurring in Chicago. The city council discussed what action to take to stem the tide of criminality, particularly crimes
such as robbery and burglary. Chief John J. Garrity submitted a proposed
ordinance that greatly increased his command over the department. On
March 11, after many months of fractious debate, the council passed by two
votes a significantly amended version of the chief's proposal. Under the new
ordinance all captains were to submit police reports of crime in their districts
directly to him. Purportedly this measure gave the chief the ability to hold the
captains responsible for their districts. The ordinance did not contain many of
the changes that Garrity was seeking. Disheartened because he received only
one deputy superintendent instead of three and did not obtain approval for a
police reserve force, Garrity complained, "I might as well quit before I start."[8]

Garrity decided to go forward and agreed to accept full responsibility for crime in Chicago.

One month later, Democratic State's Attorney Maclay Hoyne made a series of sensational charges against the Thompson Republican political machine. Hoyne said that in return for support in the primary elections Thompson had promised an "open town" to the operators of vice and gambling resorts. He claimed that the powers at city hall were perpetuating whole-sale violations of vice and gambling laws and the police were permitting these illegal practices to continue unchecked.[9] No charges were brought before the grand jury.

Regardless of the reorganization of police by the city fathers or the grand-standing, political posturing of the state's attorney, violations of Prohibition were to be found everywhere in the city. Liquor and beer were flowing freely in thousands of saloons and blind pigs. Nightclubs, restaurants, and hotel dining rooms were serving alcoholic beverages. Entering the fight, federal agents began to investigate all levels of the liquor trade while the city police were hoping to avoid charges of malfeasance by making token arrests. On November 9, 1920, federal warrants issued for Mike de Pike Heitler and three others charging the sale of liquor, forgery of a permit, and conspiracy to violate the Prohibition Act. Ten warrants were issued for South Side saloon and resort operators for violation of the Prohibition laws. No mention was made by the feds or the press of Torrio, Colosimo, or Stetson.[10]

Torrio and Colosimo continued to provide beer and liquor to the saloons in the Levee and in Burnham and other south and west suburbs. Covertness and secrecy were employed, and payoffs were made to mayors, police officers, and deputy sheriffs. Because of the time he was spending with his new wife and his "uptown" friends, Big Jim was willing to let Torrio manage the brewery and bootlegging operations. Although he still was not well known as a vice boss, Torrio rode on Colosimo's reputation. Big Jim was considered by the Levee operators and others in the vice business to be a very powerful chieftain who had political connections at the ward and city levels and even with state officials. They accepted Torrio as Colosimo's man. While Colosimo turned his attention elsewhere, Torrio decided to move quickly and decisively to improve his situation significantly.

Torrio had little to fear from the federal enforcement agents. A scant 134 investigators were responsible for policing Illinois, Iowa, and a section of Wisconsin. Without the assistance of local police agencies, the feds couldn't begin to control an operation as widespread as the distribution network of Torrio and Colosimo. In addition, there were gangs on the west and north sides of Chicago that also were entering the bootlegging field. By bribing and suborning public officials and police on the local level, Torrio ensured that his operations would be free from municipal enforcement interference. How well Torrio succeeded can be learned from an admission by Chicago Police Chief Charles C. Fitzmorris in November 1920, "Sixty percent of my police are in the bootleg business."[11]

A major shooting occurred in early 1920 that involved Colosimo's associates and gang members. Maurice "Mossy" Enright, a gangster and big-time union boss, heard that "Dago Mike" Carrozzo, a member of the Colosimo gang, was making threats against Enright's life. Wanting to resolve this matter before he was the loser, Enright and two of his followers shot at Dago Mike and Frank Chiaravaloti in the Vestibule café in the Levee. Miraculously not wounded in the shootout, Carrozzo and Chiaravaloti fled.

Michael "Dago Mike" Carrozzo was born in Italy in 1909. He came to the United States, settled in Chicago, and was hired as a bodyguard for Colosimo. He earned Jim's trust by working as a hustler and a talent scout for Colosimo's brothels. Colosimo made him business agent of Street Laborers' Union No. 361, the street-sweepers union of which Edward Lynch, who was sponsored by Enright, was president. Big Tim Murphy, a powerful and ruthless union boss, coveted the street-sweepers union. On September 23, 1919, due to strenuous efforts by Murphy, Carrozzo was elected president of the union by a near-unanimous vote. At twenty-six years old, he was the youngest man ever to be elected at that time to a union presidency in Chicago.[12]

Murphy decided that Enright, who still wielded substantial clout in the union, had to be permanently eliminated to prevent him from retaking control of the union. A secret meeting was held in Colosimo's Café where fateful decisions and plans were made. On February 4, 1920, as Enright parked in front of his home at 1110 W. Garfield Boulevard, he was shot dead by two blasts from a sawed-off, double-barreled shotgun fired through the window of a passing Chalmers sedan. Enright had a loaded revolver in his pocket, but he never had a chance to draw it. This cold-blooded street murder was committed on orders of "Big Tim" Murphy by James "Sunny Jim" Cosmano, a member of Colosimo's gang. Among those arrested was Frank Chiaravaloti, who was connected to Colosimo and, in fact, was engaged to Big Jim's sister-in-law.[13]

Within a few hours of the shooting, Carrozzo and Murphy were arrested by Chicago detectives and held in County Jail without bond. State's Attorney Hoyne identified the actual shooter as Cosmano, who was living in the Levee at 1811 S. Armour Avenue. Cosmano had been given the position of foreman of the street sweepers in the First Ward by his longtime friend Colosimo. His colorful criminal history included being shot in 1912 by killers working for Torrio; they were resolving the Black Hand extortion threats that had been received by Colosimo.

In the investigation of Enright's murder, Detective Sgt. Charles Gratton learned that Carrozzo had secretly gone to Buffalo, New York, before Enright's murder. He had returned two weeks before the shooting with a man known only as Tommy the Wop, who was reputed to be a shotgun-wielding hit man. A squad of detectives from Chicago went to Burnham to search for Tommy in resorts operated by Torrio. They failed to find any trace of Tommy.

On February 16, the grand jury returned indictments against Murphy, Cosmano, Carrozzo, and James Vinci. Assistant State's Attorney John Prystalski charged that Vinci was the driver of the murder car and that Cosmano fired the shots that killed Enright. A series of trials of the defendants was planned. The first was against Vinci, who had confessed to driving the murder car but later recanted. He charged that brutal tactics were employed by state's attorney's investigators to obtain the confession. Vinci was found guilty and sentenced to fourteen years at Joliet state penitentiary. As the case against Murphy, Carrozzo, and Cosmano was being readied for prosecution, the state's attorney discovered that the two key witnesses against the three defendants had disappeared. The case against the three was eventually *nolle prossed*. Carrozzo held a celebration at Colosimo's Café on the night of his release from jail. On December 28, Vinci's conviction was overturned by the Illinois Supreme Court. In a second trial Vinci was acquitted.[14]

While the case ended unsatisfactorily, the police and the state's attorney were in agreement that Enright was shot because of a conspiracy by labor leaders and Colosimo to control several unions. Enright's murder was the last criminal activity in which Colosimo was known to have an involvement.

Chapter Thirty-Four

MURDER!

Big Jim Gets Hit

1920

Case number	3326
Name	Colosimo, James
Age	45 years
Ethnicity	Italian
Employment type	High white-collar
Business owner	Restaurant
Date of offense	May 11, 1920
Date of death	May 11, 1920
Address	2126 S. Wabash Ave.
Location description	In entrance to his cafe
Type of homicide	Intentional murder
Type of death	Homicide
Method of killing	Gun
Related to Prohibition	Yes

— Chicago Police Department Homicide Record Index

As May began, the Jaysee Orchestra under the direction of Peter De Quarto was playing each evening at Colosimo's Café. The customers ate, drank, laughed, and danced throughout the nights. The staff rushed among the tables, serving the drinks and meals. In front, the cop who was there each evening paced back and forth. None of the patrons or staff could have imagined what was going to occur in only a few days.

On Monday, May 10, state Sen. Francis P. Brady, Republican leader in the First Ward, met Big Jim on the street. Big Jim complained to Brady that "they" wouldn't let him cheat regarding Prohibition, but Brady wasn't concerned because Colosimo was always crying when he was making money. Brady said everybody knew that Colosimo, backed by Alderman Michael Kenna, was selling liquor despite the Eighteenth Amendment.[1]

In the early hours of Tuesday morning, May 11, Big Jim won twenty-three hundred dollars during a big crap game on the second floor of the café. A well-known West Side gambler was the big loser. He left muttering threats against Colosimo. Pleased with his winnings, Jim went to his home on Vernon Avenue and went to bed.

Later that same morning, Torrio phoned Colosimo at his home. He told Colosimo that he had made arrangements for the delivery of two truckloads of especially good whiskey to the café. Torrio said Jim had to be at the restaurant to personally receive the shipment. Jim had not planned to be at the restaurant that afternoon and objected to going. Torrio persuaded Jim that he had to be there personally to pay for the load. Reluctantly Colosimo agreed to meet the trucks.[2]

That afternoon was cloudy; the temperature was forty-five degrees. The wind was blowing twenty-eight miles an hour from the northeast. As the clock neared 4 p.m., Colosimo prepared to leave his home on Vernon Avenue. Dale had planned to go shopping that afternoon with her mother. As Jim kissed his wife goodbye, he said he would send the car right back. As he steered the long Pierce-Arrow through the South Side streets, Chauffeur Woolfson sensed that his boss was agitated. Colosimo was carrying his .38-caliber pearl-handed revolver in his right hip pocket. Some insiders later claimed that he also was carrying $150,000 in cash.

After arriving at the restaurant, Jim said hello to an employee and went directly to the small office in the rear of the café. Bookkeeper Frank Camilla was sitting at the desk working on some papers. As Colosimo entered the room he asked, "Hello Frank, what's going on?" Frank answered, "Nothin.'"[3] This exchange was the standard way the two men greeted each other for several years. After a brief discussion of business, Colosimo pointedly asked if anyone had called. Frank replied, "Nope." Colosimo grabbed the phone off the desk and tried to call his attorney. He had trouble with the call but finally reached De Stefano's secretary. She said her boss wasn't in the office. Colosimo told her to have De Stefano call him at the café. Jim walked out of the office and went to the back room of the restaurant. He spoke briefly with two kitchen employees who were preparing food for the early dinner trade. Then he walked from the back room through the dining room toward the front of the restaurant, heading to the small vestibule inside the ornate front doors. He pushed open the mirrored door leading to the foyer.

As Colosimo entered the small lobby, two loud gunshots rang out. Jim

crumpled to the floor. Only fifteen minutes had passed since he had entered
the restaurant. He was laying face down on the porcelain tile floor, blood running from a bullet wound in his head. Within minutes, he was dead.

All seven employees in the restaurant heard the two loud reports and
began to search for the source. The noises sounded different from the usual
sounds of the restaurant. Chef Antonio Caesarino, who had worked for
Colosimo for twenty years, opened the back door and looked into the alley
behind the café. He saw nothing that could have made the noises. Waiter
Louis Gus Stadleman guessed that the sound had come from the foyer and
went to the front to investigate. Seeing Jim's body, he frantically ran out to
Wabash Avenue looking for anyone fleeing the scene. All he saw were the lines
of autos and streetcars containing workers heading from downtown to their
homes. The copper was not on duty this early in the evening.

Bookkeeper Frank Camilla later told the police:

> Mr. Colosimo entered my office about 4:10 p.m. I was alone there. The
> chef, Antonio Caesarino; the cook, Joe Gentile; and the pantryman, Joe
> Tozzi, were in the service room adjoining, preparing for our 5:30 table
> d'hote. As is his daily custom, Mr. Colosimo, walked into my office and
> asked about the receipts for the night before and whether or not I had
> started a balance. Then he went to the telephone and called the office of
> Rocco De Stefano, his lawyer and one of his closest friends. He failed
> after considerable effort to get Mr. De Stefano and left word for the
> lawyer to call him at once.[4] He then left my office and walked east toward
> the entrance door and turned through the east doors which led to the
> north room.
>
> I don't know how long he was in there but it seemed only an instant when
> I heard two sharp reports. I thought at first it was the bursting of an automo-
> bile tire, but there was something so insistent about them that I determined
> to go outside and see. I walked out the door leading to Wabash Avenue. I saw
> nothing unusual and turned to re-enter. But there was a spring catch and I
> could not get in. I then walked to the north room entrance, stepped in,
> and stumbled over the body of Mr. Colosimo in the half darkness. I
> turned him over and saw the blood and yelled for help. Then I telephoned
> for the doctor. Someone else must have called the police.[5]

Alerted by waiter Camilla's yelling, chef Caesarino and the other employees rushed to the foyer. They stood uncertainly around Jim's body, aghast at
the scene. No one touched the body that had been their boss. Someone ran
back to the office to call the neighborhood doctor. It was 4:25 p.m. Big Jim
Colosimo, the first vice lord of Chicago, lay dead in the vestibule of his

restaurant at 2126 S. Wabash Avenue. Manager Abraham "Abe" Arends phoned the Harrison Street police station to report the shooting.

When the phone rang in Dr. Robert Cunningham's small office at 2204 S. State Street, barely a block from the restaurant, he picked up the black receiver and said his name. Someone shouted into the phone, "Get down to Colosimo's! Jim's shot!" Cunningham didn't need any other information. He had known Jim Colosimo for some time and occasionally had patronized the restaurant. He grabbed his medical bag and rushed down the wooden stairs to State Street. He hurried to the corner and turned west on Twenty-second Street. As he neared the restaurant, an employee standing at the north door waved him into the foyer.

Dr. Cunningham found Colosimo face down, his head pointing toward a phone booth and his feet pointing to the front door. The doctor checked for a pulse and found none. He found no sign of life and did not attempt any life-saving measures or call an ambulance. He saw a bullet hole behind Colosimo's right ear with powder burns around the entry hole. A large amount of blood had oozed from the hole onto the floor. As he examined the body, he noticed that Colosimo's clothing was not disturbed. He found a fully loaded revolver in the dead man's right hip pocket. In other pockets, the doctor found $120 in currency, a gold pocket watch, and a diamond ring. If Big Jim had been carrying thousands of dollars to pay for the liquor shipment, it was gone by the time the doctor arrived. The employees still milled around gaping at the lifeless body.

Cunningham walked into the dining room and noticed that there was a table set for one person. He checked a small cream pitcher on the table and found that the inside was wet from cream recently poured. The doctor also noticed a dozen bloody footprints that went from the dining room in the direction of the kitchen, but it was not clear to him whether these belonged to the killer or one of the employees.

After receiving the phone call from restaurant manager Arends, the desk sergeant at the Twenty-second Street District Station dispatched every available officer to Colosimo's Café. Several officers jumped into the back of the patrol wagon. The driver raced east on Twenty-second Street, gong sounding. Shortly after the first officers shouldered into the foyer, one of them phoned the Twenty-second Street station to verify Colosimo's murder. The desk sergeant contacted Capt. Michael F. Ryan, Superintendent John J. Garrity, the homicide squad, and the coroner's office. A squad of a dozen uniformed officers from the Twenty-second Street District Station, led by Lt. James McMahon, reached the scene. The police found a number of persons milling about inside the restaurant and moved them onto the sidewalk. Sirens and gongs sounded across the Levee. Police squads and patrol wagons began pulling up in front of the restaurant. The clamor drew crowds, and soon the sidewalk and the street were crowded with spectators. Friends of Colosimo, former employees, and Levee characters arrived. The word raced from person to person throughout the Levee.

Superintendent Garrity, First Deputy Chief John Alcock, Chief of Detectives Mooney, Detective Lt. Michael Hughes, and Coroner Peter M. Hoffman reached the scene. Sgt. John Norton, head of the homicide squad, brought his entire unit of twelve detectives. None of this show of law-enforcement officials was of any help to Big Jim.

The homicide detectives conducted a crime-scene search. They noted that the lobby contained a wooden phone booth with a nickel pay phone behind a mirrored door to the north and a small checkroom to the south. In between was a mirrored glass door leading to the main dining room. One bullet had gone through a lower door panel of the phone booth, entered a heavily plastered wall, and dropped down to the building's foundation. The detectives speculated that the most likely scenario was that the killer had hidden in the coatroom. When Colosimo entered the foyer, the killer fired two shots from the doorway of the coatroom. Because the detectives quickly assumed that the killing was an ambush, they did not consider that Colosimo and the killer may have been talking together in the small lobby before the shots were fired.

Captain Evans, the department's fingerprint expert, painstakingly checked the small entry room for prints. He found four distinct prints on the outside knob of the door leading to the north room and dusted the prints with a special powder to make them visible for photography. The police photographer set up a bulky camera on a sturdy wooden tripod. He used flash power and glass slides in wooden holders to take photographs of the body, the entry room, and the fingerprints that Evans had dusted. The coroner's physician and technicians from his office examined the body and released it to Orme's Funeral Parlor at Twenty-second Street and Michigan Avenue.

Moving their search into the restaurant the detectives saw that one table contained four used glasses. One glass contained beer. A waiter claimed it was near beer. The other glasses were empty. Frank Griffin, assistant bookkeeper, told the detectives that a party of two men and two women had been seated at the table and left about one hour before the shooting. Gathering the employees who were in the restaurant, the detectives transported them to the Twenty-second Street station for questioning. Taken to the station were:

Frank Camilla, head bookkeeper,
Frank Griffin, assistant bookkeeper,
Gus Tozzi, cook,
Joseph Gavilla, waiter,

Louis Stadleman, waiter,
Gus Tastalena, kitchen helper, and,
William Long, Negro porter.

The restaurant staff was questioned for hours by the station detectives, homicide detectives, and state's attorney's investigators. They were held overnight and released the next day.

De Stefano had telephoned the restaurant, returning the earlier call that Colosimo had made to his office. When he was told of the shooting he rushed to the scene. He was soon joined by a battery of legal heavyweights from the state's attorney's office, including George T. Kenney, secretary and personal assistant to State's Attorney Hoyne, and Assistant State's Attorneys John Prystalski, James O'Brien, and John Owen. The state's attorney's men left the café and went to the Twenty-second Street station. Prystalski, O'Brien, and Owen, yielding to the persistent cries for information from the band of reporters crowding around the front desk, held an impromptu press conference. They said that they suspected a connection between Colosimo's murder and the shooting of Enright only a few weeks earlier. The assistant state's attorneys said Colosimo was one of the men who was handling the behind-the-scene defense of those who had been charged with Enright's murder.

Meanwhile, the city detectives learned from their interviews that in recent years Colosimo had been protected by bodyguards when he had gone abroad. They also learned that seven months earlier he had received four Black Hand letters. The last came in November 1919 and directed Colosimo to leave ten thousand dollars at an appointed place at midnight. Jim had reportedly decided to handle the matter himself. He wrapped a one-dollar bill around a roll of paper and left the package at the designated spot at the designated time. Colosimo hid nearby and waited with a revolver in his hand. At midnight a man picked up the package. Jim moved quickly from his hiding place to fire a shot at the extortionist, but the unknown man had swung aboard a passing streetcar before Jim could act.

Detective Anthony Gentile, a longtime friend of Jim, told the press of a recent change in Colosimo's behavior. Gentile recalled:

> I can't imagine how a man could change more. I knew Jim for ten years, and I never passed his place when he did not give me the cheeriest kind of greeting. But lately it changed. I saw him Saturday night and said, "Hello, Jim." At first he didn't appear to see me. Then he stuck out his hand, but it was limp—the old, warm grip was gone. I'm certain that something was preying on his mind. His appointment to meet some one at the Café at

the hour he was killed, the gun in his pocket and the nervous farewell he gave his wife, all show he was going to meet trouble.[6]

The detective, knowing Jim normally went to the restaurant at seven in the evening, surmised that the 4 p.m. appointment was part of the murder plot.

Detectives were dispatched to the haunts of known Levee gunmen. They found several and took the surprised gangsters into custody. By late evening thirteen suspects had been arrested and subjected to rough questioning. The suspects were released one by one, except for Joseph and Jose Moresco, two of Victoria Colosimo's brothers. The police continued to question them in the hopes that they would admit that the murder was in retaliation for Colosimo's divorce from their sister and parsimonious financial settlement. The theory was fallacious, and the brothers were eventually released without charges.

A number of reporters went to the home on Vernon Avenue to question Dale Winter. They found the recent bride in hysterics. When she was able to speak she said Jim had left her to go to an appointment at the café. Through her tears she repeated her husband's last remarks: "You don't need to earn a living now. You can rest and study, and rest and sing, and rest, and perform in the Auditorium." She added that she and Jim often talked about her future and the "thing we were silliest about was my becoming a great singer some day."

The detectives arrived on Vernon Avenue after the reporters. They scooped up Dale, Jim's sister, and Isadore Piatti, an opera singer who was at the Colosimo home. The three were taken to the chief's office at city hall for questioning by senior officials in the police department and state's attorney's office. Again weeping hysterically, Dale denied that her husband had received any threats. Through her tears, she said Jim was not in fear of anyone. Abe Arends, manager of Colosimo's, and his assistant Harry James, arrived at city hall to comfort Dale. When the questioning was finished, they took a disconsolate Dale home.

The new widow returned to the Colosimo home after midnight and found a persistent reporter for the *Daily News* waiting there. He managed to talk his way into an interview with the woman the papers called the "sobbing little widow." Dale told the reporter:

> Jim left in his car for the Café shortly before 4 o'clock so that I could go shopping. A short time after he had been driven away I received a telephone message that he had been shot. I learned that he went to the Café and after telephoning the office of attorney De Stefano he went to the kitchen and on coming back, apparently to leave the Café, he was shot.

He often said he was unhappy and that he needed me. But I wouldn't go with him until we were married and I told him so. I loved him though—I loved him with all my heart. But after he obtained his divorce I married him. And he was as good as gold to me. During our honeymoon at West Baden I learned to know him better than anyone has ever known him, I think. And he had a heart of gold—pure gold. If I hadn't loved him before, I loved him then, I just couldn't help it. And to think he has been killed. We were so happy.

I'll learn things I never wanted to know about him. I've refused to know them. Couldn't they keep them out of all the talk? You can't know how completely Jim kept all of that away from me. I didn't care about what he had been. All I cared about was what he was when he was with me. He was my god. Really and truly he was my god. All of us around him were little things—nothings. I'm nothing without him.

I should say I suspect everyone. That is a terrible thing to suspect everybody—those near—the people I have heard about vaguely—and others who have been in his past.[7]

The *Daily News* article ended, "And so as she had glided skillfully away from leering, tipsy patrons of Colosimo's when she was the 'queen of the cabaret,' she glided skillfully away from the black knowledge in order to keep her own memory of Big Jim as white as possible."[8]

On Wednesday, Dale was questioned again by detectives, and this time she remembered that she and Jim had been threatened by Victoria Colosimo. Dale said: "She walked into the restaurant one night and told us that if we didn't stay away from each other, she would kill us—Jim and me. We tried to quiet her. At last she told us she didn't mean it and to forget it. But I didn't believe her—and neither did Jim."[9]

The press coverage was spectacular and expansive. The newspapers responded with a fury and printed a series of extra editions that newsboys hawked in front of Colosimo's Café and throughout the Levee and the downtown area. Each paper tried to top their competition with newer bulletins. A reporter for the *Herald and Examiner* wrote that Jim was worth a million dollars. A reporter for the *Evening Post* wrote that when the police examined Jim's body they found a keyring with a diamond estimated to be seven carats. The *New York Times* headed their story "James Colosimo Slain at Restaurant Door."[10] The Italian language newspaper *L'Italia* reported, "Colosimo had operated a nightclub frequented by *bon vivants* of high and low society who spent a merry time there." The paper stated that Big Jim derived "his stupendous income" from the café. In a highly critical statement reflecting the Italian Catholic viewpoint the paper reported that

Colosimo had divorced his wife in order to carry on with a younger woman, an entertainer at his club.[11]

Several of Jim's old friends met at Pat O'Malley's saloon on Polk and Clark streets in the heart of Little Italy. This beer parlor was chosen because twenty years earlier Colosimo, when he was a nobody, came in and drank large ten-cent schooners of beer at the long, polished mahogany bar. After several visits he was accepted by the regulars and enjoyed occasionally sitting down for pinochle with the owner. At the time Jim had recently been promoted to fore-man of a white-wing street-sweeping crew that did alleys in the downtown area, which meant he had little to do during his eight-hour shift. The regulars recounted how when Jim was tired he would "catch a little kip" in the base-ment of a bakery across the street.

The *Tribune* editorialized on the evil conditions in the Levee:

> Whatever the motive of the murder of "Big Jim" Colosimo, the crime fur-ther advertises the fact that there is a considerable region hereabouts where law is not. Or rather there is a law, but it is not the law of the land enacted by legislatures and applied by courts. The law this region knows is the law of the jungle. It issues not from the lips of judges but from the smoking mouths of automatics or sawed-off shotguns. Its officers are gun-men, Camorrists, labor sluggers, the dive keeper's henchmen.
>
> Colosimo belonged to this extralegal world that has no respect for any law but its own.[12]

Because of the many coarse descriptions in the press of his beloved friend as a vice lord, gang boss, and mobster, De Stefano rose to defend the dead man. He met with reporters to describe the character of the man who grew up in his family's apartment. De Stefano explained, "There never was a man, sub-jected daily to temptation as he was in his position, who proved himself more scrupulous and honest. He was a good man and generous to a fault. Take the case of his former wife's family. He practically imported all of them. He col-lected more money in the Liberty Loan drives than any man in his ward. He gave liberally to every Red Cross and YMCA drive. Jim would always listen to someone in trouble. He never betrayed a confidence. Everyone loved him. I remember once he took one of his singers, a fellow named Prati, to West Baden with him. Prati was sick at the time, and Jim paid all of his expenses while he was recovering. I can cite numerous other cases where he paid the hospital expenses and doctor bills of his sick employees."[13]

On May 13, homicide detectives went back to the scene of the murder to conduct a reenactment of the events in the café when Colosimo was killed. Lt. James McMahon described what he believed was the sequence of the events.

He explained: "Jim had walked into the foyer to talk in private with the mysterious stranger. The pair talked briefly. Jim either became angry or disgusted and decided to end the conversation quickly. Jim turned away to re-enter the restaurant. The killer drew his revolver and fired with his gun only a short distance from Jim's head. Jim went down fast with a bullet in the brain. As Jim fell the killer's second shot went wild. The killer fled silently out the front door and disappeared."

A few days later Big Jim was laid to rest in Oak Woods Cemetery. Michael Iarussi, whose card stated he was a funeral director, embalmer, and auto-livery driver handled the arrangements. The Colosimo family was charged $2,500 for the embalming and casket and $125 for an electric cross and torches used during the wake. Later, Colosimo was moved to a private Gothic-style mausoleum with black iron gates in the front and a stained-glass window in the rear. The vault and mausoleum cost $6,500. No one else ever was placed in the mausoleum.[14]

Rocco De Stefano still was grieving deeply over the loss of his friend since boyhood when he learned that his mother, Emmanuela De Stefano, had died shortly after learning of the sad news of the murder of Colosimo—her "foster son" Jim, whom she had raised from the time he came to Chicago at age twelve.[15]

An advertisement in the entertainment section of Chicago daily newspapers that co-incidentally appeared on the day of Jim's death read:

Colosimo's—Finest Italian Restaurant in Chicago
Table de Hote Dinner $1.50—Cabaret and dancing

There was no mention of the deadly event that was going to take place that evening. Never again would the café be filled with world-class celebrities; never again would the spotlight beam on the angel of the cabarets; never again would the man in the white three-piece suit move between the tables projecting Italian gusto. The first vice lord of Chicago was dead.

Chapter Thirty-Five

INVESTIGATING IN ALL DIRECTIONS

How Not to Solve a Crime

1920

THE VENGEANCE of Frank Raszina, escaped convict, sent up for life for the murder of Colosimo's friend, to which the café man testified.

THE JEALOUSY of Arthur Fabri, a fellow entertainer of Dale Winter, who loved her before she married Colosimo.

THE REPRISAL of the Arnstein-Sullivan bond robbers for the arrest of two members of the band who were habitués of the Wabash avenue resort.

SOME CONNECTION with the murder of "Moss" Enright and Edward Coleman.

THE SPITE, possible, although doubtful, of the first Mrs. Colosimo over the romance of her husband and the youthful and pretty cabaret singer.[1]

— Colosimo murder theories, *Chicago Evening Post*

On the day after the murder, Coroner Peter M. Hoffman convened an inquest at Orme's Undertakers on the edge of the Levee. Friends of Colosimo, police officers, newspaper reporters, and Levee characters crowded into the small room. The coroner empanelled a six-man jury and announced that Dale Colosimo would not be present due to illness. He added that the police had advised him that they needed more time to conduct a thorough investigation. He said that the detectives had said they had no evidence to offer for the inquest. Hoffman then solemnly announced that, due the circumstances, he was continuing the hearing indefinitely. Coroner Hoffman and Luigi Colosimo signed the death certificate. Less than ten minutes had elapsed, probably the all-time record for a five-star, front-page murder inquest. The disappointed throng slowly filed out and milled around in front of the funeral parlor until they saw Hoffman escorting the jurors to the nearby Colosimo's Café. The mob of curious followed to 2128 S. Wabash Avenue.

At the restaurant, Hoffman brought the jurors into the entry area where the murder had taken place. The coroner had notified some press in advance because newspaper photographers already had set up their bulky cameras in the foyer. Hoffman knelt on one knee and pointed a revolver at the phone booth door. Amid a fusillade of flashes, he reenacted his version of what had taken place.

One initial murder theory followed by the detectives was that Victoria Colosimo had developed a strong grievance against her former husband and had gotten her revenge. A police search on the night of the murder had failed to locate the first Mrs. Colosimo. Lt. Michael Hughes of the detective division said: "I am convinced that when we find Mrs. Moresco we will learn that the murder was the result of a family quarrel. Her brothers, we suspect, were not satisfied with the money settlement following the divorce."[2] Investigators learned that following the divorce Victoria's brother William started a loud argument with Colosimo in the café. The quarrel grew so violent that a waiter got a revolver and stood by Jim's side. Lt. James McMahon said he couldn't locate William but had found and arrested another brother, James, on the day of the shooting. While James Moresco was being questioned, the detectives vainly searched for Victoria. They were unsuccessful. She seemed to have disappeared.

A few days later reporters located Victoria in California where she had been living since the divorce. She had told the police how to reach her. In a long-distance phone conversation Victoria somehow managed on her say-so alone to persuade the detectives that she was not involved in any murder plot. She suggested that the police investigate the goings-on at the gambling room above Colosimo's restaurant where high-stakes gambling took place night and day. She hinted that Colosimo may have been slain as the result of a gambling feud. The police investigated Victoria's gambling theory, as well as the Moresco family vengeance theory, and both were discarded. After several days in jail and several intensive interrogations. Victoria's brother James was released.

Detective Sgt. Anthony Gentile had a theory about the murder. After interviewing employees at the restaurant, he concluded that Arthur Fabri, the musician who had helped Dale's career, might be the guilty party. Café employees had told Gentile about Fabri's romantic interest in Dale, and the sergeant surmised it could have been a crime of passion by a discarded lover. When Gentile learned that Fabri had moved back to his hometown of Grand Rapids, Michigan, he requested assistance from the police in that town. The Grand Rapids police reported back that Fabri had not been seen in town since last summer when he had returned home from Camp Grant to visit his wife, a local girl.[3] When detectives learned that Fabri was living in New York, Gentile's theory was summarily dismissed.

A hapless drifter known as Frank Razzino[4] turned into a likely suspect when someone recalled that in 1906 he had shot and killed a friend of Big Jim Colosimo. At Razzino's trial, four Colosimo employees gave damaging testimony that sealed Frank's fate. He was sentenced to be hanged at Joliet state penitentiary, but before Razzino could be executed he was judged insane and sent to the state mental hospital in Menard, Illinois. Having been recently discharged from the hospital, Razzino had been seen on Twenty-second Street just weeks before Colosimo was shot. An initial search by detectives failed to produce Razzino. They did manage to locate Arthur Rockhill, a New York theater representative who was in Chicago on the night of the murder. He told an amazing story. Rockwell said he had been walking along south State Street near midnight on May 11 when he saw an obviously intoxicated man stumble and sit down on the concrete. The man asked for a match, and Rockwell gave him one. When the drunk took it, a revolver dropped from his pocket. The man mumbled something about having killed that "God damn dago." Rockhill was taken to the bureau of identification and shown mug shots. He identified a police photo of Razzino as the drunken man. Immediately, additional squads of detectives joined the hunt for Razzino. The police department's daily bulletin described Razzino as "wanted in connection with Colosimo's murder." Newspaper headlines blared "Colosimo Foe Identified as Death Boaster" and "Ex-Convict Hunted as Feud Killer." Razzino was eventually spotted and arrested, but, after intensive questioning, he was cleared of any involvement in Colosimo's murder.

Grasping at the proverbial straw, the police came up with a new suspect, Antonio Villiano, whom they described as a close friend of Victoria Colosimo. Although he lived in Los Angeles, informants whispered to the police that he had been in the Levee area around the time of Colosimo's murder. Subsequent investigation proved that Villiano had not left Los Angeles.

A fanciful theory that was never substantiated was that Big Jim had been the organizer in a one-hundred-thousand-dollar wine purchase that went badly. On behalf of a number of his countrymen, he had placed the order and made the payment to a St. Louis dealer in contraband alcohol, so the story went. When the wine was received by the participants, more than three-fourths of the bottles had spurious labels and contained only water. The disappointed purchasers demanded their money back, but Jim reportedly could not obtain a reimbursement. Italian gossipers mused that the dissatisfied customers caused Colosimo's murder. Savvy homicide detectives laughed and discarded the theory almost as soon as they heard it.

Lieutenant McMahon from the Twenty-second Street District Station told the police reporters that he was certain that Colosimo had gone to the restaurant on the fateful day to meet an unknown man at 4 p.m. McMahon wondered aloud why Jim had not taken Dale and her mother with him on the trip to the restaurant so that the two could have continued on in the chauffeured car to do their downtown shopping. In addition, when Colosimo entered the restaurant the first question he asked was whether anyone had called for him. Lieutenant McMahon suggested that learning the identity of the man that Colosimo was to meet could solve the mystery of his murder.

Early in the investigation, but overshadowed by more sensational matters, Joe Gabreala,[5] a porter at Colosimo's Café, phoned the South Clark Street District Station to report that he had information about the murder. Gabreala said that, between 3 p.m. and 4 p.m. on May 11, he noticed a man with his hands in his coat pockets who was pacing nervously between the north and south dining rooms in the restaurant.[6] Seeking further details detectives went to Gabreala's apartment at 216 E. Twenty-second Street. Gabreala told them his attention was attracted to the mystery man by "his queer actions and nervousness." Gabreala asked the man, "What can I do for you?" "Nothing," he answered. The man turned away from Gabreala and continued his pacing. Gabreala left work just before the shooting. He walked home and went to bed. The next morning when he read in the newspaper of the killing he made his call to the police.[7]

The homicide dicks scrambled to search for this suspect. For the first time in the case they had a real suspect who might actually have been the killer. Gabreala told the police that the man was a white American male, twenty-four years old, 145 pounds, tall, slender, dark hair, rosy cheeks, blue eyes, and wearing pants with cuffs and a tight-fitting gray overcoat. From informants in the Levee the detectives learned that the description fit Frankie Yale, a tough New York City gang leader and friend of Johnny Torrio. One informant claimed that Torrio had paid ten thousand dollars to his Brooklyn friend to murder Colosimo. There was a persistent rumor that Yale was in Chicago on the day of the murder.[8] The Chicago police made a request to the New York police to pick up Yale. When Yale was arrested in New York in late May, two detectives and Gabreala took the train to New York. A police lineup that included Yale was arranged. Gabreala was asked if he could identify the man he had seen at Colosimo's Café. The porter became frightened and refused to select anyone.

The Chicago detectives learned nothing from questioning Yale. They left New York without placing a charge against him. When the detectives returned to Chicago they complained that the New York City police had hampered their investigation. The detectives said they were not allowed to interrogate Yale unless there were New York officers present.[9]

Lieutenant McMahon, never out of theories, told the reporters of his newest idea regarding the murder. He said that the manner in which Colosimo was killed indicated the murderer was a drug addict or insane. Unfortunately, McMahon failed to provide an explanation of how he had reached this conclusion. On May 14, he announced that a Levee underworld character and drug addict known as Gordon the Jew was being hunted by his detectives. McMahon said that Gordon had hung around Colosimo's Café for almost twenty years. During that time, Jim had generously given Gordon handouts. McMahon had an informant who said that in recent months Jim turned down the requests for money, which caused Gordon to make threats against the restaurant owner. Unfortunately, Gordon was never found, and nothing came of this incredible line of inquiry.

Despite the fact that it had occupied the front pages every day, Mayor Thompson showed little interest in the Colosimo slaying. He made no comments to the press and took no visible part in the investigation. He was so unconcerned that he and his political partner Fred Lundin left town on May 14 for a two-week cruise on the Mississippi, Ohio, and Tennessee rivers. This pleasure jaunt included all of his cabinet heads and thirty-four ward committeemen who were members of the Republican Central Committee. Diamond Joe Esposito, a powerful South Side politician who soon would become another gangland victim, also joined the jolly vacationing "sailors."[10]

By late May the police were running out of leads and theories. They found one more that led them to question William Sullivan, alias Chubby Lardner. Sullivan had been in Colosimo's Café several weeks before the murder drinking with a party of women. Because he began to create a disturbance, he was given the bum's rush to the front door by the waiters. Sullivan put up fierce resistance that resulted in him getting a thorough beating by the staff. Sullivan had vowed vengeance and thus unwittingly made himself a suspect. He was detained but was quickly cleared.

On May 18, State's Attorney Hoyne told reporters he had ordered his chief investigator Morris Wilson to vigorously investigate the Colosimo murder. Hoyne said he wanted Victoria Colosimo questioned as soon as she returned to Chicago. Not to be outdone, Police Chief Garrity revealed that he had received a new clue from three Italians but declined to reveal their identity or the clue. He issued a general order commanding all officers working on the case not to disclose any information to the press. He said that death threats had been received by several witnesses, causing them to become fearful of cooperating with the investigation. He said it would be necessary to shield all witnesses.[11]

On May 21, Victoria Colosimo returned by train from the West Coast. Meeting her at the railroad station was Rocco De Stefano's wife and a virtual phalanx of newspaper photographers, reporters, and bystanders. After being photographed and interviewed, the two women began to leave the station. Sgt. John Norton and Detective Anthony Gentile stopped them on the platform and insisted that Victoria accompany them. The group went to the state's attorney's office where Victoria was questioned for several hours by assistant state's attorneys and investigators. The following day Victoria vehemently denied to the press that she was married to Tony Villiano.[12] She described him as a friend. Speaking like a woman scorned, she said: "I am nobody's wife, but I am the widow of Jim Colosimo. I haven't seen him [Antonio Villiano] since last February, when I left Chicago. I have not married, and I am still the widow of Jim Colosimo. I am here to fight for my rights. Dale Winter never was Jim's wife. He got his divorce while I was in California. I knew nothing about it, because the papers were never served on me. The divorce is void."[13]

For the next six months the investigation continued with little direction and no positive results. Each month there were fewer leads to follow and fewer detectives assigned to the case. On December 8, Deputy Coroner Charles F. Kennedy resumed the inquest into Colosimo's death. Porter Joseph Gabreala from Colosimo's Café testified about the mysterious man he had seen in the restaurant on the day of the murder. He gave a detailed description of the man but said he did not know the man's identity. De Stefano rose to his feet and shouted out: "This man is not telling the truth. He and other witnesses are not telling all they know. I believe he knows who shot Colosimo. I believe that it is possible that the New York suspect was the man and Gabreala was afraid to identify him. Perhaps Gabreala feared that he too would lose his life if he told the truth. He is really the only one who can identify the killer."[14]

Neither De Stefano nor Kennedy could shake Gabreala. The last witness was a police officer from Chicago who testified that the department had no clues or leads concerning the identity of the killer. Deputy Coroner Kennedy asked the jurors to render a verdict. They returned an open verdict, which meant that the jurors couldn't determine anything other than Colosimo had been murdered by parties unknown. Kennedy said that this verdict could be amended if new information was developed in the future.[15] Death certificate No. 32805 was issued by the coroner's office. The cause of death was given as "hemorrhage and injury to the medulla oblongata due to a bullet wound of head."[16] The medulla oblongata is the smaller and lower portion of the brain stem that controls autonomic functions, including the cardiovascular and respiratory systems. The killer's single bullet had ended Jim's life in an instant. He was most likely dead before he hit the floor of the foyer.

Two days later, De Stefano called a press conference. He said the failure of Gabreala to identify the suspect was due to fear of the Black Hand. De Stefano said that the inability of the police to protect witnesses who could testify against Italian criminals was responsible for the long list of unsolved crimes against Italians in Chicago. He emphasized, "I will not rest until Jim Colosimo's murderer is brought to justice."[17]

On December 14, De Stefano called the press again to announce that he had new information. He said that one hundred and fifty one-thousand-dollar bills that Big Jim had obtained by selling securities and gems before his murder had disappeared and could not be located. De Stefano said that Colosimo had shown these thousand-dollar bills on the day before he was murdered to Michael Potson, his business partner in the café. The attorney explained that Colosimo had been transferring his wealth into cash so that he could purchase a residence on Lake Shore Drive for himself and Dale. According to De Stefano, Big Jim's intention was to reform and lead a cultured life among the wealthy patrons of his café.

Before the reporters could close their notebooks De Stefano said he had more to say. He announced that bookkeeper Frank Camilla had been investigating the murder and had information about the killer. Camilla had learned that thirty minutes after the shooting the killer took a cab from Colosimo's Café to a downtown railroad station. Camilla had reported that the taxi driver had left town after the murder. De Stefano said his name was Louis Santuzzi. During Camilla's investigation he had learned that Santuzzi had returned to Chicago. He had been located by Camilla, and arrangements had been made to have Santuzzi appear at De Stefano's office the following day. De Stefano and Santuzzi were then going to police headquarters to look at a photograph of Frankie Yale. De Stefano told reporters he surmised that immediately after the killer shot Colosimo he took $150,000 to $175,000 from Big Jim's pocket and fled in Santuzzi's dirty brown cab to catch the next train to the East Coast. De Stefano hoped to clinch the identification of the murderer from Santuzzi's description of his passenger.[18] Unfortunately Santuzzi did not arrive the next day at the lawyer's office. The *Daily News* had printed Santuzzi's name in the evening edition of their paper and Santuzzi, apparently terrified, was said to have fled in the early morning hours from his lodging on west Twenty-second Street. No one ever heard from Santuzzi again.

In mid-December 1920 the case heated up for the last time. Police Chief Charles C. Fitzmorris, who had been appointed by Mayor Thompson to replace Garrity on November 10, 1920, announced that he had a new informant who had important information about the Colosimo murder. Fitzmorris said: "Someone in Chicago had contracted for the murder with a major Black Hand organization in New York City. The agreement specified a payment of $150,000 for the killing with $20,000 going to the gunman and $130,000 to the Black Hand gang. On the day of the murder Frankie Yale and another man came to Chicago. They killed Colosimo and were then given $150,000 which Colosimo had earlier placed in a tin box in his office. Shortly after the killing the pair returned to New York with the money."[19]

The informant, who claimed he had seen the murderer, said that the primary motive behind the killing was to remove "the powerful Levee lord whose influence and ramifications extended far into the political and official life of Chicago." The informant said that after the shooting the gunman fled north on Wabash Avenue to Twenty-first Street and took a taxi to the Illinois Central station in time to catch a 6 p.m. Michigan Central train to Buffalo.[20]

Chief Fitzmorris sent a telegram to New York police requesting the arrest of the "Italian who it is believed shot Big Jim Colosimo to death."[21] The chief sent detectives to New York to assist the police there in following the new lead. The Chicago detectives were seeking Frankie Yale and an accomplice who was believed to have stood guard while Yale shot Colosimo. Despite a search, Yale could not be located.[22] The Chicago detectives returned home empty-handed, complaining that influential New Yorkers were hiding Yale.

Chicago Police Department Case No. 3326 on the Colosimo murder was filed away. The report dryly recounted the facts of the killing and categorized the case as a "homicide, intentional murder."

Al Capone, offering a suggestion many years after Colosimo's death, explained the root of the problem, "Colosimo had a lot of money" and "Johnny wanted a big cut." Capone alleged that Johnny Torrio thought that Jim was "growing soft." During a violent argument one night in the small office in the back of Colosimo's restaurant, Big Jim slapped Torrio so hard that he fell backward to the floor. Later Big Jim explained: "That bum thinks he's my partner. He only worked for me."[23]

Today, the answer to why Colosimo was murdered can be deduced from what happened after the killing. One man had wanted to take over the very successful vice empire that Big Jim had created over a period of almost twenty years. One man had the vision to see what tremendous opportunities national Prohibition was going to bring. One man had reached a point in his career where it was time to become the boss. One man had sufficiently bribed the Chicago police so that they never investigated his link to the murder. This was the man who immediately after the murder assumed unchallenged command of Colosimo's vice empire.

This was the same man who had wept openly when he was told of Jim's murder. "Big Jim and me," he said, "were like brothers."[24] This was the man who had connections in New York that could supply an experienced killer who was not known to the staff of Colosimo's restaurant or to the Chicago police.

This man was Johnny Torrio, who on May 12, 1920, became the head of Colosimo's vice operations, bootlegging operations, and all of the other criminal activities that had made Big Jim Chicago's first vice lord.[25]

Chapter Thirty-Six

WHAT HAPPENED
TO THE CASH?

Dividing Up Big Jim's Estate, What Little There Was Left

1920

Instead of disclosing an estate of a half a million dollars, the famous cabaret king's attorney, Rocco De Stefano, searching high and low, has found only some liberty bonds, a few other securities and some jewelry, which, with the value of his interest in the restaurant, will not amount to more than $1,000,000.

— *Chicago Evening Post*

Like most of the immigrants of that period, James Colosimo left no will, but his intestate death was not the most serious concern confronting the heirs. The real problem was the difficulty in locating his assets. The money and valuables that were found after his death seemed far too meager for a vice chieftain. British journalist and author Collinson Owen, writing in England in 1931, offered an explanation: "It was understood that for a long time the Black Hand had exacted heavy payments from him." Owen did not mention who it was that "understood" this, nor did he give any evidence supporting his assertion. Perhaps Black Hand payments could have diminished some of Big Jim's resources, except Owen goes on to report that Colosimo had Johnny Torrio slaughter the Black Handers that had been shaking him down and then relaxed and took life easy.[1] It seems highly unlikely that Big Jim Colosimo, vice lord of the Levee, made any payments to Black Handers.

Attorney Rocco De Stefano did not delay in filing the papers seeking to open Jim's estate. On the morning of May 17, a hearing was held in the court-room of Probate Judge Henry Horner[2] in the county building. Detectives, reporters from the city's six daily newspapers, and a crowd of spectators filled the courtroom. Six claimants for Colosimo's estate testified. Two key players, Dale Winter and Luigi Colosimo, were joined by other members of the Colosimo and Moresco families. In the course of the proceedings Winter fainted twice, once in the courtroom and once in the hall outside the courtroom.

Luigi Colosimo, speaking Italian with Sgt. Anthony Gentile translating, said he lived at 3156 S. Vernon Avenue and that he was Jim's father. Luigi testified he had married three times. His first wife was Santa, with whom he had one child named Antonio, now forty-nine. Following Santa's death Luigi married Giuseppina, and they had had four children: Francesco, Maria who had married Vincenzo Petroco, Bettina who had married Franco Ciraldo, and a son named Vincenzo, later known as Big Jim. After Maria died, Luigi married Ursala, who died without bearing children. Luigi listed the survivors of James Colosimo as Dale Winter Colosimo, Victoria Moresco, Antonio Colosimo, Francesco Colosimo, Maria Colosimo Petroco, Bettina Colosimo, and himself. For the record Luigi explained how Jim had married and divorced Victoria Moresco and then married Dale Winter. Luigi said he learned of Dale and Jim's wedding from a letter dated April 17, 1920, that Jim had sent from Indiana. Luigi concluded his testimony by stating that Jim had had no natural or adopted children.[3]

De Stefano told the judge that as a longtime adviser and friend of Colosimo, he was in the best position to interpret Jim's wishes concerning his estate. De Stefano added that before Colosimo's death, Jim had discussed providing bequests to the Knights of Pythias Orphans' Home and a scholarship fund for the high-school education of poor boys. Subsequently, Judge Horner appointed De Stefano as administrator of Colosimo's estate and issued an order allowing De Stefano to open the safes and vaults belonging to Colosimo. Neither the Knights of Pythias nor the scholarship fund was ever mentioned again.

On May 16, De Stefano went to the Illinois Trust and Savings Bank, the Fidelity Vaults, and the Michigan Avenue Trust Company to collect the contents of Jim's safe-deposit boxes. Observing the box openings were Dale Winter, Luigi Colosimo, and Leroy Wilner, a representative from state Attorney General Burndage's office. The keys to the boxes had not been found, so a professional safe expert was hired to drill open the boxes. De Stefano revealed nothing concerning the contents of the boxes to the reporters who followed the party from bank to bank, saying that every item would be recorded and every paper carefully read before he released any information. A lock expert also drilled the safe in the office at Colosimo's Café.

Meanwhile, Victoria Colosimo said in an interview with the *Chicago Daily Journal:*

Jim is dead and I won't besmirch his name. Until he met Dale Winter he was good to me and I won't say ill of the dead because of the times he was good to me. But the people that are concerned in many of his affairs and who all seem to have turned against me now will have reason to regret. When I go back it will be with a carefully planned campaign. I will rock Chicago. This is not idle talk. Those who understand will know what I mean. For twenty years I was Jim Colosimo's confidant, and at times his adviser. If they who are fighting me want to test it, I am ready for a fight to the finish. I am an Italian. Jim was an Italian. I am not afraid. I will be protected but I will have my own [protection].[4]

On May 24, Dale Winter Colosimo went to a Probate Court hearing concerning the estate. She carried a green-covered document, which she planned to present in court. The document waived all her claims against the estate. It also relinquished her dower right, widow's award, widow's rights, and all other benefits and claims. She said she took this action to preserve Colosimo's estate in its entirety so that a suitable monument or mausoleum could be erected in the memory of her departed husband. Before entering the courtroom she made clear to the reporters her position concerning her late husband's money, her thoughts, and her plans for the future. Although virtually penniless, Dale said, "All I want of Jim is the memory of him. I don't want his money or the things he gave me. I'm going to sing again. Maybe I'll sing better. I know now there isn't much to life except giving something to others. There'll never be anything in my life except singing and remembering and singing."[5]

Dale, represented by De Stefano,[6] presented her document to Judge Horner. Dale's renunciation read: "I, the grantor, Dale Winter Colosimo, for and in consideration of the sum of $1 and the further consideration of love and affection which I cherish and hold dearly for James Colosimo, now deceased, and his loveable memory, I, the undersigned, Dale Winter Colosimo, hereby and herewith forever waive, relinquish, release, surrender and quit claim all my rights, titles, interest, and benefits which I may have by reason of my marriage, to all of his estate both real and personal, including any interest in the restaurant business, jewelry, merchandise, cash, etc."[7]

After reading Dale's renunciation, Judge Horner indicated that he was deeply concerned over her abjuration of her widow rights. Dale replied she was taking the action "so that there remains no grounds for the belief on the part of anybody that she married Big Jim for his money."[8] De Stefano explained that Dale was retaining her engagement and wedding rings. He added that the Colosimo family had agreed to "take care" of Dale, but in response to the judge's questions, admitted that he was unable to show any proof of this plan. Judge Horner shook his head gravely over Dale's actions and reluctantly accepted the renunciation but said he wanted additional information before he would allow the document to be formally recorded. Dale reserved the legal right of bearing the name of Colosimo to respect his memory as his grief-stricken and bereaved widow.

On the same day as the court hearing, Victoria Moresco accepted a $12,500 payment from the estate.

On May 29, a brief legal proceeding took place across the Atlantic Ocean in a courtroom in Petilia Policastro, Cosenza, Calabria, Italy. A somber group assembled in this stately chamber of justice. Present were Consul General of the United States Francis B. Keene, two representatives of the Department of Justice, a representative of the Ministry of Foreign Affairs, a notary, the collector of filing costs, the clerk of the court, the president of the tribunal, and the two required witnesses. Appearing before the presiding judge, Antonio Colosimo, Francesco Colosimo, and Maria Colosimo agreed to have their father, Luigi Colosimo, act as their general attorney in all matters relating to the handling of Big Jim's estate. The judge agreed and signed the formal documents. The clerk added the seal of the court. The document was sent to the United States.

Meanwhile, De Stefano continued his search for the Colosimo fortune. So far, De Stefano said he had found less than $50,000 in cash and bonds. He reported that twelve keys had been found on Colosimo's body, but that he had only been able to account for two of them. What doors the other ten keys opened never was determined. De Stefano had found one safe-deposit key that he could not match with a corresponding bank. Although De Stefano promised steadfastly that he would search and search until he found the full estate, he gave up in one month.

On July 24, Jacob Verburg, assistant to Probate Judge Horner, reported that an inventory of Colosimo's belongings received from administrator Rocco De Stefano showed property valued at $81,945. That amount included a half interest in Colosimo's Café valued by De Stefano at $25,000.[9] The inventory included bonded whiskey valued at $3,500. The heirs to the Colosimo estate sold the thirty-five barrels of whiskey that had been found in a government-controlled warehouse to Mike Potson for $2,232. On August 18, the heirs of Colosimo's estate gave Dale Winter Colosimo three Ambassador Hotel bonds worth $3,000 and one diamond lavaliere worth $3,000.

Also in August new information about Colosimo's financial affairs came to light. A few weeks before his death Big Jim had purportedly engaged in some unusual banking business with President Warren C. Spurgin of the Michigan Avenue Trust Company at Michigan Avenue and Twenty-second Street. There was no factual information, only verbal allegations, as to exactly what the banking business consisted of. Shortly after Colosimo's murder, it was discovered that Spurgin had fled Chicago leaving the bank insolvent. Spurgin had engaged in bad loans and illegal activities with bank funds. The information about Colosimo's dealings with Spurgin came from Torrio, Bloom, Joe Grabiner, and Izzy Lazarus. They suggested that Colosimo may have deposited $100,000 with Spurgin shortly before his death. No record could be found of any such transaction at the bank. Spurgin was indicted by the Cook County grand jury but was never apprehended. No money ever was obtained from the bank.

Adding more darkness to the tragic ending of Big Jim, Mayor Thompson revoked the cabaret, restaurant, and cigarette licenses of Colosimo's Café on October 27. The police acted promptly now that Colosimo was not around and shuttered the restaurant. Mayor Thompson said that he had received complaints of liquor being sold in violation of Prohibition. Rumors in political circles suggested that the actual reason behind the closing was that Kenna and Coughlin were supporting Michael Igoe for state's attorney while the mayor's candidate was Judge Robert E. Crowe. De Stefano announced that as the direct result of the action by the mayor and chief the value of the restaurant dropped to $5,000 from its earlier appraisal of $25,000.

The official record of Probate Court for Colosimo Café that was filed on October 30 showed assets at $8,133 and liabilities at $3,000.

On February 25, 1921, De Stefano filed a final statement of Colosimo's estate. There were no real estate holdings because the residence and the restaurant property had been transferred to family members many years before. The personal property in Colosimo's estate was listed as:

Forty-five U.S. Liberty bonds	$14,500.00
Two notes secured by a trust deed signed by Mary Aducci and husband on July 1, 1919	$10,000.00
Checking Account at Michigan Avenue Trust Company	$8,197.72
Cash in safe-deposit vault, Michigan Avenue Trust Company	$4,000.00
Receipt for 50 barrels (1630 gallons) bonded whiskey	$3,500.00
Diamond lavaliere	$3,000.00
Three Ambassador Hotel bonds	$3,000.00
Platinum ring with five karat diamond and small diamonds, garnets, and emeralds	$2,500.00
Receipt for U.S. Liberty bonds	$2,500.00
Pearl stickpin	$1,500.00
Equitable Life Assurance Society of the U.S. policy	$1,478.86
Interest on U.S. Liberty bonds	$537.81

Cuff buttons set with diamonds	$350.00
Platinum chain with pearls	$200.00
Suspenders with gold attachments set with eight diamonds	$200.00
Three unset diamonds	$110.00
Cash from person of the deceased	$101.33
Collar buttons set with diamonds	$100.00
Platinum chain set with pearls and onyx	$100.00
Stickpin set with one diamond and nine rubies	$100.00
Two Automobile Service of Illinois shares	$100.00
Interest coupons	$83.12
Platinum chain set with eleven small stones and greenstones	$75.00
Stickpin set with one diamond and three pearls	$75.00
Garters with gold clasps and buckles set with six diamonds	$60.00
One Sportsman Club of America bond	$50.00
Oak Woods Cemetery refund deposit	$37.00
Stickpin set with four small diamonds, eleven emeralds and sapphires	$35.00
Fifteen chip diamonds	$30.00
Pearl-handed Revolver	$25.00
American flag set with rubies, diamonds and emeralds	$20.00
Clerk of the Criminal Court refund check	$10.00
Full dress buttons	$10.00
Leather pocketbook with gold border	$10.00
Pair of onyx and pearl buttons	$10.00
Pearl cuff button set with small diamonds	$10.00
Platinum chain set with pearls and onyx	$10.00
Three onyx and pearl shirt studs	$9.00
Gold chain	$5.00
Gold match safe	$5.00
Gold pencil and case	$5.00
Gold ring	$5.00
Four full dress pearl studs	$4.00
Leather card case with gold border	$3.00
Collar button set with blue stone	$1.00
Gold cigar cutter	$1.00
Gold handle knife	$1.00
Gold cigar lighter	$ .50
Total	$56,665.34

The audit of the property in the closed Colosimo Café did not contain any hints of the colorful restaurant and nightclub that had once featured the Singing Angel.

North Room
42 tables, 1 upright piano, 1 high chair, 1 ticket box, 1 waiters cabinet

South Room
29 tables, 1 grand piano by Bush & Gertz, 1 music cabinet

Office
1 oak desk, 1 filing cabinet, 1 typewriter, 1 adding machine, 1 couch, 1 book rack, 1 small safe, 6 small pictures, 1 check protector

Kitchen
2 cash registers, 2 cashier's chairs, 1 water cooler, 1 water filter, 2 coffee urns, 1 hot water urn, 1 dish-washing machine, 1 gas range, 1 broiler, 1 hot-water tank, 6 enamel pans, 5 enamel strainers, 5 stew pans, 1 knife cleaning machine, 5 chairs, 1 table, 1 cook's work-stand, 1 meat block, 1 garbage can, 2 large copper pans, 2 small copper pans, 1 large heavy tin boiler, 12 heavy kitchen utensils, 3 dishpans, 3 mop pails, 5 spaghetti strainers, 7 spaghetti sauce strainers, 22 waiters trays, 1 plunger

Dishes
3 two-foot platters, 68 assorted platters, 75 dinner plates, 83 soup plates, 267 small plates, 22 sugar bowls, 12 water bottles, 53 sets of salt and pepper shakers, 26 glass match stands, 75 cups, 104 saucers, 72 creamers, 168 butter chips, 12 cruets, 14 tea pots, 11 celery trays, 2 gravy dishes, 8 large salad glasses, 1 butter cutter, 1 pencil sharpener

Plated Silverware
24 oyster forks, 87 soup spoons, 137 tea spoons, 172 forks, 177 knives, 24 streak knives, and miscellaneous silverware and equipment

Glasses
229 water glasses, 318 split glasses, 30 snit glasses, 36 Tom Collins glasses, 18 fancy glasses, 112 ice cream dishes

Miscellaneous
   2 cheese machines, 12 cheese grinders, 1 ice box, 1 ice-cubing
   machine, 1 bottling apparatus for manufacturing soda water

The Colosimo family received the following amounts from the proceeds
of the estate:

Luigi Colosimo, father	$733.33
Francesco Colosimo, brother	$366.66
Bettina Colosimo Ciraldo, sister	$366.67
Antonio Colosimo, half-brother	$366.67
Maria Colosimo, sister	$366.67
Total	$2,200.00

A surprise reopening of the hunt for the missing Colosimo fortune came
in November 1921. The heirs gave a contract to Michael Potson to search for
Big Jim's money. The contract provided that Potson would receive a portion
of any funds he recovered. Potson estimated that the missing estate amount to
be $250,000 to $500,000 in cash and $250,000 in securities. He began his
search by checking the walls in the family home on Vernon and in Colosimo's
Café for a hidden cache. When he found nothing, Potson offered a reward of
$15,000 for information that would reveal the whereabouts of the missing
funds, but there were no takers. Potson then revealed for the first time that,
only a few days prior to Colosimo's murder, he had accompanied Big Jim to
the bank. As they left the bank, Colosimo gave Potson a box to carry to Jim's
home. Once inside the house on Vernon Avenue, Jim "laughed and asked me if
I knew what I had been carrying. Then he opened the box before me and
pulled out 250 $1,000 bills. He counted them and played with them like a boy
while we sat there in the living room of his home."[10] Potson never located the
$1,000 bills nor any of Jim's "fortune."
   Starting in the early 1900s, Big Jim made an estimated fifty thousand dollars a month, untaxed, from his resorts and brothels. In addition, he was likely
skimming from the payments for protection from the other resort and gambling house operators. Add the income from the café and the gross is more
than ten million dollars. Where did it go? Did father Luigi carry packages of
currency back to Colosimi in his suitcases? Did Torrio grab the cash after the
sudden demise of the Levee's whoremaster? No one has ever presented a rea-
sonable explanation of the disappearance of Colosimo's fortune or the hundreds of thousands of dollars that Big Jim allegedly had on hand at the time of
his murder.

Chapter Thirty-Seven

THE END OF THE LEVEE AND BIG JIM

Vice and Colosimo Flourished; Their Success Wrote Their Doom

1920

> *In exchange for three weeks' marriage with a beautiful singer, Jim Colosimo lost his empire, his first wife and his life. One only hopes that Dale sang that well.*[1]
>
> — Norman Mark, *Mayors, Madams, and Madmen*

The closing of Levee—first in 1912 and more emphatically in 1914—marked the end of the segregated vice district in Chicago. Many other American cities had similar vice areas in the early 1900s.[2] Following Chicago's lead, one by one, the red-light districts across the United States were shut down.[3]

Starting in 1914 the Levee in Chicago slowly deteriorated into a slum. The resorts lost their patrons and closed their doors. The cribs were torn down or used for homeless shacks. Prostitution grew more decentralized, emerging across the city in seedy neighborhoods and nightclub areas. While roadhouses rose in numbers and popularity, those employing professional prostitutes significantly decreased. The brothel-dominated prostitute caste disintegrated and disappeared. Ladies of the evening were no longer imprisoned by force or poverty within chattel houses. Some began working in apartments controlled by organized crime; some in rooms on their own; a few worked the taverns; and the lowest strolled the streets near the downtown or night-life sections.

The killing of Colosimo ended the era of a first-generation powerful Italian gang, union, and political boss who ran vice and criminal activities in Chicago and the suburbs. The only reminder of his importance was the bouquet of red carnations left once a year at the door to the mausoleum in Oak Woods Cemetery where Big Jim was interred. Even that noble practice by an unknown person stopped in the late 1980s. Today, mourners and sightseers passing by the gray burial monument with the bent iron gates no longer remember Big Jim or his famed café. His name and his role in Chicago's vice history had faded from memory.

The first vice lord and the ladies of the Levee were gone.

EPILOGUE

What Happened to All Those Persons and Places After Colosimo Was Shot

Colosimo's Café

The first evidence of the existence of a restaurant operated by James Colosimo at 2126 S. Wabash Avenue can be found in advertising directories and telephone books beginning in 1911. Paul Bergamini, Big Jim's head waiter, filed an application on behalf of Colosimo for a liquor license on October 27, 1914.[1] The age of the two conjoined buildings where the restaurant was located is not known. One preposterous estimate, by reporter John H. Thompson in the *Chicago Tribune*, would have placed it in 1834, a year after founding of the city.[2]

On June 29, 1918, Michael Potson, the restaurant manager, purchased from Colosimo a half-share in the restaurant.[3] When Jim was murdered in 1920, the estate and his heirs, Luigi Colosimo and his four children, acquired Jim's half-interest in the business. The five new half-owners had only begun to settle the estate's affairs when, on October 28, 1920, Mayor William Thompson ordered Colosimo's Café summarily closed, purportedly for selling whiskey during Prohibition.[4] Rumor was that Thompson was punishing Aldermen Michael Kenna and John Coughlin for supporting Michael Igoe for state's attorney over Thompson's own candidate, Judge Robert Crowe. The place was reopened with a restraining order and a Superior Court injunction denying the city's power to license restaurants.[5] The injunction was ultimately sustained by the Illinois Supreme Court.[6] After several years, Luigi Colosimo and his family sold their half interest to Potson and returned to Italy.[7]

Potson retained full control of the business until its demise, always keeping the well-known name Colosimo's Café. Potson was born D. Mihail Bogodlou in Asia Minor around 1880 and immigrated to the United States in 1900. By 1906 he had worked his way up from selling pistachio nuts to buying a restaurant and pool hall at 2015 S. Clark Street. Along the way he earned a reputation as a shrewd operator and a big-time gambler.[8]

The wet bar and upstairs gambling at Colosimo's attracted the attention of federal enforcement agents. In 1926 and again in 1928 a federal judge padlocked the place for a year for Prohibition violations.[9] In 1929 federal agents swooped in and rounded up Ralph "Bottles" Capone (Al Capone's brother) and his friends.[10] In 1932 federal agents again "halted the revels" at Colosimo's and arrested six patrons.[11]

When Prohibition ended, Potson kept Colosimo's popular with musical reviews and ice shows, along with its traditional opera singers in an air-conditioned venue.[12] Colosimo's Café continued into the middle forties, but by then Potson's reputation as a gambler had begun to get in the way. Hollywood comedians Abbott and Costello sued Potson over gambling losses they sustained in the second-floor gambling room. The federal government indicted Potson on a broad range of gambling charges and in 1948 sent him to prison. He was paroled in October 1950. Eventually, he moved to Encino, California. He died on September 29, 1955.[13]

After several failed attempts by outsiders to acquire the restaurant and after a fire swept through it in January 1953, the Church of Divine Science took over the property. The Church redid the interior and held services there. Because of the slum-like condition of the premises, the City of Chicago sued to raze the property. On February 7, 1958, wreckers leveled Colosimo's. Even after its death, the café managed to make a headline. A relic hunter acquired a still that had been found in the basement only to be charged by the federal government with possession of illegal equipment. Eventually the government backed off because it was discovered that the still no longer worked.[14]

Victoria Colosimo

Victoria Colosimo, nee Moresco, divorced by Big Jim Colosimo in February 1920, was living in Los Angeles at the time of the murder. After returning briefly for the police inquiry, she returned to Los Angeles and within the year married her boyfriend, Antonio Villiano, a Naples-born bartender and grocer.[15]

It was a stormy relationship. Villiano was involved in a damage suit for assaulting Victoria's landlord in December 1920. In 1925 Victoria sued her husband for divorce, but later dropped the suit.[16] On April 30, 1930, the U.S. Census found the pair still living in Los Angeles at 3622 W. Jefferson. They had no children.[17] In December 1930 Victoria again sued Antonio for divorce, this time charging him with flourishing a gun and threatening to kill her and her sister who was living with them. Despite their marital problems, they apparently remained together until he died on June 21, 1944, in Los Angeles. Victoria was listed as his wife on his death certificate. He died of pneumonia.[18]

Two years later, Victoria married again, this time to a man named Reeg. Nothing is known about Reeg except that he died before Victoria. She died as Victoria Reeg on December 24, 1964, in Los Angeles General Hospital of arteriosclerosis vascular disease. She was eighty-five years old. She was buried at Holy Cross Cemetery.[19]

Rocco De Stefano

Rocco De Stefano, Jim Colosimo's attorney and one of his closest friends, mourned his mother and Big Jim in the days after the murder. His mother, who had raised Jim as a part of her family during his adolescent years, died on May 16, 1920, at the age of seventy-two. Her obituary reported, "Colosimo's death proved a shock to her and hurried the end."[20]

Rocco was convinced that Jim had been killed by the Sicilian Black Hand, a notorious extortion fraternity. He argued this theory forcibly at the coroner's inquest in December 1920. He was able to obtain support from State's Attorney Robert Crowe in urging victims of the Black Hand to come forth and make reports of their incidents.[21] A news story after Rocco's death said he had "aided in exposing and suppressing the notorious Mafia Black Hand Society."[22]

Throughout his career as an aggressive criminal defense lawyer, Rocco drew the respect of his legal colleagues. His clients sometimes were from the criminal element, sometimes from the wealthy. In 1914, in perhaps the most spectacular of his cases, he caused the Illinois Supreme Court to set aside a finding of guilty and the death sentence on behalf of Sabella Nitti-Crudelle, who was poor, illiterate, and accused of murdering her husband. The court found that she had not "received a fair and impartial trial."[23] In 1921 De Stefano was chosen as a director of the Lawyers Association of Illinois.[24] In 1931, the Justinian Society of Advocates, an Italian American legal organization, honored him on his thirty-fifth anniversary as a lawyer with a banquet at the Morrison Hotel.[25] During his career, he served as assistant corporation counsel, assistant attorney of the Cook County Forest Preserve District and special assistant state's attorney. He was appointed as an assistant attorney general by Gov. Henry Horner in 1933.[26]

On August 8, 1936, Rocco's second wife, Bessie, died at the age of fifty. She was buried in her birthplace, Farmington, Missouri.[27] The following year Rocco, who had long been active in the Elks, was elected "esteemed leading Knight" of Greater Chicago Lodge No. 4. Before he could succeed automatically as Exalted Ruler, and after a long illness, he died at Mother Cabrini Hospital on April 2, 1938. He was sixty-two years of age. Final services were held at Holy Rosary Church and he was buried in Calvary Cemetery.[28]

Minna and Ada Everleigh
When Mayor Carter Harrison Jr. closed down the Everleigh Club in October 1911, the sisters Minna and Ada Everleigh retired with an estimated one million dollars in cash and two hundred thousand dollars in jewelry—a considerable amount in 1911 dollars for two young ladies in their thirties. After the closing, they left promptly on an extensive European tour. They later returned to Chicago in hopes of retiring quietly and privately to their favorite pastimes, theater-going and writing poetry. Because they were too well known in Chicago, they moved to Manhattan, changed their last name to Lester (which probably was their original surname) and lived out the remainder of their lives in luxury and privacy. Minna died on September 16, 1948, in New York at the age of seventy. Ada died on January 3, 1960, in Virginia at the age of eighty-four.[29]

Carter Harrison Jr.
After his fifth term as mayor, in which he parted with Aldermen Kenna and Coughlin and closed down the Levee, Carter Harrison lost the 1915 Democratic primary to Robert M. Sweitzer. Sweitzer, in turn, was defeated by the Republican candidate, William "Big Bill" Thompson.[30]

In World War I, Harrison, anxious to serve but too old for military service, became a captain in the American Red Cross and served in field hospitals just behind the front lines. An avid cyclist, fisherman, and big-game hunter, he traveled extensively after the war with his wife in Europe and Africa. He kept in touch with the political scene though he never again sought elected office; and in 1933 President Franklin Roosevelt appointed him collector of internal revenue for the northern district of Illinois, a task he performed for eleven years before retiring permanently from public office at the age of eighty-four.[31]

He and his wife, Edith, were patrons of the symphony and opera. They had acquired a substantial art collection, which Harrison donated to the Art Institute of Chicago. It included works by Gauguin, Cassat, Monet, and Toulouse-Lautrec. A proud and outspoken man, Harrison wrote two autobiographical works, *Stormy Years* and *Growing up with Chicago*, which continue to provide insights into the history of the early twentieth century. He died sitting at the dinner table on Christmas Day, 1953, at the age of ninety-three. [32]

Maclay Hoyne
Grandson of a founding trustee of the City of Chicago, son of an attorney who served as president of the Chicago Bar Association, halfback on the Williams

College football team, Maclay Hoyne was in his eighth year as Cook County state's attorney when Big Jim Colosimo was murdered.[33] He and his staff had amassed an impressive record of more than five thousand felony convictions in his eight years in office. In that time he had received several hundred threatening letters, culminating on May 23, 1920, with an attempt on his life.[34]

A protégé of Carter Harrison Jr. with extensive political experience, Hoyne won two successive terms as state's attorney. He sought the Democratic nomination for mayor in 1919. He ran as a third-party candidate, splitting the Democratic vote and handing the election to Thompson.[35] In 1920 he sought a third term as state's attorney, but the intra-party wounds of 1919 had not healed, and he failed to gain the nomination. He did not take the defeat graciously.[36]

Hoyne pursued the practice of law until a new opportunity for public service came when the Democrats secured control of the Sanitary District in 1926. Despite the old tension between Hoyne and new Sanitary District Chairman Timothy Crowe, Hoyne accepted an appointment as head of the district's legal staff.[37] The district was riddled with patronage and corrupt payroll practices, and Hoyne got caught in the crossfire. During his three-year tenure as chief lawyer for the Sanitary District, Hoyne provided valuable service on a working committee representing Chicago during the Great Lakes diversion conferences. At issue was how much Lake Michigan water could be diverted by Chicago to dispose of its sewerage.[38]

In 1932 disciplinary proceedings were brought before the Illinois Supreme Court by the Chicago Bar Association for hiring and payroll practices in the Sanitary District in 1927–1929. Hoyne was one of fifty-five lawyers cited. Despite his claim that he had no authority or responsibility for hiring and firing, and despite eloquent pleas on his behalf, on December 24, 1932, Hoyne was suspended from practice for one year.[39]

Hoyne returned to private practice and remained at it until a few weeks before his death. He died in his home of uremic poisoning on October 1, 1939. He was survived by his widow, Marie, and two sons, Thomas Maclay Hoyne II of Winnetka and Francis J. Hoyne of Flossmoor.[40]

Michael Kenna and John Coughlin

Before Alderman John J. "Bathhouse John" Coughlin died on November 11, 1938, he and his aldermanic colleague, Michael "Hinky Dink" Kenna, had ruled Chicago's First Ward and dominated much of Chicago politics through the mayoralties of Hempstead Washington, John Hopkins, George Swift, Carter Harrison Jr., Edward Dunne, Fred Busse, William "Big Bill" Thompson, William Dever, Anton Cermak, Frank Carr, and part of the mayoralty of Edward Kelly—eleven mayors and forty-six years. As children, they were raised when Chicago was a city of horses; as senior aldermen they officially approved the opening of Chicago Municipal Airport (now Chicago Midway International Airport) in 1927.[41]

Coughlin died of pneumonia at the age of seventy-eight. He had been an alderman of the First Ward continuously since 1892. Kenna died on October 11, 1946. He had held the post of alderman from 1897 to 1922 and 1939 to 1943, but he had held the more powerful post of First Ward Democratic Central Committeeman from his first election to this position in 1892 until he resigned because of age in 1944.[42]

Kenna and Coughlin ran the notorious First Ward Ball and made a living from selling protection from the police to operators of vice and gambling establishments. They successfully fought the attempt of traction magnate Charles Tyson Yerkes to "buy" the Chicago City Council for his streetcar lines.[43]

Coughlin and Kenna were friends and colleagues, but they were quite different. Coughlin loved the outdoors and frequently traveled to Colorado where he owned property and a stable of horses. He was indifferent to religion. He remained single all of his life. When he died, his estate was probated at $22,500, enough to provide a $100-a-month lifetime income for his sister, Katherine. Kenna was quiet, retiring, and careful with his money. He was married but had no children. He was a devout and practicing Catholic. His estate amounted to a substantial $928,270. He left the majority of it to his twenty nieces and nephews.[44]

John Patton

From the moment John Torrio visited Burnham in 1907 and made a deal with Johnny Patton, the village president, the town flourished as a major center for vice and earned the reputation of "having more red-light houses and prostitutes per capita than any other comparable spot in the world."[45]

After Colosimo's death, Patton was promoted to a vice boss for Torrio in the west suburban towns of Cicero and Stickney.[46] He continued as a vice chief under Al Capone and later under Capone's successors. He retired in 1949 after forty-two years in the twin roles of Burnham village president and mob viceroy for the suburbs.[47]

As did many of his mob associates, Patton became interested in horse racing. On September 22, 1931, Patton obtained a lease from the Illinois Central Railroad for land in Cicero. The property had formerly served as a dog track owned by mob bosses Jake Guzik and Frank Nitti. On May 2, 1932, the land was opened as a half-mile horse racetrack, known as Sportsman's Park. The *Chicago Tribune* described it as "an elaborate affair with a swanky clubhouse and attractive racing strip . . . that many say is the finest half-mile racing plant in America." Edward J. O'Hare and John Patton, president and secretary-treasurer, respectively, admitted that they owned 85 percent of the stock in the track.[48]

On November 8, 1939, O'Hare, by then known as a "millionaire front man" for the mob and the mob representative at Tropical Park in Florida, was shotgunned to death gangland style at Ogden Avenue and Rockwell Street in Chicago.[49] Investigations led to revelations that O'Hare was one of the syndicate's "most valuable men" alongside John Patton and Frank Nitti.[50] The following year, John L. Keeshin, trucking magnate, bought out Patton and heirs of the deceased O'Hare to gain sole control of Sportsman's Park.[51]

John Patton died on December 23, 1956, at his farm home near Earl Park, Indiana, after a three-year illness.[52]

Rev. William T. Stead

Rev. William T. Stead drowned at sea in the *Titanic* disaster in 1912. Stead was planning to visit the United States to speak on world peace at a conference in New York City. William Howard Taft had asked Stead to appear at the conference, which was to be held at Carnegie Hall.

When the *Titanic* struck the fateful iceberg, Stead helped several women and children into the lifeboats. After all the boats had gone, Stead went into the first class smoking room, where he was last seen sitting in a leather chair and reading a book.

In 1886, Reverend Stead had written an article titled "How the Mail Steamer Went Down in Mid-Atlantic, by a Survivor." In the story a steam ship collides with another ship. Many persons on board lost their lives due to a shortage of lifeboats. Stead wrote, "This is exactly what might take place and will take place if liners are sent to sea short of boats." In 1892, Stead wrote another story about a maritime disaster, this one titled "From the Old World to the New." In the article Stead told how the steam ship *Majestic* rescues survivors of a ship that had hit an iceberg.

William Hale Thompson

One of the most flamboyant and controversial mayors in Chicago history, William Hale "Big Bill" Thompson was in the middle of his second term when Jim Colosimo was assassinated. He had defeated reform candidates in the elections of 1915 and 1919. He lost to reform candidate William Dever in 1923 but defeated him in 1927. In 1931 he was overwhelmingly beaten by Bohemian immigrant Anton J. Cermak. In 1939 Thompson tried to get the Republican nomination for mayor but the result was a "humiliating, complete, and final" defeat.[53]

While holding the post of mayor, Thompson was vigorously pro-German and anti-British. He encouraged book burning and tried to force the Chicago

Public Library board to prune books that he found unacceptable. He was
widely reputed to be financially connected to Al Capone. He was indicted for
bribery and corruption of the Board of Education. In the trial Thompson was
defended by Clarence Darrow and found not guilty.[54] After Thompson died,
investigators from the offices of the state attorney general and state treasurer
found $1,466,250 in U.S. currency and $36,000 in gold certificates in his safe-
deposit boxes.

The *Chicago Daily News* called him "a practical politician of the first mag-
nitude . . . his success was based on deception and distraction. He was the most
amazingly unbelievable man in Chicago's history." And the *Chicago Tribune*'s
legendary Col. Robert R. McCormick said: "He was intelligent, clever, and a
fighter. I can remember the times he made a monkey out of us."[55]

William Hale Thompson died of a heart attack on March 19, 1944, at the
age of seventy-four.[56]

John Torrio

John Torrio stepped up after Colosimo's death to operate his vice operations
and organize and direct illegal liquor trade, primarily beer, in Chicago, Burnham, and Cicero. With the aid of young Al Capone, Torrio quickly amassed
great power and considerable wealth. The *Chicago Tribune* reported that for
his mother Torrio had purchased a seaside estate in Italy and staffed it with
servants. The newspaper said Torrio measured his profits in "hundreds of
thousands."[57]

A few years later, in a rare moment of bad judgment, Torrio was arrested
by federal Prohibition agents in connection with his purchase of the Sieben's
Brewery on Chicago's Near North Side. The arrest was a setup arranged by
archrival Dion O'Banion. The federal government convicted twenty-two
Chicago hoodlums for the crime, including Torrio. On November 25, 1925,
while the indictment was pending, the powerful and ruthless O'Banion was
murdered. The killing took place in O'Banion's flower shop on Clark Street
across from Holy Name Cathedral in broad daylight. Torrio had ordered the
murder and had brought in Frankie Yale as the lead killer. The Chicago Beer
Wars began in earnest.[58]

Barely seven weeks later, while returning in the late afternoon from a
shopping trip with his wife and brother-in-law, Torrio was attacked and shot
numerous times by men from the North Side Gang in front of his residence.
As the assassins fled, his wife, Anna, helped drag the bleeding Torrio to the
front door of their apartment. He was taken to Jackson Park Hospital where
his condition turned critical. But two weeks later he was strong enough to
appear in federal court to request that he serve a pending nine-month jail sentence for the Sieben's incident in the Lake County Jail, deemed by him a safer

harbor than the Du Page County Jail to which he had been sentenced. After serving the sentence, Torrio quietly disappeared from Chicago.[59]

He recuperated from his wounds with a trip to Europe and then returned to New York. He developed real estate interests in St. Petersburg, Florida.[60] Little is known of him until 1931, when he was subpoenaed and brought back to Chicago to testify before a federal grand jury in Al Capone's income tax trial. He said nothing of importance and remained quiet for the next several years. Then, in October 1935, two major New York crime figures, Arthur "Dutch Schultz" Flegenheimer and Louis Amberg, were killed in gangland fashion. The press reported that Torrio had become the power behind the scenes in the New York mob. He was indicted for the murders but never tried.[61]

In 1936 the Alcohol and Tax Division of the Internal Revenue Service secured sufficient evidence to have Torrio arraigned on a charge of defrauding the government of $250,000 in alcohol taxes. Three days later, Anna bailed out her husband with $100,000 in cash.[62] The indictment languished. A year later another federal grand jury indicted Torrio for income tax evasion and conspiracy. In a surprise turn of events he pleaded guilty. He was sentenced on April 13, 1939, to two and a half years in prison and forfeit of his $100,000 bond.[63] He served the sentence in Leavenworth federal prison and was released on parole in November 1941.[64] He remained comparatively quiet after that, although newspapers carried a story in 1954 that he was in Chicago "with authority to speak for the Mafia" in mediating the feud between Chicago crime barons Tony Accardo and Paul Ricca.[65]

Late in life, Torrio and his wife retired to a residence at 9902 Third Avenue in Brooklyn. He died in his barber's chair of a heart attack on April 16, 1957, and was buried in Greenwood Cemetery.[66] The event was unnoticed for three weeks. After Torrio's death, Anna returned to her birthplace to live in the Cincinnati suburb of Mariemont, and on July 30, 1964, at the age of seventy-four, she died of peritonitis in the Glass Nursing Home in Cincinnati. Her body was shipped to Brooklyn and was interred alongside her husband.[67]

Dale Winter
After Colosimo's death, Dale Winter, married for only twenty-five days, retired to live with her mother. She kept her stage name and in March 1921 in Chicago she filled in as the lead in the Chicago company of *Irene*, the most successful Broadway musical of the decade. She again was the lead when the company played Cincinnati for two weeks.[68] It became her signature role. She sang the role for a sixteen-day Broadway revival in 1923 and often in the years that followed.[69]

In November 1924 she married Henry Duffy, a thirty-year-old Broadway actor and producer.[70] The couple moved to California where Duffy built a

large and successful string of legitimate theater houses in San Francisco, Los
Angeles, and other cities on the West Coast. Dale frequently appeared in his
productions, and they formed and co-owned the Duffy Players.[71] In the early
thirties, Dale presented Henry with two children who lived to become successful, one as a physician and the other in theater.[72]

But the Great Depression and the coming of movies dealt a death blow to
the legitimate theater. Most of Henry and Dale's theaters closed before the
end of the thirties, and they filed for separate bankruptcy in 1941. In 1945
they were divorced. In the forties, Henry produced at least one successful
musical in New York, but he died at the age of seventy-one of cancer, virtually penniless, at the Motion Picture Country Home in Woodlands California on November 17, 1961.[73] Dale, meanwhile, was cast in a few
forgettable films in the early forties, but she was already in her midfifties and
inexperienced before the unforgiving camera. There would be no more film
roles. She married and survived two men of wealth, Herschel McGraw and
Edward S. Perot. The second husband, Perot, died on June 25, 1963, in Santa
Barbara.[74] Twenty-two years later, on November 28, 1985, Dale died in Santa
Barbara "after an extended illness." Her obituary noted that she was "a mem-
ber of the Coral Casino, The Little Town Club, and Birnam Wood Golf
Club" as well as a practitioner for her last twenty-four years with the First
Church of Christ, Scientist.[75]

Glossary of Period Terms

B-girl—bar girls who worked in dance halls and solicited male customers to purchase watered-down drinks for them.

B-highballs—drinks ordered by dance hall and bar girls when they were with male customers. The drinks were either non-alcoholic or severely watered down.

bagman—collector in a vice organization. A bagman collects weekly and monthly protection dues from vice-resort and gambling-house operators. The money is split by the boss of the local political organization and the district police commander. The bagman may be an agent of the police or the political leader.

bagnio—see *house of prostitution*.

bar girls—see *B-girls*.

bawdy house—see house of prostitution.

billy—short for billy club, a small handheld weapon used by police to forcibly subdue prisoners. It was used in blows to the head. Most were made of leather, and some contained lead.

Black Hand—usually a group of Italian and Sicilian blackmailers who preyed on businessmen in the Italian community in the immigrant cities east of the Mississippi River during the late nineteenth and early twentieth centuries. While many historians and true-crime writers describe this Black Hand as an organized group, some even suggesting that it was controlled from Italy or Sicily, Dr. Robert Lombardo, in his well-researched and scholarly work, explains that the blackmailers were unorganized opportunists in numbers of cities who took advantage of the fear they engendered with their crude letters in the Italian immigrant community and the tradition of these new citizens not to bring their troubles to the police. The fear was not imaginary, as there were countless bombings, shooting, stabbings, and murders committed by Black Hand gang members to prove they were deadly serious about their demands for money from the small merchants and wealthy businessmen who were their victims. The name was derived from the drawing of a black hand on the extortion note. In Italian *Mano Nera*.

blind pig—saloon or tavern running illegally during Prohibition years. Later used to describe an establishment selling alcoholic beverages without the proper licensing. Blind pigs operated clandestinely and did not have signs outside advertising the nature of their business. The location of blind pigs were almost always known to the police and accordingly had to pay off the police or the local politicians to continue operation. Their locations also were known to everyone in the neighborhood.

blocks—designation used in Chicago to indicate the smallest geographical unit. A block was usually two rows of buildings or houses separated by a narrow alley with streets on all four sides. A block was approximately one-eighth of a mile in length and one-sixteenth of a mile in width.

bluebloods—wealthy and elite persons. See *bluestocking*.

blue laws—legislation with a Puritanical bent; e.g., the Illinois midnight-closing law on Saturdays and the all-day closing on Sundays for saloons. Proponents of blue laws favored strict law observance and were opposed by supporters of a wide-open town. Blue laws were anti-vice, anti-wild dancing, and anti-liquor in nature and always in opposition to any saloon activities on Sundays. Usually promoted by church groups.

bluestocking—person who was a wealthy resident of the Gold Coast and North Shore with strong, personal concerns about the improvement of Chicago. The word comes from the French *bas blue*. A person with gentility, class, and manners. See *bluebloods*.

blind—see front.

boater—round straw hat with a wide band worn by men from Memorial Day to Labor Day.

boodle—bribe or illicit payment to a politician or public official to gain favor.

booking—procedure in the arrest process. After being arrested a person is taken in custody to a police station where the desk sergeant completes an arrest form and places the person in the station lockup until he/she is released on bond or goes to court. In Chicago during the years 1890 to 1914 it also was used to describe the interview visit that a plainclothes officer conducted with each new girl at a house of ill-repute. The officer listed the girl's name, age, and other information. This booking meant entering the name of new prostitutes on the station's books. The process was a bogus operation to conceal the actual age of new girls under eighteen. The girls had been carefully instructed by the madam or by their cadets to lie about their ages.

brass knuckles—metal appliance that was placed over the fingers to land a forceful blow against an opponent in street fights. The device consisted of four metal rings welded together that were slipped over the fingers of the user's strongest arm. Sometimes used by police officers. Possession of brass knuckles was a crime.

brothels—see house of prostitution.

bully pulpit—advantageous position of public authority or public visibility for making one's views known. Politicians, elected officials, ministers, and organization officials can make use of their position of authority by speaking or writing in this manner when attempting to accomplish an objective.

bum's rush—forceful throwing a drunk or other unwanted person out of a bar usually by bouncers or waiters, also used for pushing a person rapidly out of any place where his presence is no longer wanted.

bum steer—false information, bogus information.

bunco—variety of crooked confidence games and gambling games. Also, bunko.

bunco men—men employed by gamblers to work in their operations, usually as steerers.

cadets—procurers working for brothel operators and madams who identified likely young girls at train depots and elsewhere as possible recruits for houses of prostitution, an integral part of the infamous white slave trade. Term used interchangeably with pimp.

cappers—see *steerers*.

catch a little kip—Chicago slang for sleeping, usually when the person should be working, sometimes practiced by police officers on the midnight shift and politically sponsored workers.

cathouse—see *house of prostitution*.

chippies—streetwalkers, a common slang used in America in the nineteenth century to describe common prostitutes.

clout—political power, as in the ability to get things done through political relationships.

colored—name given to African Americans by many whites in the late-nineteenth and early twentieth centuries.

come-alongs—special devices, similar to handcuffs, used by early police officers to attach to an arrested subject and pull the subject forcibly along the sidewalk to the station or police call box. One form was a metal ratchet cuff that could be tightened around the suspect's wrist as needed by the officer. Another involved two small, flat pieces of metal linked by a short, thin chain. An officer held the two pieces of metal in his hand and twisted the chain around a prisoner's wrist. Further twisting by the officer caused pain with the intention of subduing an unruly prisoner.

coop—see *hole*.

cop, coppers—police officers

corner—see *going to the corner*.

creaker—wooden device used by early Chicago police officers to summon aid from nearby officers, first used in 1857. An officer in need of help would activate the creaker, and the noise would be heard by nearby officers on patrol. Mostly used in the nighttime when there was less street noise.

cribs—lowest class of houses of prostitution, a room in a cheaply constructed wooden, one-story building. The room would contain a single bed, a wooden chair, a small table with a wash basin, and sometimes a dresser. The room would front directly on a street.

cut whiskey—popular practice during Prohibition in which water, coloring, and flavors were added to real whiskey to make two to three gallons of cut whiskey from one gallon of genuine whiskey. The process also was known as cutting. Provided an economic advantage to the seller when the buyers thought they were purchasing the "real thing."

demimondaines—women kept or protected by wealthy lovers. In the context of the book it is simply a fancy way of saying ladies of the evening.

dicks—detectives.

dive (boxing)—as in "take a dive" was an expression using in boxing to indicate that one of the two fighters in a match would be instructed by his manager to deliberately lose the fight.

dive (economic)—used to indicate a business in the Levee that was a low-down disreputable type of place, usually a saloon serving five-cents-a-glass, twenty-five-cents-a-shot saloon to bums, drunks, and lowlifes.

dollar houses—houses of prostitution where the charge to spend a few minutes in a sex act with a prostitute was one dollar.

drayman—driver of a heavy horse-drawn cart without sides used for haulage. The cart was called a dray.

drys—individuals, organizations, and states that were in favor of the prohibition of alcoholic beverages. The Woman's Christian Temperance Union (WCTU), one of the major "dry" organizations, was founded in Evanston, Illinois, the next town north of Chicago. While the WCTU managed to keep Evanston as dry as a bone; Chicago was wet as the ocean.

downtown—commercial, business, and entertainment section of Chicago.

dummy—person who applied for and/or held a liquor license on behalf of the true business operator. *Front* and *frontman* are synonyms. Also used in real estate deals to hide the true ownership of property.

expositions or exposition shows—weekly events staged in the back rooms of certain brothels in which two prostitutes, usually of considerable size, engaged in no-holds-barred wrestling matches. Their costumes were scanty, and the patrons paid a sizable admission fee. Sometimes expositions meant sexual acts between two women or a woman and a man.

fall houses—vice and gambling houses selected by vice bosses to be used for fake vice raids by the police. All-important patrons were advised to leave the premises before a raid, and only a few whores and a stand-in madam were arrested.

faro—card game operated by a dealer and usually two helpers. The players wagered on the unseen top card of the dealer's deck. The game often featured a mechanical device from which the top card was selected. While the game could be operated honestly, it frequently was crooked. The cheating was accomplished by card manipulation through the dexterity of the dealer or by the house-controlled workings of the mechanical box. Faro was a popular card game during the early days of the frontier and was common in early Chicago. The gambling houses featuring this game were often known as faro banks. The play was done on a faro table.

fix—maneuver behind the scenes to thwart justice so that an arrest or trial would result in the defendant being freed despite the charges or evidence against the person. Usually involved bribing the arresting officer, investigating detective, prosecuting attorney, or judge.

fixer—person who was used to obtain a verdict (not guilty or discharged or dismissed) acceptable to the defendant in criminal cases. The lawyer representing the defendant usually handled paying the fixer his required fee. In turn, the fixer would split his fee with the judge or police officer or both. Sometimes the fixer accomplished his task by having a strong political pull with the party currently in power in the mayor's office.

flats—apartments in multistory rental buildings.

flop house, flops—dilapidated frame structures where persons who had no regular residence and little money lived in Chicago's early years. The earliest rent was five cents, but it moved up to twenty-five cents over the years. In later years these buildings were known as skid-row hotels that charged one dollar for one small room with a bed and table and wire screening for a ceiling. Frequently used by beggars and drunks.

footpads—criminals who operated on foot and robbed their victims usually by physical strength. Usually worked in dark streets, alleys, or gangways.

front—legitimate business operated to disguise an illegal or quasi-illegal operation. The legal operation was most frequently in the front of a building while the illegal business was in the rear, hence the name "front." Most commonly used for gambling joints.

frontman—person who served as the visible head of a gambling house or prostitution resort. The frontman operated the vice activity for the true boss or bosses who sometimes were local political figures or wealthy individuals and did not want their names openly linked with illegal activities.

fooey lawyers—shyster lawyers working in the Levee who dealt primarily in criminal cases.

fork over—act of giving something to someone that a person might otherwise not want to do, as in "He had to fork over his share of the winnings." Usually involved duress.

gamahucher specialists—prostitutes around the time of the Civil War.

girls—women, regardless of age, who worked in a house of prostitution.

go-between—person who operates between criminals and law enforcement seeking to obtain favors for the criminals from the police or courts. See fixer.

going to the corner—act by a woman leaving a dance hall to go to a nearby hotel for prostitution.

Gold Coast—Michigan Avenue (Lake Shore Drive) north from the Chicago River to North Avenue and the adjacent streets east and west of Michigan Avenue. Beginning in the early 1900s the area where many of Chicago's wealthy citizens resided.

goody-goody two-shoes—reformer, churchgoer, sweet and virtuous person, derogatory title given by a person engaging in a vice or inappropriate political or governmental activity to describe a reformer or social activist. Sometimes a goody-goody two-shoes was used derogatorily to describe a social activist with wealth or social position. Often shortened to goody two-shoes.

goodtime girls—women workers in saloons who would mingle with male customers and encourage them to buy them drinks. The women were very friendly and easy-going. If the men wanted to dance or drink, the women obliged. If the men wanted to go upstairs or in back, the women were willing to go for a price.

greenhorns—Persons who are not familiar with the culture of an area, new arrivals, persons who could be easily deceived or tricked, immigrants.

grizzly bear—crude dance with strong sexual movements that came to the Levee around the turn of the century from the Barbary Coast in San Francisco. Very popular with the patrons of the saloons and dance halls, but Alderman Kenna was opposed to the activity. Kenna made Ike Bloom stop the dance in Freiberg's Dance Hall and forced the police to halt it in other places in the vice district.

Guinea—Italian immigrants. Used derogatorily by non-Italians, primarily by the immigrant Irish to taunt Italians into fights.

habeas corpus—writ usually served on the police to bring a person who it is said is being held unlawfully before a judge.

hack driver—man employed as a taxi driver. Originally, a taxi was horse drawn. Taxi drivers were sometimes called hackneys or hackeys.

hackney—coach or carriage for hire.

Hall—slang, referring to Chicago's city hall, the seat of municipal government.

harebrained—a person with no more sense than a hare; foolish, stupid.

heavies—rough and tough guys with big muscles and heavy builds. Used by political organizations on election day to intimidate, physically harm, or kidnap opponents and their supporters.

hit man—hired killer.

hole—location inside of a business (barber shops, restaurants, saloons, bakeries, theaters, etc.), which was used by foot-patrol officers to spend most or part of the tour of foot-patrol duty for resting, talking, sleeping, or playing cards. Most commonly used on the midnight tours of duty. Frequently the place of business would be closed for the day, but the officer had a key from the management with which to let himself into the premises. Also known as the coop.

home brew—alcoholic beverage made in the home. In the 1920s this product ranged from wine to beer to gin. The early producers were Italian immigrants who made wine from grapes in their kitchens, bathrooms, bedrooms, basements, and garages. Experiments with gin, so-called bathtub gin, came soon after but sometimes with deadly results for the drinkers depending upon what evil stuff had been used to make the brew. Persons who were chemically inclined produced beer, but only for use by themselves and friends because it could not be made in sufficient quantity for it to be commercially viable.

house—see *house of prostitution*, see *resort*.

house of ill repute—see *house of prostitution*.

house of prostitution—premise in which the sale and consummation of sexual acts for money takes place.

in the know—having special knowledge of an event in progress or about to occur, persons who have inside or secret information about a matter.

jackies—sailors.

jackrollers—street thieves who specialized in grabbing the unwary from behind, usually around the neck. While holding their neck, the jackroller would grab the victim's wallet and run off. Sometimes the victim received a vigorous clout to the head. The thief used surprise and strength to get the money; usually no weapon was used. The crime took place in dark alleys and along lonely stretches of sidewalk. The name was popularized in penny novels and in *The Jack-Roller* by Clifford R. Shaw of the University of Chicago.

joints—saloons, dives, and resorts.

key—dates, names, addresses of persons, police officers, and officials who were cited as involved in vice activities in the report of the Chicago Vice Commission. The commission completed its report in 1911 and submitted it to the city council. The key was kept locked in a safe-deposit vault, and a number of specified commission members had to be present for the key to be read by approved individuals.

L—elevated electric railway system that operated on the north, south and west sides of Chicago. Also called the Rapid Transit, the company was created through bribes to aldermen to obtain the rights to construct an elevated transit company over the city streets. The lines converged on the downtown area from their respective started points and encircled the business district in a steel rectangle commonly known as the Loop which then became a nickname of the downtown business and commercial district. See *Loop.*

Levee—area when spelled with a capital *L* meant Chicago's infamous segregated vice district centered around Twenty-second and State streets. With a small *L* it meant a vice and saloon district.

lid—term used to describe a period when the police were suppressing vice or gambling, as in "the lid is on" meaning that the police were enforcing the laws. "The lid is off" meant that the police were taking protection money and vice was running freely.

Loop—nickname for the main business district of Chicago also known as downtown. The nickname came from the fact the elevated railway lines made an elevated, steel rectangle around the downtown area running above Wells Street on the west, Van Buren Street on the south, Wabash Avenue on the east and Lake Street on the north. The Loop allowed the L trains to return to their respective starting points. See *L.*

low-rent district—originally a literal expression relating to a section with low housing costs but later became slang for anything that was at the lower end of the economic scale.

macques—used by the *Tribune* to describe members of the crowd outside the Turf where Dannenberg's raiders were making arrests on July 16, 1914. Presumably the *Tribune* was using a colloquial for *maquereaux.* See *maquereaux.*

Mann Act—federal criminal statute passed in 1910 that forbade, under heavy penalties, the transportation of women from one state to another for immoral purposes. Bill was introduced by Republican Congressman James Robert Mann from McLean County, Illinois.

Mano Nera—see *Black Hand.*

maquereaux—French procurers and operators of whorehouses both in France and in the immigrant cities in the United States in the late nineteenth century and early twentieth century. They were active in the First Ward in Chicago at the turn of the century.

marked money—genuine currency on which police or prosecutors have made small notations or markings so that the bills can be identified in court in cases involving bribery, corruption, and blackmail.

miscreant—evildoer, villain.

Near North Side, Near West Side—Chicago terminology for geographical locations in the city. The land immediately north of the Chicago River was known as the Near North Side and the land immediately west of the south branch of the river was known as the Near West Side. The exact limits of these designations changed over the years but it was essentially the territory within two to four miles of the river.

Nellie bar the door—slang term meaning "anything goes."

night sticks—wooden club carried by uniformed police officers on patrol that were approximately one foot long and one-and-a-half inches in diameter. Clubs were used to subdue unruly arrestees. Frequently made from oak or hickory.

nightwalker—woman who walks the streets between dusk and dawn for illegal purposes such as a streetwalker. The activity is termed night walking. See streetwalker.

nolle prosequi—legal term meaning discharged for want of prosecution. Used by the prosecutor when he/she wants the case dismissed because the state does not wish to proceed, usually for want of evidence. Also used in the past tense after the act had been completed as nolle prossed.

ordinances—laws passed by a council or board of elected representatives of an incorporated city, town, or village that apply only to conduct within the community that passed the ordinance. Examples are ordinances that deal with disorderly conduct, soliciting for prostitution, and petty theft. County governments also can pass ordinances.

open town—also called wide-open town, a term used to describe a local environment in which saloons, gambling, and prostitution could operate with relative immunity from legal controls.

padrone—person who exploitatively employs or finds work for Italian immigrants in America.

pander—procurer of women for prostitution. Person working in the white-slave traffic. Also panderer.

panel house—vice resort which had one or more of its bedrooms specially constructed with a concealed wall panel that could be opened while a customer was engaged in sex. An accomplice of the madam would reach into the room through the panel and remove the wallet and cash from the customer's trousers that the prostitute had conveniently placed on a chair next to the panel. A bedroom so equipped was called a panel room.

patrol wagon—originally a simple, wooden open wagon that was horse-drawn. It was used by the police for transporting officers to the scene of an incident or for transporting prisoners to the station. Originally, it was manned by a driver who was not a police officer and a uniformed police officer. A large clapper gong was mounted on the side which could be sounded when the wagon was hurrying to an emergency call. In later years, it was driven by a gasoline motor. Later versions were fully enclosed. Nickname was paddy wagon.

pimp—see *cadet*.

plainclothes—police officer working in civilian dress, not in uniform.

plum job—in political usage meant a job which involved little technical skill, no physical labor, no accountability, and very little work. These jobs were held only by persons with strong political support. These positions usually had vaguely written job descriptions. The lack of supervision meant the employee could begin late and leave early or on some days not work at all. Only patronage workers whom the alderman believed were very important at election time were given these jobs. Example—a street or sidewalk inspector.

Prairie Avenue—street of stately, costly, and extremely well-furnished residences where Chicago's first society ladies, the wives of very wealthy husbands, resided. The first home in this section was built in 1836 and the last in 1900. Prior to, during, and after the Columbian Exposition in 1893 the neighborhood of homes of many of Chicago's earliest millionaires. The area included the 1800 and 1900 blocks of South Prairie Avenue, the 1800 block of South Indiana Avenue, and 211–217 East Cullerton Avenue. This district was adjacent to the Levee.

precinct—lowest level of political subdivisions of the city of Chicago. A group of precincts comprised a ward, the next higher level political subdivision.

precinct captain—Democrat or Republican political workers in the precincts of the wards of the city. The head of each political party's workers in a precinct is called a precinct captain. The precinct captain is responsible to the committeeman of his/her party of the ward. In the early years, there were some precinct captains from splinter parties.

pull—see *clout.*

ratted on—squealed, informed the authorities.

red-light district—neighborhood where prostitution can be found operating openly, also known as a segregated vice district. This is an area where the soliciting for or act of prostitution is not the basis for police action. In the United States the expression was first used in the early 1890s. The term comes from the practice of using a red light in the front or hallway or window of a building to signify that prostitution is available inside. Some historians claim that the expression can be traced to a bible story about Rahab who was a prostitute that lived in Jericho. Rahab cooperated with spies working for Joshua. She marked her house with a scarlet rope. There were many red-light areas in the United States over the years although they are no longer existent. A partial listing includes the Levee, Chicago; the Block, the Combat Zone, and Scollay Square, Boston; Venus Alley, Butte, Montana; East Colfax Avenue, Denver, Colorado; Sunset Boulevard and Western Avenue, Hollywood, California; Hotel Street, Honolulu; Storyville, New Orleans; the Tenderloin and Times Square, Manhattan; Northern Liberties, Philadelphia; Marcy Street, Portsmouth, New Hampshire; Commercial Street, Salt Lake City; Sepulveda Boulevard, San Fernando Valley, California; Barbary Coast and the Tenderloin, San Francisco; Beacon Street, San Pedro, California; the Reservation, Waco, Texas; and Fourteenth Street and Vermont Avenue NW, Washington, D.C.

resort—see *house of prostitution.*

roadhouse—location in the county where alcohol and food were served and where there was generally dancing and prostitution. It was an invention of the early 1900s caused by the automobile. A newer version of a stagecoach inn with emphasis on having a good time. One- or two-story wooden structures built along highways in unincorporated areas and in some small towns that offered dining, drinking, dancing, girls, and gambling. There were small bedrooms for short visits of a sexual nature. Some had bedrooms for the women workers.

ropers—see *roping, roping in,* and *steerers.*

roping—rapping on the windows by prostitutes to attract the attention of potential customers.

roping in—using a variety of persuasions, ploys, and gimmicks to lure visitors and unknowing locals to visit a specific resort or gambling joint.

rubber—man who works in a bathhouse and gives massages and rubdowns.

ruffiano—pimp, bully, ruffian. One who swaggers, a brutal, violent person.

Sands—spit of sand on the north side of the mouth of the Chicago River. A decrepit slum where murderers, robbers, bums, and drunks built and lived in crude wooden shacks. Also living there were tough whores and tougher bartenders, all plying their sordid trade. Torn and burned down by Mayor Long John Wentworth and a band of police and rowdies.

salumi—sausage, ham, bacon from Calabria.

scapegoat—person who is made to take the blame, usually in a criminal case, while others escape prosecution. Frequently not the most important of the offenders.

scarlet sisters—prostitutes.

schooners—giant glasses of cold beer of the type served at Kenna's Workingman's Exchange from 1897 to 1920, also known as tubes, scuttles, goldfish bowls, shuppers, and flagons. The glass was always clear and not colored.

show raids—police raids of houses of prostitution and gambling joints designed to convince the press and the public that these vice locations were not being protected by local government, which, of course, they were.

show-up—common police practice in which a suspect in a criminal investigation is placed in a line with similar persons. A witness or witnesses to the crime are asked if they can pick the person they had seen from among the lineup.

slummers—persons from other parts of the city and suburban areas who visited the Levee to see the excitement and what was going on.

sotto voce—very softly, literally "under the voice."

statutes—laws passed by a state legislature that apply only to conduct within the state that passed the law. Criminal statutes deal with crimes of violence, crimes of theft, crimes involving sex offenses, including prostitution, etc.

steerers—persons hired by a gambling house or a brothel to direct visitors or the unwary to the gambling house or brothel. The technique was known as roping.

Strand—small strip of whorehouses on Chicago's Far Southeast Side patronized heavily by steel workers from the nearby mills.

streetwalker—prostitute who plies her trade on the public way. In the late 1800s, if a streetwalker engaged in vice activity on the street in the evening, she was called a nightwalker.

strong-arm robbery—crime committed on the street or alley in which the victim is physically grabbed and held while the victim's money is stolen. This crime was usually committed by a single, strong assailant; in other cases two persons attacked the victim, one holding the victim's arms while the other took the money or valuables. See *jackrolling*.

skylarking—person who plays actively and boisterously, person who frolics and is lighthearted and gay.

tally-ho—a fast coach drawn by four horses. The name came from England where it described the four-in-hand coach used to go between Birmingham and London.

tenderloin—a low-income neighborhood with apartments, cheap hotels, saloons, brothels, and gambling joints. Frequented by lowlife characters and criminals. Commonly used to describe a seamy section in New York City at its peak between the late 1800s and early 1900s and also used to describe similar districts in other places, such as San Francisco.

third degree—rough treatment, verbally and/or physically, of a subject during an interrogation by police intended to cause the person to provide information or to confess to a crime. In policing, early use of the term was attributed to certain rough detective practices in the New York City Police Department. The phrase was first used in law enforcement in the late 1800s.

tin horn—person who insiders and people in the know consider small and insignificant or not the real thing. Most commonly used in the expression "tin horn gambler" meaning a would-be or wannabe gambler who pretends to be important but actually has little ability, influence, or money.

trick—act of prostitution, in later years the nickname used by prostitutes to denote a customer.

Unione Siciliana—Sicilian American organization formed in New York City in the late 1800s as a fraternal group. It offered insurance policies and social services for Sicilian immigrants and their families. Chapters developed in many cities east of the Mississippi River where there were concentrations of Italian immigrants. Evolved into an organization that was active in political activity and in promoting Italian candidates for public office. In later years, the Unione was infiltrated by gangsters and hoodlums who were involved in prostitution, shakedowns, extortions, kidnappings for hire, and murder in Italian communities. In 1918, New York gang leader Frankie Yale (Uale) became president of the Unione. Yale is alleged to have murdered Jim Colosimo and Dion O'Banion in Chicago at the request of Johnny Torrio.

wagon—see *patrol wagon*.

ward—political subdivision of the city of Chicago. Each ward is divided into precincts.

wets—individuals, organizations, and states that were opposed to the prohibition of alcoholic beverages and believed in minimal restrictions on the sale of beer and alcoholic beverages.

wisenheimer—a smart aleck, a wise guy.

white wing—persons in Chicago in the late 1800s and early 1900s who were employed by the city for the purpose of sweeping the streets and picking up garage along the curbs. The employees wore white uniforms, including a military-type billed cap. The white wings worked in the City of Chicago Department of Sanitation. The jobs were obtained through political favoritism.

vice trust—term variously used by reformers, crusaders, and newspaper reporters to describe a secret cartel behind the vice and gambling in the Levee during the late 1800s and early 1900s. Many times the newspapers identified specific individuals as members of the trust. Their number ranged from three to more than a half-dozen depending upon the particular revelation. The Vice Trust purportedly controlled the protection racket in the Levee in which saloon owners, brothel madams, and gambling-house operators had to pay weekly fees to the police and ward leaders in order to remain in business.

Volstead Act—popular name for the Thirteenth Amendment to the U.S. Constitution, which prohibited the manufacture, transport, distribution, and sale of alcoholic beverages including beer and whiskey. Act took effect in 1920.

wide-open town—see *open town*.

Workingman's Exchange—saloon opened and operated by Alderman Michael "Hinky Dink" Kenna on State Street in the center of downtown Chicago. Had a long wooden bar and the world's largest stein of beer. Also a quite lavish free lunch for the drinkers.

yokel—derogatory term for a visitor to a city who was from the country, sometimes a farmer.

NOTES

Names of Chicago newspapers are short-
ened: *Chicago Tribune* is *Tribune*, *Chicago
American* is *American*, *Chicago Record-
Herald* is *Record-Herald*, *Chicago Daily
News* is *Daily News*, *Chicago Inter-Ocean* is
Inter-Ocean, *Chicago Journal* is *Journal*,
Chicago Daily Times is *Daily Times*, *Chicago
Herald* is *Herald*, and *Chicago Herald and
Examiner* is *Herald and Examiner*. The
Chicago City Directory published by Lake-
side Press, Chicago, is shortened to
Directory.

INTRODUCTION

1. Paul James Duff, *Side Lights on Darkest Chicago* (Chicago: M. Haynes,
   1899), 36–37.
2. Lincoln Steffens, "Chicago: Half
   Free and Fighting On," *McClure's
   Magazine*, October 1903.
3. Carl Sandburg, *Chicago Poems* (New
   York: Henry Holt, 1916).
4. Ibid.

CHAPTER ONE

1. *Tribune*, May 13, 1920.
2. "The Murder of Colosimo," *Illinois
   Policeman and Police Journal*
   (March–April 1947): 26.
3. Jack Lait and Lee Mortimer, *Chicago*

Confidential (New York: Crown,
   1950), 231; Alson J. Smith, *Syndicate
   City* (Chicago: Henry Regnery,
   1954), 162.
4. The presence of the Sicilian dele-
   gation at the funeral provides com-
   pelling evidence of the strong
   position Colosimo, a Calabrian, held
   in the Italian community in Chicago.
   The Sicilians had a direct tie with
   Jim because they provided homemade alcohol and wine for Jim's
   bootlegging operations in 1919 and
   1920.
5. "The Murder of Colosimo," 26.
6. *New York Times*, May 16, 1920.
7. *Tribune*, May 16, 1920.
8. John Kobler, *Capone* (New York: Putnam's Sons, 1971), 73.

CHAPTER TWO

1. Ovid Demaris, *Captive City* (New
   York: Pocket Books, 1969), 105.
2. One colorful story handed down
   from generation to generation on
   the origin of the name Colosimi was
   that Greeks and Albanians came to
   the river in the valley and yelled back
   to others who were following them,
   "*cola siamo*," meaning "here we are."

The town's name was supposedly
derived from that shout. Source:
e-mail to the author from Christiana
Colosimo, "My Family History,"
October 2006.

3. Margaret Watkins, e-mail to the
   author, November 1, 2005.

4. Maria Colosimo, phone conversation
   with the author, October 19, 2006;
   Debbie Colosimo Hormel, e-mail to
   the author, January 24, 2007;
   Christina Colosimo, "Family History," 2006.

5. Birth and baptismal records,
   Colosimi, Italy.

6. SS *Alsatia*, Manifest, 1891.

Chapter THREE

1. Clem Yore, "The Women Who
   Walk," *Songs of the Underworld*
   (Chicago: Charles C. Thompson
   Co., 1914), 55.

2. F. M. Lehman and N. K. Clarkson,
   The White Slave Hell (Chicago:
   Christian Witness, 1910), 203.

3. Walter C. Reckless, *Vice in Chicago*
   (Chicago: University of Chicago
   Press, 1933), 1, 2.

4. Troy Taylor, *Bloody Chicago* (Decatur,
   IL: Whitechapel Productions Press,
   2006), 15.

CHAPTER FOUR

1. Lait and Mortimer, *Chicago Confidential*, 164.

2. *Directory*, 1894.

3. Giovanni E. Schiavo, *The Italians in
   Chicago* (Chicago: Italian American
   Publishing, 1928), 33–34.

4. Curt Johnson and R. Craig Sautter,
   Wicked City (Highland Park, IL:
   December Press, 1994), 84. Hank
   Messick, *The Private Lives of Public
   Enemies* (New York: Dell, 1973), 36.

5. Schiavo, *Italians in Chicago*, 43.

6. "The Murder of Colosimo," 24.

7. Ibid.

8. *Tribune*, November 28, 1912.

9. *Tribune*, August 13, 1895.

10. George Ade, *The Old-Time Saloon*
    (New York: Ray Long & Richard R.
    Smith, 1931), 7–8.

11. Kobler, *Capone*, 43–44.

CHAPTER FIVE

1. Hal Andrews, *X Marks the Spot*
   (Chicago: Spot Publishing Co.,
   1930), 4.

2. Johnson and Sautter, *Wicked City*, 84.

3. Ibid.

4. Robert M. Lombardo, "The Genesis
   of Organized Crime in Chicago,"
   Criminal Organizations 10, No. 2
   (Spring 1996): 13–21.

5. *U.S. Census*, 1900.

6. *Tribune*, April 18, 1901.

7. Ibid.

8. *Tribune*, April 24, 1901.

9. Antonio Napoli, *The Mob's Guys*
   (College Station, TX: Virtual-
   bookworm.com Publishing,
   2004), 9.

10. Robert Fitch, *Solidarity for Sale* (New
    York: Public Affairs, 2006), 138.

11. Johnson and Sautter, *Wicked City*, 87.

12. George Murray, *The Legacy of Al
    Capone* (New York: G. P. Putnam's
    Sons, 1975), 73–74.

13. Napoli, *The Mob's Guys*, 7.

14. Fitch, *Solidarity for Sale*, 138.

15. James B. Jacobs, *Monsters, Unions and
    Feds* (New York: New York Univer-
    sity Press, 2006), 47; author's per-
    sonal investigative reports.

CHAPTER SIX

1. Emmett Dedmon, *Fabulous Chicago*
   (New York: Atheneum, 1983), 261.

2. James L. Merriner, *Grafters and Goo Goos* (Carbondale: Southern Illinois University Press, 2004).

3. Reference Service, Chicago Public Library, March 7, 2007.

4. In Chicago's early years two aldermen were elected to represent each of the city's thirty-four wards, but in 1923 this number was reduced to one. From that year onward Coughlin held the post of alderman and Kenna became the ward committeeman.

5. Lloyd Wendt and Herman Kogan, *Lords of the Levee* (Indianapolis, IN: Bobbs-Merrill, 1943), 45.

6. Ibid., 75–76.

7. *Tribune*, January 26, 1895.

8. Richard Lindberg, *Chicago by Gaslight* (Chicago: Academy Chicago Publisher, 1996), 115.

9. Ibid., 116.

10. Stephen Longstreet, *Chicago, 1860–1919* (New York: McKay, 1973), 355.

11. Douglas Bukowski, *Big Bill Thompson, Chicago, and the Politics of Image* (Urbana: University of Illinois Press, 1998), 12–14.

12. Lait and Mortimer, *Chicago Confidential*, 29.

13. Years later it was revealed that many if not all of Coughlin's poems and songs were ghostwritten by John Kelley, a famous Chicago police reporter for the *Record-Herald* and later for the *Tribune*.

14. John J. Coughlin, *Dear Midnight of Love* (Chicago: John J. Coughlin, 1900).

CHAPTER SEVEN

1. Duff, Side Lights on Darkest Chicago, 3.

2. Walter C. Reckless, "The Natural History of Vice Areas in Chicago."

PhD diss., University of Chicago, 1925, 52.

3. Dr. James J. Conway, conversations with the author, 2005–6.

4. Dedmon, Fabulous Chicago, 251.

5. Kobler, Capone, 43.

6. Charles Washburn, Come into My Parlor (New York: Knickerbocker Publishing Co., 1934), 120.

7. Longstreet, Chicago, 354.

8. Peter Mannino, "Early Years," The Outfit, http://www.geocities.com/SiliconValley/1424/early_.htm.

9. Kobler, Capone, 41.

10. Reckless, The Natural History of Vice Areas in Chicago, 54.

11. Washburn, Come into My Parlor, 181–86.

12. Ernest A. Bell, Fighting the Traffic in Young Girls (Chicago: L. S. Walter, 1911), 102.

13. Samuel Paynter Wilson, Chicago and Its Cess-Pools of Infamy (Chicago: Samuel Paynter Wilson, 1910), 127.

14. Raphael W. Marrow and Harriet I. Carter, In Pursuit of Crime (Sunbury, OH: Flats Publishing, 1996), 208.

CHAPTER EIGHT

1. William Stead, *If Christ Came to Chicago* (Chicago: Laird and Lee, 1894), 6–7.

2. Dedmon, *Fabulous Chicago*, 256.

3. Stead, *If Christ Came to Chicago*, 15; Harvey Wish, "Altgeld and the Progressive Tradition," *American Historical Review* 46, No. 4 (July 1941): 813–31.

4. Dedmon, *Fabulous Chicago*, 200.

5. Lindberg, *Chicago by Gaslight*, 113.

6. Dedmon, *Fabulous Chicago*, 201.

7. Ibid., 202.

8. Lindberg, *Chicago by Gaslight*, 114.

9. Herbert Asbury, *Gem of the Prairie: An Informal History of the Chicago Underworld* (New York: Alfred Knopf, 1940), 155.

10. Dedmon, *Fabulous Chicago*, 257.

11. Wendt and Kogan, *Lords of the Levee*, 94.

12. Asbury, *Gem of the Prairie*, 155.

13. Stead, *If Christ Came to Chicago*, 255.

14. Ibid., 245.

15. Ibid., 251–53.

16. Ibid., 247–48.

17. Dedmon, *Fabulous Chicago*, 205.

18. Stead, *If Christ Came to Chicago*, 258.

19. Ibid., 259.

20. Ibid., 260.

21. Dedmon, *Fabulous Chicago*, 256–57.

22. Wendt and Kogan, *Lords of the Levee*, 91–93.

CHAPTER NINE

1. Popularly attributed to the Everleigh Sisters.

2. "Everleigh, Ada and Minna," Women in American History by Encyclopedia Britannica (Online). April 5, 2004.

3. H. W. Lytle and John Dillon, *From Dance Hall to White Slavery* (Chicago: Charles C. Thompson Co., 1912), 80–81.

4. Ibid., 81.

5. Lait and Mortimer, *Chicago Confidential*, 21–22.

6. Ibid., 23.

7. Karen Abbott, *Sin in the Second City* (New York: Random House, 2007), 32.

8. Much of the material in this chapter is from Washburn, *Come into My Parlor*. Unfortunately, some of the information must be considered highly suspect as to reliability and veracity. Similarly, in the account of their life by novelist Irving Wallace, there are numerous falsehoods that had been told to Wallace by Minna Everleigh in 1945.

9. *Tribune*, January 21, 1979.

10. Abbott, *Sin in the Second City*, 42.

11. Lait and Mortimer, *Chicago Confidential*, 23–24.

12. Ibid.

13. Ibid., 24.

14. Washburn, *Come into My Parlor*, 110.

15. Irving Wallace, "Call Them Madam," *Playboy*, September 1965.

16. Johnson and Sautter, *Wicked City*, 78.

17. Some have conjectured that Field was shot at the Everleigh Club and transported to his home on Prairie Avenue. While it makes a fanciful and colorful story, there is no reliable evidence to support the account that he was shot at the club.

CHAPTER TEN

1. *Tribune*, December 7, 1908.

2. Wendt and Kogan, *Lords of the Levee*, 153–54.

3. Ibid., 153.

4. Lewis and Smith, *Chicago*, 340, 430; Wendt and Kogan, *Lords of the Levee*, 154–55.

5. Wendt and Kogan, *Lords of the Levee*, 153–54. Some historians put the year of the first ball as 1898.

6. *Tribune*, January 18, 1954.

7. William Gleeson, *Can Such Things Be?* (Chicago: William Gleeson, 1915), 86.

8. Johnson and Sautter, *Wicked City*, 82–83.

9. Lewis and Smith, *Chicago*, 340.

10. Wendt and Kogan, *Lords of the Levee*, 156.

11. Lindberg, *Chicago by Gaslight*, 131.

12. Johnson and Sautter, *Wicked City*, 81–82.

13. *Record-Herald*, December 10, 1907.
14. *Tribune*, September 29, 1908.
15. *Tribune*, September 30, 1908.
16. John Clayton, "The Scourge of Sinners: Arthur Burrage Farwell," *Chicago History* (Fall 1974): 68.
17. *Tribune*, September 30, 1908.
18. *Tribune*, December 14, 1908.
19. Johnson and Sautter, *Wicked City*, 97.
20. *Tribune*, December 23, 1908.
21. *Tribune*, December 7, 1909.
22. Lewis and Smith, *Chicago*, 341; *Tribune*, December 9, 1909.
23. *Tribune*, December 10, 1909.
24. Illinois Association for Criminal Justice, *The Illinois Crime Survey* (Chicago: Illinois Association for Criminal Justice, 1929), 846.

CHAPTER ELEVEN

1. Lawrence Binda, Big Bad Book of Jim: Rogues, Rascals and Rapscallions Named James, Jim and Jimmy (Lincoln: University of Nebraska Press, 2003), 18.
2. Dedmon, *Fabulous Chicago*, 289.
3. Andrews, *X Marks the Spot*, 4.
4. Cook County Clerk, film #103034, No. 349222, July 22, 1902.
5. Lait and Mortimer, *Chicago Confidential*, 164.
6. Johnson and Sautter, *Wicked City*, 84.
7. Robert J. Schoenberg, *Mr. Capone* (New York: William Morrow and Co., 1992), 42.
8. Giovanni Schiavo, *The Truth About the Mafia* (New York: Vigo Press, 1962), 195.
9. *Daily Journal*, April 14, 1908.
10. Lombardo, "The Genesis of Organized Crime in Chicago," 12.
11. George Kibbe Turner, "The City of Chicago, A Study of the Great Immoralities," *McClure's Magazine* 18 (April 1907): 583–88.
12. "The Murder of Colosimo," 24.
13. Johnson and Sautter, *Wicked City*, 85.
14. *L'Italia*, March 29, 1914; Wendt and Kogan, *Lords of the Levee*, 139; John P. Gavit, *Americans by Choice* (New York: Harper and Brothers, 1922), 372.
15. *American*, August 1, 1949.
16. Andrews, *X Marks the Spot*, 4.
17. Johnson and Sautter, *Wicked City*, 85–87; Jay Robert Nash, *Encyclopedia of World Crime* (Wilmette, IL: Crime Books, 1989), 394. No support could be found for the lottery and grape distribution activities other than the two prior citations that did not contain any facts or references.
18. *Time*, October 11, 1926.

CHAPTER TWELVE

1. Norman Mark, *Mayors, Madams, and Madmen* (Chicago: Chicago Review Press, 1979), 151.
2. Records of the Probate Court of Cook County, IL, Document 195, File No. 64561. In re estate of James Colosimo deceased, May 17 1920.
3. There is no record substantiating that Luigi Colosimo had a cousin in Chicago named Gennaro Colosimo. Nor is there any record that Luigi ever lived anywhere in Chicago except with his son Jim.
4. *World's Annual Sporting Records* (Chicago: 1905, 1911). Dr. John J. Binder, associate professor, University of Illinois, Chicago, provided the copies of the covers of the 1905 and 1911 *World's Annual Sporting Records*.
5. *Directory*, 1905.
6. *L'Italia*, December 19, 1908. (This clipping came from Dr. John Binder.)
7. *Directory*, 1905–12.
8. The mortgage was paid off in 1919.

Luigi Colosimo sold the property in 1926.

9. The legal ownership of the property at 3156 S. Vernon Avenue changed several times. In 1914, after the shooting of Sergeant Birns and the arrest of Jim Colosimo, attorney Rocco De Stefano, Jim's friend and confidant, recommended that all property be moved out of Jim's name. On August 1, 1914, Colosimo conveyed the title of the property at 3156 S. Vernon through a series of transfers to John Torrio and finally to his wife, Victoria. In 1920 another change occurred. When Colosimo divorced Victoria Moresco, his wife of many years, attorney De Stefano brokered an agreement between the parties. In the deal, Victoria conveyed the title for Vernon Avenue to Jim's father, Luigi, on February 2, 1920. After Jim's murder, Luigi continued to live in the house and hold title to the property until all of the probate and estate questions were resolved. On June 21, 1927, Luigi sold the property to a person outside the family. Over the years various owners came and went. Eventually, the house was torn down, and the land became and remains a city park. Mothers pushing strollers and kids playing baseball have no idea of the great vice lord who once owned the land beneath their feet.

10. *U.S. Census*, 1910.

11. *World's Annual Sporting Records* (Chicago: 1905, 1911).

12. *Directory*, 1913–20.

CHAPTER THIRTEEN

1. Josiah Flynt, "In the World of Graft," *McClure's*, 1901, 329.

2. Ibid., 330.

3. *Tribune*, May 23, 1903.

4. Eugene Stevens, *Wicked City*

(Chicago: G. E. Stevens & Co., 1906), 55.

5. *Record-Herald*, September 25, 1908.

6. *Record-Herald*, September 21, 1908.

7. Clifford G. Roe, *Panders and Their White Slaves* (New York: Fleming H. Revell Co., 1910), 177–80.

8. *Daily News*, January 31, 1910, and October 28, 1910; Roe, *Panders and Their White Slaves*, 181–82.

9. Joseph Spillane, "The Making of an Underground Market: Drug Selling in Chicago, 1900–1940," Journal of Social History (Fall 1998): 27–47.

CHAPTER FOURTEEN

1. Clem Yore, *Songs of the Underworld* (Chicago: Charles C. Thompson Co., 1914), 34.

2. William Burgess, *The World's Social Evil* (Chicago: Saul Brothers, 1914), 79.

3. *Tribune*, November 29, 1909.

4. Johnson and Sautter, *Wicked City*, 85.

5. Ibid., 86.

6. Murray, *Legacy of Al Capone*, 340.

7. *Tribune*, September 26, 1909.

8. *Tribune*, November 15, 1910.

9. Asbury, *Gem of the Prairie*, 269.

10. Messick, *Private Lives of Public Enemies*, 29.

11. Humbert S. Nelli, *The Business of Crime* (Chicago: University of Chicago Press, 1976), 119–20.

12. Ibid., 122.

CHAPTER FIFTEEN

1. *Record-Herald*, October 19, 1909.

2. Washburn, *Come into My Parlor*, 106.

3. Marrow and Carter, *In Pursuit of Crime*, 208.

4. Washburn, *Come into My Parlor*, 238.

5. Bell, *Fighting the Traffic in Young Girls*, 257.

6. *Record-Herald*, May 23, 1907; *Tribune*, July 23, 1909; *American*, July 28, 1909; *Daily News*, July 29, 1909.

7. *Tribune*, October 1, 1909; *American*, October 11, 1909.

8. *Tribune*, October 1, 1909; *American*, October 11, 1909.

9. *Tribune*, October 12, 1909.

10. Rodney "Gypsy" Smith was born in 1860 of gypsy parents near Epping Forest, England. His mother died when he was very young. Rodney's father was so impacted by his wife's death that he was converted in a mission and became an evangelist and brought members of his gypsy tribe into religion. Rodney grew up in this primitive religious atmosphere and grew to be a strong-minded, fiery evangelist.

11. *American*, October 12, 1909.

12. *Record-Herald*, October 19, 1909.

13. *American*, October 16, 1909.

14. Ibid.

15. Washburn, *Come into My Parlor*, 106–7.

16. Ibid., 107; *Record-Herald*, October 19, 1909; *American*, October 19, 1909.

17. *American*, October 14, 1909.

18. Ibid.

19. Ibid.; *Inter-Ocean*, October 14, 1909.

20. *Tribune*, December 28, 1909.

CHAPTER SIXTEEN

1. Lehman and Clarkson, *White Slave Hell*.

2. *U.S. Census*, 1910.

3. Lehman and Clarkson, *White Slave Hell*, 407.

4. *Daily News*, January 31, 1910.

5. *Daily News*, March 5, 1910.

6. Leigh B. Bienen and Brandon Rottinghaus, "Learning from the Past, Living in the Present: Understanding Homicide in Chicago, 1870–1930," *Journal of Criminal Law and Criminology* 92, nos. 3–4 (2003): 486.

7. *Daily News*, April 5, 1910.

8. *Daily News*, August 25, 26, 1910.

9. *Daily News*, April 29, 1910.

10. Lehman and Clarkson, *White Slave Hell*, 21.

CHAPTER SEVENTEEN

1. *Summary of Penal Ordinances of Chicago* (Chicago: T. H. Flood & Co., 1914), 34, 96.

2. *Daily News*, January 5, 1911.

3. *Daily News*, January 26, 1911.

4. *Daily News*, January 24, 1911.

5. *Daily News*, February 13, 1911.

6. *Daily News*, April 4, 1911.

7. Burgess, *World's Social Evil*, 259–60.

8. George J. Kneeland, "Commercialized Vice," *Proceedings of the Academy of Political Science in the City of New York* 2, No. 4, Organization of Social Work (July 1912): 127–29.

9. Report of the Vice Commission of Chicago, *Social Evil in Chicago* (Chicago: Vice Commission of Chicago, 1911).

10. Washburn, *Come into My Parlor*, 190.

11. Report of the Vice Commission of Chicago.

12. Burgess, *World's Social Evil*, 225–26.

13. Washburn, *Come into My Parlor*, 190.

14. Graham Taylor, "The Story of the Chicago Vice Commission," *The Survey*, May 6, 1911, 239–47.

15. Washburn, *Come into My Parlor*, 190.

16. Virgil W. Peterson, *Barbarian in Our Midst* (Boston: Little, Brown and Co., 1952), 93.

17. *Daily News*, April 17, 1911.

18. *Daily News*, June 24, 1911

19. Ibid.

20. *Daily News*, May 2, 1911.

CHAPTER EIGHTEEN

1. Ray Hibbeler, *Upstairs at the Everleigh Club* (Chicago: Volitant Books, n.d.), 128.
2. Lait and Mortimer, *Chicago Confidential*, 23.
3. Kobler, *Capone*, 44.
4. *Record-Herald*, October 25, 1911.
5. *Daily News*, October 24, 1911.
6. *Daily News*, October 25, 1911.
7. *Daily News*, October 30, 1911.

CHAPTER NINETEEN

1. Messick, *Private Lives of Public Enemies*, 32.
2. Patricia Jacobs Stelzer, "Prohibition and Organized Crime: A Case Study, an Examination of the Life of John Torrio," MA thesis, Wayne State University, 1997, 3.
3. Ibid., 5–9.
4. Ibid., 9.
5. Elmer I. Urey, *Tax Dodgers* (New York: Greenberg, 1948), 61.
6. Stelzer, "Prohibition and Organized Crime," 8.
7. Ibid., 10–12.
8. Ibid., 12.
9. *Tribune*, December 11, 1907, 12.
10. Jack McPhaul, *Johnny Torrio* (New Rochelle, New York: Arlington House, 1970) 79; Nelli, *Business of Crime*, 78.
11. Kobler, *Capone*, 37.
12. *Tribune*, August 14, 1911.
13. On April 10, 1911, the *Chicago Daily News* published an article stating that the term *Black Hand* was created by an imaginative New York City newspaper reporter. The reporter, while working on a kidnapping case, was examining several extortion notes in a police station on the east side of Manhattan. In one of the notes he saw a crudely drawn hand holding a stiletto against a heart. The reporter secretly wrote "Mano Nero" on the note in handwriting similar to that used by the author of the note. According to the *Daily News*, it was at that moment that the phrase "Mano Nera" was first used. The reporter achieved a beat over his colleagues, the paper increased circulation, and ultimately other newspapers used the same word in their stories of kidnapping and extortion in New York's Little Italy. The name was quickly adopted by Italian criminals in their extortion letters. Another suggestion as to the source of Black Hand is that it comes from the name of a secret Spanish society of anarchists formed to assassinate monarchs and chiefs of state. The concept later spread to other countries, particularly the Balkans.
14. Robert M. Lombardo, "The Black Hand," *Journal of Contemporary Criminal Justice* 18, No. 4 (November 2002): 393–408. Many reporters and writers have explained Black Hand crime as a stage in the evolution of traditional organized crime in the United States. If the Black Hand was truly an apparatus of the organized crime syndicate, Colosimo, the leading and undisputed Italian ganglord in Chicago, would not have been a target of the extortionists. Dr. Robert M. Lombardo of Loyola University, the first academician to seriously study the Black Hand has clearly refuted the theory that the traditional Italian crime syndicate evolved from the Black Hand extortion racket. According to Lombardo, the Black Hand was nothing more sinister or complex than a few, unconnected criminal groups of Italian immigrants who used fear to extort money from their countrymen.

15. *Tribune*, November 23, 1911. Chicago Police Department, *Homicide Records, 1870–1930*, cases 33448 and 3349.

16. *Tribune*, November 23, 1911; December 4, 1911.

17. See notes 15 and 16.

18. Kobler, *Capone*, 85–86.

19. *Directory*, 1913.

20. McPhaul, 126.

21. Messick, *Private Lives of Public Enemies*, 32; Kobler, *Capone*, 64.

22. John H. Lyle, *The Dry and Lawless Years* (Englewood Cliffs, NJ: Prentice Hall, 1960), 36.

CHAPTER TWENTY

1. Civil Service Commission, City of Chicago, *Final Report Police Investigation* (Chicago, 1912).

2. *Chicago Committee of Fifteen Records*, 1.

3. Civil Service Commission.

4. *Daily News*, January 15, 1912.

5. Robert O. Harlan, *The Vice Bondage of a Great City* (Chicago: Young People's Civic League, 1912), 18–19, 20–22, 28.

6. Ibid., 36.

7. *Tribune*, August 31, 1912.

8. McPhaul from an undated *Herald-American* clipping, 64.

9. *Inter-Ocean*, September 29, 1912; *Daily News*, September 28, 1912.

10. Clayton, "Scourge of Sinners," 74–75.

11. Marrow and Carter, *In Pursuit of Crime*, 374.

12. *Daily News*, September 30, 1912.

13. *Daily News*, October 1, 1912.

14. *Tribune*, February 8, 1901.

15. *Record-Herald*, October 4, 1912.

16. Ibid.

17. Ibid.

18. *Daily News*, October 4, 1912; *Record-Herald*, October 4, 1912.

19. *Daily News*, October 5, 1912.

20. *Post*, October 4, 1912.

21. Reckless, *Vice in Chicago*, 5.

22. Asbury, *Gem of the Prairie*, 300.

23. Lindberg, *Chicago by Gaslight*, 142.

24. *Daily News*, October 9, 1912.

25. *Record-Herald*, October 5, 1912; *Post*, October 7, 1912.

26. *Daily News*, October 6, 1912.

27. *Record-Herald*, October 7, 1912.

28. *Tribune*, October 7, 1912.

29. *Daily News*, October 29, 1912.

30. *Record-Herald*, November 19, 1912,

31. *Daily News*, December 2, 1912.

32. Reckless, *Vice in Chicago*, 95–96.

CHAPTER TWENTY-ONE

1. *Daily News*, January 11, 1913.

2. *Tribune*, March 20, 1913.

3. Richard Lindberg, *To Serve and Collect* (New York: Praeger 1991), 131; *Tribune*, July 18, 1914.

4. *Daily News*, April 22, 1913.

5. Lindberg, *Chicago Ragtime*, 154.

6. Lindberg, *To Serve and Collect*, 109.

7. *Daily News*, April 12, 1913.

8. *Tribune*, June 13, 1913; *Daily News*, June 13, 1913.

9. *Tribune*, July 4, 1913.

10. *Tribune*, July 9, 1913.

11. *Tribune*, January 3, 1914.

12. *Tribune*, January 9, 1914.

13. *Tribune*, February 26, 1914; *Daily News*, July 17, 1914.

14. *American*, July 18, 1914,

15. *Daily News*, July 2, 1914.

16. *American*, July 14, 1914; *Daily News*, July 17 1914.

17. *Daily News*, July 15, 1914.

18. Ibid.

19. Kobler, *Capone*, 57.

CHAPTER TWENTY-TWO

1. Lindberg, *Chicago by Gaslight*, 144.
2. *American*, July 17, 1914; *Daily News*, July 17, 1914; July 18, 1914.
3. *American*, July 17, 1914; *Daily News*, July 17, 1914; *Tribune*, July 17, 1914.
4. *American*, July 17, 1914; *Daily News*, July 17, 1914.
5. *American*, July 17, 1914.
6. *Daily News*, July 17, 1914.
7. *Tribune*, July 17, 1914.
8. Ibid.
9. *American*, July 17, 1914, July 18, 1914; *Daily News*, July 17, 1914.
10. *American*, July 17, 1914.
11. Ibid.
12. *Daily News*, July 18, 1914.
13. *American*, July 18, 1914.
14. *Tribune*, July 17, 1914.
15. *Daily News*, July 18, 1914.
16. *American*, July 20, 1914.
17. *Daily News*, July 17, 1914.
18. *Daily News*, July 20, 1914.
19. *Daily News*, July 18, 1914.
20. *American*, July 18, 1914.
21. *Tribune*, July 23, 1914.
22. Ibid.
23. *American*, July 18, 1914.
24. *Daily News*, July 20, 1914.
25. *Daily News*, July 18, 1914.

CHAPTER TWENTY-THREE

1. *Tribune*, July 19, 1914.
2. *American*, July 21, 1914.
3. Ibid.
4. In the following years, Colosimo was arrested twice more. In April 1917, when detectives from First Deputy Westbrook's office were making a series of raids in the Levee, they arrested Colosimo, his manager "Abit" Arends, and ten waiters after the officers found a quantity of liquor in a service bar at the café after the closing hour. In 1919, after an incident outside one of his resorts in Burnham, during which he punched and assaulted a *Tribune* reporter, he was arrested on a subpoena issued on the reporter's complaint.
5. *American*, July 20, 1914.
6. *Daily News*, July 20, 1914.
7. *Tribune*, July 20, 1914, January 21, 1914.
8. *American*, July 21, 1914.
9. *Daily News*, July 21, 1914.
10. *American*, July 22, 1914.
11. *Fort Wayne Sentinel*, July 22, 1914; *American*, July 21, 1914.
12. *Daily News*, July 21, 1914.
13. *American*, July 22, 1914; *Tribune*, July 21, 1914.

CHAPTER TWENTY-FOUR

1. *Daily News*, July 21, 1914.
2. *American*, July 21, 1914.
3. *American*, July 22, 1914.
4. Ibid.
5. *American*, July 24, 1914.
6. *Daily News*, July 22, 1914.
7. Ibid.
8. *American*, July 23, 1914.
9. *Daily News*, July 25, 1914.
10. Ibid.; *American*, July 27, 1914.
11. *American*, July 28, 1914.
12. *American*, July 29, 1914.
13. *American*, July 30, 1914.
14. *Daily News*, July 31, 1914; *American*, July 31, 1914.
15. *Survey*, August 8, 1914, 476, 477.
16. *L'Italia*, August 16, 1914.

CHAPTER TWENTY-FIVE

1. Lindberg, *To Serve and Collect*, 134.
2. Asbury, *Gem of the Prairie*, 314.

3. County refers to the roughly four hundred square miles of unincorporated area of Cook County that existed in 1900.

4. *Tribune*, May 4, 1916.

5. Johnson and Sautter, *Wicked City*, 104.

6. Records of the Circuit Court of Cook County, IL, dated October 21, 1914, United Breweries Company vs. James Colosimo et al., #311934.

7. Kobler, *Capone*, 56.

8. Lombardo, "The Genesis of Organized Crime," 13; Matthew J. Luzi, "From the Boys in Chicago Heights," 2003.

9. Nelli, *Business of Crime*, 122.

10. *Tribune*, May 4, 1916.

11. Johnson and Sautter, *Wicked City*, 105.

12. *Tribune*, May 7, 1916.

13. *Tribune*, February 8, 9, and 10, 1916.

14. *Tribune*, November 24, 1916; Kobler, *Capone*, 57.

15. In January 1921, Al Capone, who at that time was a foot soldier for Johnny Torrio, was arrested as the proprietor of two locations in Burnham where slot machines were found. He used his alias Al Brown when he went to court.

CHAPTER TWENTY-SIX

1. Longstreet, *Chicago*, 469.

2. *Tribune*, January 14, 1916.

3. "The Wreck of Commercialized Vice," *The Survey*, February 5, 1916.

4. Andrews, *X Marks the Spot*, 4; Binder, *The Chicago Outfit*, 9.

5. "Diamond Joe" Esposito was shot to death on the sidewalk in front of his home in 1928.

6. Washburn, *Come into My Parlor*, 244–45.

7. *Tribune*, July 21, 1914.

8. Schoenberg, *Capone*, 44.

9. Lindberg, *To Serve and Collect*, 138.

10. Charles J. Masters, *Governor Henry Horner, Chicago Politics, and the Great Depression* (Carbondale: Southern Illinois University Press, 2007), 44.

11. Lombardo, "The Genesis of Organized Crime," 12.

12. Thomas M. Coffey, *The Long Thirst* (New York: Norton & Co., 1975), 33.

13. *Daily News*, August 25, 1919.

14. John Landesco, "Organized Crime in Chicago: Part III of the Illinois Crime Survey" (Chicago, 1919), 852.

15. Lawrence Bergreen, *Capone* (New York: Simon and Schuster, 1994), 86.

16. *New Republic*, November 6, 1915, 7–8.

17. Lindberg, *To Serve and Collect*, 138.

18. *Report of the Senate Vice Committee* (Springfield: State of Illinois, 1916), 23, 28, 42.

19. Schoenberg, *Capone*, 45.

20. Bukowski, *Big Bill Thompson*, 33–34.

21. *Tribune*, October 3, 1916.

22. *Tribune*, October 6, 1916.

23. *Tribune*, October 24, 1916.

24. *Tribune*, October 24, 25, 1916.

25. *Tribune*, October 25, 1916.

26. *Tribune*, January 10, 1917.

27. *Literary Digest*, January 27, 1917, 179.

28. Bukowski, *Big Bill Thompson*, 53.

29. Ben Hecht, *Gaily, Gaily* (New York: Doubleday, 1963).

30. *Survey*, January 20, 1917, 462–63.

31. *Tribune*, December 19, 1917.

32. Ibid.

33. *Tribune*, January 12, 1918.

34. Bukowski, *Big Bill Thompson*, 53–54.

35. *Tribune*, January 13, 1918.

CHAPTER TWENTY-SEVEN

1. Asbury, *Gem of the Prairie*, 312.
2. Washburn, *Come into My Parlor*, 134.
3. John J. Binder, "Chicago," *American Mafia*, http//www.americanmafia.com/Cities/Chicago.htm11.
4. Andrews, *X Marks the Spot*, 4.
5. Washburn, *Come into My Parlor*, 136–38.
6. William J. Helmer and Rick Mattix, *The Complete Public Enemy Almanac* (Nashville, TN: Cumberland House, 2007), 85.
7. Johnson and Sautter, *Wicked City*, 85–86.
8. Some Chicago historians have incorrectly assumed that the Italian vote was the largest in the First Ward.
9. Ibid., 85.
10. *Indianapolis Sentinel*, July 18, 1895.
11. Mark Prow, e-mail to author, June 14, 2005. Mark Prow is the grandson of Lafe Prow.
12. Ibid.

CHAPTER TWENTY-EIGHT

1. *Tribune*, March 25, 1917.
2. *Tribune*, May 12, 1920.
3. Charles A. Sengstook Jr., *That Toddlin' Town* (Urbana: University of Illinois Press, 2004), 114.
4. *Directory*, 1913 and 1914.
5. *American*, July 18, 1914.
6. *Tribune*, July 19, 1914.
7. Johnson and Sautter, *Wicked City*, 88.
8. Hecht was a frequent customer and a reporter for the *Chicago Daily News*. He wrote a daily column named "1001 Afternoons in Chicago." He later wrote the script for the movie *Scarface* based on the life of Al Capone and co-authored the play *The Front Page*, which parodied the corruption in the Cook County Sheriff's office.

9. After Lyle became a crusading judge seeking higher office he turned against Colosimo and claimed he used his countrymen's fear of the Mafia to extort money from opera singers.
10. Lyle, *Dry and Lawless Years*, 30, 33.
11. *Tribune*, January 13, 1918.
12. A more recent example of the restaurant's fame was a line in the hit movie musical *Chicago* in which a naive young female singer implored her boyfriend to get her hired as a singer at "Big Jim Colosimo's."
13. *Tribune*, July 1, 1919.
14. "Early Years." *The Outfit*, Peter Mannino, http://www.geocities.com/SiliconValley/1424/early_.htm. February 16, 2000.
15. Walter Noble Burns, *The One-Way Ride* (Garden City, NY: Doubleday, Doran & Co., 1931), 2–4.
16. Longstreet, *Chicago*, 473.
17. Kobler, *Capone*, 40.

CHAPTER TWENTY-NINE

1. *Herald and Examiner*, January 22, 1917.
2. Kobler, *Capone*, 65–66.
3. *Herald*, January 22, 1917.
4. Kobler, *Capone*, 66.
5. *Herald*, January 22, 1917; Washburn, *Come into My Parlor*, 139–40.
6. *Tribune*, January 23, 1917.
7. *Tribune*, January 29, 1917.
8. Ibid.
9. *Herald and Examiner*, May 16, 1920.
10. Ibid.
11. *Daily News*, May 13, 1920.
12. *Tribune*, May 12, 1920.
13. Burns, *One-Way Ride*, 3–4.
14. Coffey, *Long Thirst*, 34.

CHAPTER THIRTY

1. National Commission on Marihuana and Drug Abuse, "History of Alcoholic Prohibition," (Online), September 15, 2005.
2. *Tribune*, May 21, 1919.
3. James H. Rossenau and Otto Czempiel, *Governance Without Government* (Cambridge, England: Cambridge University Press, 1992), 205.
4. Ibid., 205.
5. Ibid.
6. William M. Tuttle, *Race Riot* (Chicago: University of Illinois Press, 1996), 240–41.
7. *Tribune*, September 16, 1918.
8. Lait and Mortimer, *Chicago Confidential*, 156.

CHAPTER THIRTY-ONE

1. Kenneth Allsop, *The Bootleggers and Their Era* (Garden City, NY: Doubleday & Co., 1961), 29.
2. *Daly News*, August 26, 1919.
3. National Commission on Marihuana and Drug Abuse.
4. *Tribune*, September 24, 1917.
5. Sheriff Traeger failed to mention that his politically appointed, untrained, and unprofessional deputies likely were receiving a steady flow of protection money for not raiding these locations.
6. *Tribune*, May 19, 1918.
7. *Tribune*, July 20, 1918.
8. *Tribune*, October 23, 1918.
9. Dennis E. Hoffman, *Business vs. Organized Crime*, Chicago Crime Commission, December 1, 1989.
10. Bergreen, *Capone*, 86.
11. Bukowski, *Big Bill Thompson*, 78–80.
12. Ibid., 81.
13. Edward Behr, *Prohibition* (New York: Arcade Publishing, 1996), 177.

14. *Tribune*, May 21, 1919.
15. *Tribune*, June 6, 1919.
16. Records of the Circuit Court of Cook County, IL, Marie Kerrigan vs. James Colosimo dba Colosimo's Café, June 9, 1919 to May 7, 1921, #B53212; Records of the Probate Court of Cook County, IL, Document 195, File No. 64561, In re estate of James Colosimo deceased, May 17 1920.
17. *Tribune*, May 22, 1919.
18. *Tribune*, May 19, 28, 29, 1919.
19. Ibid.
20. *Daily News*, June 14, 1919.
21. *Tribune*, June 18, 1919.
22. *Daily News*, August 26, 1919.
23. Bob Skilnik, *The History of Beer and Brewing in Chicago 1833–1978* (St. Paul: Pogo Press, 1999), 122–23.
24. Ibid., 123.
25. Ibid.

CHAPTER THIRTY-TWO

1. *Daily News*, May 17, 1920.
2. Gregory S. Gatsos, *History of the West Baden Springs Hotel* (French Lick, IN: Springs Valley Herald, 1985), 95.
3. *U.S. Census*, 1920.
4. *Tribune*, May 12, 1920.
5. Ibid.
6. *Daily News*, May 13, 1920.
7. Court records in Los Angeles showed that Victoria Moresco had married Antonio Villiano.
8. Records of the Circuit Court of Cook County, IL, dated March 31, 1920, #B00059. Colosimo vs. Colosimo.
9. Ibid.
10. *Tribune*, March 31, 1920.
11. Ibid.
12. Mark Prow, e-mail to author, June 14, 2005.

13. Gatsos, *History of the West Baden Springs Hotel*, 51.
14. McPhaul, 148. A search of the April and May issues of *Variety* failed to produce this article.
15. *Tribune*, June 19, 1938.

CHAPTER THIRTY-THREE

1. *Tribune*, February 11, 1920.
2. Schoenberg, *Capone*, 61.
3. William Helmer, *Public Enemies* (New York: Facts on File, 1998), 7.
4. There is no factual evidence establishing exactly when Capone arrived in Chicago. He had been arrested in New York in 1919, so the earliest he could have come to Chicago would have been in the end of that year or the beginning of 1921. Fred D. Pasley (*Al Capone* [Binghampton, NY: Ives Washburn, 1930], 9), who knew Torrio and Capone and who authored one of the first true crime books on Chicago, wrote in 1930 that Capone came to Chicago in 1920. Capone biographer Lawrence Bergreen wrote that Capone came to Chicago in 1921 (Bergreen, *Capone*, 87).
5. Dr. John J. Binder, Mars Eghigian Jr., Jeff Thurston, e-mails to author, January 2 and 5, 2007; *Tribune*, June 14, 1931.
6. "The Murder of Colosimo," 24.
7. *Tribune*, January 16, 1920.
8. *Daily News*, March 11, 1920.
9. *Daily News*, April 2, 27, 1920.
10. *Daily News*, November 11, 1920.
11. Kobler, *Capone*, 69.
12. *Tribune*, February 5, 1920.
13. Napoli, *The Mob's Guys*, 56.
14. *Daily News*, February 4–20, 1920; May 3–12, 1920; May 18–19, 1920; May 24, 1920; *Herald and Examiner*, April 23–24, 1920; *Tribune*, September 24, 1919; February 11, 1920;

April 15, 1940; June 25, 1940; Westbrook Pegler, "Union Constitution Lets Labor Bosses Rule Without Vote," *Mansfield, Ohio, News Journal*, July 15, 1948.

CHAPTER THIRTY-FOUR

1. *Daily News*, May 13, 1920.
2. Kobler, *Capone*, 70. There is a similar story reportedly told by South Side gang boss Jim O'Leary that Torrio had discussed this plot with him.
3. Schoenberg, *Capone*, 63.
4. Attorney Rocco De Stefano later explained that the 4:15 p.m. call to his office had been in reference to an abstract of title to a piece of property. De Stefano said that the two had talked the night before about a business matter involving the property.
5. *Herald and Examiner*, May 12, 1920.
6. *Daily Journal*, May 13, 1920.
7. *Daily News*, May 12, 1920.
8. Ibid.
9. *Herald and Examiner*, May 13, 1920.
10. The only other mention made by the *New York Times* of the Colosimo murder was a short article headed "All Classes Mingle at Colosimo's Funeral." That article described the crowds of political figures and common masses that were present at Big Jim's last passage.
11. *L'Italia*, May 22, 1920.
12. *Tribune*, May 13, 1920.
13. *Daily Journal*, May 13, 1920.
14. Records of the Probate Court of Cook County, Document 195, File No. 64561. In re estate of James Colosimo deceased, May 17, 1920.
15. *Journal*, May 17, 1920.

CHAPTER THIRTY-FIVE

1. *Evening Post*, May 13, 1920.

2. *Evening Post*, May 12, 1920.

3. *Daily News*, May 13, 1920.

4. Some newspapers spelled his name as Raszina.

5. The newspapers used various spellings for this name.

6. *Daily News*, May 12, 1920.

7. Ibid.

8. In 1931 Walter Noble Burns, a long-time Chicago newspaperman, wrote the *One-Way Ride*, a nonfiction book about the gangsters in Chicago. In the book, Burns tells of a rumor he had heard about Colosimo's murder. Burns said that Torrio had paid Yale ten thousand dollars to murder Colosimo. He also said that the Chicago police had picked up Yale "by accident" in a sweep of suspected persons on the day after the murder but released him without charge the following day. John Kobler in his book *Capone* repeated the rumor and added more details. Kobler claimed: "Into a police dragnet the day of the murder blundered the veteran Five Pointer and executioner Frankie Yale. He had been about to board an eastbound train when the police stopped him. They could not connect him with the murder at that time, however, and they let him go on to New York." Bill Helmer and Rick Mattix, two of the greatest crime historians of the gangland era, state in their book *The Complete Public Enemy Almanac* that Yale was in Chicago on the day of the murder.

9. *New York Times*, July 2, 1928.

10. *Tribune*, May 16, 1920.

11. *Evening Post*, May 18, 1920.

12. The name Villiano also appears in some newspaper articles as Villiani.

13. *Evening Post*, May 21, 1920.

14. *Tribune*, December 9, 1920.

15. Ibid.

16. Coroner's Report #32805, County of Cook, May 15, 1920.

17. *Tribune*, December 11, 1920.

18. *Daily News*, December 15, 16, 1920.

19. *Tribune*, December 14, 1920.

20. *Daily News*, December 13, 1920.

21. Ibid.

22. *Tribune*, December 15, 1920.

23. "The Murder of Colosimo," 25.

24. Coffey, *Long Thirst*, 35.

25. Among the distinguished historians, newspapermen, and crime researchers who believed that Torrio hired Yale to murder Colosimo were Robert J. Casey, famous Chicago newspaperman; Judge John Lyle, crusading reformer who ran for mayor of Chicago; Kenneth Allsop, Prohibition-era historian; Stephen Longstreet, Chicago historian; George Murray, Chicago newspaperman; Lawrence Bergreen and Robert J. Schoenberg, Capone biographers.

CHAPTER THIRTY-SIX

1. Collinson Owen, *King Crime* (London: Ernest Benn Ltd., 1931), 133–34.

2. Judge Horner was elected governor of Illinois in 1933. He served until 1940, when he died in office.

3. Unless otherwise noted, all of the information in this chapter is taken from the records of the Probate Court of Cook County, IL, Document 195, File No. 64561. In re estate of James Colosimo deceased, May 17 1920.

4. *Daily Journal*, May 17, 1920.

5. *Tribune*, May 26, 1920.

6. De Stefano was representing everyone else in the estate matter as well

as serving as administrator of the
Colosimo estate. No one seemed
concerned about a conflict of interest.

7. Ibid.

8. *Daily Journal*, May 26, 1920.

9. The other half interest was owned by
Michael Potson.

10. *Herald and Examiner*, November 27,
1921.

CHAPTER THIRTY-SEVEN

1. Norman Mark, *Mayors, Madams, and
Madmen* (Chicago: Chicago Review
Press, 1979), 153.

2. Atlanta, Baltimore, Cleveland,
Kansas City, Louisville, Minneapolis,
Newark, New York, Philadelphia,
Pittsburgh, Portland (Maine and
Oregon), Richmond, Shreveport,
and Syracuse to name a few.

3. Reckless, *Vice in Chicago*, 1, 2.

EPILOGUE

1. City of Chicago, Application for
Liquor Licenses, 1914, second
period, October 27, 1914. It is highly
probable that Colosimo's Café had
licenses for the years 1911, 1912, and
1913, but there are no records available for these years.

2. *Tribune*, October 17, 1950.

3. Michael Potson deposition of August
10, 1920.

4. *Tribune*, October 28, 1920.

5. *Tribune*, February 27, 1921.

6. *Tribune*, February 28, 1921

7. *Tribune*, July 6, 1922.

8. *Tribune*, October 4, 1955

9. *Tribune*, February 2, 1926; May 28, 1928.

10. *Tribune*, June 26, 1929.

11. *Tribune*, June 18, 1932.

12. *Tribune*, February 4, 1934; October
14, 1934; November 15, 1936; May
2, 1937; August 11, 1946.

13. *Tribune*, October 4, 1955.

14. *Tribune*, July 30, 1947; January 22,
1953; July 20, 1953; October 4,
1955; November 16, 1957; March
10, 1958.

15. *Tribune*, December 24, 1920. Other
reports indicate that she had married
Antonio before Colosimo's death.

16. *Tribune*, December 16, 1930.

17. U.S. Census of Population, 1930:
Los Angeles, CA enumeration district 272.

18. Certificate of Death, State of California, # 44–0043336.

19. Certificate of Death, State of California, # W-148075.

20. *Tribune*, May 17, 1920.

21. *Tribune*, December 11, 12, 1920.

22. *Tribune*, April 3, 1938.

23. *Tribune*, June 17, 1924.

24. *Tribune*, February 6, 1921.

25. *Tribune*, December 21, 1931.

26. *Tribune*, December 2, 19, 1933.

27. *Tribune*, August 9, 1936.

28. *Tribune*, April 3, 1938.

29. *New York Times*, September 17, 1948;
Encyclopedia Britannica Online,
retrieved August 27, 2007.

30. *Tribune*, December 26, 1953.

31. Ibid.; "Biography of Carter H. Harrison IV," Newberry Library, Inventory of Carter H. Harrison Papers,
pp. 1637, 1637–1953, bulk
1840–1850.

32. *Tribune*, December 26, 1953.

33. *New York Times*, October 2, 1939;
Time/CNN internet, *Time*, December 13, 2007.

34. *New York Times*, May 25, 1920.

35. Wendt and Kogan, *Lords of the Levee*,
168–71.

36. *Tribune*, September 1, 1920.

37. *Tribune*, December 3, 1926.

38. *Tribune*, March 25, 1929; September 22, 1929.

39. *Tribune*, December 24, 1932.

40. *Tribune*, October 2, 1939; *New York Times*, October 2, 1939.

41. *Tribune*, November 12, 1938; Municipal Reference Library, City of Chicago, "Centennial List of Mayors, Aldermen and Other Elective Officials of the City of Chicago, 1837–1937."

42. *Tribune*, August 23, 1892; October 12, 1946; October 13, 1946.

43. *Tribune*, October 13, 1946.

44. *Tribune*, November 12, 1938; January 13, 1939; October 20, 1946; August 9, 1947.

45. *Tribune*, December 24, 1956.

46. *New York Times*, December 25, 1956.

47. *Tribune*, December 24, 1956.

48. *Tribune*, April 20, 1932.

49. *Tribune*, November 29, 1939.

50. *Tribune*, November 11, 1939.

51. *Tribune*, July 16, 1940.

52. *Tribune*, December 24, 1956; *New York Times*, December 25, 1956.

53. Wendt and Kogan, *Lords of the Levee*, 354; Chicago Public Library, Municipal Reference Collection, "The Mayors of Chicago."

54. Wendt and Kogan, *Lords of the Levee*, 213, 273, and passim; *Tribune*, March 31, 1944; April 1, 1944.

55. Wendt and Kogan, *Lords of the Levee*, 356–57.

56. *Tribune*, March 20, 1944.

57. *Tribune*, January 25, 1925.

58. *Tribune*, January 25, 26, 28, 1925.

59. *Tribune*, February 9, 10, 1925.

60. *Tribune*, June 17, 1931.

61. *New York Times*, October 26, 28, 31, 1935; November 1, 1935.

62. *New York Times*, April 23, 24, 29, 1936; *Tribune*, April 23, 26, 1936.

63. *New York Times*, April 11, 13, 1939; *Tribune*, April 13, 1939.

64. *Tribune*, 1941.

65. *Tribune*, May 1954.

66. *New York Times*, May 8, 1957; *Tribune*, May 8, 1957.

67. Ohio Department of Health, Certificate of Death: Anna T. Torrio. Records of Greenwood Cemetery.

68. *Appleton Post-Crescent*, March 30, 1921.

69. *Nevada State Journal*, May 14, 1921.

70. *Tribune*, November 21, 1924.

71. *Arcadia Tribune*, June 19, 1931; "Cinema Treasures," Cinematreasures.org/theater/5492; "El Capitan," American Theater Organ Society (www.atos.org); Internet Broadway Database (www.ibd.com: Irene).

72. California Birth Index, 1909–1995.

73. *Santa Barbara News-Press*, May 4, 1961; *Tribune*, January 19, 1961; *New York Times*, November 21, 1961.

74. California Death Index, 1940–1997: Herschel McGaw; Social Security Death Index: Herschel McGaw; *New York Times*, June 27, 1963, obituary, Edward Sansom Perot.

75. *Santa Barbara News Press*, December 1, 1985; California Death Index, 1940–1997: Dale Winter Perot.

BIBLIOGRAPHY

This bibliography is limited to books, periodicals, reports, newspapers, and other items actually used in the development and writing of The First Vice Lord. *Primary research sources were official records from numerous cities, counties, states, and the federal government, as well as records in Italy. Secondary sources were contemporary newspapers and magazines. Other sources included books, articles, reports, and interviews with descendants of persons who lived in Chicago and Colosimi during Jim Colosimo's lifetime.*

BOOKS
Abbott, Karen. *Sin in the Second City*. New York: Random House, 2007.
Ade, George. *The Old-Time Saloon*. New York: Ray Long & Richard R. Smith, 1931.
Allsop, Kenneth. *The Bootleggers and Their Era*. Garden City, NY: Doubleday & Co., 1961.
Andrews, Hal. *X Marks the Spot*. Chicago: Spot Publishing Co., 1930.
Asbury, Herbert. *Gem of the Prairie: An Informal History of the Chicago Underworld*. New York: Alfred Knopf, 1940.
Bell, Ernest A. *Fighting the Traffic in Young Girls*. Chicago: L. S. Walter, 1911.
Bergreen, Lawrence. *Capone*. New York: Simon and Schuster, 1994.
Behr, Edward. *Prohibition*. New York: Arcade Publishing, 1996.
Binda, Lawrence. *Big Bad Book of Jim: Rogues, Rascals and Rapscallions Named James, Jim and Jimmy*. Lincoln: University of Nebraska Press, 2003.
Binder, John J. *The Chicago Outfit*. Chicago: Arcadia, 2003.
Bukowski, Douglas. *Big Bill Thompson, Chicago, and the Politics of Image*. Urbana: University of Illinois Press, 1998.
Burgess, William. *The World's Social Evil*. Chicago: Saul Brothers, 1914.
Burns, Walter Noble. *The One-Way Ride*. Garden City, NY: Doubleday, Doran & Co., 1931.

Cherrington, Ernest H. *The Evolution of Prohibition in the United States of America.* 1920. Reprint, Montclair, NJ: Patterson Smith, 1969.

Chicago City Directory. Chicago: Lakeside Press, 1894–.

Coffey, Thomas M. *The Long Thirst.* New York: Norton & Co., 1975.

Dedmon, Emmett. *Fabulous Chicago.* New York: Atheneum, 1983.

Demaris, Ovid. *Captive City.* New York: Pocket Books, 1969.

Demlinger, Sandor, and John Steiner. *Destination Chicago Jazz.* Chicago: Arcadia, 2003.

Duff, Paul James. *Side Lights on Darkest Chicago.* Chicago: M. Haynes, 1899.

Fitch, Robert. *Solidarity for Sale.* New York: Public Affairs, 2006.

Gatsos, Gregory S. *History of the West Baden Springs Hotel.* French Lick, IN: Springs Valley Herald, 1985.

Gavit, John P. *Americans by Choice.* New York: Harper and Brothers, 1922.

Gleeson, William. *Can Such Things Be?* Chicago: William Gleeson, 1915.

Harlan, Robert O. *The Vice Bondage of a Great City.* Chicago: Young People's Civic League, 1912.

Hecht, Ben. *Gaily, Gaily.* New York: Doubleday, 1963.

Helmer, William J. *Public Enemies.* New York: Facts on File, 1998.

———, and Rick Mattix. *The Complete Public Enemy Almanac.* Nashville, TN: Cumberland House, 2007.

Hermann, Charles H. *Recollections of Life and Doings in Chicago.* Chicago: Normandie House, 1945.

Hibbeler, Ray. *Upstairs at the Everleigh Club.* Chicago: Volitant Books, n.d.

Hoffman, Dennis E. *Business vs. Organized Crime.* Chicago Crime Commission, December 1, 1989.

Illinois Association for Criminal Justice. *The Illinois Crime Survey.* Chicago: Illinois Association for Criminal Justice, 1929.

Jacobs, James B. *Monsters, Unions and Feds.* New York: New York University Press, 2006.

Johnson, Curt, and R. Craig Sautter. *Wicked City Chicago.* Highland Park, IL: December Press, 1994.

Kobler, John. *Capone.* New York: Putnam's Sons, 1971.

Lait, Jack, and Lee Mortimer. *Chicago Confidential.* New York: Crown, 1950.

Landesco, John. *Organized Crime in Chicago: Part III of the Illinois Crime Survey.* Chicago: n.p., 1919.

Lehman, F. M., and N. K. Clarkson. *The White Slave Hell.* Chicago: Christian Witness, 1910.

Lewis, Lloyd, and Henry Justin Smith. *Chicago: The History of Its Reputation.* New York: Harcourt, Brace, 1929.

Lindberg, Richard. *Chicago by Gaslight.* Chicago: Academy Chicago Publisher, 1996.

———. *To Serve and Collect.* New York: Praeger, 1991.

Longstreet, Stephen. *Chicago, 1860–1919.* New York: McKay, 1973.

Lytle, H. W., and John Dillon. *From Dance Hall to White Slavery*. Chicago: Charles C. Thompson Co., 1912.

Lyle, John H. *The Dry and Lawless Years*. Englewood Cliffs, NJ: Prentice Hall, 1960.

Mark, Norman. *Mayors, Madams, and Madmen*. Chicago: Chicago Review Press, 1979.

Marrow, Raphael W., and Harriet I. Carter. *In Pursuit of Crime*. Sunbury, OH: Flats Publishing, 1996.

Masters, Charles J. *Governor Henry Horner, Chicago Politics, and the Great Depression*. Carbondale: Southern Illinois University Press, 2007.

McPhaul, Jack. *Johnny Torrio*. New Rochelle, New York: Arlington House, 1970.

Merriner, James L. *Grafters and Goo Goos*. Carbondale: Southern Illinois University Press, 2004.

Messick, Hank. *Private Lives of Public Enemies*. New York: Dell, 1973.

———, and Burt Goldblatt. *The Mobs and the Mafia*. New York: Ballantine Books, 1972.

Murray, George. *The Legacy of Al Capone*. New York: G. P. Putnam's Sons, 1975.

Napoli, Antonio. *The Mob's Guys*. College Station, TX: Virtualbookworm.com Publishing, 2004.

Nash, Jay Robert. *Encyclopedia of World Crime*. Wilmette, IL: Crime Books Inc., 1989.

Nelli, Humbert S. *The Business of Crime*. Chicago: University of Chicago Press, 1976.

———. *Italians and Chicago, 1880–1930*. Oxford: Oxford University Press, 1970.

Owen, Collinson. *King Crime*. London: Ernest Benn Ltd., 1931.

Peterson, Virgil W. *Barbarian in Our Midst*. Boston: Little, Brown and Co., 1952.

Reckless, Walter C. *Vice in Chicago*. Chicago: University of Chicago Press, 1933.

Roe, Clifford G. *Panders and Their White Slaves*. New York: Fleming H. Revell Co., 1910.

Rossenau, James H., and Otto Czempiel. *Governance Without Government*. Cambridge, England: Cambridge University Press, 1992.

Sandburg, Carl. *Chicago Poems*. New York: Henry Holt and Co., 1916.

Schiavo, Giovanni E. *The Italians in Chicago*. Chicago: Italian American Publishing, 1928.

Schoenberg, Robert J. *Mr. Capone*. New York: William Morrow and Co., 1992.

Sengstook, Charles A., Jr. *That Toddlin' Town*. Urbana: University of Illinois Press, 2004.

Skilnik, Bob. *History of Beer and Brewing in Chicago, 1833–1978*. St. Paul: Pogo Press, 1999.

Smith, Alson J. *Syndicate City*. Chicago: Henry Regnery, 1954.

Stead, William. *If Christ Came to Chicago*. Chicago: Laird and Lee, 1894.

Stevens, Eugene. *Wicked City*. Chicago: G. E. Stevens & Co., 1906.

Taylor, Troy. *Bloody Chicago*. Decatur, IL: Whitechapel Productions Press, 2006.

Turner, George Kibbe. "The City of Chicago: A Study of the Great Immoralities." *McClure's Magazine* 18 (April 1907).

Tuttle, William M. *Race Riot*. Chicago: University of Illinois Press, 1996.

Urey, Elmer I. *Tax Dodgers*. New York: Greenberg, 1948.

Washburn, Charles. *Come into My Parlor*. New York: Knickerbocker, 1934.

Wendt, Lloyd, and Herman Kogan. *Lords of the Levee*. Indianapolis, IN: Bobbs-Merrill, 1943.

Wilson, Samuel Paynter. *Chicago and Its Cess-Pools of Infamy*. Chicago: Samuel Paynter Wilson, 1910.

Yore, Clem. *Songs of the Underworld*. Chicago: Charles C. Thompson, 1914.

JOURNAL ARTICLES

Bienen, Leigh B., and Brandon Rottinghaus. "Learning from the Past, Living in the Present: Understanding Homicide in Chicago, 1870–1930." *Journal of Criminal Law and Criminology* 92, nos. 3–4 (2003).

Kneeland, George J. "Commercialized Vice." *Proceedings of the Academy of Political Science in the City of New York* 2, No. 4, Organization of Social Work (July 1912): 127–29.

Lombardo, Robert M. "The Black Hand." *Journal of Contemporary Criminal Justice* 18, No. 4 (November 2002): 393–408.

———. "The Genesis of Organized Crime in Chicago." *Criminal Organizations* 10, No. 2 (Spring 1996).

Spillane, Joseph. "The Making of an Underground Market: Drug Selling in Chicago, 1900–1940." *Journal of Social History* (Fall 1998).

Wish, Harvey. "Altgeld and the Progressive Tradition." *American Historical Review*

DISSERTATIONS

Reckless, Walter C. "The Natural History of Vice Areas in Chicago." PhD diss., University of Chicago, 1925.

Stelzer, Patricia Jacobs. "Prohibition and Organized Crime: A Case Study: An Examination of the Life of John Torrio." MA thesis, Wayne State University, 1997.

PAPERS

"Biography of Carter H. Harrison IV," Newberry Library, Inventory of Carter H. Harrison Papers, pp. 1637, 1637–1953, bulk 1840–1850.

Colosimo, Christina. "My Family History." 2006.

Municipal Reference Library, City of Chicago. "Centennial List of Mayors, Aldermen and Other Elective Officials of the City of Chicago, 1837–1937."

NEWSPAPERS

Arcadia Tribune

Chicago American

Chicago Daily Journal

Chicago Daily News

Chicago Daily Post
Chicago Daily Times
Chicago Herald and Examiner
Chicago Inter-Ocean
Chicago Record-Herald
Chicago Sun-Times
Chicago Tribune
Indianapolis Sentinel
L'Italia
New York Times
Santa Barbara News

PERIODICALS
"Billy Sunday's Advocacy of Vice Districts." *The Survey*, January 15, 1916.
Clayton, John. "The Scourge of Sinners: Arthur Burrage Farwell." *Chicago History* (Fall 1974).
Flynt, Josiah. "In the World of Graft." *McClure's*, 1901.
"The Murder of Colosimo." *Illinois Policeman and Police Journal* (March–April 1947).
Taylor, Graham. "The Story of the Chicago Vice Commission." *The Survey*, May 6, 1911.
"The Wreck of Commercialized Vice." *The Survey*, February 5, 1916.
Wallace, Irving. "Call Them Madam." *Playboy*, September 1965.

NEWSPAPER ARTICLES
Pegler, Westbrook. "Union Constitution Lets Labor Bosses Rule Without Vote." *Mansfield, Ohio, News Journal.* July 15, 1948.

REPORTS AND RECORDS
California Death Index, 1940–1997.
Certificate of Death, State of California.
City of Chicago.
Chicago Committee of Fifteen, *Records*.
Chicago Police Department, *Homicide Records, 1870–1930*.
Circuit Court of Cook County, Illinois.
Civil Service Commission, City of Chicago, *Final Report Police Investigation*, (Chicago, 1912).
Cook County Clerk.
National Commission on Marihuana and Drug Abuse. "History of Alcoholic Prohibition." (Online) September 15, 2005.
Nevada State Journal.
Ohio Department of Health, Certificate of Death.
Penal Ordinances of Chicago. Chicago: T. H. Flood & Co., 1914.
Probate Court of Cook County, Illinois.

Records, Circuit Court of Cook County, Illinois.
Report of the Vice Commission of Chicago. *Social Evil in Chicago*. Chicago: Vice Commission of Chicago, 1911.
Summary of Report of the Senate Vice Committee. Springfield: State of Illinois, 1916.
Social Security Death Index.
U.S. Census, 1900 and 1910.

BOOKLETS
The Everleigh Club, 1900–1911 Illustrated. 2nd ed. Chicago: n.p., n.d.
World's Annual Sporting Records. Chicago, 1905, 1911.

SHIP MANIFESTS
SS *Alsatia*
SS *Statendam*

SONGS
Coughlin, John J. "Dear Midnight of Love." Chicago: John J. Coughlin, 1900.

INTERNET
Binder, John J. "Chicago," *American Mafia*. http//www.americanmafia.com/Cities/Chicago.html.
Everleigh, Ada and Minna. "Women in American History" Encyclopedia Britannica online. April 5, 2004.
Mannino, Peter. "Early Years." *The Outfit*. http://www.geocities.com/Silicon Valley/1424/early_.htm. February 16, 2000.
National Commission on Marihuana and Drug Abuse. "History of Alcoholic Prohibition." September 15, 2005.

INTERVIEWS
Dr. John J. Binder, Mars Eghigian Jr., Jeff Thurston, e-mails to author, January 2, 5, 2007.
Christina Colosimo, interviews in person, by phone, by letter, and by e-mails, 2005, 2006, 2007.
Christina Colosimo's mother, Elizabeth Mascara, by phone, October 31, 2006. Mark Prow, e-mail to author, June 14, 2005. Mark Prow is the grandson of Lafe Prow.

INDEX

K

Kamradt, Paul M., 212
Keene, Francis B., 256
Keeshin, John L., 269
Kelley, "Polack Ben," 148
Kelley, John, 289
Kelly, Edward, 267
Kelly, Paul, 128-129
Kenna, Michael "Hinky Dink," 12, 19-20, 22, 40, 42-50, 56, 58, 59, 61, 65, 68-75, 79-80, 85, 89, 92-93, 100, 107, 111, 113-116, 118-119, 122-124, 137, 143, 148, 161, 165-169, 178, 180, 182, 199, 210, 214-215, 228, 234, 257, 263, 266-268, 278, 283, 285
Kennedy, Charles F., 248
Kennedy, William P., 214
Kenney, George T., 238
Kerrigan, Marie, 215-216, 299
Kersten, Judge, 161
King, Wincey, 72
Kneeland, George J., 110
Knights of Pythias, 20, 254
Knights of Pythias Orphans' Home, 254
Kogan, Herman, 45-46
Kostner, Joseph O., 19
Kotecki, Maximilian, 74
Krum, Morrow, 216
Kucharski, Joseph, 146

L

Laborers International Union of North America, 42
Lait, Jack, 33, 81
Lake County Jail, 218, 270
Lame Jimmy, 67-68
Landesco, John, 228
Langon, Frank, 154, 163
Lardner, Chubby, 247
Lardner, Ring W., 198-199
LaSalle Hotel, 145
Laurenzana, Italy, 34
Law and Order League, 67, 71, 73, 110, 121, 136, 141
Lawyers Assn. of Illinois, 265
Laymen's Evangelical Assn., 105
Lazarus, Izzy, 257

Leathers, Billy, 81
Leavenworth federal penitentiary, 271
Lederer, George, 202
Lehman, F. M., 109, 111-112
Leo family, 26
Leslie, Aimee, 122
Levee Committee of Fifteen, 90, 139-140
Levene, Mae, 203
Lewis, "Dago Frank," 81, 141, 163
Lewis, John, 39
Liberty Loan drives, 241
Lincoln Park, 65
Lindberg, Richard, 171
L'Italia, 84, 168, 240
Little Cheyenne, 31
Little Green House, 55
Little Town Club, 272
Little, Ed, 141
Little, George, 80, 160
Livingstone Hotel, 202
Lombardo, Robert, 273
Long, William, 238
Longstreet, Stephen, 177
Los Angeles General Hospital, 265
Los Angeles, Calif., 222, 245, 264-265
Lower, Elton, 154
Lundin, Fred, 247
Luthardt, William H., 182
Lyle, John H., 198
Lynch, Detective, 141
Lynch, Edward, 230
Lynch, Patrolman, 140

M

Mabee, Melbourne, 154
Macklin, Chesterfield Joe, 44-45
Madame Butterfly, 203
Mafia, 190, 265, 271
Maggi, Alfred, 19
Majestic, SS, 269
Malbaum, Charley, 163
Maletta family, 26
Mancuso family, 26

Manhattan Brewery, 219
Mann Act, 100, 280
Mann, James Robert, 280
Maraca family, 26
Marcovitz, A., 139
Mark, Norman, 83, 261
Marks, William, 208
Marshall Ventilated Mattress Co., 114
Marshall, Thomas, 138
Martin, Gladys, 54
Martin, Judge, 40
Mascaro family, 26
Mason, Billy, 43
Maurice "Mossy" Enright, 230
Maxim's, 145
Mayors, Madams, and Madmen, 83, 261
Maypole, George, 19
McCann, Edward, 91-92, 102-104
McCarthy, Hugh, 209
McCarthy, J. T., 129
McClellan, George B., 128
McClure's Magazine, 90
McCormack, John, 199
McCormick, Robert R., 160, 270
McDonald, Michael Cassius, 47, 77
McGavick, Alexander J., 74
McGoorty, John P., 223
McGraw, Herschel, 272
McInerney, Alderman, 118
McKay, Dwight, 19
McKee, Frank A., 216
McMahon, James J., 167-168, 236, 241, 244, 246-247
McWeeney, John, 119, 124, 135-136, 138, 142, 145-146
Memorial Church of Christ, 118
Mercy Hospital, 153-154
Merlo, Mike, 19, 21
Merriam, Charles E., 113-115, 139, 214
Merrill, Detective, 152-153, 155, 157
Messick, Hank, 127

Reckless, Walter, 142
Reeg, Victoria, 265
Regnella, Raymond, 17
Repakes, John, 39
Republican Central Committee, 247
Republican National Convention, 175
Republican Party, 115, 185
Review of Reviews, 57
Rexford, Edward, 19
Rhinegold Saloon, 146
Rica, Frank, 42
Ricca, Paul, 271
Riley, Harrison B., 139
Ringling Brothers Circus, 70
Rizzuto family, 26
Rock Island Railroad, 130
Rock River Conference, 182
Rockhill, Arthur, 245
Rodrick, Ike, 18, 20
Roe, Clifford G., 85, 97-100, 107
Romagnono, Tony, 39
Ronga, Anthony, 19
Rooney, Judge, 168
Roosevelt, Franklin D., 20, 266
Rosenberg, Michael, 19
Rosenwald, Julius, 110
Rothschild, Sam, 185
Ruffo, Titta, 19, 198-199, 203, 223
Ryan, Michael F., 142-144, 146, 149, 151-152, 154-156, 158, 161, 163, 166-168, 236

S
Saffo the Greek, 157, 162-163, 166-167
Saints Peter and Paul Church, 74, 110
Salvation Army, 106, 136
Sampson, Detective, 152
Sandburg, Carl, 14
Sands, the, 31
Santa Maria Incoronata Catholic Church, 18
Santuzzi, Louis, 249
Sappho brothel, 54
Saratoga brothel, 178

Schaffner, Charles, 219
Schubert, Bill, 163
Schuettler, Herman F., 115, 154, 184, 208
Schultz, "Dutch," (Arthur Flegenheimer), 271
Scrivner, George, 175
Seventh Regiment Armory, 68, 104-105
Seventh Street Armory, 101
Shaw, Clifford R., 279
Shaw, Vic, 54, 122, 138
Shaw's bordello, 54, 138
Shea, Detective, 141
Shippy, George M., 91-92, 102-103
Side Lights on Darkest Chicago, 9, 51
Sieben's Brewery, 270
Silver Dollar Saloon, 141
Silver, George, 19
Simms, Edwin W., 110, 213
Sloop, John C., 152-153
Small, Len, 225
Smith, Captain, 184
Smith, Rodney "Gypsy," 12, 101, 104-106
Smitz, Harry, 217
Society for Social Hygene, 110
Solberg, Marshall, 168-169
Solon, Frank W., 39-40
Sons of Temperance, 211
South Clark Street District Station, 246
South Park Avenue Methodist Episcopal Church, 203
Spadoni, Giacomo, 19, 203, 223, 225
Spanish-American War, 103, 144
Speedway Inn, 176, 212
Spencer, Georgie, 54, 80, 157
Sportsman's Club, 181-182
Sportsman's Park, 268-269
Spring, Joseph, 155
Springfield, Ill., 125, 139
Spurgin, Warren C., 256-257
St. Adelbert's Cemetery, 166
St. Anthony de Padua Hospital, 161

St. Louis, Mo., 68, 96, 98-99, 123, 131, 245
Stadleman, Louis Gus, 235, 238
Starek, Detective, 107
State Line Inn, 212-213
Stead, William T., 12, 57-58, 60, 90, 269
Steele, Percival, 114-115
Steffens, Lincoln, 9
Steinberg, Jacob, 213
Stetson Brewery, 218
Stetson, Joseph, 218-219, 229
Steward, LeRoy T., 74, 92, 103-108, 111, 115, 119
Stickney, Ill., 173, 210, 268
Storyville, 282
Street Laborers' Union, 230
Sullivan, William, 247
Sumner, Dean, 110, 118
Swan's Billiard Hall, 153
Swanson, Lillian, 200
Sweitzer, Robert M., 179, 214, 266
Swift, George B., 68, 267
Sykes, Tillie, 156

T
Taft, William Howard, 100, 269
Talerico family, 26
Tammany Hall, 128
Tastalena, Gus, 238
Taylor, Agnes, 97
Taylor, Chief City Prosecutor, 40
Taylor, Graham, 110
Tennes, Mont, 20
Tetrazzini, Luisa, 199
Thompson, John H., 263
Thompson, William Hale "Big Bill," 12, 22, 48, 177, 179-182, 184, 198, 208, 214-215, 227, 247, 249, 257, 263, 266-267, 269-270
Thrasher, Samuel P., 177, 209
Thurston, Harry, 53
Time magazine, 65, 81
Times Square, 282
Tip Trust, 216
Titanic, RMS, 269
Toman, John, 19